DATE DUE

NOV 3 0 1999			
NOV 2 2 2000			
MAR 1 3 2001			
JUN 0 4 2004 OCT 1 9 2004			
FEB 1 7 2005			
MAR 1 8 2005			
MAY 2 7 2005			
JUL 2 7 2006 SEP 2 3 2007			
DEC 0 4 2007			
NOV 2 3 2010			

DEMCO 38-297

Polish Americans and Their History

Polish Americans

AND THEIR HISTORY

Community, Culture, and Politics

Edited by

John J. Bukowczyk

University of Pittsburgh Press

Published by the University of Pittsburgh Press, Pittsburgh, Pa. 15260
Copyright © 1996, University of Pittsburgh Press
Manufactured in the United States of America
Printed on acid-free paper
10 9 8 7 6 5 4 3 2 1

Preparation of this volume was supported by a Wayne State University (WSU) Small Research Grant and by subventions from the WSU Department of History, the WSU Polish Studies Program, and the Polish American Historical Association, all of which are gratefully acknowledged.

LIBRARY OF CONGRESS CATALOGING-IN-PUBLICATION DATA

Polish Americans and their history : community, culture, and politics
   / edited by John J. Bukowczyk.
      p.   cm.
   ISBN 0-8229-3953-3 (alk. paper)
      1. Polish Americans.   I. Bukowczyk, John J., 1950– .
E184.P7P6848   1996
973'.049185—dc20   96-10070

A CIP catalog record for this book is available from the British Library.

For Mieczysław Haiman
(1888–1949)

Contents

Preface		*ix*
Pronunciation Guide		*xv*

1. Polish Americans, History Writing, and the
   Organization of Memory 1
   John J. Bukowczyk

2. Labor, Radicalism, and the Polish-American Worker 39
   William G. Falkowski

3. Family, Women, and Gender: The Polish Experience 58
   Thaddeus C. Radzilowski

4. Polish Americans and Religion 80
   William J. Galush

5. Jewish Emigration from Poland Before World War II 93
   Daniel Stone

6. Polonia and Politics 121
   Stanislaus A. Blejwas

7. Displaced Persons, Émigrés, Refugees, and Other
   Polish Immigrants: World War II Through the
   Solidarity Era 152
   Anna D. Jaroszyńska-Kirchmann

8. Post–World War II Polish Historiography on
   Emigration 180
   Andrzej Brożek

Notes		*193*
List of Contributors		*271*
Index		*273*

Preface

IN 1942, A SMALL GROUP OF POLISH ÉMIGRÉ SCHOLARS, WHO
had fled to the United States in order to escape the Nazi onslaught,
joined together in an attempt to preserve and advance Polish learning and
culture despite the subjugation of their homeland. Assisted by Americans
and joined by American Poles, the émigrés founded the Polish Institute
of Arts and Sciences in America (PIASA). But PIASA's founders, as part
of a worldwide Polish diaspora, also recognized both the need and the
opportunity to encourage scholarship not only on Poland and its place in
world civilization but also on the immigrant population of which they
were a part. In 1942, PIASA accordingly organized a Commission for
Research on Polish Immigration, which soon acquired organizational independence from its parent body as well as a new name, the Polish American Historical Association (PAHA).

One of America's older and larger scholarly organizations devoted to
studying the history of an ethnic group, PAHA dates its founding to those
perilous yet hopeful days of World War II. PAHA continues to maintain
a vital presence in both Polish-American affairs and in the American historical profession, and in the fifty years that have elapsed since its founding, the structure of this field, the composition of its practitioners, and
the scope of their interests have changed repeatedly, as has the place that
ethnic Americans and ethnicity have occupied in American culture and
society. In the past two decades, in particular, historical study of Polish-
American culture, community life, and politics has reached a new critical
plateau. Informed and cross-fertilized by methodological, theoretical, and
historiographical developments in the wider historical discipline, Polish-
American history writing has joined in dispelling the melting-pot myth
and has engaged what increasingly seems a central concern of both humanists and social scientists in our own time: the evolution and meaning
of multiculturalism in America.

In order to mark its fiftieth anniversary, PAHA has organized this volume of eight original historical and historiographical essays that, it is

hoped, will be of interest and use to scholars and students of the ethnic experience as well as to Polish Americans committed to the critical examination of their own rich history. The essays in this volume pursue, to a greater or lesser measure, three objectives. First, most attempt to offer a concise summary or synthesis of various aspects of Polish-American life, particularly subjects whose history has been most transformed in the past two decades by exciting new research in the field. Second, those essays covering subjects that have enjoyed extensive prior scholarly attention also seek to present a broad historiographical review of the historical literature in each of these areas; they examine how fifty years of scholarship have reoriented our comprehension of the experience of this large and important American immigrant and ethnic group. Third, while examining the current state of this field and focusing on the ways it has developed and currently is practiced—by Polish-American and other scholars in the United States—most of the essays have tried to identify promising territory for further exploration in order to broaden and deepen our grasp of the Polish portion of America's multi-ethnic history.

The volume begins with an introductory essay by John J. Bukowczyk, which lays a groundwork for understanding contemporary Polish-American historical scholarship by looking at how Polish Americans have developed, organized, and used historical memory. The volume next explores Polish-American economic and social life. William G. Falkowski grapples with a growing literature on Polish-American workers and immigrant radicalism, again countering the once held stereotype that America's "new immigrants" formed an inert mass when it came to labor struggles and politics. By contrast, Thaddeus C. Radzilowski outlines the state of research on the subject of immigrant women and families, both of which are areas of study still in their infancy.

The emphasis of the volume gradually shifts to consider the social and cultural sides of the Polish immigrant experience. William Galush examines one of the richest areas of recent Polish-American history and historiography, developments in religion (both institutional and popular). One special feature of this volume, achieved by the inclusion of an essay by Daniel Stone, is an attempt at integrating the history of Poland's Jewish emigrants into a Polish-American history writing that hitherto has focused almost singularly on Poles from the Roman Catholic tradition and its offshoots. Stanislaus A. Blejwas meanwhile looks critically at Polish-American involvement in American politics.

The last two essays both broaden and internationalize the scope of the volume. In a more monographic presentation reflective of the paucity of prior research on her topic, Anna D. Jaroszyńska-Kirchmann explores the uncharted terrain of post–World War II Polish emigration. This volume also aims to encourage the cooperation and collaboration of Polish-American and Polish scholars, a movement previously aided by the thaw in the Cold War and now given increased momentum by Poland's recent emergence from the Soviet political sphere. Accordingly, we are honored to include in this volume an essay by the late distinguished Polish scholar Andrzej Brożek, which reviews post–World War II Polish scholarship on the Polish emigration to the United States. Professor Brożek's unfortunate death during the latter stages of this volume's preparation makes his contribution especially valuable, as it may be his last published work.

In assembling these essays that accomplish so much, it must be conceded that this already long volume contains unfortunate gaps, only some of which reflect gaps in the extant scholarship. Wittingly, the volume does not review the subject of assimilation and acculturation, as we have concluded that space might allow us to update but would not allow us to improve substantially upon the outstanding historiographical treatment of the subject, *Polish-American Community Life: A Survey of Research* (1975), by sociologists Ewa T. Morawska and Irwin T. Sanders. Research on anti-Polish prejudice and discrimination, and on Polish-American education and social mobility as well, has remained slim enough not to support a reconnaissance at this time. It is regrettable that immigrant secular culture—both high culture and popular culture—has received only passing attention here. One commissioned contribution on this subject failed to materialize in time to be included (and too late to be replaced). In general, it also might be noted, this area remains underresearched by historians, although the reader is alerted to the recent work by professor of English Thomas S. Gladsky, *Princes, Peasants, and Other Polish Selves: Ethnicity in American Literature,* which at least treats a portion of that vast domain.

The subject of intergroup relations—particularly relations between Polish Americans and African Americans—likewise deserves broader treatment than it has received here and there in some of the essays. Thus far little research throughout the field of immigration and ethnic history has looked at this crucial problem, although some comparative studies of Poles and other groups at last have begun to appear. Similarly, the reader will notice that the young "interdiscipline" of cultural studies has yet to touch research in Polish-American history (save, perhaps, for some explorations of immigrant popular culture—on the polka, for example). Given the newness of "cultural studies," this may cause no surprise, but less defensible is a general absence of "gender" as a category of analysis and explanation in recent Polish-American scholarship, even in works focusing on women. The decline of women among the ranks of Polish-American scholars may help explain this *brak*, which, it is hoped, soon will be remedied.[1] More understandable, none of the essays treats immigrant children, a topic only now being addressed by Polish scholar Adam Walaszek and perhaps others; while the volume also forgoes the subject of Polish immigrant involvement in agriculture in America, not for its lack of importance but owing to the small attention this topic has received from scholars, which thus deters a historiographical overview. Finally, neither the expression of what might be called "suburban ethnicity" nor subjects pertaining to the Solidarity-era emigration have been discussed here (nor, it seems, very much yet elsewhere). Both remain topics for vital future research.

Having admitted some of the shortcomings of this undertaking, I should offer a few words on its merits. The volume incorporates the revisionist scholarship generally abroad in the discipline in the 1970s and 1980s, identifies new subjects and historical actors in a previously circumscribed narrative, and explores new themes, methodologies, and (perhaps most provocatively) new analytical paradigms and perspectives, including class. In short, the volume assesses a subfield and a history as both have reached a milestone.

Many debts are incurred in the organization of a volume such as this. I first would like to thank the scholars who, at the developmental stage of this project, generously lent their names to this still untested undertaking. Included among them are Ronald Bayor, John Bodnar, Kathleen Neils Conzen, Nora Faires, Victor Greene, Thaddeus Gromada, Thomas Napierkowski, Stephan A. Thernstrom, and Robert H. Zieger. Among this group I especially would like to give credit to our friend and colleague the late George Pozzetta, who on many occasions proved himself a friend of PAHA but, alas, whose untimely and unexpected passing has taken him from us before the conclusion of the project.

Before these essays took shape, most were presented in preliminary form at the 1991 annual meeting of the Polish American Historical Association in Chicago, Illinois. Included among the chairs and commentators who willingly served at this venue and who deserve special thanks are Margo Anderson, James Barrett, Leonard Chrobot, Nora Faires, Donna Gabaccia, Laurence Glasco, Victor Greene, Christiane Harzig, John Kulczycki, Deborah Dash Moore, Thomas Napierkowski, Joseph John Parot, George Pozzetta, John Rury, and Andrew Yox. The long gestation period for this project offered many scholars an opportunity to provide useful advice on its conception and organization, and a few have remained steady participants in its execution. On this count, thanks go to James S. Pula, Stanislaus Blejwas, Thaddeus Radzilowski, and especially to Nora Faires, for their knowledgeable and strategic support, and to Mary E. Cygan, Dennis Koliński, and Dominic A. Pacyga for their contributions. In a more material vein, I also would like to thank the Wayne State University Office of Research, Department of History, Department of German and Slavic Languages and Literatures, and Polish Studies Program for support of this volume; several Wayne State University administrators, including Frank Corliss, Daniel Graf, Donald Haase, Garrett Heberlein, and Alan Raucher for their personal support; former PAHA treasurer Peter D. Slavcheff for keeping PAHA organizationally sound enough to see this work to fruition; and graduate research assistant David R. Smith for making PAHA a model of administrative efficiency during the two-year PAHA presidency of this volume's editor (1990–1992). I am also grateful to the staff of Wayne State University's Purdy/Kresge Library.

Finally, perhaps a word is in order about the dedication of this volume. Although he was not a "professional" historian, Mieczysław Haiman was a thorough researcher, a gifted archivist, and a prolific writer on Polish-American subjects. He was one of PAHA's founders and its first president, and the organization was in large measure his creation. In marking our fiftieth anniversary with the publication of this volume, we commemorate PAHA but also honor our intellectual forebear. We dedicate this volume to Mieczysław Haiman, with enduring thanks. To our beloved PAHA, we happily add the traditional toast *"Sto Lat!"* (May you live a hundred years).[2]

Pronunciation Guide

THE ACCENT IN POLISH ALWAYS FALLS ON THE PENULTIMATE syllable. For aid in the pronunciation of Polish words and names, please consult the following key:

> c is always pronounced as ts
> ch very nearly like a gutteral h
> cz as ch
> g is always a hard sound, like g in get
> i as ee
> j as y
> rz like French j, as in *jardin*
> sz as sh
> szcz as shch, with both sounds enunciated
> u as oo
> w as v
> ć as ch
> ś as sh
> ż, ź both as zh, the former of higher pitch, the latter deeper
> ó as oo
> ą, ę as French en
> ł as w
> ń changes -in to -ine, -en to -ene, and -on to -oyne

Americanized Polish names and terms typically have dropped Polish diacritical marks, for example, Pułaski would become Pulaski. This pronunciation key was taken from John J. Bukowczyk, *And My Children Did Not Know Me: A History of the Polish-Americans.*

Polish Americans and Their History

I

Polish Americans, History Writing, and the Organization of Memory

John J. Bukowczyk

Here is the epoch of Slavic immigration. Since the Poles are here in the majority, therefore a beautiful future is awaiting them . . . and I guarantee this to you, that here in America a "Second Polish History will begin."

Bishop J. L. Spaulding (1901)

STATELESS, COLONIZED, AND CONQUERED PEOPLES IN MODERN times have derived appreciable political vitality and strength from nurturing their national myths, manufacturing historical memory, and transmitting narratives—sometimes heroic, sometimes tragic, sometimes chiliastic—to succeeding generations who they hoped would become the patriots and nationalists of the future. Poles were not "stateless" in the sense that, for example, Gypsies or Basques either never have had or have not yet succeeded in forming a nation-state of their own. But as a conquered and colonized nation-in-the-making (with their country's political administration inadequately bureaucratized and centralized; its populace sharply divided by class, region, religion, and in this sense perhaps "prenational"; and its geographical position as a borderland conducing to geopolitical complexities), the Poles nonetheless have shared a longing for a national homeland, united, sovereign, independent, and puissant. Like other oppressed peoples, they too have looked to history as a means of sustaining and advancing their national aspirations. Thus, Poles believed that, although subjugated and partitioned by its neighbors, Poland possessed an existence as a nation and as a state that anteceded, and might as easily succeed, contemporary international political arrangements and exigencies.

The power of historical myth and memory as an engine of Polish nationalism has remained a leitmotif in Polish affairs through a second world war and through a fifty-year postwar era of a different kind of national subjugation. American Poles have partaken of these movements since the nineteenth century. In the words of the slogan placed on the masthead of the Polish immigrant newspaper *Echo z Polski:* "First, you should know your ancestral history—both its defeats and its glories." But American Poles also have developed their uses of Polish-*American* history, uses related to each other and to their life as ethnic Americans.[1] Rev. Wacław Kruszka, celebrated as the "Nestor of Polish-American historians," argued that the history of "what our immigrants had accomplished is not only pleasant and interesting, but is also very useful because it develops a complete human being by cultivating and fostering all three powers of his soul: memory, intellect, and willpower." As the celebrated Polish comic dramatist Aleksander Fredro (1793–1876) observed, "History is life's model"; and in the early 1900s Kruszka too thought that history—of the good and the bad—provided lessons both moral and practical. For the "young Pole raised in America," Kruszka believed, "a Polish American history will teach him . . . how he must live in this country in order not to lose his faith and nationality."[2]

Kruszka's contemporaries—allies and enemies alike—amply demonstrated the practicality of Polish and Polish-American history, discovering its many political and ideological uses in the various national struggles at home and abroad in the decades ahead. The development of (first) immigrant and (later) Polish-American history writing, attendant organizational growth, and the evolution of Polish studies in America cut to the core of America's cultural mosaic and American political pluralism. Whatever the immigrant and ethnic experience, it is through the social construction and ideological formulation of that experience (and respective reconstructions and reformulations) that immigrants and ethnics have developed connections—among themselves, to their communities, to their ancestral and adoptive homelands: to God, Country, and Polonia.[3]

This essay examines the recovery, manufacture, and use of the past as related to the organizational, social, and political development of Polish America from the nineteenth century through our own time. By the late twentieth century, professional historians of Polish-American extraction have continued to ask questions of their history. Those questions are rooted in the past but also hold contemporary political and personal meaning for them. The questions they pose involve the definition of ethnicity in modern America, but also the meaning of America itself as both a society and an ideal. These questions involve an understanding of themselves both as historians but also as human beings, as "ethnics" but also as Americans.

Problematizing the Mass Migration

Polish-American history writing—and the development of Polish-American history as (variously) ideology, culture, and politics—began at the crossroads of Polish mass migration and Polish nationalism in the late nineteenth century. Since the 1790s, Poland had been divided and absorbed by its three neighbors, Prussia, Russia, and Austria. By the 1880s, not long after large numbers of Poles had begun to migrate "for bread" *(za chlebem)*, writers in all three Polish partitions already had started to monitor emigrant conditions abroad and to study the mass exodus of their countrymen and countrywomen. Poles founded several specialized journals and periodicals that focused on the subject of emigration.[4] Researchers such as Leopold Caro, Franciszek Bujak, and Józef Okołowicz sought to measure the volume of the migration or assess its causes and consequences. Others, like Stanisław Kłobukowski, also tried to describe emigrant life abroad, in Brazil as well as in North America.[5]

Depending in large measure upon their economic interests or political position, economists, politicians, churchmen, political reformers, and Polish nationalists either encouraged or condemned the peasant exodus. Critics considered emigration an economic and political ill because it reduced the rural labor supply, raised the price of agricultural labor, and drained away potential recruits to the Polish nationalist cause, the very lifeblood of the shackled Polish Nation. Conversely, some supporters considered emigration a political and social "safety valve"; even Polish National Democratic *(Endek)* leader Roman Dmowski, a nationalist opponent of the emigration, eventually concluded that emigrant Poles who sent money from abroad back to Poland served the national cause by providing capital for economic development and, when organized, political support overseas. Emigration thereby offered rural Poles an opportunity to improve their tenuous material circumstances and become part of the political Nation.[6]

As these attitudes gained currency, Poles began to accept the emigration and, by 1914, appreciated its political and economic utility. World War I did bring Poland's "resurrection" as an independent nation-state, thanks to transcontinental political machinations, American and French patronage, and Polish political mobilization, especially in the United States (in the coinage of the Polish National Alliance, Poland's so-called Fourth Partition). Not surprisingly, after the war the new Polish state and its new Polish academic establishment took especial interest in the emigration. This interest gave rise to several new journals and a succession of studies, which, while cognizant of emigration as a demographic and economic hemorrhage, no less appreciated that Poland could receive considerable political and economic support from Poles who lived abroad, *Polonia zagraniczna*.[7] This collective noun reinforced the notion that Poles should remain bound both to each other and to their homeland, the *ojczyzna*.

Most of these writings constituted more of a policy debate than a historical discourse. The real historiography of Polish emigration (and immigration) accordingly begins on this side of the Atlantic. As the Polish exodus seemed a problem to some Europeans, their arrival—and that of other so-called new immigrants—presented an even greater problem in the eyes of most American observers. Social investigators such as Emily Greene Balch, Peter Roberts, and Robert E. Park took a charitable interest in the Poles and sought to ameliorate their social conditions and Americanize them.[8] The problem of immigrant adjustment and the social problems of "dysfunctional" immigrants received extensive exploration by sociologists William I. Thomas and Florian Znaniecki in their monumental work, *The Polish Peasant in Europe and America,* the cornerstone of the discipline's so-called Chicago School and probably the most influential work dealing with Polish immigrants written in the twentieth century.[9] With the outbreak of World War I, the fact that unnaturalized immigrants born in Poland's German and Austrian partitions technically classified as "enemy aliens" touched issues involving America's internal security and prompted new inquiry of clearly political inception. Meanwhile, the interest taken by Protestant evangelists in the Poles stemmed from the latter's growing numbers and largely Roman Catholic religious affiliation, which made them an alluring subject for proselytizing.[10]

By contrast, the era's racialist and immigration restrictionist literature subsumed Polish immigrants in its pseudo-scientific analysis and frothing diatribes. General studies of the "new immigration" also took note of the Poles, but this work divided into roughly the same categories and followed basically the same thematic lines. At best, it depicted Poles and other "new immigrants" as Americans-in-the-making, either aspiring to Anglo-conformist ideals or, if simmering in a "melting pot," set to boil until taste, odor, and texture had blanched out. At worst, textbook writers reduced these immigrants to "wretched refuse," the offal better left out of the potage. Woodrow Wilson's characterization of the "new immigrants," which appeared in his *History of the American People,* typifies the genre. "Throughout the century," Wilson wrote in 1901 while still a Princeton history professor,

> men of the sturdy stocks of the North of Europe had made up the main stream of foreign blood which was every year added to the vital working force of the country. . . . But now there came multitudes of men of the lowest class from the south of Italy and men of the meaner sort out of Hungary and Poland, men out of the ranks where there was neither skill nor energy nor any initiative of quick intelligence; and they came in numbers which increased from year to year, as if the countries of the south of Europe were disburdening themselves of the more sordid and hapless elements of their population.[11]

After the 1920s, American scholarship on the Poles and other so-called new immigrants softened considerably as "progressive" historians developed a faith in eventual assimilation. Even so, into the early 1960s, after two decades of textbook references to America as a "melting pot," most history texts continued "to talk about 'the immigrants' as distinct from 'us Americans.' "[12]

Commemorating and Politicizing Immigrant History: The Pre–World War I Era

Most Polish immigrants probably would not have recognized themselves in these versions of their past, assessments of their present condition, and prescriptions for their future in America. Moreover, peasant or priest, artisan or intellectual, Polish immigrants possessed their own historical sense and produced their own histories much at variance with these renditions of their passage from Europe's "teeming shores" through Liberty's "Golden Door." Peasant historical tales—recalling epidemics, wars, prophetic or magical incidents—circulated in rural popular culture and formed part of the peasant oral tradition.[13] Typically of local relevance and immediacy, these tales followed patterns and served functions that merit further investigation. In America, the survival—or creation—of reminiscence doubtless eased the pain and guilt of separation, reinforced ties to loved ones, village, and perhaps Nation, and helped make sense of the decision to emigrate.

Later in America, immigrants met with another type of local history in the form of parish commemoratives and the yearbooks of a myriad of societies, clubs, organizations, and fraternals. Published to mark a significant parish or institutional anniversary (and in the former case, probably written by the pastor), these often impressive though largely formulaic tomes served a dual function, which helps to account for their proliferation, longevity as a form, and apparent popularity. For their makers, the parish commemoratives, in particular, raised funds, enhanced social status, shored up pastoral authority and legitimacy, and buttressed the hegemonic aspects of both Church and religion.[14] As a shared, and eventually routinized, community event, their publication reinforced community identity and cohesiveness and social recognition from members of other Polish immigrant communities (particularly those with shorter histories). This genre differed little in character or function from mainstream, boosterish, national or local histories, save for a measure of defensiveness. Also, in contrast to mainstream history texts that presumably spoke to a universal audience, these works aimed inward, even as they perhaps curried the favor and patronage of organizational or ecclesiastical superiors.

The relationship between Poles (particularly the Polish immigrant clergy) and their church (its hierarchy specifically) grew increasingly strained as Polish numbers in America mounted and as churchmen wrestled with rising immigrant demands in the late nineteenth century. These centered first on the issue of "lay trusteeism," that is, lay control over parish property. Second, influenced by the widening movement known as Cahenslyism, Poles also petitioned for representation and equality *(równouprawnienie)* in the hierarchy of the Roman Catholic Church in America and for the appointment of Polish bishops.[15]

With these struggles and the period's broader ideological and political conflicts providing a backdrop, Polish immigrant intellectuals and publicists began to write and to use their history not in order to buttress the status quo as the yearbooks continued to do, but to challenge it. On the local and popular level, lay trustee fights, pitting priests and parishioners variously against each other, often invoked competing versions of local and parish history.[16] On the national level, the campaign for Polish-American bishops—"polyglot bishops for polyglot dioceses" (this from the title of a celebrated article by Wisconsin cleric, Rev. Wacław Kruszka)—resulted in Polish America's (Polonia's) first and most distinguished history, Kruszka's *Historya polska w Ameryce* (Polish history in America).[17] Kruszka's thirteen-volume history offered ample evidence as to the development and maturation of Polish settlement in America and itself became an argument for the Poles' greater recognition by the Church and incorporation into its affairs.[18] But Kruszka did not write Polish-American history for contained, institutional purposes. Instead, he prescribed a social vision that embraced an incipient cultural pluralism. This national idea, whether addressing ecclesiastical affairs or secular national questions, commanded early and lengthy discussion and debate in the pages of Polonia's expanding press in the late nineteenth and early twentieth century.[19] Early Polish-American book publishing also found a market in Polonia for historical works that developed Polish national myths, sentiments, and themes. The Dyniewicz Publishing Company in Chicago, for example, printed historical novels by Henryk Sienkiewicz and Władysław Reymont, although such work constituted only a small portion of the firm's printing volume (and that of its successor, the Smulski Publishing Company), in which elementary school primers and readers written in Polish apparently predominated. In Toledo, Antoni Paryski built what has been called a "publishing empire," printing (actually reprinting) virtually anything available.[20]

During these years, the division of Polonian politics into warring ideological factions and the intensification of Polish nationalist politics on both sides of the Atlantic yielded additional historiographical signposts on the road toward both a mature Polish-American community and an independent Poland. By the end of the nineteenth century, Polonia's intelligentsia included the priests of several European-educated orders, among whom numbered both Polish Jesuits and members of the influential Chicago-based Resurrectionist congregation. After 1885, Polonia also acquired its own American-grown pastoral leaders when, in that year, Rev. Józef Dąbrowski, a veteran of the January Insurrection of 1863, established Detroit's SS. Cyril and Methodius Seminary, Polonia's first institution of higher education.[21] The schismatic religious movements of the era also coalesced into a third ideological tendency, institutionalized in the Polish National Catholic Church; while an assortment of Polish socialists, anticlericalists, and nationalists also joined the ideological fray. Of the last genre, the influential and numerous works of journalist Stanisław Osada, meanwhile, perhaps stand out among the books, articles, and pamphlets produced by members of these competing ideological factions and pointed Polonia toward the armed struggle for Polish independence.[22] Yet the road to independence both began and ended in a fork: the question of Polish identity.

Polish Americans' relationship to Poland, Polish politics, and Polish culture has remained a major theme in Polish-American historiography since probably the 1890s. This nationalist ferment produced a secular nationalist institutional analogue to Detroit's Polish Seminary with the founding, in 1912, of a Polish National Alliance–sponsored educational academy (later Alliance College) in Cambridge Springs, Pennsylvania, which never achieved within Polonia the social, cultural, or political influence of the former. In the explosive matter of identity, meanwhile, opposing historical salvoes in the form of general and organizational histories were fired back and forth by writers attached to Polonia's competing clericalist, nationalist, and indeed Polish National Catholic and socialist camps. These works spoke to Polish national aspirations abroad, but their publication also involved the political legitimacy that a properly turned historical account can either deny or convey. As for immigrant identity, contemporary immigrant history writing unavoidably addressed what recent historiography has identified as Polonia's central ideological issue of the period: whether the immigrant was a Polish Catholic or a Catholic Pole. Embedded therein lurked the fundamental and dangerous question: What is a *true* Pole? The enduring answer that Polonia forged, both Polish *and* Catholic (which identified Polish nationality with Roman Catholic religion), has exercised baneful effects that perhaps have outweighed this formula's considerable social and political advantages.[23]

One of these effects has been the marginalization or exclusion of non-Catholics—atheists, agnostics, the immigrant left, Polish Protestants, and Polish Jews—from most historical studies of Polish immigration. What we therefore have called Polish immigration history actually has been Polish ethnic history—the study of ethnic group formation, development, and decline in more recent years. From a technical standpoint, this narrowing of subject has not been entirely inappropriate. First, the field has evolved in the admittedly limiting American social context in which ethnicity in large measure became "ethno-religion." Second, since most migration from "Poland" occurred while the country was still partitioned, that is to say, before its re-creation as an independent state with "subjects" or "citizens," it was not "Poles" who emigrated but various ethnic peoples who left it—Polish, Jewish, Ukrainian, and so on (and this sidesteps the issue of regional identities and affiliations). The omission of the *Polish* emigrants' "non-Polish" counterparts nonetheless has had us write only part of a complicated story rather than a comprehensive history.[24]

When we move from the clash of nationalist ideas and ideals to the arena of popular nationalist agitation and mobilization, we find history, politics, and immigrant identity no less intertwined. Yet mass nationalist politics in Polish America drew principally upon neither the immigrant nor even the ethnic saga during the late nineteenth and early twentieth centuries. Rather, the immigrants' politically compelling myths, images, and symbols on one hand derived from Poland's messianic nationalist tradition, crystallized in the writings of Adam Mickiewicz, Julius Słowacki, and others, and on the other hand came from Polish Roman Catholic religious traditions like the "miracle" at the Swedish siege of Częstochowa and from Poland's glorious pre-partition days—in short, from Polish history. Prewar Polonia's largest popular nationalist political manifestation illustrated both these symbolic sources: in July 1910, in a celebration with unabashedly anti-German political content, Poles throughout the United States commemorated the five-hundredth anniversary of the Polish victory over the Teutonic Knights at the Battle of Grünwald.[25]

Toward a Polish-American Identity and History: The 1920s and 1930s

With Poland reestablished as an independent state at the end of World War I, American Poles and their history reached a critical abyss over which, once having leapt, they could no longer retreat. At one blow, Polish independence and reunification had destroyed the raison d'être of Polonia's prewar political life. For those who had located their identity in their connection to Poland—and stated the intention to return—Polish independence presented a hard decision and underscored a terrible point: only a few Poles returned to the new Poland.[26] As immigrant leaders grew disillusioned with 1920s Poland, they settled upon a new political slogan that embodied their new attitude: *Wychodźtwo dla wychodźtwa* (Emigrants for themselves). Immigrant history writing reflected this reorientation as "Poles in America" later became "American Poles" and, still later, "Polish Americans."

The wartime and postwar Americanization campaign and, beneath it, the more pervasive, enduring, and seemingly inexorable process of assimilation pushed forward this transit in self-ascribed identities. About the survival of Polish culture under immigration conditions, Polish novelist Henryk Sienkiewicz in the 1870s had already opined:

> But what about the second, third and fourth generations? What of the children born of German, Irish, or American mothers? Sooner or later they will forget. They will change everything, even their names, which English teeth find too difficult to chew and which interfere with business. How long it will take is difficult to say. But just as Poland disappeared, so will

this same sad fate inevitably befall her children who, today, are scattered throughout the world.[27]

Sienkiewicz might have been overly pessimistic about Polish descendants' willingness or ability so thoroughly to remake themselves, and he might likewise have been overly optimistic about the willingness of the native-born and other groups to accept and to amalgamate (intermarry) with the Poles, or the willingness of the Poles to amalgamate with them. But certainly assimilation had advanced considerably by the 1920s, especially as immigration-restriction legislation halted the culturally reinvigorating influx of large numbers of Poles. With the process of assimilation so palpable, researchers in the 1920s and 1930s—both American and Polish American—began to produce sociological studies patterned on the "community studies" model, which examined social change within Polonian communities, and especially among the so-called second generation, the first Polish generation born in the United States. In this genre, the work of Theodore Abel and of Niles Carpenter and Daniel Katz stands out. While few in number, these professional social science works—produced increasingly by university-educated Poles and Polish Americans—continued into the 1950s, suggesting that at least a handful of academic professionals had changed their attitudes about this large ethnic group: from a social problem, Polish Americans had become an object of scholarly interest.[28]

Polish immigrant publicists, politicians, educators, and intellectuals themselves recognized the force of assimilation. At the extreme, assimilation threatened to overtake Polonia's youth, on whom depended (Polonian leaders believed) Polonia's future as a "community," as a social, political, economic, and cultural formation. Polonia's elders tried to confront the assimilation problem head-on by stressing the preservation of culture and its intergenerational transmission through, among other tactics, the commemoration of Polish and (increasingly) Polish-American history. In part, the commemorative journal as a genre proliferated because, as Polish immigrant settlements matured, they simply had more anniversaries to celebrate. Yet, by reifying and thereby glorifying the immigrant past, these publications tried to create a historical core around which the now multigenerational Polish-American community might cohere and thereby endure. As early as 1905, a new Polish-American periodical called *Orędownik Językowy* (The language advocate), edited by Rev. Bolesław Góral, had railed against the creolization of Polish, the use of Polonized English words. But the campaign did not meet with much success; it seems not to have realized that peasant immigrants probably lacked the Polish vocabulary to describe many of the things, hitherto unfamiliar to them, that they now encountered in the urban industrial world.[29] Yet even while organizing or encouraging youth activities within the ethnic fold and arranging Saturday schools aimed at fostering the maintenance of the Polish language, in the 1920s Polish-language newspapers began to print "youth columns" in English, the language increasingly preferred by young Polish Americans.

Faced with American realities and having decided to stay here, Polish-American leaders and intellectuals—stigmatized by the hyphen—shifted their energies toward the attainable goal of winning recognition in their adoptive country. Their social status doubtless had increased as they figured in wartime politics, one of whose puzzles was the Polish issue. Despite the racialist climate that had spawned immigration restriction legislation in the 1920s, Poland's restoration to statehood under the terms of the Treaty of Versailles enhanced Polish Americans' national recognition by transforming them into a potential, if untapped, American foreign policy resource.

The growth of Slavic studies in the United States in the 1920s lends support to this contention. Though Slavic studies as a field in colleges and universities dated back to the late nineteenth century, it reportedly "developed slowly and aroused little interest" until World War I. Withal, interest in Russian surpassed that in Polish studies, which were pursued largely by a handful of amateurs and hobbyists. In the mid–nineteenth century, poet James Gates Percival (b. 1795) produced Polish translations and wrote articles on Polish history and literature; still later in the century, Jeremiah Curtin (b. 1840) published translations of Sienkiewicz's novels, which circulated widely. In the 1890s, study of Slavic (and Polish) subjects took a more serious turn. At Harvard University, historian Archibald Cary Coolidge taught Russian and Polish history, oversaw the creation of Harvard Library's venerable Slavic collection, and in a paper presented in 1895 to the American Historical Association urged increased study of Slavic civilization. Courses in rudimentary Polish appeared elsewhere as well with, for example, instruction beginning at Notre Dame University in 1909. Coolidge student Robert Howard Lord (1885–1954), himself for a time on the Harvard faculty, published *The Second Partition of Poland* in 1915.[30]

Yet only after World War I increased curiosity in and familiarity with Poland did Slavic studies in American colleges and universities expand appreciably. At the University of California, Slavist George Rapall Noyes (1873–1952) and his assistants translated the Polish messianists—

Mickiewicz, Słowacki, and Krasiński. At Columbia University, John Dyneley Prince introduced Polish into the curriculum. At Dartmouth, Eric Kelly, author of *The Trumpeter of Krakow,* taught Polish translation and, for a brief time, enticed Canadian-born Slavicist William J. Rose to serve on the faculty. In a few institutions Polish library holdings grew markedly, most notably at Stanford University with the founding in 1919 of the Hoover War Library (the Hoover Institution on War, Revolution and Peace), whose materials derived from postwar relief work in Eastern Europe. In the meantime, Wisconsin Poles pressed to have Polish offered at the University of Wisconsin (which they achieved in the 1930s); Illinois Poles temporarily installed University of Cracow professor Roman Dyboski at the University of Chicago; and Detroit Poles engineered the appointment of Polish scholar Thaddeus Mitana at the University of Michigan. In a similar vein, in 1940 the University of Pittsburgh dedicated its Polish Room as part of the Nationality Rooms Program housed at that institution's Cathedral of Learning (the structure was begun in 1926 and the first set of rooms completed between 1938 and 1957).[31] The appointment at Columbia of Arthur P. Coleman in 1927 marks a watershed for the Slavic studies discipline. Characterized as "the first American of non-Slavic origin to receive a doctorate in Slavic languages in the United States," Coleman with his wife, Marion Moore Coleman, spilled forth a steady stream of writings on Polish culture in America during the next four decades, focusing especially on Poland's nineteenth-century political émigrés and on the American experiences of Polish-born actress Helena Modjeska (Modrzejewska) and Polish novelist Henryk Sienkiewicz.[32]

Although numerous, these attempts at institutionalizing Polish studies remained limited in scope and depth. While perhaps winning prosperous middle-class Poles (now including many college-educated professionals) some approbation from America's cultural elite, the foregoing had little impact on the status hierarchy within Polonia, in which the Polish-American elite still remained connected (perhaps more so than some would have liked). In 1926, Chicago Poles organized a Polish Arts Club, the first of a string of cultural clubs that came to life in the next couple of decades. Oriented toward the works that composed Polish "high culture" (fine arts and belles lettres), these groups buttressed the social status of Polonia's social elite by distinguishing its members from what some of them may have disparaged as the hybrid kiszka-beer-and-polka culture of their working-class co-nationals.[33] Often university based, these organizations afforded Polonia's social elite a point of contact with their native-born social betters, access to the bottom rung of a longer and higher social status mobility ladder, and thus a possible escape from what scholars have called the ethnic "mobility trap."

In 1925, the "distinctively Polish-American" Kosciuszko Foundation, organized by Professor Stephen P. Mizwa (Mierzwa)—himself a "poor Polish farmer" who had immigrated and advanced himself—represented a more artful and ambitious linkage of Polonian middle-class aspirations and America's citadels of learning, one accomplished through the medium of American and, later, Polish-American philanthropy.[34] Through tuition scholarships and reduced rates on Polish-American line steamships, the Kosciuszko Foundation supported Poles who wished to study in America and American students of Polish who wished to deepen their knowledge of the language and culture through study abroad. The Foundation also promulgated Polish history and culture by publishing biographical works on Poles and by hosting Polish commemorative events including a Paderewski testimonial dinner in honor of the tenth anniversary of Polish independence and a Copernican quadricentennial program in 1943 to mark the four-hundredth anniversary of Copernicus's death.[35]

The promotion of Polish history and culture in the 1920s and 1930s had four characteristics. First, despite signal accomplishments in a few academic settings, the level and depth of Polish studies in American colleges and universities remained fairly modest throughout the period. The onset of the Great Depression further retarded such efforts. Second, the efforts described above focused upon Polish language, literature, and culture, and decidedly not upon history. Third, to the extent that they did involve history, it was largely the history of Poland and not Polish America.[36] Finally, control over much of this activity rested in the hands of non-Poles (the possible significance of this remains to be considered).

In this manner, for most Polish Americans (who took Polish America, not Poland, as their frame of reference), achieving recognition became a problem that was more political than intellectual during the postwar period. What special strategies and tactics did this require? In the 1890s, Chicago Poles enjoyed a Polish Day at the Columbian Exposition and unveiled a statue of Kosciuszko there in Humboldt Park. In like manner, in 1910 one of American Polonia's most celebrated national/historical events of the prewar period took place. That July in Washington, D.C., Polish America's largest national gathering to date—and the first worldwide conclave of Poles—not only commemorated the Polish victory at the Battle of Grünwald but also marked the unveiling of monuments honoring American Revolutionary War heroes Casimir Pulaski and Thaddeus Kosciuszko, hyphenated but nonetheless true American patriots. Elsewhere, Poles also lobbied for the renaming of parks, streets, and bridges in honor of Polish or Polish-American figures. Such popular historical celebrations with Polish-American patriotic themes (with the emphasis on the American aspect) tried to counter negative ethnic images of themselves and their group, such as those purveyed by historian Woodrow Wilson.[37]

In the more formal historical realm, this quest for recognition saw the publication in 1939 of a *Who Is Who in Polish America,* edited by Rev. Francis Bolek. Bolek had served as chaplain in the Polish-Soviet war of 1918–1920, in which he had been taken prisoner of war by the Bolsheviks. He emigrated to the United States in 1924 and taught briefly at Alliance College (1928–1931), after which he became pastor of a Polish parish in Sharon, Pennsylvania, and later a teacher of Polish at a minor seminary in Athol Springs, New York.[38]

Polish-American history writing also reflected this mood, a tendency that blossomed in the scholarly career of Miecislaus (Mieczysław) Haiman (1888–1949), the foremost historian of American Polonia in the twentieth century. Haiman migrated to the United States in 1913 and became a citizen twelve years later. While still a journalist in the late 1920s and early 1930s, Haiman began to spin out the first of a long string of historical books and articles that linked America's Polish immigrants with civic virtue, American nation-building, and other quintessentially patriotic themes.[39] He wrote biographical sketches of Polonia's early leaders such as Rev. Vincent Barzyński, Rev. Józef Dąbrowski, publisher Władysław Dyniewicz, and Bishop Paul Rhode. His work also examined American attitudes toward Poland. In pieces on the Civil War, pioneers on the western frontier, the colonial period, and the American Revolution (one of which marked the two-hundredth anniversary of the birth of George Washington), Haiman articulated a singular message, which he wrote increasingly in English: where America happened, Poles were there.[40] In doing so, Haiman became the intellectual analogue of those immigrant businessmen and professionals—increasingly integrated into the larger American economy that operated outside, around, and increasingly into the immigrant enclave—who guided their immigrant co-nationals into citizenship, registered them as voters, and made "Americans" of them, in greater numbers and to a deeper extent than ever achieved by any Americanization campaign. For Haiman, the ideologue of Polish Americanism, as well as for many of his co-ethnic contemporaries, clearly the dreaded hyphen could serve to connect as well as to divide.[41]

Haiman also led efforts to establish a Polish-American archive and museum. As early as 1928, a Brooklyn chapter of the Polish Roman Catholic Union (PRCU), the large Chicago-based fraternal, had urged the PRCU to create a Polish museum in America. Seven years later, the PRCU, under president Joseph L. Kania, finally committed to the idea and appointed Haiman—at the time editor of *Naród Polski* (The Polish Nation), the PRCU's official organ—as its curator. The centerpiece of the early holdings of the PRCU Museum and Archives was the collection of papers of the Polish National Department *(Wydział Narodowy),* which had marshaled Polish-American support behind Poland's National Democratic Party, the liberal capitalist wing of Polish nationalist politics. With the founding of the installation and Haiman's tireless work, additional archival and museum materials flooded in. The invasion of Poland in September 1939 gave an unexpected boost to collection efforts as administrators at the Polish Pavilion of the 1939 New York World's Fair chose to intern valuable exhibitions at the PRCU in order to prevent them from falling into the hands of the Nazi occupation. The growth of the archive from various sources, including Haiman's personal library, made the PRCU Museum and Archives by the 1940s probably the premier research collection on American Polonia in the United States. In 1959, the museum was renamed the Polish Museum. By then, it was institutionally independent of the PRCU.[42]

Institutionalizing Polish-American History and Culture: The 1940s–1950s

The outbreak of World War II in Europe had several crucial outcomes that bear on this narrative. First, the war abruptly wrenched Polonia out of its (in large measure self-imposed) isolation from Polish affairs since the 1920s, after Paderewski's fall from political power, and caused Polish Americans once again to question the nature, depth, and extent of their ethnic ties to a Polish homeland that once again faced grave peril. Second, the war raging throughout Eastern Europe prompted American armed forces to institute training programs for military personnel in the Slavic languages. With the international crisis as a backdrop, in 1945, there were 11 colleges and universities that sponsored instruction in Polish, and 147 that sponsored instruction in Slavic history and culture (though probably most of them had a Russian focus). Finally, after the Nazi attack on the Soviet Union made the latter a British ally, Eastern European nationalities still smarting from Russian or Soviet territorial ambitions suddenly fell under suspicion of pro-Nazi sympathies. (This association, however base-less, probably colored wartime American policy vis-à-vis the region and also, by extension, American attitudes about nationality studies.) But, as Slavicist Clarence Manning has argued, when the war prompted the flight of Polish refugees here, among whom numbered several renowned Polish social scientists and historians, they served to counterbalance suspicions concerning the Eastern Europeans' political tendencies. They also exercised a profound impact on Polish and Polish-American scholarship in the United States in the 1940s and 1950s.[43]

Two scholarly institutions came to life during the war years. In 1943, an American Institute for Research in the Modern History of Poland (later renamed the Józef Piłsudski Institute of America for Research in the Modern History of Poland) was organized in New York City by a group of Polish Americans led by *Dziennik Polski* (Polish daily news) (Detroit) editor Franciszek Januszewski and several émigrés—including Poland's exiled former minister of education, Wacław Jędrzejewicz, who became the institute's first executive director. Patterned after its Warsaw-based parent body and namesake founded in 1923, the Poland-oriented Piłsudski Institute since has developed an important research collection on interwar Poland and has supported research in modern Polish history. (Though its holdings contain Polish-American nationalist materials, it has displayed little direct interest in Polonian history.)[44]

Vastly more ambitious and encompassing in scope than the Piłsudski Institute and also in New York City, the Polish Institute of Arts and Sciences in America (PIASA) was formed on May 15, 1942, by exiled Polish scholars and members of the Polish Academy of Sciences, apparently with the aid of Stefan Mizwa of the Kosciuszko Foundation.[45] According to historian and PIASA president Jan Kucharzewski, the new Polish Institute vowed "to assemble, preserve, and harness for posterity the values of a nation" and "to represent Polish thought in the world." In order to implement these goals, PIASA was organized into four Scholarly Sections, each representing a branch of liberal learning, including a section devoted to the "Historical and Political Sciences," headed by the renowned Polish émigré historian, Oskar Halecki. Its success inevitably dependent upon the support of Polish America, PIASA gradually developed an interest in American Polonia even though its founding documents had not mentioned this topic. At the first meeting of PIASA's Historical and Political Sciences Section, Halecki (who by the early 1950s would succeed to the PIASA presidency) "proposed to create a special Committee for the study of the history of Poles in the United States" and, upon approval of his proposal, enticed Miecislaus Haiman of the PRCU Museum and Archives to chair it. Christened the Commission for Research on Polish Immigration, the organization held its first conference and meeting on December 29–30, 1943, in Chicago and soon found quarters in the Polish museum there.[46]

In reviewing the Commission's early days, author Frank Mocha found, first, that it immediately stimulated scholarly activity—in history and in sociology (led by Stefan Włoszczewski)—and, second, that work on Polonia spilled beyond the Commission proper, as a parallel Commission for Research on Nationality Problems was formed. Polonia-related research popped up regularly in PIASA's History of Literature and Arts Section and proliferated in general PIASA publications and programs. By 1944, the Commission for Research on Polish Immigration had begun to meet annually at different Polish-American schools and colleges, had elected its own five-member board, and started to consider forming its own journal. The latter, christened *Polish-American Studies,* took life just as PIASA activities in this area—along with its *Bulletin*—ground to a halt, owing to the Allied withdrawal of recognition and support for the Polish government in exile in London, hitherto PIASA's main source of funding.[47]

At the Commission's second annual meeting, held at Orchard Lake Seminary in October 1944, the organization changed its name to the Polish-American Historical Commission. "The new Commission," Mocha argued, "differed from the former in that it was more egalitarian and had more members," within three years in excess of one hundred. As it included more Polish-American members, the Commission, while decidedly of émigré inspiration, became more heterogeneous—and somewhat bifurcated—in composition and cast. Though founded as "an independent scholarly society," it retained links to the Polish Institute, while the first issue of *PAS* was subvened by two older Polonian organizations, the Polish Roman Catholic Union of America and the Polish Women's Alliance of America (*PAS* was subsidized also by the Polish American Congress). In like manner, as Mocha noted, while both Haiman and *Polish-American Studies* editor Konstanty Symonolewicz (whose name is rendered variously as Symmons and Symmons-Symonolewicz) belonged to PIASA, Symonolewicz's associate editor (and the Commission's treasurer) was Rev. Joseph Swastek of Orchard Lake Seminary in Michigan.[48]

The polarity in founders' backgrounds produced a corresponding division in their respective understandings of Polish-American history and, indeed, even identity. For émigré scholars such as sociologist Stefan Włoszczewski, the Poles' transplanted culture represented a positive alternative to the "cultural vacuity" of America. Though Włoszczewski certainly recalled the Americanization traditions Haiman had pioneered, he suggested a more fundamental vision of cultural pluralism, not unlike that developed by Harvard philosopher Horace Kallen, which stressed ethnic cultural uniqueness.[49] By contrast, the Commission's assimilationist (or perhaps, more accurately, integrationist) wing, soon in the overwhelming majority, apparently had something else in mind. Though the Commission's members came overwhelmingly from the ranks of Polish America, its founders had constituted the organization as a historical society, not as an ethnic organization, opening its rolls "to all who are interested professionally or otherwise in the study of Polish American life and history." As a historical society and technically not an ethnic organization, the group facilitated aspirations for upward mobility, conformed to the realities of increased social integration, and sought to contribute to mainstream historical scholarship. A note on the journal's cover advised that "Membership is not limited to persons of Polish descent." Of symbolic significance, the Commission also welcomed to membership the spouses of its ethnically intermarried members (and "Americans" like the Colemans). In 1947, the organization became a member of the American Historical Association. It is significant that when Polonian groups convened in Buffalo in 1944 and established Polonia's umbrella political lobby, the Polish American Congress, they omitted the hyphen from the group's name, out of concern that *real* Americans would impugn their loyalty to the United States. By June 1946, the Polish American Historical Commission and *Polish American Studies* followed suit.[50]

Whereas Polonian intellectuals once had disagreed over whether to stress the Polish or the Roman Catholic elements in Polish Roman Catholic identity, Polonia's first historical society divided between those émigrés such as Włoszczewski who stressed Polish America's Polish foundations and the Polonians who emphasized its—and their—Americanism. No longer "Polish-American," many of the latter soon even distanced themselves from the phrase's unhyphenated variant. Rev. Francis Bolek—author, Polonian scholar, and prominent Haiman collaborator—spelled out this position at the organization's 1949 annual conference: "Our Polonia," Bolek observed, "cannot be anything else than *Americans of Polish descent* [italics added]." Rejecting "separatism" and "double allegiance," Bolek cited the position taken by Francis X. Swietlik, president of the Polish National Alliance, who, as chair of the Polish American delegation to the Congress of Poles Abroad, explained why American Polonia could not join the organization: " 'We here consider ourselves Americans, not

Poles.' " Swietlik, a Milwaukee-born attorney, also served as dean of the Marquette University Law School. Perhaps this difference of opinion between Bolek and Włoszczewski explains the omission of the latter's name from Bolek's *Who's Who in Polish America*.[51]

Haiman had been unique because he succeeded in spanning the organization's varied constituencies; but illness prematurely forced him to curtail his work in 1948, and he died in January 1949. By then, the World War II émigré intellectuals' influence in the organization, and on Polish-American history writing in general, while probably always exaggerated now had shriveled. With Haiman's death, the organization—in 1949 renamed the Polish American Historical Association (PAHA) and converted into an independent national society—became mostly a Polonian affair. Much of its membership and more and more of its leadership consisted of Polish Roman Catholic clergy and nuns; the latter peaked between 1955 and 1956 at 90 percent. (This is not meant to suggest that the clergy formed a monolith during these years, although they likely shared a broad consensus on many matters.) Emblematic of this change in composition and orientation, no less of the practicalities of administration, in 1950 PAHA relocated its headquarters to St. Mary's College in Orchard Lake, Michigan, the institutional home of Rev. Joseph Swastek, its new head. The Polish (Saints Cyril and Methodius) Seminary, St. Mary's College, and a preparatory school constituted the Orchard Lake Schools. PAHA, meanwhile, retained links to PIASA.[52]

During the 1940s and 1950s, historical and antiquarian works by Polish Americans proliferated within and outside of PAHA. Through this medium, a broad cross section of Polish-American hobbyists, antiquarians, genealogists, collectors, and academic historians—both men and women—involved themselves in (and in some measure took ownership and control of) the writing of their history and, with it, the creation of an ethnic identity. During these years several Polish-American journalists, including Karol Wachtl, Arthur L. Waldo, and Alphonse Wolanin, published a variety of useful studies; while the Polish-American press often published historical, documentary, or antiquarian articles.[53] By the early 1950s, PAHA itself had recruited a total of four hundred members. This democratization, Mocha argued, resulted in an "unevenness"—and diminution—of standards in the early years of *Polish-American Studies,* as the journal published pieces that "were short, not sufficiently thought out, and of little scholarly value." Mocha's harsh claim—that these "accurately reflected the state of Polonia research in America in this period"—should not obscure the fact that this early Polonian work itself serves as a valuable primary document, which speaks to the popular intellectual climate of Polish America at midcentury.[54]

Three observations shed light on PAHA organizational and scholarly activity during this era. First, a large portion of the organization's work and its members' scholarly output carried on prewar filiopietistic and antiquarian interests, albeit often based on careful research. In 1958, for example, *Polish American Studies* published a symposium on the contributions of the small group of Polish artisans who had settled at Jamestown, while other numbers of the journal included articles on Revolutionary War general Casimir Pulaski, Poles who had fought in the American Civil War, actress Helena (Modrzejewska) Modjeska, and similar topics. A similar orientation pervaded Polish America beyond the confines of the organization. In 1955, for example, the Polish Arts Club of Buffalo funded a Polish Room at the University of Buffalo Library as a "show-piece and a functional research center on Poland"; while Polish enclaves elsewhere dedicated public monuments to Kosciuszko, Pulaski, Copernicus, and other Polish or Polish-American personages.[55]

Serious scholarly works, at least in part, shared the motivations that inspired these efforts. During this period, PAHA undertook to compile a Polish-American encyclopedia under the editorship of Rev. Bolek and Rev. L. Siekaniec, OFM. The encyclopedia was to have included ten broad topic areas—historical background, the Polish community, education, literature, the press, social life, structure of the Polish community, economic life, qualities of Polish-American character, and relationship of immigrants to Poland and the United States—although planned subtopics did not always fit easily under the topic to which they were assigned. The 1947 PAHA annual meeting scrapped this model, however, in favor of a standard alphabetical format as prepared by Rev. Bolek. Only a first volume, covering entries beginning with the letters A and B, ever saw publication. By celebrating Polish culture and broadcasting the accomplishments of group members in America—Polish-American "firsts" and "bests"—Polonian writers challenged nagging nativist stereotypes, claimed social status, and sought public recognition and acceptance. Meanwhile, much Polish-American historical study continued in local venues such as parish and organizational commemoratives and Polish-American newspaper columns; but since many of these and other Polish-American studies appeared in Polish, they remained inaccessible to America's English-speaking historical profession.[56]

Second, during its first fifteen years between 1944 and 1959, priests and nuns wrote over half of the articles and miscellaneous short essays published in *Polish American Studies* and perhaps also a substantial portion of the era's Polish-American historical scholarship in general. Among the roughly twenty clerics who contributed articles during the 1940s and 1950s were Rev. Ladislaus J. Siekaniec, Rev. S. Zielinski, and the prolific Rev. Swastek. About thirty-five nuns also published pieces during this period, including several who contributed repeatedly: Sr. M. Liguori, Sr. M. Catherine, Sr. M. Nobilis, Sr. M. Accursia, Sr. M. Edwina, and Sr. M. Beatrice. Like their lay counterparts, they produced many sound, credible studies; and their historical interests extended beyond religious subjects.[57]

Historical pieces on religious topics steadily made up about a fifth of the articles and essays published by the journal between 1944 and 1959 (and almost 30 percent between 1951 and 1954). During this time, both PAHA and *PAS* in some measure thus served as ethnic analogues of the American Catholic Historical Association and its official organ, the *Catholic Historical Review,* which, between 1945 and 1960, published not a single article or essay pertaining to the Catholicism of Poles or any other of the "new" immigrants. A few articles in the latter dealt with issues and topics obliquely related to the so-called new immigrants, although none mentioned the latter specifically. It is not clear how many Polish Americans were members of the Catholic Historical Society or, likewise, whether any tried to publish historical pieces in the journal. It is interesting that the standard history of the American church, Monsignor John Tracy Ellis's *American Catholicism,* mentions Poles per se only in a single paragraph on the Polish National Catholic schism. To extrapolate from census figures and Polish National Catholic and Roman Catholic church membership statistics, in the 1950s Polish Americans comprised between 11 and 15 percent of American Catholics.[58]

Third, and especially striking, women—both religious and lay— quickly achieved wide representation in the ranks of PAHA. In 1947, they comprised 35 percent of the membership (of PAHA's 89 female members, 71 percent [63] were nuns). After 1947, membership lists were no longer published in the journal, and it thus becomes difficult to estimate the percentage of female members.[59] Nonetheless, during the 1950s, women annually held between 35 and 61 percent of the officer and council positions (an overwhelming majority of female officers and council members were nuns). Articles and miscellaneous short essays by Polish-American laywomen and nuns (the latter effectively subvened by Polonia's extensive system of parishes and parochial education) similarly made up an impressive 41 percent of the contents of *Polish American Studies* during the decade (57 of 138 pieces were written by women; of these, 63 percent [36] were authored by female religious).[60] Yet articles written concerning women comprised only about an eighth of the titles in the journal's first fifteen years. Of these, the overwhelming majority (85 percent) treated religious subjects, principally institutional histories of female religious congregations or brief biographies of the nuns who founded them, and all but two were written by female religious.

Although this scholarship was hardly "engendered," as scholars now understand the term, the nuns who examined the history of their female-controlled religious institutions might be seen as proto-feminist. But this remains an ambivalent proposition. The Marian tradition did represent a Roman Catholic variant of the women's sphere, which empowered the women who embraced it. At the same time, the sisterhoods formed a part of a hierarchical and male-dominated church and some of them, like the Felicians, adopted a self-abnegatory rule that, it might be argued, denied their corporeal dimension as women. Meanwhile, outside PAHA during these years, female participation in ethnic cultural and historical studies grew. In 1948, sixteen Polish-American cultural clubs established the American Council of Polish Cultural Clubs, in which many secular Polish-American women were active. Also during that year, the Felician Sisters' Madonna College in Livonia, Michigan, became a senior college; and six years later, with the same status, Holy Family College was founded in Philadelphia by the Sisters of the Holy Family of Nazareth.[61]

Overshadowing (and one might fairly say overdetermining) Polish studies and Polish-American history writing in the late 1940s and 1950s, however, was the position of Poland in—and, with it, the relationship of Polonia to—America's deepening Cold War. Already in 1941, Arthur Coleman organized the American Association of Teachers of Slavic and East European Languages; its émigré members quickly gave that body an anti-communist cast. With the establishment in July 1944 of Poland's pro-Soviet Lublin government, Miecislaus Haiman—and probably much of Polonia's academic elite—rushed to criticize Polonia's small but vocal left-wing as "communistic" and, in so doing, embraced the ideological stance that in the main characterized Polonia's intelligentsia and political leadership throughout the Cold War years. Polish scholars in America also protested postwar American foreign policy that accepted Poland's new status as a Soviet satellite. In 1946, for example, Oskar Halecki joined other Polish-American leaders to bring up Poland's situation at the Paris Conference of Great Power Foreign Ministers. In 1949, the Kosciuszko Foundation threatened to suspend its exchange program with Poland for 1949–1950 "until more favorable conditions prevail." Coleman, meanwhile, succeeded in mobilizing the Polish American Congress and much of Polonia to oppose establishment of Columbia University's Adam Mickiewicz Chair of Polish Culture because its funding came from Poland's communist government. Coleman resigned in protest after the chair was filled. In 1950 he became president of Alliance College, and in 1954, eventually bending to pressure, Columbia University resigned the gift and reduced the chair to adjunct status.[62]

Through this episode, historian Stanislaus A. Blejwas has argued, Polonia's anti-communist academic and political leaders "effectively obstructed the development of Polish studies in the United States." Yet Blejwas also fairly observed that "The second World War and the Cold War were the 'god-parents' of East Central European studies in the United States." Policy and strategic concerns and international events stimulated growth in two areas. The first was called "area studies."[63]

Wartime political considerations doubtless had caused the framers of area studies in the early 1940s "to accent the Soviet version of the relations between the nationalities of the Soviet Union, and the old Russian concept of a single Russian people." By the 1950s, scholars such as historian Wacław Lednicki had begun to emphasize "the role of the fellow travelers, who imposed on Slavic studies a special [Russian] character." Slavicist Charles Jelavich argued that grouping East Central Europe with Russia as an "area" made sense only in the contexts of linguistic or Soviet studies, although he conceded Russian influences on both Poland and Bulgaria. Reviewing the development of the discipline in 1969, Jelavich argued that, except for the immediate postwar period, the "decisive influences" on most of the countries of East Central Europe came from the West not from the East and accordingly recommended steps to remedy "the neglect of the proper appreciation of Western influences in this area."[64]

Anti-Soviet Polish specialists who wished to reorient the field accordingly identified two tasks. First, they needed to disabuse Americans of the stereotype (dating back to the nativist late nineteenth century) that "the Slavic countries, especially Poland, are countries of a very thin stratum of more or less cultivated landlords with the rest of the population . . . of illiterate peasants," and, by extension, that Soviet occupation was accomplishing the education—and civilization—of an inchoate, unwashed, pre-political rural society. Second, they needed to "rectify and correct historical perspectives, and explain to the American people the cultural differentiation . . . behind the 'Iron Curtain' " so as to undercut Soviet—and vaguely Pan-Slavic—arguments that the Soviet satellites belong together.[65] In addressing both these issues, they had to confront the chronic invisibility of Poland in European history texts and outlines published in the United States (a condition reminiscent of the historical treatment of the Polish immigrants). In 1954, historian Wacław Lednicki wrote:

> One need only glance through any of the books on the political and cultural history of modern Europe, any book on general European history used in our colleges, to see what a humble place is given to the Slavic countries. In a volume of nine hundred pages one may find perhaps ten pages on Poland, Bohemia, and the other Slavic nations. Generally Poland is mentioned in connection with the partitions only, so that the reader is really not aware at all of what it was that was partitioned. . . . [T]here exist in this country all kinds of college outline manuals published by various scholars. These outlines are of an essential importance for the student as they purport to give the basic information in each of the fields covered. . . . In [one] outline of three hundred pages, pre-war Poland has eleven lines devoted to it and post-war Poland has six lines. Bohemia and Hungary together have twelve lines. In addition to this, Czechoslovakia has twelve lines, which she owes to Munich.[66]

International developments soon boosted the efforts of the anti-Soviet Polish specialists, so that in 1954, for example, Columbia University established an Institute on East Central Europe (the same year it dropped the controversial Mickiewicz Chair), and in 1965, the American Council of Learned Societies organized a Subcommittee on East Central and Southeast European Studies. Indiana University and the University of Washington also established such programs. Between 1946 and 1965, master's and doctoral degrees awarded for work on Poland comprised fully a quarter (107) of the total master's and doctoral degrees conferred in Eastern European studies by major American institutions responding to one survey.[67]

The second growth area, stimulated by defense considerations, was language training. In 1955, according to a survey conducted by Professor Sigmund Sluszka, the Polish language was taught in about twenty-four American colleges, universities, and government training schools and in three Canadian universities. "[T]he total college student enrollment that year in Polish courses was 377," the study found, "plus 3,227 in higher institutions of other types. In addition, there were 819 students in public high schools and 189,567 enrolled in parochial schools at the pre-college level." With the United States still smarting from the successful launch of the Soviet satellite *Sputnik,* in August 1958 Congress enacted Public Law 85-864, the National Defense Education Act (NDEA), whose several language initiatives included language instruction, language institutes and centers, and a graduate fellowship program.[68]

If Russian and, relatedly, Polish studies benefited from the NDEA, support for language and area studies also came from other quarters with fewer official or determinate Cold War links. Foundations and nonprofit organizations funded language-training grants and fellowships. These included the Rockefeller and Carnegie corporations, the Social Science Research Council, the American Council of Learned Societies (for faculty), the Ford Foundation Area Fellowship Program (for graduate students), the Institute of International Education, and the Inter-University Committee on Travel Grants (whose functions, after 1969, were taken over by International Research and Exchanges Board, or IREX). Several area and foreign-language studies organizations also arose, like the American Committee of Slavicists (ACS) in 1957 (which consisted of the chairs of Ph.D.-granting university departments in Slavic languages and literatures) and the American Association for the Advancement of Slavic Studies (AAASS) in 1958. In 1955, a special "conference" of Slavic and Eastern European historians had been formed within the American Historical Association. The Mid-European Studies Center of the National Council for a Free Europe also operated in the postwar years but had shut down by the mid-1950s. The Library of Congress published an *East European Accessions List,* while journals and periodicals on the subject also multiplied.[69] In 1956, the Polish Institute of Arts and Sciences in America established the *Polish Review,* and several other journals came to life as venues for articles concerning Poland and other countries in the region. Slavic studies at Roman Catholic—and especially Jesuit—institutions also grew. Among these were Marquette, Notre Dame, and Fordham, where Oskar Halecki was on the faculty.[70]

For several reasons, these public and private initiatives affected the development of Polish studies in the United States far less than might have been anticipated. First, chronic weaknesses combined with several inherent disabilities reduced the effectiveness of area studies programs focusing on Poland and East Central Europe. The former included the inadequacies (and the linguistics slant) of language-training programs, limited course offerings, and "a lack of fellowship support in view of the difficulties of the field." The latter included the "need for many languages" that lengthened East Central European studies master's and doctoral programs and consequently tended to winnow enrollments and reduce access to all but those students with linguistic skills derived from ethnic backgrounds. (At many key institutions, Polish studies were at least spared the "inadequate library facilities and difficulties in acquiring primary materials" that hampered the study of most other countries in the region.) Secondly, these initiatives shared the preoccupation with the Soviet Union—Russia—that characterized the Cold War years. Between 1959 and 1966, for example, the Office of Education made 1,497 National Defense Foreign Language (NDFL) awards in East European languages. Although Polish fared better than its Eastern European counterparts, it garnered only 4.4 percent (66) of the NDFL awards, 82 percent (1,228) of which went to support Russian language study. Historian Stanislaus Blejwas observed that, "Available teaching positions listed under the rubric 'Russia and Eastern Europe' " similarly have "tend[ed] to be awarded to Russian specialists." By the early 1970s, the study of the area by North American scholars had approached "maturity," but, as Blejwas remarked, "the NDEA, which was crucial for the development in area studies in general, is all but extinct." Strategically, other "areas" (of the Third World now) had become hotter spots.[71]

From Cultural Pluralism to the "New Ethnicity"

However disabling these influences during the postwar years, from the standpoint of immigration and ethnic history writing, a third weakness weighed even more heavily. To whatever extent the foregoing developments actually had encouraged the development of Polish studies, they accomplished nothing immediate for scholarship on Polish America. But the postwar climate of cultural pluralism also opened a window for serious, legitimate consideration of the groups that constituted (and "groupness" that characterized) the mosaic of American society. Cold War foreign policy concerns, the Civil Rights movement, and the Nazi Holocaust together helped delegitimize racialism and usher in cultural pluralist perspectives. In this environment, Polish-American social mobility, assimilation, and mainstreaming in the post–World War II years had yielded a handful of university-educated Polish-American historians and social scientists, many American-born, who began to produce professional scholarly studies on Polish immigration topics. Among this group were historians Jerzy Lerski, Victor Greene, and Joseph A. Wytrwal; sociologists Roman L. Haremski and Helena Znaniecka Lopata; and, in folklore/anthropology, Harriet Pawlowska and Helen Stankiewicz Zand.[72]

By the early 1960s, Polish-American scholarship gradually began to reflect these influences. First, cultural contacts with Poland like the academic exchanges sponsored by the Kosciuszko Foundation continued; meanwhile, the death of Stalin and the rise of Khrushchev in the Soviet Union and of Gomułka in Poland paved the way for greater Polish contacts with Polish America and with American academe.[73] Nonetheless, the Polonian—and Polish—scholarly circles would not feel the full impact of these contacts for a decade. Second, interest in Polish-American history remained strong. By 1963, for example, PAHA claimed over six hundred members and over one hundred additional subscribers, modest figures when considered in terms of potential membership (several million Americans of Polish descent) but still representing a 300 percent increase in fifteen years. Third, the professionalization of Polish-American scholarship continued, with publication of works by Joseph W. Wieczerzak, Richard Kolm, Danuta Mostwin, and others.[74]

An increasing secularization accompanied this trend. Although, for example, male and female religious still accounted for over half of PAHA's membership in the early 1960s, their representation in officer and council positions had dropped from its mid-1950s peak of 90 percent to about 66 percent. By the late 1960s the figure began to dip below 50 percent. The content of *Polish American Studies* also mirrored this change, as the journal featured somewhat fewer articles on religious topics and markedly fewer pieces by male and female religious. In the 1950s, about 52 percent of the articles and essays published in *Polish American Studies* were written by male and female religious; for the 1960s the figure stood at 34 percent. Religious subjects slipped less sharply during the same period, from 26 to 22 percent. Additionally, whereas women still comprised about a third of PAHA's members in the early 1960s, secular women had become relatively visible in Polish-American scholarly circles, and writing on secular topics made up 70 percent of the pieces on female topics published in the journal during the 1960s. At the same time, the percentage of pieces on women published in the journal declined slightly from 12 percent in the 1950s to 9 percent in the 1960s.[75]

Given Polish-American scholarship's long associations with Roman Catholicism which continued through the 1960s, perhaps it is no surprise that the celebration of the millennium of Christianity in Poland (1966) became a rallying point for Polish—though not specifically Polish-American—cultural revival in the United States. While the millennial observance featured many largely religious events, millennium contests, commemorative pubications, and some essentially civic celebrations, most focused on the history and culture of Poland. Much of this activity that involved Poland and Polish culture was antiquarian and filiopietistic in orientation. None of the activities reviewed in a 1968 St. Mary's College symposium, for example, treated the history of the Polish experience in America.[76]

Roughly coterminous with the millennial commemoration and thematically if not directly linked to it, other initiatives also took place that increased Polonia's visibility in America. Among these were the organization, under PIASA auspices, of an important scholarly conclave in New York City in 1966; the founding of the Polish National Catholic Church Commission on History and Archives in 1967; a large Polish folklore exhibit at the Library of Congress in 1971; and the establishment of an endowed Chair in Polish Language and Literature at Harvard University, funded by the Jurzykowski Foundation in 1971. Save for the PNCC archival and documentation efforts, which themselves took place before the backdrop of the Roman Catholic millennial observances, these initiatives all focused primarily or exclusively on Polish rather than Polish-American culture and history. This had changed by the late 1960s, as Polish Americans joined with other descendants of America's new immigrants in an ethnic cultural revival known as the "new ethnicity."[77]

Although historians have laid this ethnic revival to a variety of causes (including the unfolding of "Hansen's Law"), no consensus has formed around any single explanation—the so-called ethnic revival has yet to inspire serious studies or analyses of its origins and significance.[78] Ethnic Americans doubtless drew some inspiration from the Black Pride movement and the attendant increase in recognition of African-American culture and history. But, it will be recalled, the Polish millennial observance, a landmark in Polish ethnic revival, roughly coincided with the beginnings of the Black Pride movement and took place well before the media sensation produced by the publication and later television serialization of Alex Haley's *Roots* (1976) had generalized an awareness of the Black Pride phenomenon throughout contemporary American mass culture. Exclusive of the African-American experience (as Michael Novak and others have shown), ample influences, both internal and external, conduced toward white ethnic alienation and ethnic revival in post–World War II America. Writing in 1971, sociologist Rev. Leonard Chrobot, perhaps the most notable contemporary Polish-American proponent of the "new ethnicity," celebrated the anti-materialist values and corporatist bonds of the ethnic "community" as a positive alternative to "the common enemies . . . of all racial, ethnic, religious, and economic groups—Mass Culture, and its atomization of the individual, and the Corporate State, with its assumption that the Gross National Product is more important than the quality of human life." In tracing the roots of Polish-American ethnicity, Chrobot unearthed a fundamental question of identity. In addressing the question Who am I?, Chrobot tried less to connect Polish Americans to American society (a time-honored aim of Polish-American integrationists) than to reconnect them to each other—and to themselves.[79]

Legislative developments at various governmental levels, meanwhile, both channeled and encouraged an assortment of ethnic heritage activities that followed logically from sentiments such as Chrobot's. In 1969, Representative Roman Pucinski, a Polish-American Democrat from Chicago, introduced into the House an ethnic heritage studies bill, which Congress ratified in 1972 as an amendment to the Higher Education Act of 1965. The act authorized the establishment of a National Advisory Council on Ethnic Heritage Studies, the creation of ethnic heritage studies programs, and the development of ethnic studies curricular material and teacher training. In this "polyglot nation," Pucinski noted, "made up of many diverse ethnic groups, many religions, many nationalities, and many races . . . we find relatively little or no material about the various ethnic groups that came here and made this country great, and put this country together, and gave us this great land of ours."[80]

The amendment fostered a recognition of ethnic contributions and cross-cultural understanding, and significantly it also aimed to "afford to students opportunities to learn about their own ethnic heritages." Between 1974 (the first year of funding under the act) and 1976, the federal Ethnic Heritage Studies Program supported over a dozen projects— largely curricular—that featured Polish-American participation or developed Polish-American materials. Several state legislatures also enacted ethnic heritage bills; Illinois, Michigan, and several municipalities also supported ethnic studies in their various school curricula. America's bicentennial in 1976 became a focal point for such ethnic activities, with programs by private and public organizations, such as the Smithsonian Institution's "A Nation of Nations" exhibit in Washington, celebrating "our nation's cultural diversity as well as the 200th anniversary of the American Revolution."[81]

The ethnic revival and, more specifically, the passage and implementation of the ethnic heritage studies act became the occasion for an upsurge of interest—both scholarly and popular—in the history, culture, and social life of America's white ethnic enclaves. With regard to Polish Americans, local and individual initiatives abounded. At the institutional level, the University of Minnesota's Immigration History Research Center (IHRC) from 1964 and Philadelphia's Balch Institute for Ethnic Studies from 1971 developed research collections on Polish immigration. In 1971, the IHRC and the Center for Research Libraries in Chicago jointly inaugurated an ambitious Polish Microfilm Project, which aimed to microfilm some forty Polish-American newspapers. The microfilm project, which took place under the auspices of the Ethnic Records Microfilm Project, was initially supported by funds from the Alfred Jurzykowski Foundation and the National Endowment for the Humanities and was endorsed by PIASA and the Kosciuszko Foundation.[82] The Chicago Historical Society similarly housed the newly created Oral History Archives of Chicago Polonia, a large collection created in 1976 through Ethnic Heritage Studies Program funding, while the Milwaukee Urban Archives at the University of Wisconsin–Milwaukee's Golda Meir Library acquired a substantial oral history collection from a 1980–1981 Polish-American archives project.[83]

Scholarship on Polish Americans increased as research resources grew. Polish Americans were featured in several national conferences, while new research guides surveyed Polish-American serials, archival sources, and historical and sociological literature.[84] The period also witnessed an explosion in monographic research, some of it gathered and published in solid essay collections, and the publication of several general Polish-American histories, which together, although often still filiopietistic, rendered the history of Polish America more widely accessible and thus provided a basis for subsequent scholarship of a more critical nature.[85]

During this period, Polish-American priests, nuns, and filiopietistic and antiquarian lay writers continued to cede influence and prominence to more professionally trained lay, albeit still amateur, scholars (among them Henry Archacki, Francis C. Kajencki, Edward Pinkowski, Celia Wong, and Joseph A. Wytrwal). In addition, with the huge expansion of interest and opportunities in ethnic heritage studies in the United States, and later the contraction of Slavic studies here, Polish-American scholars trained in Polish or Russian history, language, or literature (often with NDFL fellowship support) gravitated toward Polish-American topics, typically bringing outstanding linguistic skills with them. Among these were M. B. Biskupski, Stanislaus Blejwas, Daniel Buczek, Thaddeus Gromada, Thomas Napierkowski, Lawrence Orton, and Thaddeus Radzilowski. Moreover, a contingent of younger scholars formally trained as primarily American historians (some but not all of Polish-American ethnic backgrounds) now connected their own study of Polish-American ethnic enclaves and Polish immigration to the mainstream of American social-historical inquiry.

Since the early days of the Polish American Historical Commission, sociologist Konstantin Symmons-Symonolewicz had called for research in Polish-American social history, but his views had little impact on Polonian scholarship during his time. While precursors of Polonia's version of the "new social history" did exist in the work of Harriet Pawlowska, Helen Stankiewicz Zand, and others, only with the publication of Victor Greene's *The Slavic Community on Strike: Immigrant Labor in Pennsylvania Anthracite* in 1968 did a historian assay the first sustained critical look at working-class Polish immigrant life "from the bottom up."[86] To be sure, scholars continued to examine more "traditional" topics like the Polish nationalist movement, associational life and electoral politics, immigrant military and government service, and Poland–United States foreign relations.[87] But, following Greene's example, more researchers began to study day-to-day immigrant life and social affairs. The most concentrated scholarly dialogue critically examined Polish-American trusteeism and independentism.[88]

While still engaging questions posed by traditional institutional history, this scholarship offered a fresh revisionist perspective. Yet the earmark of Polish America's "new social history" was its fascination with the Polish immigrant as peasant and industrial worker. Whereas in the 1950s historian Wacław Lednicki had underscored the need to disabuse Americans of the stereotype of the Pole as unwashed peasant, historians of Polonia found value in the experiences of the ordinary immigrant and won professional recognition for studies of work, families, strikes and unions, community life, popular culture, and popular religion at a time when research on such topics was in vogue.[89] Contrary to this trend and reminiscent of the variant of cultural pluralism advocated by Stefan Włoszczewski, in 1969 Polish-American scholar Richard Kolm, calling for the development of a biculturalism, urged Polish Americans to

> Change from the static base of folk-cultural identity to a dynamic . . . socio-cultural distinctiveness based on the conscious cultivation of unique values and patterns. . . . Change from exclusive emphasis on the past, to include the contemporary living Polish culture as it evolves in Poland and among Poles abroad.

Given the temper of the times and the prevailing climate of opinion, clearly Kolm remained a minority voice, one that went largely unheard.[90]

Filiopietists within Polonia disdained this emphasis on commonplace subjects previously associated with those nativist "Polack" stereotypes they had worked so hard to dispel. In defense of anthropologist Paul Wrobel, whose work on one Polish neighborhood in Detroit came under especially sharp attack, historian Thaddeus Radzilowski identified the anti-working-class theme in the filiopietists' critical onslaught. In a short essay that became a defining moment in recent group scholarship, Radzilowski expressed the sensibilities underlying the new historiographical movement, which he christened the Detroit School (after the subject of Wrobel's work and the Detroit origins of Wrobel and several of Polonia's revisionist scholars).[91] While the scholars whom Radzilowski included in the so-called Detroit School held a variety of ideological orientations, uniting their work, Radzilowski proposed, lay "a common belief in the centrality of the Polish American working class experience to any understanding of American Polonia":

> The approach [which Radzilowski called "implicitly anti-elitist"] is self-consciously (and at times defiantly) proletarian in its affirmation of the validity of the culture and history of the world of the working class immigrant, the ethnic neighborhood, the Polka band, the parish festival and local club *against* the rejection of these things by upper and middle class Polish Americans. While not escaping the nostalgia and the filio-pietism (sometimes quite subtle and sophisticated) that informs for better or worse most of immigrant and ethnic studies, they are also interested in failure, suffering and defeat.

In rejecting "whiggish Polish American historiography" and its central theme, "the progressive and inexorable *embourgeoisement* of the Polish immigrant and . . . his successes along the way," and in "affirming the value of their grandparents' and parents' experiences in themselves," Radzilowski argued:

> these scholars also reject the notion that Polish American working class people are either incomplete Poles because of their lack of interest in Polish high culture or incomplete Americans by virtue of their failure to do better in the race for success, their desire to remain in the old neighborhoods, and their adherence to largely pre-industrial mobility and status strategies.

Radzilowski saw the Detroit School as underscoring the transformative, synthetic, and original (rather than derivative) nature of the Polish-American ethnic experience. "In essence," its practitioners "see the Polish American working class from its beginnings, as a new social and cultural entity, a people *sui generis*."[92]

Polish-American history writing derived considerable energy and vitality from this flurry of vaguely politicized and certainly self-conscious scholarly work. In this vein, several distinguished essay collections and two new synthetic works—ironically, one by a Polish-American historian, the other by a Pole—attempted to integrate new scholarly interests in an interpretation of the Polish-American experience.[93] Meanwhile, programs that supported scholarly exchanges or research abroad—such as those sponsored by the Polonia Research Institute at the Jagiellonian University in Cracow, the Kosciuszko Foundation, and a few American universities—encouraged a cross-fertilization between Polish and Polish-American scholars that was later regularized through academic conferences. Though variously sponsored, probably the most notable of these was the October 1980 conclave on "Poles in North America," held in Toronto under the auspices of the Multicultural History Society of Ontario. The ongoing research program of the Polonia Research Institute and other bodies as well as other special scholarly projects no less have aided scholarly collaboration (among the latter, the ambitious Ecclesiastical Institutions Project, directed by historian Daniel Buczek and co-sponsored by the Catholic University of Lublin [KUL], outlined a massive undertaking—still unrealized—to write the history of Polish-American religious life in the style of the French *Annales* School). In the 1980s, for example, the Labor Migration and Labor Newspaper Preservation projects, both directed by historian Dirk Hoerder and sponsored by the University of Bremen in Germany (a country intimately linked with Polish emigration and immigration), repeatedly have brought together an assortment of Polish, Polish-American, and other scholars for research, conferences, and publications.[94]

The vitality of Polish-American history to group members also has, in the last two decades, sparked the formation of new historical organizations such as the Polish Genealogical Society in 1978 and the Polish American Re-Enactors Association in 1991 (the latter organized by Civil War buffs). Nonetheless, despite an aging and declining membership, PAHA continued to sustain numbers that have swung between 500 and 750, still making it Polonia's principal historical organization. As such, PAHA also witnessed important changes in the 1970s and 1980s, which reflected the evolution of Polish-American historical practice. First, the secularization of the organization intensified during the period. By the late 1970s, for example, priests and especially nuns held fewer officer and council positions, while the key PAHA offices also devolved into secular hands. Second, along with PAHA's secularization (perhaps, more specifically, a de-clericalization), came a rise in ecumenism among the clergy and nuns still active in the organization. Typifying this tendency, in 1970 PAHA elected Joseph Wieczerzak as its first Polish National Catholic president. Third, the professionalization of PAHA continued in the early 1970s: the group moved its headquarters from Orchard Lake Seminary to the Polish Museum in Chicago, incorporated in 1972 as a 501(c)(3) nonprofit organization, and became an affiliate of the American Historical Association. (While PAHA had, of course, been an AHA "member" since 1947, its new status as an "affiliated society" gave it a special institutional status with respect to—and a special institutional relationship with—the AHA. Presumably so as to emphasize its scholarly legitimacy, when listing its officers and council members in *Polish American Studies,* PAHA also began to indicate earned academic degrees, typically the Ph.D. These efforts at professionalization were carried out under the leadership of its longtime executive secretary, Rev. Miecislaus Madaj.) Fourth and by contrast, during the period, women held fewer PAHA officer and council posts, which is a trend not fully explained by the drastic decline in nuns holding such positions.[95]

The evolution of PAHA's journal, *Polish American Studies,* during these years reflects these trends. Under Frank Renkiewicz, its first secular editor since Haiman, after 1971 the journal abandoned its filiopietistic tendencies and began to publish refereed scholarly articles that conformed to the professional standards of the historical discipline. As for its contents, the journal published fewer articles and essays written by priests and almost none by nuns; and it included fewer pieces on religious subjects, more of which had lay authors. *Polish American Studies* also published fewer articles and essays either by or about women. Of the latter, nearly all treated secular subjects; more and more were written by men.[96]

Histories: Political, Personal, Existential

As the Polish American Historical Association might have served elements of Polonia's clergy as a professional alternative to the American Catholic Historical Association during the 1950s, by the 1980s it had become, at least at its core, the secular analogue for a group of Polonia's university-educated, politically fairly liberal, professional men. As a vehicle for upward mobility, self-preservation, and professional sociability for working-class male scions of peasant immigrants "for bread," PAHA perhaps at least temporarily had "engendered" a social and ideological space and thereby rendered it less than hospitable to its university-educated and perhaps increasingly gender-conscious female members and potential members who might have found other, more comfortable and personally and politically affirming professional venues elsewhere. For PAHA as an organization, this represented an inestimable loss. Meanwhile, having constructed and reified PAHA's modern existence in the commemoration of those immigrants who had come "for bread," the organization's secular leaders at once inadvertently also might have cut it off from another source of renewal, namely, the various newer groups of post–World War II immigrants and their descendants who possess interests and histories connected to contemporary Polish affairs, not the peasant and working-class past PAHA memorialized.

In embracing that past, PAHA—and the secular, male, Polish-American scholars who led it during the previous two decades—blended the sensibilities of the "new ethnicity" with the methods, problems, and interests of the "new social history." Yet, also awash in the complicated historiographical and ideological crosscurrents of American academe during the 1970s and 1980s, Polish-American (and PAHA) scholars also encountered, willingly or not, both "new left" and "radical history," subdisciplines and viewpoints that have had a profound effect upon historical inquiry in the United States throughout the period (and no less upon their own work). The more they have done so, the more eclectic and amorphous the Detroit School seems to have been, such that perhaps either it never really was a school or it did not remain so for long. A more systematic rift along traditional, left/right ideological lines, for example, seems all along to have differentiated practitioners of the Detroit School. While all may have romanced Polish immigrant working people and their popular culture, the so-called new ethnicity that helped inspire their research and activism sustained corporatist, anti-modern, anti-materialist themes sharply at odds with the "new left"/vaguely or basically Marxist orientation of some Detroit School scholars. Rev. Leonard Chrobot, for example, disavowed what he called the "decidedly Marxist" view, "that class struggle and group conflict is the *inevitable lot of the human condition* [sic]." Chrobot's formulation, of course, represents a quaintly existential distortion of class analysis.[97]

While recent professional Polish-American history writing therefore has been as politically informed as the history produced in, by, and for Polonia during the epic struggle for Poland's resurrection as a nation-state, and while its practitioners certainly have apprehended that, by writing the history of their own working-class forebears, they have claimed legitimacy for themselves, most have taken neither Poland nor even (principally) Polonia but rather the United States (and increasingly the American historical profession) as their frame of reference. In this sense, the history of Polish America, however developed and accomplished, perhaps has lost its traditional ideological and political raison d'être. Neither memory nor myth, ideology nor politics, it has become in large measure (and for better and for worse) just another subfield of the historical discipline. Perhaps it suffers the same fate that, many academic historians lament, has befallen most academic historical writing, becoming for most Polish Americans irrelevant to their lives.

While surveying the last twenty years of Polish-American history writing, its professionalization and reorientation, we nonetheless also would do well to recall an observation, made in another context, and consider its applicability vis-à-vis the practitioners of this subfield: the personal is political.[98] Can the scholars who research and write about a subject so inextricably linked to their own formation—both as scholars but also as persons—approach Polish-American history truly as "disengaged" professionals? In our time, perhaps we now can concede that the historian-as-subject cannot disconnect himself or herself from the subjectivity of personality, class, gender, race, ethnicity, culture, ideology, time, place, and so on. However objectified and professionalized, how might Polish-American history writers not mine their own and others' work for subterranean insights of personal and therefore political value?

In this intimate historical practice, these historians join their personal and political queries with introspections more existential (and religious): "*D'où venons-nous? Que sommes-nous? Où allons-nous?*" The roots of these and other such ruminations trail down into the verdant soil of the nineteenth century, that terra incognita of individual self-discovery as well as the collective discovery of national aspirations. Posing them in the here and now helps such "Poles"—typically of the so-called third or fourth generation—confront still salient questions, such as What is a Polish American? But also, and perhaps now more elementally, What is an American?[99]

Questions concerning identity are political questions because identity—both self-ascribed and ascribed—influences social location and structures social relations and vice versa. The recent social construction of "white European" as an ascriptive category should not obscure the fact that working-class white ethnics—even those privileged by their male gender—have suffered considerable marginalization and marginality (a not-quite-rightness, an out-of-placeness) akin to that experienced in some social arenas by persons of color and by women. For such white ethnic Americans (and scholars among them), the advantages conferred by their "white" skin have been compromised by vestiges of their class backgrounds and by their "unpronounceable" surnames (the latter perversely retained). They operate in professional milieus in which they seemingly continue to constitute, numerically and proportionally (and disproportionately), a minority, though not legally so defined. (It is perhaps revealing that, in one 1984 study of academics of working-class backgrounds, none of the interviewees had Eastern European surnames and few had parents in blue-collar occupations. Most would be considered lower middle class; all, save one, were male.)[100] Meanwhile, the scholars of the Detroit School have had additional, political reasons to celebrate Polonia's—and their own—immigrant peasant working-class roots. By underscoring their own group's victimization, they might distance themselves from complicity in the oppression of racial and ethnic minorities in which their forebears may have taken little or no part. They thereby also might claim the moral superiority associated with and the compensatory benefits accorded to the innocent and the victimized.

A recent work by English professor Thomas S. Gladsky deftly commingles these various themes—the political and the personal, identity and society, the individual and the community, ethnicity, assimilation, and marginality. In doing so, his work *Princes, Peasants, and Other Polish Selves: Ethnicity in American Literature* represents a rich and pioneering exploration in consciousness and in the social construction of ethnic—and American—realities and possibilities. Gladsky focuses upon

> the dialogue between majority *and* minority cultures, *and* the internal dialogue of descent writers working out their own literary images while reflecting upon their ethnic heritage. . . . In effect, descent writers have decided that ethnics are indeed the bearers of something, which—ironically but not surprisingly—is America as it might be.[101]

As Gladsky has cemented together a fragmented record to form a mosaic of contemporary relevance, other humanists have assayed kindred undertakings. Joan Micklin Silver—director of *Hester Street*, a film depiction of Jewish immigrant life on New York's Lower East Side—also reconstructed the trials of a Polish immigrant boy, Janek, and his family in a poignant short documentary/docudrama set in early twentieth-century Brooklyn, *The Immigrant Experience: The Long, Long Journey* (1972). The film was produced by Linda Gottlieb, and historian Thaddeus Gromada served as historical consultant to the project. Polish émigré filmmaker Marian Marzynski, meanwhile, has deconstructed immigrant recollection and narrative in films such as *God Bless America and Poland Too* (1990) and *Welcome to America* (1984).[102] Another film, *After Solidarity: Three Polish Families in America* (1988) by Gaylen Ross, examined the mixed experiences of America's Solidarity-era Polish immigrants. Historian Thaddeus Radzilowski consulted on the project. Meanwhile, a 1983 film by George Corsetti, Jeanie Wylie, and Richard Wieske, *Poletown Lives!*, examined the campaign by members of a Detroit Polish parish to save their church and homes from the wrecker's ball of a reindustrialization project. In like manner, though much more preliminarily, the essays in this volume also begin a sorting of historical pieces in order to determine where we have been so as to decide where we might go from here.

Against Gladsky's lyrical and optimistic reconnaissance that speaks to the conditions and consciousness of Polish America's historians, one ought yet to consider the future of Polish-American (and Polish) history in America in structural and institutional terms. For structural and institutional reasons, that prognosis seems, from a social scientist's vantage point, far more guarded. In present-day America's multicultural climate, however refreshingly it breaks with a nativist and racist past, white ethnic groups like the Polish Americans—who have had histories and experiences decidedly distinct from America's stereotypical Puritan and Cavalier ancestors—have been made, and have allowed themselves, to disappear within the designations "white European" or "Euro-American." In short, "ethnic" has come to mean a "non-white," protected, "minority" group.

Meanwhile, with the end of the Cold War and the fall of the Soviet Union, the history of Poland (an important and unreliable Soviet ally) and, by extension, the history of the Polish diaspora (once a key component of America's Cold War lobby) both might seem increasingly irrelevant to contemporary geopolitical realities. Similar domestic institutional effects that resulted from the thaw in United States–Soviet relations in the 1970s along with the Third World's rising geopolitical importance invite this speculation. Given how heavily race and power weigh upon popular thinking, moreover, the fall of the USSR—perceived (however wrongly) as a Slavic superpower—might be expected to produce disinterest in, and perhaps dismissal of, Slavic studies in general. It remains to be seen whether the growth of business opportunities in the region's new capitalist economies or a new crisis involving the countries of the former Soviet Union will counterweigh these tendencies.

This sense of irrelevance is likely, unless professional, secular Polish-American scholars link their work to the mainstream of American scholarship, claim a place for Polish Americans in America's multicultural rainbow, and forge useful connections to Polish and Polish-American affairs. But it is also likely unless Polonia finds uses in that version of memory rendered by its professional scholars. The latter, alas, may lie out of our hands; the former, perhaps not.

2

Labor, Radicalism,
and the Polish-American Worker

William G. Falkowski

The peasants of Catholic Europe, who constitute the bulk of our immigration of the past thirty years, have become almost a distinct race, drained of those superior qualities which are the foundation of democratic institutions.

—John R. Commons, *Races and Immigrants in America*

ALTHOUGH NEGATIVE, RACIALIST STEREOTYPES OF THE SO-called "new immigrants" long have colored historical treatments of Southern, Central, and Eastern European immigrant workers, in recent years scholars have produced a host of increasingly sophisticated studies concerning the role of Polish immigrants and their descendants in the process of working-class formation. To be sure, the complexity of this work is underscored by the tremendous diversity of the Polish immigrant experience in both the Polish homeland and the United States. Poland's tripartite division by Prussia, Austria, and Russia fostered divergent patterns of political, social, and economic development. And conditions in each partition changed over time. Compared to the first sizable wave of immigrants who arrived in the United States in the 1870s, the respective backgrounds of immigrants who arrived later were even more differentiated. The vast majority of Polish immigrants, however, were of peasant origins.[1]

Most Polish immigrants to the United States, some with families, made their ways to small and large cities, usually settling in ethnic enclaves near industries.[2] In some locales, Polish immigrants comprised a large portion, or even the majority, of the workforce. Men found jobs, usually as un-skilled laborers, in different industries. The experience of women who worked for wages differed from that of the men. Polish immigrants worked in both small and large mills, mines, and factories that employed different types and levels of technology along with various styles of labor management. Some industries in which they worked dominated particu-lar cities and others were part of a more diverse local economy. A few Polish immigrants became shopkeepers and smaller numbers entered the professions. Regardless of their pre-emigration backgrounds, Poles who arrived in the United States during different decades encountered consid-erably different situations. And second-, third-, fourth-, and even fifth-generation Polish Americans, many of whom have found themselves working in the same factories as their immigrant forebears, have each contended with new configurations of societal forces.

Making generalizations about the immigrant experience consequently has become an increasingly precarious venture. Nevertheless, drawing and expanding upon the pioneering work of David Brody, Victor Greene, Herbert Gutman, and David Montgomery, recent interpretations of the Polish-American experience have linked a broad amalgam of social history concerns—including family, gender, religion, community, and culture—with labor activity, making the field ever more challenging and invigorat-ing.[3] This essay updates earlier historiographical articles by Victor R. Greene (1976) and Frank Renkiewicz (1982) and concentrates on major works published in the past fifteen years that deal more than tangentially with Polish Americans.[4] Although Polish-language literature exists on the topic of the Polish-American working class, English-language materials generally are more attuned to the theoretical debates at hand and conse-quently occupy the focus of attention here.[5]

One of the most extensively contested issues regarding Polish immi-grant workers concerns how the sojourners' Old World backgrounds shaped their perceptions and behavior in the United States. For the most part, recent scholarship effectively challenges stereotypical notions, rooted in an older immigration and labor history, that depict inchoate and undif-ferentiated peasant newcomers as passive victims of American capitalism and as major impediments to unionization. Echoes of earlier scholarship, however, still continue to reverberate in the current historiographical landscape. For example, Stanley Aronowitz's disparaging dismissal of Pol-ish immigrant workers reflects the earlier genre: "Italian and Polish peas-ants provided a perfect labor force for an industrial system that demanded complete subordination of the worker to his rationalized pre-ordained tasks and to supervision. The awe of established authority was carried over from Europe by these immigrants. . . . These workers were imbued with the inevitability of social domination."[6]

Although most other recent scholars agree that these immigrants were actually ingenious in plotting their own course amid a turbulent industrial environment, significant differences of interpretation emerge as to how and to what extent immigrants' Old World dispositions characteristically animated and sustained them in their daily lives. Such consideration of immigrant motivations and strategies of adaptation is also closely linked to parallel concerns regarding immigrants' receptivity to unionism and radicalism.

In a series of books and articles, John Bodnar moves beyond the unilinear, dichotomous postulates of modernization theory whereby immigrants progressively shed a tradition-bound mentality and accept modern values of materialism, individualism, and progress.[7] Instead, he presents a more dialectical model allowing for both persistence and change. Polish immigrant and working-class culture in this context is seen not simply as a residue of the past but rather as a fusion of the past with the present, based on immigrant adaptation strategies shaped through interaction with the wider American environment. Arguing that the economic context of immigrant working-class existence also widely nurtured values antithetical to those commonly associated with modernity, Bodnar concludes that the worldview of Slavic working-class immigrants and their descendants was and remained primarily family-centered, defensive, and survival-oriented. Relying heavily upon oral history interviews conducted in Pennsylvania, Bodnar has documented among immigrants and their progeny a persistent anti-materialist ethos that looked askance at individual initiative and advancement.[8]

Bodnar also contends that the Polish-American working class was essentially conservative in its outlook and behavior—conservative in the sense that these workers were primarily concerned with defending what they perceived as their right to a steady job that provided security for their families. Recognizing that they often engaged in labor protest when aggrieved, he maintains that their demands were still characteristically defensive. Although Bodnar's immigrant workers generally did not assimilate middle-class values, they certainly did not struggle for workers' control of the production process. Bodnar concludes that Polish immigrants' willingness to involve themselves in labor organizations varied as to particular unions' receptivity toward the immigrants.[9]

By contrast, Ewa Morawska has criticized Bodnar's "working-class realism" as being "one-dimensional, flat, and tensionless." Instead, she emphasizes the "gain-instrumental orientation" of Polish immigrants in their "mobilization for economic and cultural advantage," stimulated prior to their emigration by the commercialization of agriculture and the introduction of capitalism in partitioned Poland.[10] Morawska's observations on working-class formation are predicated upon her studies of the steel town of Johnstown, Pennsylvania. Although efforts were made to unionize steelworkers there in the 1890s, and again with the 1919 steel strike, it was not until 1941 that Johnstown's workers in "little steel" were finally organized. In contrast to Bodnar's contention that immigrant workers employed primarily defensive adaptive strategies, Morawska depicts them as individualistic (albeit family-centered), advancement-conscious "penny capitalists." Morawska consequently argues that their willingness to join unions only developed as their sense of well-being became attendant upon their relative economic and social standing in the ethnic enclave rather than based on comparisons to the quality of their former lives in Poland.[11]

Over the span of the past decade, John Bukowczyk has contributed prolifically to our understanding of immigrant working-class culture and its impact upon class formation.[12] While maintaining the view that rural culture exerted a resilient influence on Polish immigrant workers' consciousness and behavior, he insists that this culture was neither monolithic nor static. He also locates significant cultural differences among Polish immigrants in the variegated class composition of the Polish peasantry and divergent political, social, and economic histories of each partition. In response to persistent notions of the torpidity of peasant culture, he maintains that particular facets of rural culture yielded contradictory tendencies among the immigrants, both before and after their decision to emigrate.[13]

For example, while the Poles' religiosity was capable of breeding an outlook of fatalism resulting in habits of docility and submissiveness, it could also sustain "a focus for community solidarity" and provide "a source of human worth impervious to degradation." Religion was thus a double-edged sword. It could act to mitigate discontent and militancy, but it could also serve to propel and bolster the immigrants' resolve and ability to resist exploitation. On the secular level, the enduring cultural legacy of feudalism similarly engendered both deferential and rebellious dispositions.[14]

Bukowczyk also devotes considerable attention to the relationship between the Polish immigrant middle class and working class. Acknowledging that an assortment of shopkeepers, businessmen, and professionals in

Polish settlements supported strikers, he rejoins that such demonstrations of ethnic-based solidarity also fostered a wide range of economic and political clientage relationships that bolstered the power of the middle class within the immigrant enclave and vis-à-vis the wider local society. Maintaining that ethnic consciousness was manipulated by Polonia's middle class to advance its own ideological agenda of personal advancement, he contends that workers' reciprocal political and economic support of middle-class leaders defused the maturation of working-class consciousness.[15]

Bukowczyk also argues that "the docility of Polish immigrant workers was observed most often in the 1880s, and their comparative assertiveness most frequently noted after 1900." He posits that this progression resulted not only as a response to transformations in American industry, but also because immigrants who arrived after 1900 were more likely to have some experience with rural populist and urban left-wing political movements in partitioned Poland. If the Polish immigrant working class was not imbued with a full-fledged ideology of labor radicalism, he reasons, it was more the outcome of capitalist repression and co-option than the result of a lack of potential. Even then, Bukowczyk posits, the Poles' willingness to fight for the well-being of their families and communities was indicative of a radical, alternative vision of society.[16]

My study of class formation in late nineteenth-century Buffalo Polonia situates the rise of working-class protest primarily in the immediate context of American political, social, and economic conditions. Given that late nineteenth-century American capitalism did not squarely fit the bill of rational and efficient (that is, what is typically considered "modern") enterprise and cognizant of the antipathies exhibited toward immigrants by most labor unions, I argue that their forms of protest necessarily were shaped in the context of limited possibilities. Examining numerous such instances of unrest—including the Luddite-like destruction of street-paving machines, the rout of Count Rybakowski's contingent of Coxey's Army, and Leon Czolgosz's assassination of President McKinley—I insist that the Poles' expression of discontent was pre-eminently derived from their conception of American rights.[17]

I also examine the attitude of labor toward Poles in regard to strike activity on the Buffalo-area waterfront in the 1890s. Initially recruited as scabs, Poles walked off their jobs over a wage dispute and the suspension of their free beer-break privilege. The union responded by welcoming the Poles to a festive celebration of workers' solidarity but failed to welcome them into the ranks of the union. By the end of the decade, the Poles,

employed as freighthandlers, gained membership in the union and responded in full solidarity to a walkout by Irish grainscoopers. Their determination to stay out on strike after other workers returned to work having
partially won their demands, however, only earned them the animus of
the union and of the Irish bishop who had played a leading role in mediat-
ing the dispute. I conclude that the posture of union officials toward
Polish workers in Buffalo was essentially self-serving, effectively precluded
the possibility of the Poles' active union participation, and severely re-
strained them in seeking redress of their grievances.[18]

If conditions after 1900 proved more conducive to the infusion of eastern and southern European immigrants into the labor movement, in numerous earlier instances immigrant Poles already amply had demonstrated
their union mettle. Leon Fink details how unskilled Polish ironworkers
in Milwaukee and adjacent Bay View rallied to support the Knights
of Labor in the mid-1880s. He argues that the Knights' ability to build
interethnic unity was predicated upon an ideology of "common-
denominational Americanism" based upon a working-class reformist political agenda shared by both skilled and unskilled workers.[19]

Determined to effect reform and emboldened by the eight-hour campaign of 1886, Polish Knights on strike marched in protest a day after the
Haymarket Riot and confronted government troops in Bay View. The
militia opened fire, killed five Poles, and wounded many others. The
Poles' militancy consequently was viewed as excessive by the Knights'
more "respectable" leaders and skilled rank and file. Fink argues that, as
local public officials relied increasingly upon repressive measures against
organized labor, solidarities between skilled and unskilled workers disinte-
grated. In effect, Poles considered the union's leaders too conservative,
and union leaders saw the Poles as too radical. Ironically, Polish immigrant workers' loyalties, displaced from a class-based political movement,
shifted to the arena of patronage-based ethnic politics, intensifying the
ethnic rivalries that the Knights had hoped to overcome.[20]

Richard Jules Oestreicher, in a study of the development of class consciousness in Detroit prior to 1900, argues that workers, regardless of
their backgrounds, shared a "culture of opposition," given the common
denominator of wage dependence and job insecurity. He explains that
the lack of Polish immigrant workers' involvement in labor organizations
resulted from organized labor's support for immigration restriction and
many labor leaders' prejudices toward Catholicism, a point that may find
support in Gwendolyn Mink's more general analysis of working-class seg-
mentation and party alignments in the Gilded Age and early twentieth

century.[21] Indeed, when Polish car-shop workers did go out on strike in 1886 and 1891, they stayed out on strike longer than other workers. Moreover, Polish workers voted for independent labor party candidates in Detroit more so than any other ethnic group except the Germans. And Polish Democratic candidates were most likely to use class rhetoric in their electoral appeals. The paucity of Polish union members in Detroit prior to the turn of the century, Oestreicher concludes, tells us more about unions than about Poles.[22]

The Poles' willingness to become active union members and their tenacity as strikers is substantiated further in reference to Chicago's meatpacking industry by the work of James R. Barrett, Dominic A. Pacyga, and Robert A. Slayton. All three authors show that, although Polish immigrant workers initially gained employment as scabs in the industry prior to 1900, soon thereafter they responded positively to the union's call for organization.[23]

Barrett shows how new work methods allowed for greater ethnic, gender, and skill diversity in the workforce, which in turn complicated the process of working-class formation. He argues, however, that the work process actually strengthened interethnic ties because different groups were mixed in the same departments. He also maintains that the paucity of mechanization in meatpacking, in contrast to the steel industry, allowed for more sympathetic relations between skilled and unskilled workers, as did the relative lack of residential segregation among white ethnics. Although the enormity of the plants, the fierce competitiveness of the labor market, and the strident pace of their work was certainly new to immigrant Poles, they were not rendered oblivious to their being exploited. It is most significant that their shared experience enabled them to develop common grievances and respond to what they perceived as threats to their traditional family values. Barrett contends that all these factors contributed to the Poles' prounion posture and that unionization was a matter of "Americanization from the bottom up."[24] Poles also demonstrated their loyalty to an Americanism based upon interethnic and interracial working-class solidarity by their relative lack of involvement in the 1919 race riots, which Barrett has characterized as predominantly an Irish-Black political and racial confrontation. In a final assessment of their disposition, he concludes that Polish workers made good union material from the start and proved themselves even more determined in subsequent battles.[25]

While Dominic Pacyga's work follows Barrett along much of the same road, Pacyga's familiarity with Polish-language sources allows additional insights about the internal workings of Chicago Polonia.[26] His examination of the editorial stance of Chicago's Polish newspapers reveals that middle-class leaders opposed strikes when workers engaged in violence. We also learn that despite the proworker rhetoric of Chicago's middle-class Polish newspapers, they opposed working-class-based political movements such as the Farmer-Labor Party although the popular Polish-American labor leader Jan Kikulski was its candidate for city clerk in 1919. Indeed, Pacyga observes that it was easier for Polonia "to unite on the shop floor than at the ballot box."[27]

While Pacyga argues that a class-conscious, prounion, "extra-communal" outlook progressively supplanted an inward-looking, "communal" orientation among Polish immigrant workers, Slayton presents a considerably different analysis in his study of the Back of the Yards neighborhood. Slayton holds that Poles and other ethnic groups became imbued with "a new sense of nationalism" around the World War I period because of the weakness of union and socialist alternatives. This new orientation, according to Slayton, further undermined class-based solidarities. Middle-class ethnic leaders depended on ethnic divisions to sustain their positions and had no real interest in confronting the packers.[28]

The leading role of Poles in the founding of United Textile Workers of America (UTWA) Local 753 and their involvement in the strikes of 1912 and 1916 in the small company town of New York Mills is examined by James S. Pula and Eugene E. Dziedzic. The authors argue that experience in multifaceted parish and secular organizations bolstered the Poles' ability and willingness to organize as workers. They also contend that the strikes ameliorated internal community divisions, allowing for concerted action beyond the confines of the ethnic group into the American mainstream.[29] To be sure, by 1916 the Poles had won company recognition of their union and many of their demands.

Pula and Dziedzic present considerable evidence in support of their view. The Poles, constituting a majority of the workforce in the mills, took the initiative to organize and join the UTWA, affiliated with the American Federation of Labor. The local's officials were Poles and its first president was a leading member of the local branch of the Polish Roman Catholic Union. Union meetings were held at a Polish tavern until a *Dom Robotniczy* (Workers' Hall) was built. The Poles' parish priest, Polish businessmen, fraternal leaders (many of whom were employed in the mills themselves), and radical newspaper editors all supported the union. Frictions certainly did exist between individuals and groups within the Polish settlement, but they were at least temporarily attenuated for the greater cause.[30]

David J. Goldberg examines the response of Polish immigrant textile workers to organizing efforts by the Amalgamated Textile Workers of America (ATWA), led by the radical Christian pacifist A. J. Muste and sponsored by the Amalgamated Clothing Workers of America (ACWA). Goldberg examines why unionization efforts ultimately faltered in Paterson, Passaic, and Lawrence between 1916 and 1921. He argues, as Slayton does, that intensified nationalisms generated by the experience of World War I muted interethnic cooperation in unionization efforts. He also contends that Poles were generally less receptive than other immigrant groups to the ATWA.[31]

While Goldberg pays scant attention to the Poles in Paterson, noting only that a Polish branch of the Socialist Party attended a 1919 strike meeting, he devotes more detailed consideration to the Poles in Lawrence. He notes that the local press derided the local Polish National Catholic Church as "Bolshevik headquarters" and considered the Poles' Roman Catholic pastor "almost pro-socialist." Rejecting the UTWA's initial leadership of the 1919 strike and prior to the ATWA's entry into the struggle, Polish and Lithuanian workers were more likely to support the 1919 strike than Irish, German, and French-Canadian workers. During the course of the sixteen-week strike, workers accepted the ATWA's leadership, which managed to negotiate some gains albeit without formal agreement or union recognition. By 1921, unable to halt blacklisting practices and hit hard by the Palmer Raids, the ATWA shut down its Lawrence office. Goldberg attributes the union's failure largely to its inability to provide the type of radical leadership Lawrence's workers expected.[32]

Goldberg deals most extensively with Poles in Passaic where they constituted the largest immigrant group and filled all levels of the occupational hierarchy, in contrast to their Polish counterparts in Lawrence and Paterson. He posits that Passaic's Poles were particularly adverse to outside labor organizations as a result of counterproductive struggles between the Industrial Workers of the World (IWW) and Daniel DeLeon's Detroit-based IWW during a failed strike in 1912. Goldberg also argues that the absence of a strong Polish immigrant middle class in Passaic allowed priestly power to predominate and deter Poles from exploring socialist alternatives.[33]

When workers in Passaic waged what amounted to a general strike in 1919, the area's textile workers established their own independent union with mixed-ethnic, mill-based locals. Poles, however, did not rise to lead the union. They chose, instead, to support the leadership of a Czech anti-clerical socialist. To explain this, Goldberg contends that Poles "did not produce . . . leftist, assertive, and self-confident leaders." After the failure of the 1919 strike, Passaic's textile workers opted to join ranks in the founding of the ATWA. Despite the assertion that Poles distrusted outside unions, "especially one that was Jewish-led and socialistically inclined," Goldberg does not reveal any evidence to indicate that Polish workers resisted joining the ATWA, although he makes it clear that the Polish middle class, including priests, clearly refused to have anything to do with the new union. In any event, the union failed to make any significant headway for the rank and file. Goldberg contends that the union's failure resulted only partially from the mill owners' effective blacklisting policies, government repression, and the vacillation of the ATWA's leadership in regard to calling another strike. Maintaining instead that ethnic divisiveness spawned by WWI-era nationalisms mostly undermined the union's efforts, he emphasizes Polish middle-class resentment toward local Jewish shopkeepers and what he terms the "frenzied activity" of Passaic's Poles in response to Pilsudski's successful defense of Warsaw against the Bolsheviks. Despite his pronounced emphasis on Polish anti-semitism, he briefly notes that Passaic's Polish workers ardently supported the leadership of a Jewish Communist Party strike organizer in 1926.[34]

Mary Cygan's work on the place of socialism in American Polonia and the role of immigrant socialism in the American left between the 1880s and the 1940s challenges the idea that Polish immigrants were essentially and pervasively conservative. She also disputes characterizations of the immigrant left as being European-centered and thus incapable of contributing to a viable American working-class movement.[35]

Cygan shows that although Polish leftists harbored concern about political developments in their homeland, most maintained close ties with American socialists. By 1912, the Polish Section of the Socialist Party (PS-SP) consisted of 134 locals and 2,500 members. Lest anyone readily conclude that this might indicate a relative lack of radical potential, Cygan points out that the membership of the Jewish Federation of the Socialist Party was no larger than the PS-SP, while the South Slavic, Italian, Bohemian, Scandanavian, and Latvian Sections each numbered fewer than 1,300 members. She also shows that in 1918 the PS-SP's newspaper, the *Dziennik Ludowy* (The people's daily), could claim a circulation of 18,000, making it the eleventh so-ranked newspaper among 300 English- and foreign-language socialist periodicals in the United States. There were close to a dozen other socialist or left-leaning Polish newspapers also publishing at the same time. In regard to electoral preferences, socialist candidates were receiving 30 percent of the Polish vote in Milwaukee as early as 1902. The Polish socialist vote in Chicago, in comparison, has been estimated in the 15 percent range. Cygan also points to a thriving socialist subculture that reached many thousands of Polish immigrant workers through popular theatrical productions.[36]

Explaining how homeland politics nevertheless created factions among Polish socialists in the United States, Cygan details the contours of the battle between socialist pro-Polish-independence, nationalist Poles and another group of anti-independence Poles. Cygan shows that the pro-independence socialists managed to exert considerable influence in American Polonia evidenced by their leadership role in the Polish National Alliance and the Committee for National Defense. She also establishes that the size and impact of the anti-independence socialists—made up of former members of the Socialist Labor Party who fostered ties with Rosa Luxemburg's Social Democracy of the Kingdom of Poland and Lithuania—was miniscule in comparison. Despite their numerical weakness, however, they still gained control of the PS-SP when they successfully purged the nationalists in mid-1916 because the nationalists refused to accept the SP's anti-war line. The nationalists' prominence in Polonia also suffered a severe setback because their complicated position in support of Pilsudski's strategy (fighting with the Central Powers to defeat Russia and then joining the Allies against the Central Powers) allowed Polonia's right-wing sympathizers of Roman Dmowski's National Democrats to portray them as pro-German.[37]

Cygan also provides fresh insights in her critique of the conventional viewpoint that the foreign elements of the Socialist Party were to blame for its breakup in 1919. She points out that the seven foreign-language federations expelled from the party after the war constituted only 25 percent of the SP's membership. Reasoning that the left's capture of the party's executive committee before their purge would have been impossible without the support of American leftists who shared a Bolshevik-inspired agenda for the United States, she concludes that the SP was not so much swamped by foreigners as it was temporarily hijacked by a minority. Indeed, in regard to the Polish federation, Cygan makes it clear that it was controlled by a small minority of Polonia's socialists after the purge. She also speculates that the leadership of other foreign-language federations might not have been backed by the majority of socialists in their own ethnic group.[38]

The socialist movement in American Polonia lost its momentum throughout the 1920s but picked up steam again with the coming of the Great Depression. By the end of the 1930s, approximately 600,000 Polish-American workers were enrolled in the ranks of the Congress of Industrial Organizations (CIO). Cygan examines how a new generation of Polish socialists, many of whom developed ties to the Communist Party (CP), was instrumental in these organizing efforts. With the advent of the CP's Popular Front agenda in the 1930s, Polish-American socialists and communists learned to work together to reach the Polish-American working class through existing community and parish networks. Unlike their radical predecessors who were oftentimes zealously anti-religious, Cygan explains, this new generation of socialists "learned how to leaflet churchgoers instead of deriding them."[39]

Cygan also considers how they seized the initiative in organizing an anti-fascist coalition in Polonia during World War II but then found themselves, like their predecessors, isolated and derided because of their foreign policy stance. Instrumental in the development of the American Slav Congress to support the Allies and gain sympathy for the Soviet Union, their legitimacy in Polonia was decimated as Stalin moved to establish Soviet hegemony over Poland. In 1944, Polonia's right wing, united under the organizational umbrella of the new Polish American Congress, rose to solidify their leadership of Polonia.[40]

Margaret Collingwood Nowak's biography of her husband, Stanley Nowak, contributes a rare personalized account of the ups and downs experienced by partisans of the left in American Polonia.[41] Nowak was one of a new breed of Polish leftists raised in America who reached young adulthood around the time of World War I. Although the biography reveals little about his parents, he was radicalized early on through his exposure to actors in the Polish-American theater who imparted a love of learning and a concern for social justice. Leaving parochial school to find work in a clothing factory, he became friendly with Chicago's preeminent Polish-American labor leader, Jan Kilkuski, and Leo Krzycki of the Socialist Party, an organizer for the ACWA. In 1924, at the age of twenty-one, he journeyed to Detroit to assume the editorship of the left-wing socialist *Głos Robotniczy* (The workers' voice), whereupon he joined and later became an organizer for the Proletarian Party, a group of Michigan socialists unable to make common cause with the Socialist or either of the American communist parties.[42]

In 1936, Nowak was hired as an organizer for the United Auto Workers (UAW) through the recommendation of Leo Krzycki. Nowak proved instrumental to the success of the UAW and also to other unions in his role as organizer-on-loan to enlist the support of Polish-American workers.[43] Nowak's experience in this regard is especially revealing of the militancy of women workers throughout the city.[44] Cognizant that Poles formed the largest ethnic group in most factories throughout Detroit and realizing the difficulty involved in reaching workers on the shop floor during a time of widespread company spying, Nowak pursued the strategy of organizing Poles through Polonia's institutional networks. In establishing the UAW Polish Trade Union Committee, he won the support of many prominent fraternal leaders and Polish Democratic politicians who held important local, state, and federal offices. His greatest innovation was to buy time on a popular Polish radio show to advance the cause of the CIO.[45]

Nowak also proved successful in staking out a political career. Having won a Democratic primary as a candidate of the CIO-supported Non-Partisan League, he was elected to Michigan's state senate in 1938 where he continued to represent his primarily Polish-American constituency for several terms, despite intense Red-baiting campaigns waged against him by his opponents. A highly publicized but unsuccessful government indictment charging that he concealed communist affiliations at the time of his naturalization also failed to affect his vote-getting abilities. Despite Nowak's involvement in the American Slav Congress and his support of the Polish communists toward the end of the war, he still won reelection. It was only when he decided to give up his Michigan Senate seat and run against a longtime Polish-American incumbent for the U.S. Congress in the Democratic primaries of 1948 that he was defeated. In 1955, he was convicted on charges similar to his previous indictment and subject to deportation until the U.S. Supreme Court reversed that decision in 1958. Nowak's career nevertheless demonstrated, as Thaddeus Radzilowski has noted, that he was "as classic an example of an ethnic leader as the churchmen and businessmen with whom he contended for the loyalty of the immigrant workers and their children."[46]

In his study of Sidney Hillman and the rise of the CIO, Steven Fraser has characterized organizers like Nowak as being a "breed apart."[47] He claims that, whereas second-generation rank-and-file Eastern European workers were less enmeshed in authoritarian, deference-based networks of kin and community than their parents, their religiosity kept them largely insulated from the radical secularism of CIO cadres. Why, then, did the second generation rally under the banner of the CIO? Fraser explains that, by the 1930s, technological change transformed second-generation workers into semi-skilled machine tenders, thus widening their responsibility and capacity for exercising judgments on the job, which markedly contrasted with the unskilled first generation's experience of undifferentiated routine. This new experience had a liberating effect, while labor policies inaugurated by the Roosevelt administration bolstered ethnic support for unions. Consequently, groups like the Steel Workers Organizing Committee often resembled coalitions of ethnic fraternal societies. In Fraser's analysis, however, much of the ethnic spark that ignited the CIO had reactionary kindling. Claiming that the Association of Catholic Trade Unionists (ACTU) was greatly responsible for the entrance of Poles and Italians into the CIO, he emphasizes the organization's anti-communism and its qualms about certain secular, materialistic aspects of the New Deal.[48]

Conterminous with Fraser, Lizabeth Cohen considers how workers in Chicago managed to revitalize the labor movement under the banners of the CIO and the New Deal in the 1930s after organized labor suffered severe setbacks in the wake of the strike wave of 1919. Moving beyond Fraser's emphasis on the workplace, she underscores the broadening of workers' experience during the period and downplays the relative impact of shifts in governmental policies and the strategic initiatives and skills employed by CIO organizers.[49]

Cohen argues that labor's defeat in 1919 essentially resulted from racial, ethnic, and accompanying forms of fragmentation in workers' ranks that sustained a pervasive parochialism. She then posits that this parochialism gradually diminished upon workers' exposure to mass-consumer culture and welfare capitalism during the 1920s, although workers accepted such innovations on their own uniquely ethnic and working-class terms. With the advent of the Great Depression, however, both ethnic institutions and welfare capitalists proved incapable of alleviating the difficulties confronting workers. Ethnicity was becoming more a sensibility than a viable support system. Middle-class ethnic leaders who headed banks and fraternal insurance programs that failed during the Depression no longer could be depended upon for guidance and support. Although most workers obviously did not seek to challenge capitalism by fighting for socialism, they developed an insistence on a "moral capitalism," which certainly limited capitalist prerogatives. Confronted by the Depression, workers developed a new set of loyalties to sustain a newly emerging sense of working-class identity, further removed from ethnic and racial parochialisms, toward the Democratic Party and the CIO. "Without new kinds of commitment by ordinary factory workers," Cohen concludes, "the help of neither the state nor union organizers would have been adequate to achieve such a major breakthrough."[50]

Ronald Schatz, in his study of the struggles of the communist-led United Electrical, Radio, and Machine Workers of America (UE), considers ethnic workers during the subsequent Cold War era. He emphasizes that the battle between the left and anti-communist insurgents proved just as important a contest as that between workers and management. When Cold War politics and the UE's refusal to abide by the loyalty oath provisions of the Taft-Hartley Act contributed to the UE's expulsion from the CIO in late 1949, the Association of Catholic Trade Unionists was in the forefront of advancing the cause of the new International Union of Electrical, Radio, and Machine Workers (IUE) of the CIO. Schatz shows, however, that Polish-American workers affected by this battle did not always abandon the UE. For example, in the Erie, Pennsylvania, General Electric plant (where Polish Americans made up approximately 40 percent of the workforce, holding jobs in the lower rungs of the occupational hierarchy), the UE defeated the IUE in re-certification elections. The local's leadership, moreover, included only one Polish American out of fourteen representatives. On the other hand, there were Polish Americans who opposed the UE, and these included the president of a local in Bridgeport, Connecticut, who testified about communist influence in the union to the House Un-American Activities Committee in 1947. Some Polish-American electrical workers also turned their backs completely on both unions, such as the first president of the East Pittsburgh Westinghouse local, after management provided him a job in the company's advertising department.[51]

The democratic reform movements that arose in several unions during the late 1960s and throughout the 1970s have not yet received much scholarly attention. Only the Nyden brothers have examined the rank-and-file insurgencies that catapulted Jock Yablonski of the United Mine Workers of America (UMWA) and Ed Sadlowski of the United Steelworkers of America (USWA) into national prominence. Paul John Nyden's study deals primarily with rank-and-file opposition to UMWA union officials and policies during the years 1963–1973. Although Yablonski is credited for taking a courageous stand in challenging W. A. "Tony" Boyle for the presidency of the union in 1969 (a challenge that was defeated and that ultimately resulted in the murder of Yablonski, his wife, and daughter, and the conviction of Boyle for his involvement in it), Nyden remains largely critical of Yablonski's previous career as a union official allied with Boyle and of the role his two sons played in the Miners for Democracy movement after his death. Nyden's criticisms center, for the most part, on the Yablonski sons' purported unwillingness to stimulate real rank-and-file democracy in the union.[52]

Philip W. Nyden's treatment of the Steelworkers Fight Back group is similarly critical of the centrally directed, unsuccessful campaign of Ed Sadlowski in 1977 for the presidency of the USWA. Aside from their critical perspective, the Nydens' studies demonstrate that neither rank-and-file insurgency stressed the ethnic appeal of their candidates. In the case of Yablonski, the necessity of capturing the Southern vote loomed large in campaign strategy. Although Sadlowski's ticket was ethnically balanced, the "ski" at the end of his name was seen as a detriment in garnering African-American votes. In an unpublished oral history interview, Sadlowski also revealed that no effort had been made to mobilize Polish-American community resources, as had been so prevalent in the case of the early days of the union. In contrast, Nora Faires, drawing upon a study by Staughton Lynd, has shown that Polish-American ethnicity remained a vital source of support for Pittsburgh-area steelworkers' struggles against plant shutdowns in the 1980s. On at least one occasion, an anti-shutdown rally included songs by a Polish Falcons choir, a dance presentation by the Polish Women's Alliance, and a salute to the Solidarity movement in Poland.[53]

The foregoing studies of the Polish-American working-class experience demonstrate that the field has grown tremendously in sophistication and breadth of inquiry over recent years. At the same time, the task still remains to counterbalance divergent interpretations in a broader conception of social change. Because of the diversity of the Polish-American working class, Polish-American workers are still variously depicted as individualistic or mutualistic, apathetic or militant, conservative or radical. And when workers are conceptualized as embryonic capitalists or the like, it even appears that we are losing our analytical grip altogether. Certainly, greater attention must be devoted to achieving mutually acceptable definitions of the terminology generated by these studies.

The findings of the research discussed in this essay may appear diffuse, fragmented, and contradictory. To a considerable extent this problem arises from the subfield's newfound vigor, which is also the case with contemporary American labor history scholarship in general. Calls for a "new synthesis" have now resounded for nearly ten years among practitioners of the "new labor history," as have attempts to make the field engage—or reengage—the problems of gender and race, language and culture, politics and the state.[54] It may be small comfort, but the historians of the Polish immigrant working-class experience have been in good company as they have groped for a nuanced historical understanding of that layered, textured experience.

In order to begin their own process of synthesis and integration, these historians might do well to try a return to the basics, which in this case would mean the utilization of Polish-language primary sources. Although many materials have fallen by the wayside (especially, and most unfortunately, many radical newspapers), full or nearly full runs of publications that served a national readership are readily available. Far-flung local strikes that provided grist for editorial comment are covered in considerable detail in these sources. Polish scholars' forays into the field also provide numerous points of reference to labor-related articles written by Polish-American correspondents for Polish newspapers archived in Poland. Many other historical treasures in both Poland and the United States undoubtedly remain to be discovered and put to good use.[55]

The problem of assessing the extent and nature of Polish-American radicalism, however, proves thornier than one of terminology or utilization of source materials. It is necessary to establish some standard by which Polish-American labor activism can be measured and interpreted. Clearly, the scholarship covered in this essay amply demonstrates that Polish Americans have proven themselves unusually receptive to unionization appeals and that their militance often superseded union initiatives. Are we, then, to conclude that Polish Americans have been more militant than other groups of workers? The evidence certainly indicates that this was often, if not always, the case. However, the key question—as to whether Polish immigrant workers and their descendants were radicalized by their experience in the United States—remains. It stands to reason that if they emigrated already possessed of a certain radical potential, it could only be in the immediate context of their American environment that this potential was either realized, weakened, or abandoned. But how do we gauge that radicalism—if it indeed existed? And how has it fared over successive generations of Polish Americans in the United States?

Making matters more difficult, radicalism itself has been differentially interpreted by both scholars and activists. One person's revolutionary is often another's fool, capitalist lackey, or self-serving charlatan. Socialists, communists, anarchists, populists, and other typically designated left-wing radicals have all waged fierce battles over the correct thrust of radicalism. Many (probably most) of those who have considered themselves radicals, moreover, have indeed often acted as a breed apart. Participation and membership in radical movements often has been zealously guarded by leaders, not only out of a justified fear of government repression, but also because of a vanguard mentality. For example, consider the manner in which American radicals condescendingly and contemptuously repudiated Leon Czolgosz's claims to be an anarchist upon his assassination of President McKinley in 1901.[56]

What, then, constitutes radicalism? Sean Wilentz has with insight observed that most historians share basic assumptions, derived from Marx, that measurements of class consciousness hinge upon the strength of a working-class radical movement and political party. Disputing this method of appraisal as overly ideological and ahistorical, he argues that class consciousness should more usefully be understood as "the articulated resistance of wage workers to capitalist wage-labor relations."[57]

Although such manner of assessment fits nicely with protrayals of Polish-American workers as possessing a radical vision of society, given their values of family and community solidarity and their attendant propensity to militant labor activity, the matter of political articulation of their grievances remains problematic. If, as we have seen, socialist candidates at times received upward to 30 percent of the Polish-American vote in certain locales, most Polish Americans who voted obviously maintained Democratic and Republican loyalties. And although the evidence seems clear that, with the advent of the New Deal, Polish-American and other workers came to perceive the Democratic Party as a workers' party, most workers simultaneously advanced the establishment of a moral capitalism.

The moral capitalism supported by most Polish-American workers undoubtedly was linked to a Catholic vision, embedded in papal encyclicals and Church teachings linked to questions of labor.[58] But does this make Polish Americans conservative? Ultimately, it must be recognized that the question of what constitutes radicalism remains ideological. The idea of a moral capitalism can and should be considered just as radical as socialist, communist, or anarchist prescriptions for societal change, and perhaps even more so. The extent to which such a religious outlook continues to shape the beliefs and behavior of Polish Americans in terms of labor and class relations in American society in the remainder of the twentieth century remains to be studied.

Most studies concerning Polish-American labor history have focused upon first-generation immigrants up to the period of World War I. Although a great deal of work remains to be accomplished in this respect, general agreement prevails that much more work needs to be done in regard to the history of successive generations of Polish-American workers. Indications are, however, that the salience of Polish-American ethnicity as an explanatory variable has dissipated over time. With the advent of widespread suburbanization and the subsequent devastation of white ethnic urban neighborhoods, ethnicity seems to have become more a means of self-conscious identification and an occasional recreational pastime than a lived, daily experience.[59]

An agenda for future research certainly requires that we begin to consider more closely the transformation of working-class ethnicity, beginning with the second generation of Polish Americans. How did the values of Polish-American workers change over time? How do we explain the steady erosion of ethnic ties? Were these changes simply the result of an inexorable assimilative process or did they involve elements of external coercion and/or enticement?[60] In this respect, we especially need to examine in much greater detail the impact of anti-communism in Polish-American life. What was the legacy fostered by the involvement of Polish-American workers in labor colleges established through the initiative of the ACTU?[61] What did the move to the suburbs mean in regard to involvement in unions? What role have the media played in shaping the self-perceptions and political dispositions of Polish-American workers? Likewise, the importance of gender in the making of the labor movement and forming radical sensibilities in relation to home, community, and workplace merits greater attention. These and many other questions and considerations need to be addressed in the coming decades. Fortunately, the future prospects of Polish-American studies appear to have been enhanced now that more scholars of many different ethnic backgrounds, as evidenced by the multi-cultural sample in this essay, are beginning to show an interest in the history of a hitherto much ignored and stereotyped ethnic group.

3

Family, Women, and Gender

The Polish Experience

Thaddeus C. Radzilowski

POLISH-AMERICAN SCHOLARSHIP HAS PRODUCED A RICH ARRAY of studies on parishes, Polonias, neighborhoods, institutions—the American *okolicas* within which families and individuals worked out their status and destinies. But, unlike Italian-American scholarship, it has done very little on the history of the family itself.[1] Lois Kalloway's 1977 survey of writing and research on Polish-American topics from 1967 to 1977 notes only seven entries under the topic of family. Two of the entries are autobiographical accounts; two are master's theses; one is a doctoral dissertation on post–World War II immigration; and one is an article that touches on the historical experience of the Polish immigrant family. This last entry is part of a wider study of the history of the families of all the major immigrant groups that came as part of the great pre–World War I immigration.[2]

In the period since Kalloway's survey, only a few new important works have appeared that treat the history of the Polish-American family in detail. All of them have looked at the family in the broader context of a community or multi-ethnic study.[3] No historical monograph and only two significant articles devoted solely to the topic have been published. The most important sources and studies that deal with the subject at any length remain largely older, sociological works. In most cases, they were undertaken to address the Polish-American family as a social problem.[4]

Until recently, the basic historiographic problem for the study of the immigrant family was the question of family breakdown and social disorganization as a result of migration and resettlement in a foreign industrial city. The terms of the problem were, in fact, first delineated at length in reference to the Polish experience in America by Thomas and Znaniecki in 1919.[5] They chronicled not only the beginning of the breakdown of the family and the traditional peasant community in which it was embedded in Poland but, even more important, the acceleration of that process by migration to the United States. They saw the peasantry, removed from the institutions that had structured and guided their lives, left in the United States in a state of confusion and disorganization, attracted to hedonism and a destructive individualism without responsibility. Peasants had internalized very few social and moral values under the old order, and the absence of those values in the New World brought them to the brink of chaos. The result was a society beset by sexual license, crime, juvenile delinquency, family breakdown, and violence. Thomas and Znaniecki even predicted that "it is quite possible that informal polygamy of both the polygamous and the polyandrous type . . . will become the prevalent type of family organization among American Poles. It is already much more frequent than American social and legal institutions can ascertain." Later in the same work, they concluded, "Thus, in general, the marriage situation among American Poles looks quite hopeless when judged by the standards of the permanent and exclusive conjugal bond."[6]

Recent scholarship has generally rejected the disorganization thesis without, in the case of the Polish family, addressing directly the issues and the evidence of delinquency, marital breakup, prostitution, sexual irregularity, and violent behavior raised by Thomas and Znaniecki. Instead, the new studies argued that the break between traditional culture and the new culture was gradual rather than abrupt and that habits and institutions of the rural pre-industrial world were, in fact, successfully adapted to the new urban milieu. The immigrant family was seen as an active and independent agent that, at least in part, shaped its own destiny and the daily lives and futures of its members. In the course of its adaptation to American reality, the immigrant family also helped to transform the traditional culture of the Polish countryside into an American urban ethnicity.[7]

The ability of the Polish immigrant family to mobilize all of its resources for survival in its new urban home became the primary focus of the newer scholarship. Detailed community studies building on older sociological data have been especially concerned with the single-minded preoccupation of the Polish family with the acquisition of a bit of land and a family house. The motivation was seen to be the satisfaction of the traditional hunger for land and the status that went with ownership.

Other motives included the traditional need to stake out a place for the family in the physical and moral universe and the more modern, rational calculation of home ownership as a hedge against economic hard times.[8]

To achieve the goal of home ownership, the Polish immigrant family developed a flexible strategy that alternated between the keeping of boarders and the use of children's wages to accumulate the necessary capital to purchase a house. The father's wages usually, in themselves, were not sufficient to permit home ownership. The combined family wages were supplemented also by keeping animals (even in cities), raising vegetables, and sewing clothes at home.[9]

To cut costs and reduce mortgages, the family home initially had few amenities and was often constructed by the family members with the assistance of friends and relatives. In some areas, the new Polish homeowners resisted municipal improvements such as water, sewage disposal, and street-paving to keep taxes low enough to make the home affordable. Only after the home was paid off was it expanded, amenities added, and neighborhood improvements voted in.[10] Some scholars such as John Bodnar and Caroline Golab have seen the Polish-American family strategy as defensive and primarily traditional in orientation. Caroline Golab summed up this position:

> The names and the places may have changed but the rules and regulations stayed the same. If he could not improve the position of the family by owning land in Poland, at least he could reproduce the familiar group and its values in America by owning a home of his own. This was the true attraction of America. America allowed him to achieve here what he couldn't do in Poland.[11]

Ewa Morawska, on the other hand, has argued that, although the immigrant peasant was indeed traditional and even before migration, traditions were already being transformed by modern culture and by a market economy. These changes, she argues, made the peasant's worldview more "complex and ambivalent" than is allowed by the other interpretations. The familial economic strategy in America was adapted not only to traditional survival and security goals but also to new ones of improvement, achievement, and advantage. The family, by its activity, thus not only taught the old values but opened its members to the new ones.[12]

It is clear, in retrospect, that survival (let alone improvement) in the New World for Polish and other immigrants, once they decided to stay, was not a product of Horatio Alger individualism but of collective effort. No collectivity was more important in achieving those goals than the family. It can even be argued that the migration process actually strengthened the peasant family, whose bonds had begun to weaken in Europe as the ties to the land began to attenuate under the impact of population growth, increasing parcelization, prejudicial land policies of the partitioning powers, and the growth of a market economy. In America, the family—a smaller unit than in Europe and less embedded in and dependent on a community—was the source of survival and the major agency for securing and keeping employment. The family provided not only food and shelter but also jobs for both men and women.[13]

The majority of Poles, men and women, who came to the United States before World War I were young and single. The decision to marry in the United States, like the decision of married men to send for wives and children, was almost always a decision to stay and make one's life in the New World, to cease being a sojourner and become an immigrant. It should be noted that the decision of many young women to come to America was clearly affected by the chance to make a better marriage match than seemed possible in the village. Further, the willingness to found a family in the United States marked a recognition by the immigrants that their lives and families would be different from the traditional models with which they were raised.[14]

The situation in the New World changed the family in many ways. The woman as wife and mother played a new role. She did not have to go to her husband's family to live after the marriage. More than likely she set up an independent household soon after the wedding. If economic circumstances forced the new couple to live with family, it was usually with the wife's family. Helen Stankiewicz Zand argues that, given the relative imbalance of unmarried women to men in the immigration and the high rate of endogamy, many young Polish male immigrants had to marry American-born daughters of earlier immigrants with well-established households. As a result, it became the custom to live with the wife's family after marriage—a practice made easier by the absence of any need to lay claim to one's share of the husband's family land. According to Zand, this significantly changed the power relationship between husband and wife in the New World.[15]

The relationship was further affected by the better education, knowledge of English, and cultural sophistication of the wife in such a union. Recent arrivals—"greenhorns"—were generally not as highly prized as husbands, either by Polish immigrant women or by those of the generation born in the United States. It was widely held that "Americans" made better husbands and were less authoritarian and abusive than newcomers.

One young Polish woman in Chicago recounted that she was attracted to the man, also an immigrant, who became her husband because, "He didn't act like the boys from Europe, from the village. He acted like he was always American! He was very nice . . . in talking and acting." Another young Polish-American woman in Detroit petitioned for divorce from her abusive husband because he was a "greenhorn," and as an "American" she did not have to put up with his boorish behavior. To his in-laws, and ultimately even to his children, the immigrant son-in-law and father often remained the "greenhorn" whose authority and prestige were inferior to his wife's.[16]

The favorable marriage market for women also quickly ended the traditional dowry. It was expected, well before World War I in most Polonia colonies, that the husband would pay almost the whole cost of the wedding. A young woman writing back to her parents in Russian Poland in 1891 rejected with scorn the marriage offer of a village suitor, which included a request for a sizable dowry:

> In America if a man has three hundred dollars, then he can get married, because in Chicago the custom is that the girl's boyfriend must even buy her wedding dress and everything else that is needed for the house. The young lady has only to worry about getting to the wedding. Here they do not ask how much dowry she will receive, dear parents.[17]

The roles of husband and wife in the Polish immigrant family—whether created anew in America or established in Europe prior to immigration—also were affected by the conditions of life in the American industrial city. The long hours worked by the father, often six days a week at some distance from home, meant that more duties and child discipline fell to the mother. She also began to assume some public functions as the family representative who in her husband's absence dealt with teachers, priests, social workers, city officials, and policemen. The social life of the family and its relations with relatives, much more now with her family than with her husband's, also became more her responsibility. Zand notes that the wife often was alone and dependent on her own resources and wits to support her children and hold the family together when her husband went to another city to find work or returned by himself to Europe to seek land to buy or to dispose of family business.[18]

The newer interpretations of the immigrant family that have focused on its relatively successful adaptation and its ability to shape its own destiny to a significant degree have caused the older descriptions of disorganization and breakdown to recede into the background or even to disappear completely.[19] In the Polish case, which was the paradigm for the disorganization interpretation in the first place, the transition to the new understanding was accomplished without confronting the original thesis directly to determine its validity. The apparent strength and success of the Polish-American family in the post–World War II period seemed to prove the earlier case false and obviate the need for further investigation. As a result, we have few good studies of the Polish-American urban family in the interwar period or of the course of its transition from its beleaguered immigrant status to its position as a mainstay of ethnicity.

In the absence of good social histories of the first five decades of this century, we are thus left uncertain of the extent to which Thomas and Znaniecki went beyond or misread the evidence. We are also uncertain of the extent to which some combination of heroic effort and changed circumstances dramatically altered the fate of the Polish-American family. Thomas and Znaniecki estimated that in 1920 what today would be called an "underclass" was between one-quarter and one-third of the total of the Polish-American population. These are estimates of people who are involved in crime, live in a criminal milieu, or are otherwise associated with it. They write, "Among the settled majority of Polish American society there may be disorganization of family life, but very little real crime. The latter grows among that floating, unorganized mass of intellectually backward immigrant population which constitutes among Poles from one-quarter to one-third of the total population."[20] This is an extraordinary estimate. (The current size of the underclass in the African-American community is estimated at 10–15 percent of the African-American population.) It has yet, however, to inspire the kind of serious study of empirical data that has been the hallmark of the new social history.

The few contemporary studies that exist for the interwar period—influenced, to be sure, by the Thomas and Znaniecki thesis and the notion that Polish Americans were a major social problem—tend to support the idea of disorganization. Literary descriptions of Polish-American urban life prior to World War II, such as Clifford Shaw's *The Jack Roller* or Nelson Algren's *Never Come Morning*, paint a dismal and corroborative picture. Polish-American sources and opinion from the pre-1940 period express dismay about and a search for solutions to the problems of the family in Polonia, which were regularly exposed by the American press, governmental reports, or sensational and violent events.[21]

The social problem connected most often with the problem of the Polish family is juvenile delinquency. Thomas and Znaniecki identified it as particularly acute among second-generation youth. They note that, "it is a well known fact that even the number of crimes is proportionally much larger among the children of immigrants than among the immigrants themselves." Frederick Thrasher's study *The Gang,* published eight years after Thomas and Znaniecki's study, identifies Polish-American youth as having the majority of ethnic gangs in Chicago, more than double the number one might expect from their percentage in the population. Polish-American juveniles were involved not only in burglary, petty theft, bootlegging, and prostitution but also in serious crimes of violence. The consequences of this criminal activity became significant enough that people within the Polish community began to organize a campaign against capital punishment because so many Polish-American young men were being executed. In a letter to Jane Addams dated February 23, 1912, Dr. Anna Wrzezokowska spoke of the "orgies of blood" inflicted on Polish-American boys by capital punishment.[22] Despite its importance as a problem for Polish leaders and the community at the beginning of the twentieth century, we have no real study of juvenile delinquency, its prevalence, or its impact.[23]

If the picture of the Polish family painted by the early sociological studies is even partially true, how and why did it change over the next thirty years? Joseph Parot observes that, "the original predictions made by Thomas and Znaniecki were based on a firm foundation." The reason those predictions did not become reality, he argues, was "the incredible tenacity, courage and spirit of thousands of unknown 'Beloved Mothers' in Polonia—who in birth, work, life, and death enabled their families to survive a most traumatic immigrant period."[24]

Sociologist William McCreedy suggests another answer: the ability of the father to maintain his position in the family even when unemployed or disabled. The Polish father, in his view, was "able to maintain the image of the patriarch even during times of great stress and social mobility." The father in the Polish family, "who was unemployed was able to hang on to his children's loyalty by collecting their paychecks and maintaining economic control of the family," while conversely, "the Polish father who appeared to be incompetent and inadequate in the New World was able to hang onto his children's loyalty and attention by needing their care and trading approval for it." In Polish families the mother, according to McCreedy, is less salient than for other groups. This lack of maternal saliency, he contends, is especially true for the daughters in the family.[25]

A third series of hypotheses about the persistence of Polish-American family ties suggests religion as the key element. John L. Thomas argued in 1956 that the authors of *The Polish Peasant* failed to see that Polish values were not just socially based and hence subject to disintegration when the peasant social world began to break down, but rather had a second more important religious rooting. Those religious values were, in his view, strongly internalized. His survey of Polish families in the 1950s showed him that the conjugal bond was significantly more stable among Polish Americans than among other Catholic ethnic groups. Another sociological study of Chicago Poles completed at the same time as John L. Thomas's, which concentrated on older people who would have been young adults when Thomas and Znaniecki were doing their research, also discovered a high degree of marital stability. The researchers attributed this to the "resilience" of the Polish family and "the strong and continuing influence of Catholicism in the lives of their subjects."[26]

It is worth noting that the successful efforts of the Poles in holding together their families and overcoming the disorganization that attended immigration and first settlement was accomplished during some of the most difficult decades in contemporary history. As *The Polish Peasant* was being published, the Polish immigrant community was suffering through the immediate postwar depression and unparalleled labor strife. A social worker in Detroit spoke of "Starving Poland" on Detroit's East Side in 1921. She described serious malnutrition and even starvation especially among Polish-American children.[27]

During the 1920s, Detroit's welfare records show many families in the Polish community in a state of chronic distress. The records for 1929, the last "normal" year before the Great Depression, show families headed by fathers born in Poland as the largest single group receiving assistance (16 percent of total), with the exception of the group with native-born fathers. However, as the Polish community in Detroit was already more than two generations old by 1929, the "native white" group also contained a significant number of families headed by Polish Americans. The Poles were second in the city only to "native whites" in cases arising out of alcoholism, death in family, handicaps, work injury, marital incompatibility, child neglect, non-support, sickness, widow- or widowerhood, and imprisonment. In cases of illegitimacy, they were ahead of "native whites" but second to blacks. They constituted the third largest group of clients after blacks and "native whites" in cases of desertion, divorce or separation, insufficient income, insanity or feeblemindedness, and unemployment.[28]

The depression of the 1930s deepened immeasurably the poor conditions in Polish neighborhoods. Unemployment in some areas reached 50 percent and evictions were commonplace. By 1932 in Detroit, relief funds had run out completely, and 4,500 families a month were being turned out of their homes. In these circumstances, poverty and dislocation created rapidly deteriorating health conditions in Polish neighborhoods. The tuberculosis death rate in some Polish neighborhoods was 40–79 per 100,000—a rate exceeded only in the poorest black neighborhoods. The infant mortality rate as late as 1939–1940 in the Polish-American neighborhoods of Detroit was the highest in the city, 40–60 per 1,000 live births.[29] Conditions in the industrial neighborhoods of other American cities were comparable. Clearly, the ability of Polish Americans not only to preserve but also to strengthen families considered beleaguered even before these conditions were obtained is a remarkable story that needs much more study by historians than it has received heretofore.

The Polish family in America has a "prehistory" in the Polish countryside. The key historiographic issue of this prehistory is the way the family was affected by migration and emigration, particularly the impact of emigration on the women who were left behind. Recently, Mary Cygan has addressed the question of whether the migration "feminized" Polish agriculture. She concludes on the basis of a study of the literature on Polish agriculture and emigration, including emigrant letters, that no such phenomenon took place. According to Cygan, the emigration was rarely so large in any one area that a village was denuded of male householders and left with mainly women to do the bulk of agricultural tasks. Furthermore, married householders made up only a minority of the migrants and emigrants from the Polish lands. Most migrants were single men.[30]

Thomas and Znaniecki note that if a householder was unable to till his own land, the function was usually assumed by a male relative. They write that "as long as familial solidarity exists and the whole family is not ruined or dispersed, some collateral member, assuming the role of head of the family, usually undertakes the cultivation of the land which the owner cannot cultivate. This is regularly the case with the land of widows and orphans."[31] This was usually the case also with the land of those who had migrated, so that rarely did women assume fully the agricultural tasks their husbands left behind. At least the major heavy work was usually done by a relative or hired man.

There were only a few areas of the Polish lands in which the majority of able-bodied men left annually for seasonal employment leaving women to shoulder the responsibility for the agricultural work. Men from these areas were not involved in the long-distance migration to North America so the conditions obtained in these villages are not part of the background history of the Polish family in America or of Polish-American women.[32]

The departure of a married man sometimes for a sojourn of many years, nevertheless, did have a marked effect on the wives and families they left behind. It expanded the tasks and responsibilities of the women, even if they did not take over the heaviest agricultural work. The new duties were not always welcome, not only because they added work and worry, but also because they were not part of women's traditional roles, as Cygan notes in her analysis of letters between migrants and their families.[33] The husband's migration, more than anything else, meant that wives were left to raise their children without the presence of a father. This caused difficulties and discipline problems. Some children grew up knowing little of their fathers, if the absence was prolonged. A popular song records the lament of a returning emigrant who says that, "My children did not know me / for they fled from me, a stranger."[34] On the other hand, the husband's absence relieved wives of the burden of pregnancy and childbirth every year or two.

Migration often strained relations between the marriage partners. Husbands found it difficult to maintain patriarchal authority at a distance. Sometimes their wives even ignored their attempts to manage the family from abroad. Wives also found themselves alone for years and vulnerable to village gossip. In some cases their husbands abandoned them, but in other cases a wife refused to leave home and join her husband abroad if he decided on a long-term or permanent stay. In a few cases, wives took up with other men or abandoned their husbands.[35]

Women, of course, did not just wait at home for the men to return. They too were migrants and emigrants. They had taken part in seasonal migrations since the 1870s and by 1900 were probably the majority of seasonal agricultural migrants. Polish women, especially the younger, single ones, often traveled together in groups to work in the beet fields of Germany and Denmark or the potato or grain fields of Russian Poland. According to one observer, the women and girls would cross the Vistula River into Russian territory to work in the fields: "They would go on foot in groups of two or three score, carrying in big kerchiefs their clothes and food with them. They would leave home in the spring and return after the potatoes had been dug in the autumn."[36]

The emigration of women from the Polish countryside was driven by the same forces that caused male emigration. At the personal level, the motives of women emigrants were as varied, complex, and idiosyncratic as those in the individual stories of the men who migrated. Women went abroad because there was a better marriage market, because their wages were needed to sustain a family on the land, or because they were called or taken by husbands, fathers, and fiancés. Emigration was also for women, as for men, a chance to escape from an oppressive personal situation.[37]

The lure of modern life, the shining image of America, and the hope of material improvement in their lives drew women as strongly as it did men. One young immigrant woman, her imagination excited by stories of those who had been in America, remembered that, "nothing in Poland was good enough for me." Whenever she saw well-dressed people, she fantasized that that was how everyone in America dressed. "Why don't we have it like that?" she thought. "Let's go to America." Another young woman envious of a much poorer friend who sent back a photograph in which "she looked as pretty as a countess," decided that, "I am going to that America. I don't want to work on a farm. . . . I came to this America because I wanted to send back a photograph to show I am also such a lady."[38]

Many of the women who emigrated went to join their husbands. They often made the arrangements themselves. They sold or leased the family land, bought tickets, arranged local transportation and border crossings (which were often illegal). They were aided only by vague, often unreliable and outdated instructions from distant husbands. Women who had little experience beyond the village or who had traveled as migrants only locally and regionally now traveled across Europe and crossed the ocean alone or with small children. They carried with them much of what they owned of value.[39]

The trip to the United States could be frightening and dangerous. Police reports in cities all along the immigrant trail noted the disappearance of women without a trace. At temporary boarding houses and on trains and ships, women were subjected to sexual harassment and even rape by crews, workers, or fellow travelers.[40] A 1911 report by a Czech-American woman, who traveled in steerage incognito as an agent for the U.S. Bureau of Immigration, described in detail the difficulties faced by young women traveling on immigrant ships:

> Not one young woman in steerage escaped attack. Two more refined and determined Polish girls fought the men with pins and teeth, but even they weakened under this continued warfare and needed some moral support

about the ninth day. The atmosphere was one of general lawlessness and total disrespect for women.[41]

After arrival, single women often lived with friends or relatives. Sometimes, however, they ended up as boarders with persons whom they knew slightly or not at all. Grace Abbott counted over two thousand young Polish women or girls who came without family to Chicago in an eighteen-month period before World War I. Of these, only 81 had parents in the city and 626 came to "cousins" and "friends." The majority had no contacts in Chicago. Abbott also discovered that many of the "friends" had not known the girl at home. Many worked some distance from their place of residence and among men and women of other ethnic groups. Wherever their residence or place of employment, they found that the social networks of kinship and gossip that had exercised social control over them in the village were much weaker and less pervasive here.[42]

The young immigrant woman quickly developed a new sense of her rights and the possibilities for greater control over her life choices in the United States. She changed jobs on the advice of friends, got her own paycheck, and often negotiated with her family about how much she would keep and how much she would contribute to the common purse. She picked her own husband and arranged her own wedding, aided only by sisters or girlfriends. Her knowledge of sex and birth control, learned from co-workers, was often more sophisticated than her mother's. Some even took advantage of skills such as sewing to open their own businesses.[43] The new freedom often brought conflict and misunderstanding with parents in Europe or the United States or with relatives or siblings acting as parental surrogates here. These painful strains on familial solidarity paralleled and merged with the equally disruptive conflicts of American-born daughters with immigrant parents.[44]

The immigration experience changed the situation of married women as well. Most immigrant women made their new homes without the assistance or advice of their mothers, mothers-in-law, or aunts, in an environment that was radically different from the one they were reared in. Their children grew up without grandparents in a strange world. Immigrant mothers came to depend more on friends, neighbors, and outsiders for support. They sought advice from these sources on making a home and preparing their children to succeed in a world they did not wholly understand. For example, one elderly immigrant woman remembered that her sister was originally to be named Anna. However, the godmother—in an attempt to improve the child's chances in life—changed the child's name to Henrietta. She explained to the mother when she returned with the child from the christening that she had changed the name because "All Annas work in the stockyards. . . . I wouldn't name her Anna." In the absence of the usual network of female relatives, the women had to expect more help, support, and companionship from their daughters and their husbands than was customary. One immigrant woman turned to her oldest daughter for help in choosing proper American names for the younger daughters so that they would fit into American society. The girls born in the 1930s were named Virginia, Bernadine, and Jacqueline by their sister who was born in 1913.[45]

Married women, like their single sisters, quickly developed a new sense of their rights in the United States. They began to feel that they were entitled to a certain level of treatment and a standard of life that was often at variance with Old World practice. The files of the Chicago Legal Aid Agency studied by Thomas and Znaniecki show that Polish immigrant women were quick to turn to police and social service agencies in case of abuse, non-support, or desertion. They soon learned that they would have to develop new strategies for coping with life's problems in urban America. In the village, many of these problems were dealt with informally by gossip or recourse to family and friends. In their new homes, immigrant women came to be more dependent on public agencies for assistance and support than their sisters in the old country.[46]

Recently historians of women's experience have begun to use the metaphor of reproduction to speak of the role of women in society. The metaphor extends the meaning of reproduction from the biological realm to the reproduction of the family's ability to maintain daily life, and to the social reproduction of communal and familial networks and the creation of new "webs of signification" (to use Clifford Geertz's phrase) to give meaning and value to all aspects of human life. The work of reproduction in all these senses stands out in stark relief in the story of immigrant women, because they were pioneers in creating new social groups with institutional and familial forms that were often novel to them.[47] Polish immigrant women carried on this work of reproduction as operators of boarding houses; as teaching and nursing nuns; as founders of a myriad of local, parochial, regional, and national social, religious, educational, and insurance organizations; and most important, as wives, mothers, and relatives. It is this last form of reproductive work that Miceala di Leonardo has aptly called "kinship work."[48]

Despite the family's patriarchal forms, sometimes re-cast and actually strengthened by the immigration experience, and despite a division of labor, resources, and support that was often unequal and disadvantageous, most Polish immigrant women, like their counterparts in other ethnic groups, probably found their identities and most of life's satisfactions in their families. For all its faults, the family and the community in which it was embedded were, after all, more immediately and more consciously their own creations than anything their mothers had ever known. In a recent historiographic study of immigrant women, Donna Gabaccia has pointed out that the sources strongly support the notion that most immigrant women (and immigrant men, for that matter) identified with their families. The negative evaluation of this identification by some feminist scholars is, she notes, the product of class and cultural bias. Except for some scholarship on more recent Polish immigrants, most research on Polish immigrant women to date has generally supported Gabaccia's idea of the family as a major source of positive identity for women and the setting for most of their satisfactions and accomplishments.[49]

In the process of creating homes and families in a foreign urban world, Polish immigrants laid down the basis for the creation of key elements of Polish ethnicity in America. They had to think consciously about what it meant to be Polish and how to translate that into the rituals of daily life. They had to decide what to keep, what to abandon, and how to celebrate holidays and rites of passage in an unfamiliar environment. They shaped many of the features of personal ethnic identity around home, food, celebration, child-rearing, and marriage. This creative adaptation and new signification was done initially by young women separated from their mothers and old world communities.[50]

Polish immigrant women also formed a wide variety of formal organizations to replace the informal networks they had left behind. Even a cursory look at the history of any major Polish-American community will demonstrate that the organizational fever gripping Polish America was not confined to men. The majority of organizations women established were religiously based, but there were also many organizations tied to neighborhoods, settlement houses, and social networks. Some were founded to provide insurance, and moral and educational uplift. The fervor for association did not decline in the generation of their daughters either. Most of the organizations Polish-American women founded were local or parochial, but some also became regional and even national in scope.[51]

The most important national, secular organization founded by Polish women in the United States was the *Związek Polek w Ameryce* (ZPA) or the Polish Women's Alliance. Founded in 1898, it created a national insurance fund run entirely by women, published a women's newspaper *Głos Polek* (The voice of Polish women), ran education programs and summer camps, and established libraries for women and children in many larger Polish communities. By 1920, it had enrolled over twenty-five thousand women and the weekly edition of *Głos Polek* was read by about 15 percent of Polish-American women.[52]

During the period of immigration, the ZPA—through its education programs, political lobbying, service work, and its publications, especially *Głos Polek*—emerged as a strong voice for feminism, political reform, and progressive goals in American and Polish-American society. It favored women's suffrage and the opening of all educational institutions and professional careers to women. It championed the rights of workers and programs of industrial safety. It informed Polish women of the progress of women's causes throughout the world and in the United States. It also tried to help rural immigrant women adjust to life in an urban setting and to become aware of the latest advances in child-rearing, hygiene, education, and nutrition. Finally, the organization worked tirelessly to preserve and propagate Polish language and culture in America and to win Polish independence.[53] During the early decades of the twentieth century, a significant number of Polish immigrant women were exposed to the ZPA. As a result, they learned the message of equal rights, of the rightful claims of women to education, advancement, and a place of dignity in modern society through an important and respected source established and run by women of their own community.

The ZPA, whose founding came in reaction to the refusal of the Polish National Alliance to enroll women, resisted all later attempts to get it to merge with male-dominated Polish-American organizations. The leadership of the ZPA allowed that, at some distant future time, it might be possible for men and women to join together in the same organization, but this would only come when "the will to rule disappears from man's soul" and when he can accept a woman as a "truly completed, equal person and not as a minor child." The ZPA remains, still today, a strong and independent women's organization in Polonia and one of the largest ethnic women's organizations in the United States.[54]

No look at the organizational life of Polish-American women could be complete without an analysis of the Polish-American religious orders. The history of the religious orders is the best documented area of the story of Polish-American women, indeed perhaps of all Polish-American history. Although most of the writing on the sisterhoods falls within the genre of institutional history, it is complex and varied and contains a rich lode of material that can be mined by social historians.[55]

A few Polish-American religious orders were brought from Europe but the majority were founded in the United States by immigrant women. In addition, young immigrant women and the American-born daughters of immigrants flocked to the sisterhoods in such large numbers that within a half-century most of the European orders had become primarily American ones with the bulk of their members in the United States. The rapid growth of the religious orders represented a yet unstudied, spontaneous outburst of religious commitment from women from whom too little had been expected in the past. It clearly marks a dramatic change in the nature of peasant religiosity in the New World and provides an example of how immigration opened new religious and social roles for women that offered greater opportunities for service and commitment.[56]

The growth of the religious orders represented the mobilization of the talents of tens of thousands of Polish-American women for service to their struggling communities. They also acted as a major agency for social, educational, and occupational mobility for women who would otherwise have had few such choices. The religious life appealed to women who were interested in positions of power, responsibility, travel, social status, and education. It also represented a chance to leave home and offered an attractive alternative to marriage, domestic service, or factory work.

The women of the religious orders mobilized a significant amount of the resources and capital of their communities for investment in education, in the care of children, of the aged, sick, and destitute, and in other social services. They also mobilized family and friends to assist with the causes of their orders and the needs of the parishes, hospitals, and other institutions they served. Because they had access to or control over jobs and resources such as scholarships, they were able to contribute to the well-being and mobility of the family. Because their vocations were highly regarded in the community, nuns added to the reputation and status of their families. Thus the activities of Polish-American sisterhoods were never entirely divorced from the intense competition for status within the community.[57]

The religious orders also created networks of the parishes they served. This involved bringing together people from widely scattered Polonian neighborhoods for social and fund-raising functions and common efforts. These networks often provided, in addition, a means to exchange and transfer resources between parishes. Most orders created auxiliary organizations, drawn from the women of the parishes they served, that became one of the major sources of inter-neighborhood cooperation among Polish-American immigrant women and their daughters.

The main function of the Polish religious orders in the United States (unlike Europe) was education. They staffed the vast network of elementary and secondary schools (about a thousand at the height of the system) created by Poles in America. In fact, that system could not have existed without the religious orders. They wrote the texts for the schools and developed curricula that attempted to inculcate in their charges both a Polish Catholic consciousness and American patriotism. Through their schools, curricula, and texts, they taught immigrants and their children the meaning of Catholicism in the new American context and sought to create a Polish-American identity that would make the immmigrants feel at home in America. If the home environment created by one group of Polish-American women was one pillar of ethnicity, the educational and social service system created by another was a second. The very existence of Polonia itself is thus to a significant degree the product of the efforts of the women of the religious orders. In addition, through their schools, hospitals, orphanages, clinics, day-care centers, and old-age homes and through their commitment, education, and labor they made major contributions to the humanization of the harsh environment of the American industrial city in this century.[58]

Another area of Polish-American women's experience that has been relatively well studied is the work experience. It is a subject that has occupied historians interested in women's history, social history, and labor history because of the extensive documentation collected by corporations, government agencies, social reformers, and economists. Much of this experience is accessible without the knowledge of Polish. All of the studies that discuss the history of work by Polish-American women in the United States treat them in a broader, multi-ethnic class context and often in comparative perspective.[59]

What do we know about the working lives of Polish-American women? Almost all single women worked. Before World War I, the pay for the various jobs Polish-American women did ranged from $4 to $20 per week with some of the jobs such as domestic work including maintenance. After marriage, the rates of work outside the home dropped off sharply. However, some evidence indicates that 10–20 percent of married women did work. If there were children, a working mother usually signified a family in serious straits. The rates of employment for married women, however, varied a great deal from one area of the country to the other. In areas such as Lawrence (Massachusetts), Central Falls (Rhode Island), Passaic or Paterson (New Jersey), textile production was the major industry and employment rates for married women were much higher. In such areas, men's work paid much less, and a great many of the jobs were open primarily to women.

Many Polish-American men were attracted to work in mines, steel mills, and other heavy industries. In areas where such industries predominated, wages for men were higher, and much fewer opportunities were available for female labor. In rural or semi-rural areas, women—both married and single—and children often found employment, usually seasonal, in canning and food processing. Certain operations in meat-packing plants, which attracted Polish male labor, were also open to women. In the Midwest, Polish women went into cigar factories. In some cities such as Detroit (once a major center for cigar manufacturing), cigar making was practically dominated by Polish women. In all areas of the country Polish women, married and single, found employment as domestics.

The second generation of Polish-American women began to move, after the Great Depression, into more varied employment than had been open to their mothers. As barriers of prejudice began to fall in the 1940s and early 1950s, Polish women moved into white-collar, clerical, and retail sales positions outside the Polish community. The new opportunities required a good knowledge of English and skills such as typing or stenography.

The women who stayed home with their children did more than just care for the house, cook, and clean. They kept large gardens, raised animals, preserved food, and sewed clothing for their families. Many also earned money by working at home, doing sewing, weaving, or home manufacturing. A good seamstress could easily make as much as her husband did at the mill. A skilled seamstress made about $100 a month in 1914. Many also ran small retail businesses out of their homes. Among early Polish immigrants, the operation of a saloon in one of the rooms of the house was a common enterprise. In the Polish neighborhoods of Chicago before World War I, for example, there were over three thousand saloons, most of them home operations, often run by the woman of the house.[60]

The most common enterprise for women, especially in heavy industrial areas, was a boardinghouse. Ewa Morawska's study of Johnstown, Pennsylvania, showed that at one time or another in the family cycle, 50–60 percent of Polish-American families took in boarders. This was heavy work that involved cooking, cleaning, and laundering for as many as a dozen men. For this difficult and tiring job, wives earned from two-thirds to three-quarters of the income their husbands made in the factories.

If we have a significant amount of information on the working lives of Polish immigrant women, we have considerably less on other aspects of their public lives and activities inside and outside their communities. Most of their time and energy was obviously devoted to their families' welfare and to their work. However, there is enough scattered evidence to indicate that they could mobilize and maintain a high level of public activity for considerable periods of time when issues important to their communities arose. The creativity, intensity, and sometimes even violence of their responses demonstrate also that they were far from being the patient and submissive immigrant Griseldas of popular myth.

The accounts of social workers and settlement house staff indicate that Polish immigrant women could and did engage in political lobbying, organizing, and demonstrating on issues such as the safety of their streets, health and sanitation, and the cost of living. Mary McDowell, for example, reports on the campaign of Polish and Czech women in Chicago to get clean water and improved sewage removal in their neighborhood. Polish immigrant women went to the streets in 1915 in Hartford, Connecticut, in support of a bakers' strike for higher wages. Their response in this case was quite sophisticated. They successfully pressured the bread companies to raise wages and improve conditions for the workers without raising the price of bread.[61]

There is hardly a Polish Roman Catholic or Polish National Catholic parish that did not experience a major disturbance over issues of leadership, control of parish resources, and relationships with the church hierarchy. In many of these struggles a key role was played by women. For example, in the well-known struggle over the control of the first Polish parish in Detroit in the early 1880s, mobs of women seized control of the church to hold it for the pastor who had been ousted by the bishop and to deny it to his appointed successor. In the process, they not only defied ecclesiastical authority but also civil authority and fought the police and courts to maintain their position. The Detroit incident was only one among the first of numerous such affairs.[62]

In the bloody battles in the coalfields, the women fought with skill and courage in support of their men. In the wake of the Latimer massacre in the Pennsylvania anthracite fields in 1897, "Big Mary" Septek led a "wild band of women" armed with clubs, rolling pins, and pokers who waged a guerrilla war against strikebreakers. In one incident they routed over two hundred male washery workers. It finally required the intervention of state militia to end the "foreign women raids." During a 1910 strike in a Brooklyn sugar refinery, when threatening shots were fired at strikers, Polish women rushed into the streets holding their children on high, daring the police to shoot. Frank Renkiewicz, in his study of Polish-American workers, notes that during strikes: "Time and again, women, wives usually, bolstered the flagging spirits of their men and took the lead in demonstrations and in sustaining resistance."[63]

In many cases, the women acted on their own behalf as workers and family wage earners. It was the walkout of the Polish women weavers, in response to a pay cut, that sparked the famous Lawrence Strike of 1912.[64] Polish immigrant women showed the greatest energy and boldness when they were involved both as workers and as the defenders of their families and communities. No incident makes that more clear than the rioting in the Back-of-the-Yards neighborhood during the great Chicago packing house strike of 1921–1922 when the employers sought to cut wages and break the union. The ferocity of the attacks by Polish women astounded even the Polish press.[65]

The 1930s was another period of crisis for the Polish-American community, and ordinary Polish-American women again reacted forcefully. The activities of these women of the second generation were not without precedent; almost all of them echoed the militancy of the immigrant generation in response to the same or similar kinds of threats. The Great Depression of the 1930s, like nothing before it, attacked two of the most important pillars of Polish-American working-class life: a secure job and a home.

These had provided the fabric of respectability, pride, and dignity that held the community together. The Polish-American response to this crisis was organized with great sophistication and an awareness of class that gained wide sympathy and response from many outside the Polish community. Polish-American women also interacted more fully with women of other groups—in a more structured class response through the newly formed unions—than did their mothers. The basis of militancy for most of them, however, still remained in the ethnic community and the family.

During the 1930s, Polish-American women not only were involved in a variety of protest activities but even initiated a number. The most important was the Detroit Meat Strike organized by Mary Zuk in the Polish neighborhoods of Detroit in the summer of 1935. The strike spread to other neighborhoods and finally to other cities in the Midwest before dying out in the autumn. The strike was the brainchild of the Committee

Against the High Cost of Living, which started in the Polish enclave of Hamtramck. Throughout its existence the strike was always far more effective in the Polish neighborhoods than it was elsewhere. As it waned, the strike movement was turned into a strong political movement. It transformed itself into the People's League. The league elected Mary Zuk to the Hamtramck city council as an advocate of consumer affairs and labor. Many of the women who first began political activity in the meat strikes later emerged as leaders in the struggle for unions.[66]

During the intense period of union organization during which the Congress of Industrial Organizations (CIO) was born, evidence indicates that Polish-American women were active in a number of centers. In Detroit, building on the base created by the meat strike and the People's League, Polish-American women played a significant role in the struggle to unionize the city's workforce. Most notable was the strike of the cigar workers who conducted the longest sit-down in American labor history to win recognition of their union in early 1937. The cigar workers, about 85 percent of whom were Polish, rallied the entire Polish community behind them in a surprising show of unanimity. The Polish-American neighborhoods of Detroit were in a stage of intense mobilization over this strike when the sit-downs in the Detroit auto factories were called. The Polish-American sit-downers—who made up the largest single group of workers in the auto plants and probably a majority in some, such as Plymouth Assembly and Dodge Main—were the sons, husbands, brothers, cousins, and neighbors of the two thousand women who sat down in the cigar factories. They were clearly influenced by the spirit of militance that the women displayed in their strike and in the earlier activities on which it was built. The cigar women's strike also precipitated a wave of sit-downs by other women in laundries, restaurants, hotels, and the five-and-dime and speciality food stores in the city. Polish-American women from the same neighborhoods that spawned the meat strike and the cigar strike played a prominent role in these actions.[67]

Other Polish-American women were involved in labor actions in factories elsewhere in the city. They constituted, for example, one of the largest groups of workers at the Ternstedt plant during the highly disciplined work slowdown that forced the management to negotiate. As wives, mothers, and sisters, they also worked in the strike kitchens, children's centers, union offices, and they mobilized by the thousands for parades and demonstrations. During bitter strikes in plants near Polish neighborhoods, neighborhood women saved unionists from mounted police attacks by pouring boiling water or dirt-filled mop water on police and opening their homes to the fleeing men. The success of the union movement in Detroit clearly owes much to the courage and perseverance of the Polish-American women of Detroit.[68]

Systematic research on these and other aspects of the historic experience of second-generation Polish-American women is still in its infancy or not yet even begun.[69] We need to know these women's stories, as well as their mothers' stories, before we can speak with any confidence about the main features of Polish-American history or indeed of the history of women in America.

4

Polish Americans and Religion

William J. Galush

THE ANCIENT PROVERB "BÓG ZAPŁAĆ" (GOD WILL REPAY) SAYS
much about Polish religious sensibility. In its traditional Roman Catholic
form, religion has pervaded Polish-American existence, fostering a rich
spirituality and evoking extraordinary material sacrifices from lower-class
immigrants. As the one institution that transcended the partitions in the
period of mass immigration, the Roman Catholic Church was intimately
linked with national identity. Yet the dominant religious persuasion has
had critics: from loyalists with differing visions of an ethnic Catholicism
to independent Catholics to anti-clericals. Tensions creative and disruptive have marked the relations of Poles to religion in America.

The historiography of religious American Polonia has developed in
parallel with study of other aspects of this community. The early filiopietism—here with its characteristic emphasis on "contributions" framed
around institutional development and featuring fulsome tribute to immigrant clerics—has been largely supplanted. Drawing from developments
in the study of religion exemplified by Timothy L. Smith, Jay P. Dolan,
and others, recent historians of Polonia have shown greater concern for
laity and community, and a more critical but less partisan spirit has informed their inquiries.[1]

Clergy and Congregations

The unusual clerical dominance in the origins of the first Polish-American
parish had attractive symbolic value to later clericalist writers and certainly

confirmed their inclinations to stress the priestly role. Studies began with the colonial period and include the antebellum period, though most work is postbellum because of the pattern of Polish immigration. The reverential, even hagiographic approach to early priests may be seen in older works such as M. Torosiewicz and Mieceslaus Haiman, sometimes as part of surveys of Polonia.[2] A rare example of recent scholarly examination of an antebellum spiritual figure is concerned more with his institutional role than with his ethnicity.[3]

The more extensive discussion of clergy for the years after the Civil War had its earliest important exponent in the work of Father Wacław Kruszka. Himself an immigrant, and half brother of the publisher of the nationally read *Kuryer Polski* of Milwaukee, around the turn of the century Kruszka wrote a monumental thirteen-volume work that discussed clergy and the church extensively and reverently.[4] He reserved his criticism largely for those priests who had defected to the Polish National Catholic Church (PNCC), a denomination discussed below. Other writers such as Revs. Alexander Syski and Joseph Swastek have followed this pattern, often in the earlier volumes of *Polish American Studies,* the organ of the Polish American Historical Association.[5] The custom of publishing parish anniversary books, which serve as sources of basic factual information, has always afforded local amateur historians numerous opportunities to eulogize their spiritual leaders.[6]

Since the 1960s the emergence of more professional—and usually lay—historians studying American Polonia has redirected the study of clerics. Biography is best represented by Daniel Buczek, who has written about the Connecticut priest Father Lucyan Bójnowski. Though generally favorable in his characterizations, he presents a well-rounded portrait of a cleric who indisputably helped shape his community.[7]

More often priests appear as part of larger studies. Andrzej Brożek offers much on the life and work of Father Leopold Moczygemba in Panna Maria, Texas, perhaps the earliest Polonian colony. Anthony Kuzniewski has provided a fine examination of the career and the role of Father Wacław Kruszka in his work on Wisconsin Polonia. Victor Greene more briefly discussed numerous clerical figures in his important study of ethnic consciousness among Chicago Poles and Lithuanians. A clerical focus appears in Joseph Parot, who provides the best work on the important Resurrectionist Father Vincent Barzyński, in his study of religion in Chicago Polonia. John Bukowczyk stresses class tensions in his study of the New York area.[8] All these works offer a critical appreciation of the role of the clergy in immigrant society.

Congregations of male religious appeared in Polonia in the late nineteenth century, often in parish service. Though they sought the ideal of
living in community, the dispersed nature of their American missions
often gave them the character of seculars. The literature on these bodies
is uneven—mainly works produced by community members—and the
profusion of master's and doctoral theses found for congregations of religious women is largely absent.

A society of particular significance was the Congregation of the Resurrection. It originated in the Russian partition in the 1830s and became
active in the United States, especially in Chicago. John Iwicki, C.R., has
written one of the better narrative histories by a community member,
which is impressively researched if largely uncritical. Joseph John Parot
discusses the Chicago Resurrectionists more analytically. He argues per-
suasively that they established a "community-parish system" with numerous institutions—including a daily newspaper and a parish bank—serving
Polonia in addition to houses of worship.[9]

Less numerous than among Franciscans, the Polish presence among
Jesuits in America has been studied mainly through leading personalities.
The antebellum Father Francis Dzierożynski has received considerable
attention, though his career, of necessity, was spent in a non-Polish milieu.[10] Their important ethnically linked work came mainly in the years
1865–1914 when several dozen came to America for varying periods as
mission band leaders and occasionally as pastors. Their reports have been
recently published and offer interesting observations on Polonia by well-
educated itinerants.[11]

Smaller communities appeared in America in the prewar period, often
of important local influence. These included Bernardines, Marian Fathers, Pallotine Fathers, Paulites, and others.[12] The presence of Polish
regulars was an important source not only of clergy but of ties to the
homeland, as they retained connections with their foundations in the
old country. More easily than Polish diocesans, who increasingly received
training in American seminaries, Polish regulars were able to maintain
Polishness through separate education and community organization.

The Role of Laity and Community

The establishment of Polish parishes was a varied process, much conditioned by local leadership, community interest, and clerical attitudes, but
in America it invariably required persuasion of laypersons in the absence
of government support. Regarding congregational formation, students of

Polonia have evolved from a clericalist perspective to a more balanced view, acknowledging the activity of both priests and laity. Older histories were often written by religious scholars who were eager to demonstrate the importance of revered colleagues or who simply reflected the pre–Vatican II vision of the Church. Rev. Wacław Kruszka is an early example, followed by later priests such as Joseph Swastek and numerous nuns, along with most writers of the parish anniversary books. As early as the 1960s, Victor Greene gave some attention to the role of laypersons in his study of Slavs in the Pennsylvania coalfields. The 1970s and 1980s saw numerous works that integrated the laity more comprehensively into studies of congregations.[13]

Laypersons formed organizations that were not only important in community formation but frequently instrumental in the foundation and support of parishes. In the prewar period of massive immigration, fraternal benefit societies were the preeminent devices, dominated by men of ambition and relative affluence, and frequently they expressed pious concern.[14] The earliest were independent societies of immigrant males, which formed on homeland and American models to provide mutual aid, their simplicity of formation normally making them the first form of Polonian organization. Chicago offers an example, where the pioneer St. Stanislaus Society (founded in 1864) was instrumental in forming the first congregation, which bore the same name. Both Parot and Greene provide useful studies of the process and the rivalries engendered as competing organizations emerged with differing views of the role of religion.[15]

Polish fraternalism underwent a crucial change less than a decade later with the formation of the Polish Roman Catholic Union (PRCU) in Chicago in 1873. In his dated but still useful account, Mieczysław Haiman notes the early clerical dominance of Rev. Theodore Gieryk and the more aggressive Rev. Vincent Barzyński, who with pious laymen sought to unite Polonia in a federation of fraternal aid societies. A major goal was the "maintenance of the holy faith," and lodges were expressly linked to parishes, with membership limited to Roman Catholics.[16] More recent historians have discussed the PRCU—and its eventually larger rival, the Polish National Alliance (PNA), founded in 1880—in terms of a prewar rivalry between "clericals" and "nationalists."[17] Although broadly persuasive, this perspective relies excessively on publications and statements of national organs and leaders articulated in terms of official ideology designed to emphasize distinctiveness; conditions in smaller colonies sometimes fostered a more cooperative relationship between local PNA lodges and priests. Local variations deserve further study.[18]

Polity and Dissent

A major concern of historians looking at parishes is polity. Influenced by the work of Timothy L. Smith, Josef Barton, Jay P. Dolan, and others, students of Polonia have given increasing recognition to the significance of lay initiative and the need for clerics to persuade, not just command, in a democratic environment.[19] There has been a general recognition of the importance of the laity, but the evaluations of immigrant aspirations toward participation in parochial government has varied.[20]

More than any other Catholic immigrants, Poles revived the question of trusteeism in the years 1870–1914. Given the legendary Polish loyalty to Roman Catholicism, it is not surprising that religious dissent in Polonia took the form of independent Catholic movements rather than defections to Protestantism. The first instance occurred in Poland Corner, Wisconsin, in 1872; and subsequently a series of local conflicts rocked American Polonia. Students of the events typically describe a sequence wherein a few men of prominence would lead a dissatisfied minority to complain of pastoral tyranny, immorality, or incompetence and, receiving no "justice" from the bishop, left the Roman obedience for a separate existence. They usually added to their rationales for dissent a desire for lay ownership of congregational property and more democratic polity, and occasionally a dissatisfied priest had spiritual leadership of the effort. Historians have moved from the partisan accounts before the 1960s to more dispassionate evaluations of these instances of dissent.[21]

Since the large majority of Poles in a colony invariably remained loyal to Roman Catholicism, the independent congregations found their existence difficult, especially if they developed without a priest as leader. The result was a tendency to form supra-congregational structures under traditional forms of leadership—new denominations headed by their own bishops.

Independent Catholic denominations have attracted more attention than congregations, but the same early inclination to partisanship gradually gave way to more detached studies. Thus Paul Fox and the authors of large anniversary books published by the PNCC, which soon emerged as the preeminent dissenting movement, have framed the story as a revolt of oppressed but nationalistic and freedom-loving immigrants blessed with the charismatic and democratic leadership of Father (later Bishop) Francis Hodur in their struggle against authoritarian Irish and German Roman Catholic bishops and their Polish clerical servants.[22] Partisans of Roman Catholicism were more inclined to blame agitation by renegade priests and pseudo-intelligentsia, though Father Kruszka acknowledged some episcopal activities that gratuitously annoyed Poles.[23]

More recent historiography on Polish National Catholicism has taken a variety of perspectives, though often with a considerable degree of overlap. The establishment of *PNCC Studies* (circa 1980) by scholars within the denomination represents an impressive effort to both eschew partisanship and elevate the level of inquiry.[24] A thoughtful overview is Hieronim Kubiak's *The Polish National Catholic Church in the United States of America from 1897 to 1980,* which stresses its democratic character and the influence of the Polish left upon the founder, Father Francis Hodur. Barbara Strassberg likewise emphasizes its democratic aspects but links the movement to aspirations for a Polish state. In a briefer work John Bukowczyk has offered an interpretation of the PNCC as embodying a variation of nineteenth-century Polish messianism, combining nationalism with anti-clericalism and egalitarianism, drawing upon popular religion in addition to secular leftist beliefs.[25]

If National Catholicism has attracted much attention among students of Polonia, Polish Protestants have been virtually ignored, largely because of their modest numbers and minimal interaction with overwhelmingly Catholic Polonia. Protestant denominational historians have generally passed over them in favor of more numerous ethnic groups with which they were intermingled. Lutheran Poles came in small numbers from the Prussian partition, but their partial assimilation to German culture continued in America and they never asserted their presence in the Polish-American community.[26] Evangelism by American Protestants was remarkably ineffective among Poles, converting only a few thousand immigrants by World War I. Such trifling numbers, ostracism by many Roman Catholic compatriots, and Americanizing pressures from the sponsoring U.S. denominations promoted more rapid assimilation.[27]

The majority's quest for recognition in the larger Roman Catholic community, symbolized by the drive for a Polish-American bishop, has attracted many historians of Polonia. The religious divisions among early writers initially influenced the investigation, with Father Kruszka overstressing the Polish presence in American Catholicism to justify a cause in which he took an important personal part.[28] Interpretations by later historians have tended to place the quest for a bishop in the context of fostering ethnicity. Greene casts the movement for equality *(równouprawnienie)* as part of the development of Polish consciousness. Writing later, Kuzniewski gives more attention to the theological rationale for Polonian bishops articulated by Father Kruszka, but he also addresses ethnic concerns. Galush discusses it as part of the development of group identity and organization among Polonian clerics.[29] In the interpretation of Edward Kantowicz, the elevation in 1908 of Father Paul Rhode of Chicago as the first Polonian bishop fostered a "quasi-denomination" within American Catholicism. Although other writers do not go as far, Rhode's importance in Polonia is unquestioned.[30]

Women and the Church

Scant attention has been given to laywomen, and what little there is tends to focus on organizations.[31] A dated and filiopietistic work by Jadwiga Karlowiczowa narrates the history and leading personalities of the important Polish Women's Alliance (PWA) founded in 1898, which evolved in response to the exclusion of women from the older fraternal federations. Donald Pienkos discusses the role of women briefly in his study of the Falcons, a gymnastic military organization that was rare among Poles in that it was open to both genders, though not on an equal basis.[32] The strategies of women, organized or not, in enlarging their role in the family and in Polonian society are fertile fields for further investigation.

The study of religious communities of Polish women remains largely the province of congregational historians, fostering a tendency toward discretion and hagiography. Students of Catholic female communities in general have only begun to utilize the perspectives developed by feminist historians such as Margaret Thompson or Barbara Misner.[33] Yet nuns were unusual among nineteenth- and early twentieth-century women in having direct control of large institutions and numerous personnel. Furthermore, sisters mobilized impressive amounts of capital for major projects whose scope and purpose they largely defined.

Study of the oldest and largest Polish community—the Congregation of St. Felix (Felicians)—has undergone significant change. Older works in the form of anniversary books or graduate theses at Catholic schools fall into the category of filiopietism, though often containing important factual data.[34] The transition to professionalism can be seen in the work of Sr. Mary Jane Kadyszewski, which is both more candid and more analytical.[35] A similar situation obtains among studies of Felician institutions or educational work. The range of activity was impressive, including not only schools and orphanages but day care and homes for the aged.[36]

Many other smaller communities have been studied in similar terms, though less extensively. The first American congregation of Polonian women, the Franciscan Sisters of Chicago, has a fine descriptive book by

Sr. Anne Marie Knawa. As with the Felicians, the scope of service was broad, including hospitals and day care in addition to education. Knawa fittingly compares the foundress, Josephine Dudzik, to her contemporary Jane Addams. The Sisters of the Holy Family of Nazareth have a well-researched centennial book, and their activity among the Polish immigrants was matched after World War I with a surprising extension among non-Poles, which is unusual among Polish congregations.[37]

Ethnicity and the Clergy

A common topic in the works on religious sisters, even if discreetly discussed, is the question of ethnic separatism. Several communities had their origins in divisions, sometimes bitter but at least deeply felt, that moved Polish minorities to establish their own houses.[38] Perhaps because historians of religion and immigration have tended to ignore nuns, the playing out of ethnic sentiments among closely knit groups of women has until very recently remained unexplored by secular writers.

Mixed orders of male religious also offer an example of the salience of ethnicity within international congregations. The Order of Friars Minor (Franciscans) has a number of narrative histories by members, less elaborately researched than Iwicki but helpful for information and references. While predominantly German in the early years in America, Polish Franciscans such as Father Leopold Moczygemba—a pioneer cleric and founding member of the Immaculate Conception Province (founded in 1872)—were active among both countrymen and others. Father Ignatius Fudzinski was even elected head of the community in 1895. Still, Polish members preferred to support their ethnic orientation and satisfy lay preferences by serving Polish parishes wherever possible. In 1905 Fudzinski and his countrymen separated themselves into the ethnic province of St. Anthony of Padua while other Poles set up the Assumption province in Wisconsin, serving numerous parishes in the Midwest.[39]

Both seculars and regulars sought some collective identity on an ethnic basis in America, a novelty unnecessary in the homeland but helpful in a pluralistic communion run entirely by non-Poles. The process was uneven, hindered by intra-clerical rivalries and personality conflicts. William Galush has surveyed clerical pre–World War I organizational development, and John Bukowczyk has examined the bases of factionalism among the immigrant clergy.[40] The post–World War I years await their historian.

Ethnicity came under attack through episcopal policy in the United States, where many bishops attempted to produce an Americanized clergy

through their diocesan seminaries. The most extensive study is by Daniel
O'Neill in the St. Paul archdiocese, where Archbishop John Ireland spear-
headed the effort, but his sentiments were echoed by ordinaries elsewhere.[41]

Yet seculars did not totally lack for ethnic education. With increasing
sophistication historians have examined the Saints Cyril and Methodius
Seminary, founded in Detroit in 1886 by the activist Father Joseph Dąbrowski.[42] Although only a minority of Polish-American clerics attended,
the seminary's very existence was a call to ethnicity; it gave to its alumni
an enhanced sense of identity and a form of community consciousness.

The Social and Political Role of Religion

Benevolent activity was not limited to envowed persons; laymen—and
even more laywomen—engaged in charitable work. Pious groups and the
occasional St. Vincent de Paul society gave aid on varying bases. Historians have almost totally neglected this topic, which offers rich insights into
the role of class, values, and organizational structures in Polonia. Studies
are non-existent at present, though references appear occasionally in
works on fraternal insurance societies or parish histories.[43]

The melding of patriotism and religion, which helped foster Polonian
nationalism before and during World War I, has only just begun to be
systematically explored. Joseph Hapak mentions the role of the clergy
in the wartime Polish army, and John Bukowczyk has offered a subtle
interpretation of the interplay of faith and patriotism. The war proved a
watershed for Polonia, forcing a reexamination of its relationship with the
homeland, which led to a more American orientation in the interwar
period.[44]

Extra-Institutional Belief

Religious sentiments also expressed themselves outside the institutional
church. Polish sociologists going back to Florian Znaniecki have examined popular religion and "superstition," an inquiry that Znaniecki extended to the United States. Such persons were less often historians than
sociologists or anthropologists, and their interest in folk beliefs and practices has been persistent. The well-known publisher Anton Paryski of
Toledo printed books on magic before the war.[45] The sacred was called
upon to solemnize labor solidarity, as in the taking of an oath before a
crucifix not to scab on the eve of a strike. There was even a recorded

instance of the crucifixion of a foreman during a labor dispute. One of the few studies of popular beliefs by a historian, John Bukowczyk, argues that the new urban environment demystified existence through science and the obvious control of nature, but overall popular religion has received little examination.[46]

The institutional church sought to accommodate a variety of religious practices, usually expressed through pious societies or devotional practices such as religious scenes of persons in costumes called living pictures *(żywe obrazy)*. Up to World War I the associations typically were for women, offering opportunities not only for pious expression but also for socializing and leadership posts. Little has been written on devotional societies, but there are numerous descriptions of Polish customs. The now-classic Helen Zand series (circa 1950) in *Polish American Studies* has been reprinted as a book, and the topic has received more recent and sophisticated attention from Aleksander Posern-Zielinski.[47]

The Second Generation and the Post–World War II Period

Immigration restriction in the early 1920s greatly decreased the flow of newcomers, and despite some reinforcement after World War II through displaced persons and latecomers, Polonia became ever more a community of the American-born. Given the long-standing inclination of historians to study newcomers, the consequence has been a relative paucity of historical works about the second and later generations.[48]

Communities of religious women after World War I have received the same attention characteristic of the immigrant period: largely internal histories by members. Although important changes such as the influx of American-born women and a decline in Polish usage has been noted, the works remain largely descriptive. No one has yet examined the reasons for the large numbers entering between the wars as compared to the diminution notable even before 1960, the evolution of leadership forms, or the integration of non-Poles. The interwar Felician establishment and vigorous promotion of the Ave Maria Guild is an example of a novel interest in adult education and the confidence to pursue it independently; both suggested a larger spirit of innovation that was insufficiently examined by historians preoccupied with nuns' education of children.[49]

As in the prewar period, the clergy has attracted disproportionate attention from scholars. Daniel Buczek continued his biographical interest by studying an American-born priest in a full-length work as well as in more general surveys. He remains one of the few writers to explore the evolution of the ethnic clergy.[50] The Polish Seminary at Orchard Lake, Michigan, has been a more popular subject. Father Leonard Chrobot offers older descriptions, but the recent work by Frank Renkiewicz is a much more thoughtful overview.[51] Preaching and sermon style has been surveyed, as well as prayer books. There is a reverent biography of the Buffalo radio priest, Father Justyn Figas, O.F.M.[52]

Parochial development after World War I has been only modestly studied. The creation of national parishes virtually ceased, though some territorial ones were de facto Polish. Even this became less typical after 1945 as suburbanization dispersed Polonians. To date, Stanislaus Blejwas offers one of the few interpretations of the interwar and later parochial evolution in the context of Connecticut Polonia.[53]

Coinciding with the decline in ethnic congregational formation was a noticeable reduction in quarrels over parish polity. Whereas Buczek and others have given some attention to postwar clerical developments, the role of the laity in the second and third generation remains largely uninvestigated. Mary Cygan suggests that there were new patterns of lay behavior that modified clerical pretensions. Even in Scranton, headquarters city of the PNCC, issues that in the past might have provoked a schism at Roman Catholic parishes did not pass beyond ephemeral protest. Formation of Polish National Catholic congregations had the paradoxical effect of enhancing loyalist clerical authority because of the departure of the most vocal and contentious laypersons. Historians have not adequately explored the sharp decline in PNCC congregational formation after World War II, nor the effect of the post–Vatican II "parish advisory councils," which reintroduced into Roman Catholic parishes a measure of elected lay representation.[54]

Preservation of Polishness among clerics has remained an obvious scholarly concern but the limited amount of research suggests a diminution in the interwar period and beyond.[55] On the national level, organization of Polonian priests declined in these years, with the demise in 1936 of the last clerical journal, *Przegląd Katolicki*. Associational life for ethnic clergy remained sporadic after World War II, although the rise of the Polish American Priests Association in the 1980s may portend a limited revival of group identity. Even regulars—whose greater control of members' education and subsequent patterns of group living witnessed a dilution of identity as non-Poles entered their communities—as well as seculars were hurt by the decline in vocation from the 1960s onward.[56] Bishops subsequent to Rhode have not attracted the attention of historians to the same degree, and Kulik's work suggests that they remained secondary even in episcopal rank, serving as ordinaries in minor sees or as suffragans. The elevation of Archbishop John Joseph Krol of Philadelphia to the dignity of cardinal in 1967 was a novelty, but no Polonian bishop seems to have replicated (or aspired to) Rhode's role as national leader.[57]

The lay backbone of Polishness, the fraternal federations, became more uniformly friendly to Roman Catholicism by World War I, with the obvious exception of the PNCC's Polish National Union. But if well-disposed, the insurance societies themselves were struggling to retain members, a quest that the depression only made harder. The difficulty of attracting second-generation and later Polonians to organizations often perceived as old-fashioned made their beneficence toward religion less significant. Nonetheless, the general decline of anti-clericalism in fraternal and other forms was positive for Polish Roman Catholicism.[58]

Studies of post-immigrant Polonian religion and ethnicity tend to involve sociologists and anthropologists as well as historians, enriching the effort with diverse methodologies. They have documented the increasingly common use of English and a growing trend toward exogamy, although much of the time national parishes retained Polish in societies and sermons. Lay activity in relatively novel areas such as benevolence increased, with lay auxiliaries emerging to aid orphanages and other institutions as well as St. Vincent de Paul and other charitable associations.[59]

Such an environment was not conducive to the PNCC. Scholars are debating its prospects in a situation of declining ethnic identity. According to Kubiak, only about fifteen parishes formed after 1945, as conflict over polity within Roman Catholicism virtually disappeared and its alleged superiority in ethnicity became less attractive. Intermarriage significantly increased, and a denomination that claimed superior Polishness became noticeably less ethnic. The ecumenical movement of the 1960s improved relations with the Roman Catholic Church, but the very raison d'être of the PNCC is undergoing reconsideration.[60]

Unanswered Questions

The study of religion among Polish Americans has emphasized the immigrant generation, usually in terms of institutional development. Even among the better-studied religious, there are profitable avenues still to be explored. Histories of communities have tended to focus on leaders and institutional development. It would be beneficial to examine the evolution of membership over time in terms of age and class, the patterns of advancement within communities, and their relations with seculars. Until recently studies of nuns have proceeded with excessive concern for discretion, or conflict minimized or omitted. The development of female religious individual and community relationships with male authority figures similarly varied over time, as did internal political structures, but these topics have remained unstudied. Even examination of patterns of piety may tell us much about their spirituality.

The religious activity of the second and succeeding generations occurred in different environments as well as times. It would be advantageous for scholars to look at the American-born in the suburbs, where they often intermarried with non-Poles and attended non-ethnic churches. The post-immigrant generations are characterized by greater variety in class and education as well as in residence, but investigation of these factors has only just begun. This should also include the study of evolving lay attitudes toward polity and piety. Did the decline in dissent, especially after World War II, have a generational or a class connection? Was there a movement toward adoption of "American" Catholic devotions at the expense of the rich range of older practices, or did a synthesis emerge? In this regard, were women the pioneers rather than men? In general, the laity should be the focus of more study, to counter the historical bias in favor of clerics.

The whole topic of religion could profitably be related more effectively to other aspects of life, such as the relation of religion to labor activity, political aspirations, and indeed its relevance for the preservation of Polish ethnicity. Did the varied development and success of unionization before and after World War I involve the invocation of religion? Similarly, were political careers supported by appeals to a common ethnic religious sensibility? Finally and most broadly, how did the role of religion evolve in the crucial process of fostering an ethnic identity across the generations? These concerns could profitably inform future scholarly inquiry.

5

Jewish Emigration from Poland
Before World War II

Daniel Stone

God took a piece of Eretz Yisroel [the land of Israel], which he had hidden away in the heavens at the time when the Temple was destroyed, and sent it down upon the earth and said, "Be My resting place for My children in their exile." That is why it is called Poland (Polen), from the Hebrew *poh lin,* which means: "Here shalt thou lodge." . . . In the great future, when the Messiah will come, God will certainly transport Poland with all its settlements, synagogues, and Yeshivahs to Eretz Yisroel. How else could it be?

THE POLISH-AMERICAN YIDDISH AUTHOR SHOLEM ASCH TOLD this Jewish legend explaining the Jewish attachment to and affection for Poland, which developed over seven hundred years of Jewish history there.[1] In this legend, Asch talked of religious Jews, but the same attitude applied to modern Jewish Bundists, Zionists, and Autonomists, who tried to build a secular Zion in Poland in modern times. However, faced with the same economic pressures that drove Christian Poles out of the land in the late nineteenth and early twentieth centuries, hundreds of thousands of Polish Jews emigrated to the New World. A study of their history, immigration, adaptation, and relations with their fellow Poles fills a gap in the history of Poles in America.

Despite the volumes of scholarly and polemical literature devoted to the study of Polish Jews and Polish-Jewish relations, Polish Jews in America have never been studied as a separate group. Historians of Jews in America rarely differentiate between Jews from Poland and other East

European countries; indeed, much scholarship betrays a lack of background in Polish history. Scholarship on Poles in America similarly ignores the numerous Jews who came to America from Poland, except as occasional rivals in acrimonious debates during times of communal conflict.[2]

The present chapter seeks to invent the field of Polish-American Jewish history on the basis of existing secondary literature devoted to Jewish history and occasionally to Polish history. Where no studies address Polish Jews specifically, general descriptions of Eastern European Jews will be used. Historiographical controversies are relatively rare in this new field, except in the area of Polish-Jewish relations, and are signaled in the footnotes.

Like Polish-American history, Polish-Jewish-American history begins in the Colonial period and becomes significant in the era of mass migration during the late nineteenth century. The first part of this chapter discusses Jews in Polish history; the second (and longest) part discusses the history of Polish Jews in America; the third part discusses Jewish links with Poland that continued until the Holocaust; the fourth part discusses contacts between Polish Jews and ethnic Poles in America. Finally, the conclusions summarize the article and make suggestions for future research.

Jews in Poland

As the legend told by Sholem Asch suggests, Polish Jews considered themselves autochthonous inhabitants of Poland, and history confirms that Jews have inhabited Poland since its beginnings. Like other corporate groups in medieval and early modern society, Jewish communities in Poland enjoyed self-governing privileges by royal charter. In the seventeenth and eighteenth centuries, Jews sought new opportunities in the burgeoning "private" cities set up by nobles on their estates, generally with similar corporate rights. In the late eighteenth century and the nineteenth century, some Poles looked toward the creation of a modern Polish nation through abolition of medieval privileges, including those separating Poles from Jews; and a significant minority of Jews adopted Polish language and culture during the nineteenth century. However, economic backwardness and the loss of Polish statehood contributed to the continuing separation of most Poles and Jews. As a result, the majority of Polish Jews entered the twentieth century with a feeling of Jewish, rather than Polish, nationality. The revival of Polish statehood after World War I finally created the conditions for Polonizing Polish Jewry, especially through the public schools, but the process affected only Jewish youth before World War II broke out.[3]

The community's dominant language was Yiddish, although most Jews also spoke Polish or other local languages. As Sholem Asch's account implies, Poland-Lithuania occupied a central place in the imagination of world Jewry before the Holocaust because Poland was the place where Jews were Jews—not Americanized, Europeanized, or Sovietized Jews. Poland was home to Judaism's most important Orthodox rabbinical schools before the Holocaust. Economically backward Wilno gained recognition as the new Jerusalem, but great rabbis gave many otherwise obscure provincial cities worldwide fame. Modern Jewish secular culture also flourished here as nowhere else. Yiddish literature emerged around 1900; Yitzhak Perets made Warsaw its capital. Jewish theater, poetry, film, photography, art, music, journalism, and even sports arose. Modern Jewish historiography emerged, aided by the formation of significant Jewish libraries such as the Central Jewish Library in Warsaw and YIVO Institute (Jewish Scientific Institute) in Wilno.[4]

Nevertheless, a noticeable minority spoke Polish at home, contributing some of Poland's most important cultural figures as well as half the readership for Polish literature and half the audience for Polish theater. The 1897 census identified 14 percent of Warsaw's Jews as speaking Polish as their first language; many more spoke Polish as a second language. According to the 1921 national census, 25 percent of Jews accepted Polish nationality (a figure that may have been exaggerated for political purposes), and, according to the 1931 census, 12 percent of Jews used Polish as their mother tongue.[5]

Relations between ethnic Poles and Jews over the centuries have varied from tolerance to intolerance; the rise of nationalism in the twentieth century created particularly bad relations. Throughout Polish history, Jews lived mostly in towns and cities, following commercial and artisanal occupations. Most Jews lived modestly. A few were rich, but the industrial revolution wiped out many jobs of less fortunate Jews, and large numbers fell into abject poverty in the nineteenth and twentieth centuries.

Jewish Immigration from Poland to America

Difficulties in studying Jewish emigration from Poland to America begin with the problem of defining a Polish Jew. Jews and their descendants who emigrated from predominantly Polish-speaking regions were Polish

Jews, as were Jews who emigrated from the borderlands, especially if these areas were included in the Second Polish Republic. That means that Ukrainian, Belorussian, Lithuanian, and Russian Jews may have been called Polish Jews, depending on their orientation and on that of the observer.[6]

If it is hard to define a Polish Jew, it is doubly hard to establish Polish Jewish patterns of migration. The U.S. government collected no data on the immigration of Jews before 1899. Statistics to that date come from Jewish immigrant aid societies. In 1899, the U.S. Immigration Service started counting Yiddish-speaking immigrants as Hebrews; acculturated Jews whose primary language was Polish counted as Poles. Immigration also used a social test: no one asked the nationality of first- and second-class passengers. Furthermore, immigrants who had stopped along the way in countries such as Germany, Britain, or Canada did not count in American statistics as coming from Poland. As a result, it is difficult to specify the number of Polish Jews before 1919.[7]

About 2 million Jews came to the United States between 1881 and 1914 from the Russian and Austrian Empires, mostly from lands that had once belonged to the Polish-Lithuanian commonwealth. Of these, 1,500,000 came from the Russian Empire (most heavily from Lithuania and Belarus) and 400,000 from Austria-Hungary. The Jewish population of the United States skyrocketed from 275,000 in 1880, to 1,100,000 in 1900, 3,800,000 in 1925, and 4,700,000 in 1945.

The Polish Jewish component cannot be stated with precision, although some calculations are possible. Before 1895, about 70,000 Jews are thought to have come from Poland, mostly from the Prussian partition. Between 1895 and 1918, about 250,000 Jews came from Congress Poland and 125,000 from Galicia. About 1 million Jews emigrated from Lithuania, Belorusssia, and Ukraine; unfortunately, there is no way of establishing how many of them came from lands that were later incorporated into the Second Republic. Between 1920 and 1936, about 150,000 Jews emigrated from the reborn Polish Republic to the United States.[8]

Polish Jews came to the American colonies as early as 1712, joining their Dutch, English, and German co-religionists. Maintaining family and business contacts with other Polish Jews in England and Poland allowed some to prosper—such as Hyam Salomon, a noteworthy supporter of the American Revolution. Polish Jewish immigration grew early in the nineteenth century, principally from the Prussian Partition, and the first specifically Polish synagogue in America opened in Charleston, South

Carolina, in 1819. By 1860, eight Polish synagogues operated in New York City and six more operated elsewhere in the United States.[9]

The early history of Polish Jewish contact in America witnessed substantial Polish Jewish cooperation as many early Jewish immigrants spoke Polish and accepted Polish ways. Some Jewish participants in the 1830 Insurrection emigrated to America, joining émigré associations that accepted "every Pole emigrant regardless of position and faith." Polish Jews played a significant role in Polish-American organizations during the 1863 Insurrection, as Polonia stressed the need to liberate both Poles and Jews from tsarist oppression. A Polish Jewish immigrant published the first Polish-language paper published in America, *Echo z Polski*. In small communities lacking either a strong Polish or a strong Polish Jewish community, Jews from Wielkopolska and other western Polish areas melted into the German Jewish community.[10]

Mass migration from Eastern Europe started in 1881–1882 when the assassination of Tsar Alexander II led to pogroms and anti-Semitic laws. About 15,000 immigrants came to North America soon after. They came mostly from Belarus, even though the pogroms took place in Ukrainian New Russia and Warsaw; and this strongly suggests that Jewish emigration resulted, not so much from persecution as from

> the transition from pre-industrial and pre-modern structure in these countries to industrialization and modern organization [which] meant dislocation of people from the land, competitive pressures of new technology on handicrafts and small-scale industry and transportation, and the exposure of previously isolated communities and regions to the rest of the world.[11]

Neither the United States nor Canada took any responsibility for the new immigrants, who were left to their own resources and to charitable assistance.

The German Jewish community revealed an impressive sense of communal responsibility in aiding their poorer East European brethren. German Jews had come to America before the Civil War as poor peddlers and shopkeepers and had moved up the social ladder. This gave them the resources to set up numerous relief missions and innovative "settlement houses," providing social services in the big-city slums. Cultural differences, however, set these two branches of the Jewish community at odds for a considerable time; they eventually merged in a common Jewish-American identity.[12]

TABLE I
JEWISH OCCUPATIONAL PATTERNS

	Congress Poland 1897	Northwest Russia 1897	Immigrants 1899–1914
Laborers	42	47	81.2
Commerce	31	26	5
Service	24	18	11
Professionals	4	6	1.3

Note: Figures are percentages.

More than most other ethnic groups (including Poles), Polish and other East European Jews emigrated to the United States as families, which suggests that Jews came to stay rather than to accumulate money for an eventual return to the Old Country. Between 1899 and 1914, women and children comprised a substantially higher proportion of Jewish than of non-Jewish immigrants. Statistics put the Jewish rate of return in 1908–1914 at 5 percent and the average rate of return of all immigrants at slightly over 30 percent. Relative to population size, more than twice as many Jews emigrated from the Russian Empire as Poles; however, the proportion was reversed among immigrants from the Austro-Hungarian Empire.[13]

The economic structure of the Jews in Congress Poland was split about evenly between merchants and artisans, but mostly artisans migrated to North America. As shown in table 1, almost half (42%) the Jews in Congress Poland worked as laborers—in mining and manufacturing (37%), transport (3%), and agriculture (2%). Then a third (31%) worked in commerce, a quarter (24%) in personal services, and a fraction (4%) in professional services. Jewish occupations in Southwestern Russia (Ukraine) varied little from this pattern, but in the poorer and more primitively industrialized Northwest (Lithuania and Belorussia), more Jews worked in agriculture (4%) and mining and manufacturing (43%) while fewer earned their living in commerce (26%) and personal services (18%).[14]

Most Polish Jews barely managed to raise enough money to buy steamship tickets; they lacked capital to set themselves up in business when they arrived in America, and they took whatever jobs were available. Almost half (45%) declared no occupation on arrival, a significant figure that has not yet been interpreted. Of those declaring occupations, they called themselves skilled laborers (67%), laborers (12%), servants (11%), mer-

TABLE 2

OCCUPATION OF IMMIGRANTS, 1899–1910

	Jews with Occupations	Jews Total Group	Poles with Occupations	Poles Total Group
No occupation	0	45	0	21
Skilled trades	67	37	6	5
Laborers	14	8	75	59
Professionals	1.3	0.7	0.2	0.16
Adult literacy	n/a	74	n/a	65

Note: Figures are percentages.

chants and dealers (5%), farm laborers (2%), professionals (1.3%), and farmers (0.2%). Of skilled workers, tailors were by far the most common (37%), followed by carpenters (10%), dressmakers (10%), shoemakers (6%), and lesser numbers of clerks, accountants, painters, glaziers, butchers, bakers, locksmiths, and blacksmiths. The minuscule number of professionals mostly consisted of teachers (29%) and musicians (22%). Engineers (6%) loosely balanced electricians (5%). The percentage of clergymen, artists, writers, and scientists was all about the same (5%). Only 290 professionals (4%) practiced medicine, and 34 (0.5%) practiced law.[15]

In contrast (as shown in table 2), roughly a quarter (21%) of Poles declared no occupation on arrival. Of those declaring an occupation, 6 percent worked in skilled occupations; 75 percent worked as laborers (including farm laborers); and 0.2 percent were professionals. Taken together, 74 percent of adult Jews and 65 percent of Poles could read; male literacy rates were similar, but twice as many Jewish women read as Polish women.[16]

Scholarship on Jewish life in America concentrates overwhelmingly on New York because so many Jews chose to live in and around that city. Before World War I, 86 percent of Jewish immigrants lived in the North Atlantic states, mostly in New York (64%) and Pennsylvania (10%). The Illinois population of immigrant Jews (6%) provided the most substantial Jewish population living in close proximity to ethnic Poles; smaller communities coexisted in cities such as Detroit, Milwaukee, and Buffalo.[17] Including American-born Jews, a third (33%) of American Jews lived in New York City in 1897, and closer to half (44%) in 1927; the overwhelming majority lived in the North Atlantic states.[18]

Usually, Polish Jewish immigrants were met at the dock by relatives (often distant ones whom they had never met before) and were taken to badly overcrowded apartments in the Lower East Side of New York City. They started work as tailors within the week, probably learning on the job the minimal skills needed to perform one simple operation required for industrial tailoring. The shop may have been in the apartment of a Jew who had emigrated a few years earlier from the same town and who had saved enough money to buy two or three sewing machines. At first, workers often lived where they worked, although in time they generally took on their own apartments, renting out spaces to boarders to make ends meet.

Living conditions were appalling at first, because of poverty and over-crowding. A New York buildings inspector described a typical tenement inhabited by Polish Jews:

> In No. 76 a peddler lives, with his wife and four small children. The rooms, like the rest of this floor, are very dirty. In a corner next to these rooms a pile of garbage about two feet high lies right at the head of the stairs as you go up. The children on this floor are very poorly clad . . . nothing but a loose gown, and no underclothing at all.
>
> Rooms 77, 78, and 79 are crowded with men and women sewing on machines. . . . They work for large clothing firms.[19]

Very few of the Jews raised in these conditions got much schooling before World War I. Overcrowded schools on New York's Lower East Side turned away students or seated them three to a desk in classes of sixty to one hundred students; most Jewish children dropped out by the legal school-leaving age of twelve. The school situation began to improve after 1910, when Jews moved to new districts in Brooklyn. Nevertheless, before World War I, few Polish Jews entered high school, and of those, less than one-fifth graduated. Naturally, very few attended even the tuition-free City College of New York until the 1920s, when they enrolled in large numbers.[20]

Along with poverty, criminality played a part in Polish Jewish ghetto life before World War I. The Lower East Side slums produced numerous gangs. Violent crime was rare until the 1920s when the American-born generation took over and found themselves increasingly isolated from a Jewish community that was turning middle class. By the 1930s, the Jewish criminality rate was less than half the general criminality rate for New York City, and it declined still further after World War II.[21]

Most Jews sought legitimate employ, naturally. Impoverished Jews had been in the forefront of trade union organization in Eastern Europe and took a similar stance in freer America. Early clothing workers unions followed ethnic lines, and the clothing industry endured many strikes, particularly as manufacturing moved out of home sweatshops into factories. The terrible Triangle Shirtwaist Factory fire of 1911 provided impetus for organization; 146 workers (mostly young Jewish and Italian women) died, unable to escape because the doors were locked. The cloakmakers union strike of 1910 proved a pivotal event in organizing the International Ladies Garment Workers Union (about two-thirds of whose members were women); the Amalgamated Clothing Workers Union (two-thirds male) formed slightly later. The largely Jewish leadership, with full support of the members, reached out in solidarity to Polish, Italian, and other workers. Socialist ideology played a substantial role in broadening union membership and found wide—though far from unanimous—support among Jewish immigrants.[22] Jewish businessmen, understandably, rarely supported trade unions and socialist causes.

Polish Jewish women played an unusually active role in unions and in their community. Jewish women had already been distinct in Europe for their business activities, which stemmed, in part, from social patterns directing men toward informal religious study throughout their adult years, leaving the wives to support the family. After arriving in America, women of employable age (starting in their early teens) invariably went to work in the garment trade. The substantial female presence in the workforce led to their high involvement in trade union activities and in political causes. Married women stayed home whenever possible, contributing to family finances through piecework or by taking in boarders.[23]

Polish Jewish immigrants remained religious, for the most part, thanks to the development of Americanized forms of worship. Attendance at traditional Orthodox *shuls* declined, but after about 1910, the modern Orthodoxy and the new Conservative movement began to replace them. Polish Jewish immigrants worshiped increasingly in a traditional but non-fundamentalist manner, adopting English as the dominant language for all activities except prayer and accepting American ways of life unless they explicitly contradicted Mosaic Law. German-based Reform Judaism— which at this time aggressively repudiated many important aspects of strict observance—attracted few East European Jews. Most Jewish children in America attended public schools, adding after-hours religious study organized on modern pedagogical principles. Noticeable minorities,

TABLE 3
JEWISH OCCUPATIONAL PATTERNS

Year and City	Manual Labor	Business and Office	Professions
1890 Lower East Side	75	24.5	0.5
1905 New York City	57	40	2
1933 New York City	43	49	8

Note: Figures are percentages.

however, attended a variety of private schools including religious schools (which also taught secular subjects) and Yiddish-language secular schools.[24]

The professional Yiddish theater provided Polish Jewish immigrants with popular and specifically Jewish forms of cultural expression as early as the 1880s. The numerical high point of Yiddish theater came in 1918, when New York City alone supported almost twenty Yiddish theaters, but its popularity soon declined as the postwar generation switched to English. Many early plays portrayed emigration from the *shtetl* to the United States. After World War I, plays increasingly depicted the return visit of Americanized Jewish immigrants to their hometowns. Yiddish translations and adaptations of Shakespeare, Ibsen, and other classics also appeared, particularly in the 1920s.[25]

The Yiddish theater soon declined because ghettoized and marginal American Jewry transformed itself into a lower-middle-class ethnic American group. Blue-collar Jewish identity dwindled from about 60 percent before World War I to about 30 percent in the 1930s as American-born children moved into the workforce. Blue-collar Jewry consisted increasingly of older workers and new immigrants. After the war, East European Jews—including Polish-American Jews—made their way into the lower reaches of the middle class (as shown in table 3). Where 75 percent of the proletarian Lower East Side and 57 percent of the Jewish population of New York before World War I had worked as manual laborers, only 43 percent of New York's Jews fit that category in 1933; 49 percent worked as peddlers, clerks, sales personnel, or for big business, and 8 percent worked as professionals. Polish Jewish businesses were mostly small neighborhood shops. Jews provided almost three times the number of lawyers, dentists, and doctors than their proportion in the population would suggest, but these generally eked out an existence in marginal practices in immigrant neighborhoods. The ascent of Polish Jews into the upper middle class came well after World War II; in 1952, the majority of New York Jews still worked as office and sales staff. Jews of German origin, primarily, achieved noteworthy success in retailing, clothing manufacturing, and entertainment.[26]

Outside of proletarianized New York City, Polish and other East European Jews worked more at mercantile occupations such as peddling and shopkeeping than as factory garment workers (although the marginal level at which they functioned in early years makes the label "middle class occupations" meaningless). Census figures for 1900 describing "Russian-born Jews" coming from Poland and the lands of the Polish-Lithuanian Commonwealth, showed that 61 percent of New York Jews were employed in manufacturing (mostly the garment industry), compared with 31–42 percent of Jews who worked in manufacturing in Chicago, Milwaukee, Buffalo, and Detroit. Peddling reversed the order: 17 percent of Detroit's Jews followed this activity and only 5 percent of New York's. Similarly, shopkeeping and other business activities account for 43 percent of Detroit's Jewish occupations and 16 percent of New York's.[27]

In Milwaukee, Jews tended to collect scrap metal and rags, selling to foundries and paper mills. There were few tailors, but many shopkeepers and enough Jewish housepainters and bakers to form unions. Peddling died out quickly because of strict municipal regulations and attacks on peddlers by youngsters in Polish and German districts.[28]

Detroit immigrants lived in new one-family houses, which in time became seriously overcrowded. Municipal services such as street repair and sewage construction also became inadequate as immigration grew. Nevertheless, living conditions and the availability of work seemed better than in New York. Community sources showed that the most common occupations in 1907 were clerk (392 workers), peddler (276), tailor (116), laborer (98), clothing (96), grocer (71), travel agent (65), cap maker (55), junk peddler (54), carpenter (49), stenographer (48), machinist (47), dry goods (44), teacher (44), and shoemaker (43).[29]

The most thorough survey of any immigrant Jewish community showed that in Bridgeport, Connecticut, Polish and other immigrant Jews who had been born and raised in Eastern Europe before World War I started out as an "upper lower class" of skilled laborers (60%) with a substantial lower-middle-class minority (25%), a modest group of lower

lower class (12%) and a small group of upper middle class (3%). Younger members of the same generation who were raised in America could be found mostly in the lower middle class (57%), followed by upper lower (32%), lower lower (7%), and upper middle (5%). Constrained by the Great Depression, their American-born children showed a small decline in lower middle (55%), a modest increase in upper lower (40%), a minuscule increase in upper middle (5%), and the disappearance of lower lower. They entirely failed to penetrate the upper class. Ethnic Poles, in contrast, remained overwhelmingly lower lower class in all three prewar generations (90%, 87%, 90%) with a modest appearance in upper lower (10%, 7%, 7%) and a minimal appearance in lower middle (7%, 0.4%, 3%).[30]

Attitude toward language and culture provided the key to upward social mobility in Bridgeport. While more than half of Polish children left school at the legal leaving age of sixteen, almost all Jewish children graduated. A school official credited success to "the Jewish parent [who] is anxious for the child to speak English, go to school without exception, and is always willing to cooperate." Speaking Yiddish and Polish in Europe, Polish Jews had traditionally been bilingual and switched easily to Yiddish-English bilingualism in America, as formal religious education in Hebrew safeguarded Jewish identity. In addition, Polish and other East European Jews (even from the working class) held "values conducive to middle-class success and could, under the proper circumstances, easily return to the pursuit of trade and study" that had formed an important part of Polish Jewish life in Europe.[31] Another reason for upward mobility was Jewish investment in business and in education, whereas other groups invested in personal property. Banks ignored small businessmen, but Jewish loan societies offered start-up loans without interest or at nominal rates; fewer than 1 percent of recipients defaulted.[32]

Social change affected the status of Bridgeport's women. Working-class Jewish wives received discretionary allowances for household expenses whereas husbands in more strictly patriarchal ethnicities only doled out money for specific purchases. The first bourgeois generation went further and "for all practical purposes [appointed the] wife the purchasing agent and business manager of the family corporation," although husbands retained the final say. Women demanded and won greater recognition in the synagogues of the large Conservative movement, which abolished the Orthodox practice of segregated seating.[33]

Entering the American middle class, however, did not assure Polish and other East European Jews of security and wealth, in part because they encountered constant discrimination. Until well after World War II, Jews were barred from executive employment in most established Anglo firms and institutions; many firms refused to hire Jews even for menial tasks. In the mid-1930s, Jews provided less than 5 percent of all corporation directors. There were only three Jewish executives in the entire automobile industry and no Jewish executives in other branches of heavy industry. Fewer than 1 percent of the nation's commercial bankers were Jewish. Ivy League and other elite colleges imposed low quotas on the admission of Jewish students and rarely hired Jewish professors. Professional schools also limited Jewish entrance and Anglo professional firms restricted hiring. Hospitals often refused to let Jewish doctors admit their patients. Genteel hotels generally refused service to Jews, although they sometimes accepted Jewish conventions in the off-season. Members of country clubs, university fraternities, and other social groups blackballed Jews from membership. Discrimination continued in universities until the 1960s and in business until the 1980s.

Denied opportunities in bourgeois America, Jews of Polish and other origin set up their own middle-class institutions. They went into business for themselves. Chronically short of capital, small businesses predominated and large Jewish businesses grew more from a sense of the market (entertainment and retailing, for example) than from heavy capital investment. Jewish hospitals, law firms, and accounting offices emerged. Jewish resorts, university fraternities, and country clubs catered to the emerging Jewish bourgeoisie. In addition to serving as houses of prayer, synagogues turned into community centers, devoted to educating children and providing cultural entertainment for adults.[34]

Small cities offered better business opportunities than large cities; here, Jews could avoid or escape the proletarianization that characterized life in large metropolitan centers. Still, according to a 1950 survey, half of small-city Jews remained dissatisfied. Positive features of small-city life included economic and social prospects as well as the chances of "feeling comfortable" as a Jew. Negative factors included slender opportunities to marry within the faith, low quality of Jewish education, and poor intellectual and artistic facilities.[35]

Isolated Jews in small towns led very lonely lives. For example, Fredelle Bruser Maynard spent her childhood in rural Saskatchewan, where the world seemed "alien if not actively hostile . . . because we did not go to church or belong to clubs or, it seemed, take any meaningful part in the life of the town." "Our social roots went, not down into the foreign soil on which fate had deposited us," Maynard observed, "but outwards, in delicate sensitive connections, to other Jewish families in other lonely prairie towns" with whom they met on Sundays and holidays. She felt at home only when the family moved to Winnipeg, a city with a sizable Jewish community, during the Great Depression. The anti-Semitic attitudes she encountered from time to time in both places bothered her less than the isolation of Jewish life in a small town.[36]

Jewish Ties to Poland

Like other immigrants, Polish Jews maintained a strong attachment to their native land that took institutional form in the *landsmanshaft* organization (plural, *landsmanshaften* or *landsmanshaftn*) wherever large numbers of Jews congregated. A landsman came from the same city, town, or even street in the Old Country. Typical landsmanshaft-founding stories involved a group of men without wives or fiancées who met at the home of a married landsman to share news from the Old Country. A formal organization eventually emerged to prevent deportation of a landsman or to bury a landsman who died without family. These groups were so small in scale, that "sometimes 20 or 30 landsmanshaft congregations would share one building, each occupying a small room or corner of a room." Landsmanshaft synagogues sought "meticulous preservation of the traditional Orthodox service" free from American innovation or even practices of neighboring European communities. Benevolent associations, common to Jewish life in Poland, formed anew to help immigrants cope with the ordinary problems of life before the introduction of state-run social security.[37]

Landsmanshaften were small and companionable; thus, larger European cities spawned numerous American offspring. For example, Warsaw Jews in New York grouped themselves in, among other organizations, the Bronx Warsawer Young Men's Society, Prager Warschauer Young Men's Aid Society, Warschauer Israel Ladies' Sick Support Society, Warschauer K.U.V. Bnei Israel, Warschauer Ladies' Benevolent Society, Warschauer First Sick Relief Association, Warsawer Benevolent Society, Warshauer First Congregation, Warschawer Independent Sick Support Society, Warshauer Sick Support Society, Warshauer Young Men's Benevolent Association, and the Warshawer Progressive Benevolent Association. They also organized extended family circles such as the Warshaw Brothers' Benevolent Association and the Warschauer and Feigenheim Benevolent Society. Other Polish cities gave rise to such groups as the Dubner Young Friends' Benevolent Association, Polish Kassover Young Men's Progressive Association, and the Przemyslauer Young Men's Sick and Benevolent Association. Membership rarely exceeded two hundred.

The first landsmanshaft organization was founded by Cracow Jews in 1855 in New York City, which also spawned a women's group in 1868 and a young men's group in 1873. Although there were seven Cracow groups in New York before 1880, Mińsk became the unrivaled leader in the age of mass migration, providing thirty landsmanshaften. Cracow followed with twenty-one, Warsaw with nineteen, and Białystok with sixteen.[38] There may have been as many as 3,000 landsmanshaften with 500,000 members in the 1930s in New York City alone and more than 700 in Chicago. Smaller North American cities also produced these organizations. Most associations disappeared when the original members moved or died, but a few have survived up to the present. Landsmanshaften tended to be strongly working class in origin. Employed workers provided 75 percent of the members in 1938; 15 percent were small businessmen and 10 percent were professionals.[39]

The following expenditures of one landsmanshaft society illustrate typical activities. Between 1906 and 1931, it spent almost $41,000: to pay doctors' bills (15.3%), for sick benefits (14.2%), unspecified endowments (10.7%), charitable contributions (8.8%), the society's twentieth-anniversary celebration (8.6%), contributions to members (7.5%), theater tickets (6%), for a cemetery (5.8%), salaries (5.7%), undertakers (4.8%), printing and postage (3.8%), entertainment (2.3%), and other items (6.5%). A few landsmanshaften formed as business partnerships.[40]

Landsmanshaften joined together to form regional associations, only one of which achieved a stable institutional existence. This group—the Federation of Polish Jews (originally, in Yiddish, *Der Poilisher Farband*)—came into existence "for the purpose of strengthening the feelings of kinship between the Polish Jews of America and those who were left behind in the old home; to help the newcomers materially and socially; and to build their own hospital." The Federation enrolled about 50,000 members in the 1930s. It had been preceded by the Federation of Galician and Bucovinian Jews of America, which claimed 60,000 members in 1903. It planned "to study the political, economic and social conditions of the Jews in Galicia and Bucovina, and to devise ways and means of ameliorating those conditions through the exercise of the collective influence and energy of the Galician Jews of America." A Federation of Russian-Polish Hebrews in America also sprang up in 1908, claiming 40,000 members, "to assist Jews arriving to this country from Russian Poland." In 1937, the

United Galician Jews of America formed to protect co-religionists against persecution.[41]

In addition to landsmanshaften, many Polish Jews joined Yiddish labor fraternal orders, which combined conservative social values with radical politics. The Kolomea Friends' Organization, for example, maintained a strike fund and contributed to other unions' funds even though its members were Orthodox Jews who manufactured ritual prayer shawls. The Workmen's Circle *(Arbeter Ring)* achieved a membership of about 50,000 in 1915. Typical expenditure patterns for a local branch emphasized endowments (32%), sick benefits (32%), aid to members (23%), as well as much smaller sums for funeral expenses (5%), aid to trade unions (3%), contributions to socialist parties (2%), aid to societies (2%), and lectures (1%).[42]

Polish Jews remained strongly attached to Poland, but their Poland was a very different one from that of the Catholics—it was the Jewish Poland of the *shtetl* and the Jewish quarters of large cities. Just as Catholic Poles saw Jews as incidental to their vision of Poland, Jews saw the Catholics as incidental to theirs. Landsmanshaft "memory books" described hometowns "in a poetic manner, permeated with nostalgia for the old country." They contained descriptions of streets, fairs, marketplaces, and landscapes as well as cultural-historical reports of *shtetl* life. More complex accounts issued by fraternal orders that linked numerous landsmanshaften were more literary and even more pervaded with nostalgia, such as the musings of an immigrant who, despite his wanderings around the world, still dreamed of his hometown in Lithuania and exclaimed that "no [other] land and no city could quench my longings. No beautiful landscapes were as dear to me as the muddy courtyard of the synagogue back home." One immigrant who visited his old home in the 1930s offered these enthusiastic reflections:

> Polish is an alien language to me. Nevertheless as soon as I heard the sounds of that language I felt close to it. The feeling of the fatherland seized me. True, Poland treats its Jews as if they were step-children. But Jews have lived there for centuries and are strongly attached to it. What a pleasant melancholy and painful sweetness possessed me when I saw the Polish landscape. I felt like kissing every bare-foot Polish woman, and embracing every landsman, irrespective of whether he was a Jew or a Gentile.

Some memory books celebrated single streets in the Old Country. Paradoxically, after idealizing the Old Country, authors went on to proclaim how much better life was in America.[43]

This emotional bond with Poland took concrete form in the charitable contributions to Jewish communities in Poland. Landsmanshaften supplied financial assistance to Jewish institutions in the immigrants' towns and cities of origin such as schools, community kitchens, hospitals, and homes for the aged. Secular institutions received more money as Jews became Americanized, but special funds were always available at Passover.[44]

Landsmanshaft groups responded overwhelmingly to the destitution of Jewish Poland and other parts of Eastern Europe caused by World War I, the Polish-Soviet War of 1920, and the Russian Civil War. The Proskurover landsmanshaft seems typical. Emigrants returned to this *shtetl*, located ninety miles east of the Galician-Soviet border, in 1919 with money sewn into secret pockets in their shirts. Another mission returned the following year (despite well-publicized murders of American Jews by bandits), carrying the organization's entire treasury plus private funds—over $65,000.[45]

The American Jewish Joint Distribution Committee (known as Joint) gradually took over relief administration from the landsmanshaften, which donated $7,248,988 (more than three times their donations to American charities) to Joint and other established charities for distribution in Poland. Founded in 1914 by Jewish philanthropists of mainly German origin, Joint sent a team to the Pale after the conclusion of hostilities and found such destitution that between 1919 and 1924 it raised $45 million from large and small contributors alike. Joint originally hoped to transfer the money to Polish and American governmental agencies for distribution but then found it necessary to administer the relief itself. Local Jewish agencies, supervised by Joint's American staff, fed and housed hundreds of thousands of Jews in the war-torn Pale, rebuilding community facilities such as synagogues, schools, and hospitals.

Between 1920 and 1924, Joint handled most of the funds through its short-lived Landsmanshaft Division, providing accreditation to agents who met its conditions and assisting them in dealing with the Polish government. Other groups, such as the Federation of Polish Jews in America, also contributed.[46] Recorded landsmanshaft contributions represented about $6,000 per society or about $30 per member, six times the annual dues paid by the overwhelmingly working-class membership. Some large societies such as the Bialystoker Society, contributed tens of thousands of dollars after special levies on its members.

Joint provided direct assistance to Polish Jews even after the crisis ended. Contributions varied from a low of $400,000 in 1926 (18% of total expenditures) to a high of $3,800,000 in 1938 (33%) for such projects as vocational training, nonprofit business loans, and summer camps for children. Joint's expenditures in Poland exceeded expenditures among the war-ravaged Jewry of Soviet Belarus and Ukraine in the 1920s, the endangered German Jewry of the 1930s, and by a wide margin, Palestinian Jewry.

It is impossible to estimate how much more money was distributed privately, but the sum is likely to be substantial since landsmanshaft societies often preferred to work on their own because of their intense local focus and because of their suspicion of outsiders, particularly Jews of German origin. They sought out new members through ads in American Yiddish periodicals, eventually sending agents to the region with thousands of dollars in cash for distribution. Relief sums often consisted of $10–50 contributions from individual American immigrants to individual relatives in Poland. Enough American Jews went to Europe to prompt steamship companies to offer special discounts to relief workers. Landsmanshaft contributions to the Old World declined during the interwar period as the postwar emergency eased, as ties with the Old World slowly declined, and as the Depression hit.[47]

Money from America served as "the life preserver that kept many afloat . . . during the hard times that were so frequent" between the two world wars, contributing to the Polish national economy as well. Many Jewish families in Poland received letters, checks, packages, and even visits from American relatives. Landsmanshaft organizations continued to send funds to help maintain synagogues, buy necessities for the poor, and provide capital for the Free Loan Societies that helped keep petty businesses going. America also stimulated the imagination of the young and the adventurous. American movies played even in small-town cinemas in Poland, and children studied English. Polish-American Jews brought wondrous tales of wealth to dazzle their listeners, stimulating them to modernize—or emigrate.[48]

World War II brought new concerns, ultimately destroying the Jewish community in Poland and bringing an end to Jewish-American relations with Poland. The Nazis brutalized Jews in 1939, ghettoized them in 1940, starved them in 1941, and murdered them in 1942–1944. Perhaps 200,000 could be found in Poland at the end of the war and many survivors emigrated to Palestine or the West. The remainder settled in a few large Polish cities and contacts between them and the West diminished as the Communist regime solidified its control over the country, isolating its citizens.

During World War II, American Jews of Polish and other origin worked hard to gain assistance from the U.S. government.[49] Since the independence of the Federation of Polish Jewish and similar groups had been lost in the Great Depression, Polish-American Jews spoke primarily through the coalition of Jewish community organizations (many of them Eastern European), called the American Jewish Congress and headed by Rabbi Stephen Wise, and to a lesser degree through the influential (but strongly German Jewish) American Jewish Committee. The two organizations differed in tactics: the Committee worked behind the scenes whereas the Congress organized public demonstrations and other protests. As news of the Holocaust reached North America in July 1942, the horrified Jewish community turned to Franklin Delano Roosevelt for help; Polish courier Jan Karski's mission confirmed the reports.

Unfortunately, faith in Roosevelt was sadly misplaced. The president met with Jewish leaders and spoke sympathetically but then did little.[50] The American government could not save the majority of Jews in Nazi-occupied Europe, but it could have saved several hundred thousand refugees who had made their way to neutral countries such as Spain and Portugal, as well as the inhabitants of increasingly reluctant Nazi allies such as Hungary and Romania. Unfortunately, Britain refused to open the doors to Palestine, and no country in North or South America accepted many Jews. In 1942 and 1943, the U.S. State Department offered phoney technical excuses such as lack of shipping space for refugees, at a time when the United States evacuated hundreds of thousands of Christian refugees (including Anders's Army) to points of safety and American ships returned empty from ferrying munitions to Britain.

While the United States was still neutral in 1939–1941, Joint allocated about $3,000,000 to the relief of Jews in Poland. This money funded about 90 percent of soup kitchens, orphanages, old-age homes, and other social agencies in the Polish ghettos. Polish Jewish groups in America raised money for Joint and cooperated in helping Jews from Eastern Poland who had been forcibly relocated to the Soviet Union along with other Poles. In 1942, American Jews responded to news of the death camps by organizing public demonstrations across North America. Held in large arenas such as New York's Madison Square Garden and attended by tens of thousands of demonstrators, Jewish leaders were joined by politicians, labor leaders, and Christian church leaders in protesting mass murder. Their efforts led to the creation of the War Refugee Board, which helped about 200,000 refugees survive the war; Joint paid most of the bills, even though the refugee board was a U.S. government operation. Even at this time, Allied air command refused to bomb the rail lines and gas chambers of Auschwitz in 1944 when several hundred thousand Hungarian Jews might have been saved.[51]

The destruction of Polish Jewry in the Holocaust broke the ties that linked Polish-American Jewry to Poland. Their relatives had died, their *shtetls* no longer existed, and the Jewish quarters in cities such as Warsaw had been razed to the ground. Many Polish-American Jews came from territories that had been taken over by the Soviet Union. In the postwar world, Polish-American Jews turned their attention elsewhere. The Holocaust had convinced North American Jews that Europe, especially Central and Eastern Europe, was no fit place for Jews. Organizations such as the American Jewish Congress and the American Jewish Committee worked to overcome barriers blocking immigration to North America and Palestine; they worked for Israeli independence, as well.[52] Polish-American Jews found a landsman in the displaced persons (DP) camps or in Palestine more easily than in Poland. As before, landsmanshaft groups raised as much money as possible on their own or working through umbrella organizations—but no longer for Poland. The Polish-American Jewish community was gone and Polish-American Jews became simply American Jews.

Jews and Poles in America

Whereas Jewish links with Jewish Poland remained very strong until 1945, Jewish interaction with Catholic Poles revealed deep ambivalences and hostilities. Jewish immigrants from Poland encountered a North American Polonia that based its identity on a Catholic, and often anti-Jewish, orientation. The first major Polish-American organization, the Polish Roman Catholic Union (PRCU), was founded in 1875. The Union's more secular rival, the Polish National Alliance (PNA), accepted both Jews and socialists as members, but it too considered itself founded on Catholic principles and clerical influence remained strong.[53]

The absence of Polish Jews in Polonia is striking, in view of European Poland's substantial number of Polish-speaking Jews and even Jews of Polish nationality, although future research may change that picture. At present, it seems most likely that Jews who took on Polish nationality rarely emigrated after 1880. The Polish-language Jewish press in Poland grew continually through the late nineteenth and early twentieth centuries, but the Jewish community in America published only in Yiddish, English, and Hebrew.[54]

On the day-to-day level, Polish-Jewish relations in Europe and America were filled with ambiguities. Ethnic Poles and Polish Jews brought un-flattering images of each other from Europe. A sociological study reports that unacculturated Jews, many of whom spoke Polish in the immigrant generation, saw Polish peasants (and, by extension, immigrant workers in America) as backward, dirty, and occasionally dangerous, although they tempered their disdain with compassion. These attitudes may have repre-sented absorption of the Polish gentry's attitudes toward peasants. Polish peasants in Europe and America saw Jews as clever, but dishonest, and still liked doing business with them—carefully. In the religious sphere, Poles on one hand saw Jews as Christ-killers but on the other held learned rabbis in awe.[55] A Polish-raised Jew observed more optimistically that, in Europe, "we lived together while we remained separate and apart. . . . We needed each other, often complemented each other, and so there was reason for tolerance; but there was not much incentive for eliminating the barriers that separated us." Peasants "almost always had their 'Jew,' a merchant or storekeeper whom they believed to be honest [and] so long as that trust remained, the Jew could expect most of their business." How-ever, he agreed that "close friendships" involving meetings in each others' homes or attendance at each others' social functions "were practically non-existent." Thomas and Znaniecki's classic study of Polish peasants noted that the commercial division of labor between Poles and Jews al-lowed mutual understanding and even "a curious closeness of relations" that coexisted with "antagonism, hostility, and mistrust."[56] Hostility manifested itself in occasional fights between Polish and Jewish youths from adjoining neighborhoods and in attacks on Jewish peddlers in Polish neighborhoods.[57]

European patterns of Polish-Jewish contact continued in American towns and cities where a Polish-American proletariat met a Jewish-Ameri-can petty bourgeoisie on a daily basis. In Johnstown, a Pennsylvania steel town, East European Jewish shopkeepers served a Polish, Ukrainian, and Hungarian working-class population. One Jewish shopkeeper recalled that in the years before World War II,

> many, many foreign born mothers . . . would come in with their *babushkas* and the long dresses on, while the children waited outside . . . and they would bargain over prices. . . . They would rather shop in our store than in [American ones] because in the latter they were not well accepted.

One of Johnstown's Jewish shopkeepers spoke five East European lan-guages; he helped his customers deal with their finances and even gave advice on marriage. A Jewish peddler acted as banker and accountant for his Slavic coal miner customers. Several Jews served as interpreters in court and in government offices for Poles and other Slavs applying for American citizenship. Even the American-born children of Jewish shop-keepers picked up enough "Slavic" to help customers (probably without differentiating between Polish and other languages). Because of these close ties, Polish-American readers generally ignored campaigns in the ethnic press to "support your own" by shopping in Polish-owned stores, and even Polonia's press continued to publish advertisements by Jewish shop-keepers, lawyers, and doctors.[58]

Ambivalence characterized contact between Polish Catholics and Pol-ish Jews in the marketplace in Chicago. Louis Wirth reported that Poles and Jews in Chicago

> detest each other thoroughly [but], having lived side by side in Poland and Galicia, are used to each other's business methods. They have accommo-dated themselves to one another, and this accommodation persists in America. The Pole is not accustomed to a "one-price store." When he goes shopping it is not a satisfactory experience unless he can haggle with the seller and "Jew him down" on prices.

Indeed, "Poles come from all over the city to trade [at] the familiar street-stands owned by Jews." Thomas and Znaniecki also observed that bar-gaining formed an essential part of Polish peasant economic behavior.[59]

The creation of an independent Poland led to conflicts between Polish-American Jews, supported by other East European American Jews, and Polish Americans. These conflicts reflected abstract antagonisms that had not been moderated by personal contact since the residential and voca-tional patterns of the two groups in America tended to separate them. In addition, these conflicts stemmed from the insecurities of recent immi-grants. Inter-ethnic mixing of all kinds appears to have declined in Chi-cago during the 1920s compared with the period before World War I. Jewish and Polish groups alike sponsored American-style festivals and sports celebrations to guide Americanization into communal channels. Some Jewish organizations called for a common Jewish-American identity to supplant the particularities of the landsmanshaften. Young people re-sponded positively and created the hyphenated American identity in its Polish and Jewish variants. In Detroit, too, Jewish renters tended to move out of immigrant neighborhoods when they made money, leaving their Polish home-owning neighbors behind.[60]

Disorder throughout the Eastern borderlands of the Polish state and the eruption of the Polish-Soviet War of 1919–1920 led to anti-Jewish "excesses," the number and intensity of which are still hotly debated. Polish and Jewish communities in America became directly involved when Roman Dmowski visited America in 1918 and came into conflict with American Jewish leaders, particularly Louis Marshall, president of the American Jewish Committee. Ignacy Paderewski tried unsuccessfully to mediate. After meeting with Dmowski, Marshall and other American Jewish leaders concluded that the New Poland would be hostile to Jews and went to Paris to lobby, successfully, for the Minority Treaties, which they hoped would secure Jewish rights in Poland and other countries.[61]

The Jewish press reported the Polish-Soviet War extensively, alleging thousands of Jewish deaths, tens of thousands of injuries, and large property losses. It pointed to the involvement of Polish army units and civilians in attacks on Jews. The Polish press called Jewish allegations enormously exaggerated and argued that, in any case, incidents were the products of war, not anti-Semitism. American diplomats instructed to report on the situation in 1920 disagreed with each other (as have modern historians).[62]

Reports in the North American ethnic press created a climate of strife. Jewish groups publicized the fate of their Polish co-religionists; sympathetic congressmen, some of them Christians, introduced resolutions condemning alleged atrocities. Polish groups defended Poland's good name, attacked Jews for alleged anti-Polish activities, and even organized boycotts of Jewish stores. On occasion, street fights between Polish and Jewish youths broke out.[63] These antagonisms have lurked just under the surface up to the present and have erupted more or less vociferously, most recently over the film *Shoah* and the convent at Auschwitz.

Polish and Jewish groups fought out these conflicts primarily in the ethnic press. The Jewish-American press generally ignored Poland and Polonia, except in times of communal conflict when it usually criticized the Poles; statements favorable to Jews were noted appreciatively. In contrast, the Polish-American press paid considerable attention to the Jews.[64]

The attitude toward Jews expressed in Polonia's press defies easy classification. For example, Winnipeg, Canada, supported two long-lived Polish-language newspapers, *Gazeta Katolicka* and *Czas*. The former identified Catholicism with Polish identity, opposing Jews, breakaway Catholic groups, and secular interests. While supporting civil rights for individual Jews in the New Poland, *Gazeta* betrayed its hostility to Jews by claiming that Polish Jews were not real Poles and by attacking its opponents within the Winnipeg Polish community (including a former editor) for supposed Jewish origins. Throughout the interwar period, *Gazeta* continued to criticize Polish Jews while rejecting fascism and criticizing Hitler's persecution of Jews in Germany. The "progressive" newspaper, *Czas,* generally supported Józef Piłsudski and his moderate sympathy for Polish Jews. It condemned the rise of extreme Polish nationalism, particularly violent attacks on Jews by Polish students in the 1930s. Both papers united in opposing in the strongest possible terms attacks on Poland in the Jewish press, however.[65]

Despite these conflicts, relations between American Jewish groups and the Polish Republic were generally correct or even favorable during the interwar period. The influential American Jewish Committee, at that time composed mostly of Jews of German origin, maintained a close liaison with Polish diplomats in Washington and New York, and its allied organization, the American Jewish Joint Distribution Committee, arranged without difficulty for the distribution of financial assistance in Poland. Both groups accepted claims by Polish diplomats that the impoverishment of Jews in Poland at this time stemmed from economic modernization rather than from anti-Semitism, while they avoided too close an identification with the diplomatic positions of the new Polish state. Jewish bankers from these circles declined the urging of Polish diplomats to underwrite major investments in Poland because they deemed such investments unlikely to succeed.

In contrast, the Federation of Polish Jews reacted both more positively and more negatively to the Polish state. Under its interwar president Benjamin Winter and secretary Zelig Tygel, both of whom were born in Poland, the Federation responded positively to overtures from Mieczysław Marchlewski, the Polish consul in New York City. Marchlewski organized a joint Polish-Jewish Committee of Good Will in New York City in 1930 and gained its support for Polish diplomatic positions, particularly regarding the border with Germany. He hoped to extend the alliance into joint electoral campaigning in America and, ultimately, to gain Jewish investment in Poland. The Polish consul understood that a good relationship with Polish-American Jews could not survive without a commitment by Warsaw to improve the economic situation of Jews in Poland, particularly by hiring Jews for public service jobs in cities where Jews comprised a major proportion of the population. Warsaw ignored his suggestions.

Good relations between the Federation of Polish Jews, on the one hand, and Polish Americans and Polish diplomats, on the other, broke down after a few years when Polish diplomats failed to condemn anti-Jewish riots by nationalist students in Poland in strong enough terms to satisfy the Federation. Fearing a hostile reception and having nothing to offer American Jewish groups, Polish diplomats avoided Polish Jews in America, squandering an opportunity to cultivate potentially useful allies. In any case, the Great Depression deprived the Federation of Polish Jews of the financial ability to pursue any active policy. The American Jewish Congress, a coalition of East European Jewish groups, spoke out stridently about Jewish difficulties in Poland in the 1930s.[66]

Such conflicts between the Poles and Jews in America have generally been overly stressed in the historical literature. Polish-Jewish relations may have been significant in Poland, but in America, they provided an irritating side issue of little consequence to the life of either community. Despite sharp conflicts over Old World affairs, American Poles and American Jews (including Polish Jews) have generally gotten along in the New World. Indeed, their interests, along with Italians and other members of the great pre–World War I migration, have coincided in breaking down Anglo-Saxon domination of American life.

While Polish and Jewish communal organizations remained suspicious of one another, in the 1920s American Poles and Jews of Polish origin cooperated extensively on labor issues and politics since both groups belonged to the immigrant generation that sought recognition in America. Polish and other East European Jews separated themselves from the conservative, business-oriented, and Republican German Jewish establishment. Based in substantially Jewish clothing unions (the International Ladies Garment Workers and the Amalgamated Clothing Workers), David Dubinsky and Sidney Hillman, both immigrants from the Pale, rose to prominence in the 1920s and helped found the Congress of Industrial Organizations (CIO). This new labor federation represented semi-skilled Polish, Jewish, Italian, and other immigrant workers who had been ignored by the older American Federation of Labor (AFL). Even though the CIO itself was riddled with ethnic and religious tensions, Poles and Jews cooperated in changing the face of American unionism. Polish and other East European Jews, along with Poles and other East European immigrants, similarly participated in Roosevelt's New Deal coalition. Cooperation was particularly visible in Chicago and other cities hosting both Polish and Jewish communities. Jews and Catholics joined forces to support Al Smith's campaign for the presidency in 1928. In 1932, Franklin Delano Roosevelt's supporters formed a Foreign Language Citizens Committee of the Democratic National Committee to work for ethnic support. That support lasted throughout the 1930s and beyond.[67] Mutual political and labor efforts represented a kind of coalition-building that was common on the American scene, not a merging of the Polish and

Polish Jewish communities, as could be expected since the two groups never merged in Europe.

Conclusions

The large Jewish population of Poland played a major role in the mass migration to North America of the late nineteenth and early twentieth centuries. Like other immigrants, Jews faced harsh challenges and lived difficult lives in America, especially in the first decades of settlement. The proletarianized population of New York lived in greatest poverty until the 1920s, and the peddlers and petty traders characteristic of smaller centers did only a little better. Polish-American Jews helped themselves through a wide variety of associations and benefited from extra help from their richer German Jewish cousins. With their interest in education, Jews took advantage of general prosperity in the 1920s to begin to move toward middle-class prosperity.

Polish-American Jews Americanized and joined other Jews in a common Jewish-American identity, but they still maintained close ties with their families and countrymen in Poland. Landsmanshaften united a large percentage of American Jews in small organizations representing single towns or even streets in Poland, separating them from other American Jews. Given the modest means of their immigrant members, these organizations raised a surprisingly large amount of money for Jewish institutions in their hometowns and promoted constant personal transatlantic contact. The Federation of Polish Jews also encouraged close ties with the Polish state during the interwar period, although its weak financial position, particularly in the 1930s, forced it to merge with the American Jewish Congress. All Polish-American Jewish groups relied heavily on the expertise of the German Jewish dominated American Jewish Committee to distribute charitable contributions in Poland. Ties between Polish-American Jews and Polish Jews came to an abrupt halt with the Holocaust and the emigration of survivors. After 1945, Polish-American Jews became simply American Jews, little interested in distinguishing Poland from other Old Country regions.

Polish-American Jews interacted with Polish Americans primarily in the marketplace. Jewish peddlers and shopkeepers often set up their businesses in immigrant areas where Jewish, Polish, Italian, and other newcomers lived. Since Polish-American Jews spoke Polish and shared common cultural assumptions, Catholic Poles often preferred to shop in their stores. When the two communities Americanized during the interwar period, they often shared common trade union activities and enthusiastically joined in Franklin Delano Roosevelt's New Deal coalition. Unfortunately, old antagonisms aggravated by disagreements about the conditions of Jews in Poland pulled them apart at times.

These conclusions about Polish-American Jewish history are preliminary, because the field has never been studied systematically. Fundamental research remains to be done in a number of areas:

1. Distinguishing American Jews of Polish origin from American Jews of other origin (especially Russian and Austrian) is a crucial problem. Work needs to be done with immigration records, government records on all levels, communal records, and memoir material. Differences between men's and women's experiences should not be overlooked.

2. Jewish records pertaining to Poland should be located and studied. The records of the Federation of Polish Jews and the American Jewish Congress are most important. Another major source is the YIVO Institute in New York City; its vast resources relating primarily to Jewish life in Poland include records on transatlantic contact ranging from letters to home movies.

3. American Jewish financial assistance to Polish Jews has been well studied from the American side, but the receiving side is little documented. Polish archives can shed light on everything from governmental discussions to the tax status of recipients.

4. Polish-American organizations should be investigated to identify those Polish Jews who integrated themselves within the Polish community by preference and to understand their activities. Considering the number of fluent Polish-speaking Jews, it would be surprising if some immigrants did not choose this path in America.

5. The Polish and Jewish ethnic press should be examined more systematically. It is important to look at periods of communal peace as well as periods of ethnic conflict.

6. The New Deal era offers a promising subject of political cooperation between Poles and Jews. Municipal politics in cities with large Polish and Jewish communities such as Chicago and Detroit should be investigated. Polish-American attitudes toward and involvement in the election of Jewish governors Herbert Lehman (New York) and Henry Horner (Illinois) might prove particularly interesting.

7. Cooperation between Jewish and Polish organizations in America that were concerned with civilians in Nazi-occupied Poland

should be investigated. Both have been studied in isolation. The Polish government-in-exile and its representatives have not been studied in this regard.

Research on these and other questions will enrich and extend the portrait of Jewish emigration from Poland presented here.

6

Polonia and Politics

Stanislaus A. Blejwas

IN THE 1872 PRESIDENTIAL ELECTION, A POLE FROM VIRGINIA complained in the New York journal *Swoboda* (Freedom): "Every nationality secures for itself vested rights. Only Poles sweetly daydream—quietly as if they were not [present here] in America. Likewise, no one cares about us in America, no one knows about us, for who is aware of the dumb [*niemowa*]?" Responding to this mournful lament, a writer from Chicago replied that the nearly twenty thousand Chicago Poles, who previously had not participated in politics, had undertaken to enter the presidential election "politically as Poles from Chicago." Piotr Kiołbassa, who would go on to make a distinguished career in Chicago politics, explained further the purpose of a Polish committee to elect Grant. Freeing themselves from German patronage, Chicago's Poles were now organizing under their own banner. While the already large number of Chicago Poles made the formation of different political parties inevitable (including the creation of a committee to elect Grant's opponent, Greeley), it was still possible

> with the help of organized societies to easily come to an agreement as to the objectives mutually affecting all our fellow countrymen, whether from Silesia, Lithuania, Halicz, Mazowia, Podlesie and Great and Little Poland. . . . When it is a Polish matter, why then we Poles in Chicago are all Poles.[1]

This early exchange raised themes about Poles and politics that have echoed throughout the history of American Polonia: the bewailing of an inadequate Polish presence in American politics; the need to organize the immigrants in order to make the group's voice heard; the political potential of the large and ever-growing Polish immigration; insufficient representation in both elective and appointive offices; and the appeal for ethnic unity around a putative Polish political agenda. As Wacław Kruszka, the nestor of Polonia historians, commented:

> From the very beginning the emigration even entered American politics as Poles, together and as a united force. Their primary idea, their leading and dominant principle in politics was—in the first instance to care about Polish interest and not about the interest of American political parties.[2]

Defining just what was the "Polish interest" in American politics and how and who was to articulate it is at the heart of the history of American Polonia politics. Politics have always attracted the interest of community activists and commentaries by scholars and politicians. However, despite the importance of politics for every immigrant community, a history of American Polonia politics and political culture has not yet been attempted. The works that do exist suggest the potential structure for such a synthesis and directions for further study.

In research on American Polonia politics, the definition of "Polish interest" in American politics is the core issue. A related and crucial subtext is the question of who was a Pole, and later a Polish American, or an American of Polish origin. Such questions, as Edward Kantowicz illustrates in his study of Chicago Polish-American politics, gave rise to three types of Polish-American politics—the politics of Poland (the homeland's liberation), Polonia politics (the politics of the parishes and fraternals), and American politics. Each co-existed, often overlapping, and participation in one or another corresponded to the mental world in which the immigrant lived. Furthermore, in specific periods, one form of political activity tended to predominate, as in the period prior to and during World War I, when the politics of Poland and Polonia prevailed.[3]

Polish Nationalism and Nationalist Organizations

The burgeoning peasant immigration after the January Insurrection and the American Civil War set the stage for politics in American Polonia. Political émigrés committed to the struggle for Polish independence became alarmed. Peasants were leaving partitioned Poland while the nation confronted fierce Germanization and Russification. Unlike the political émigrés, the peasants' national consciousness was considered weak or non-

existent. Although peasants ostensibly spoke Polish, their language was a
dialect. Peasants possessed, at most, a common folk consciousness. They
identified with local customs, religion, villages, neighborhoods, and not
(as political activists and intellectuals believed) with a common national
culture. Most never consciously participated in national life, and the concept of Poland lacked "that practical definiteness and vitality" it held
for political émigrés.[4] Furthermore, many arrived fresh with memories of
serfdom and hatred for the "lords" *(panowie)*, sentiments cultivated for
political purposes by Poland's partitioners. The fear was that in America
this valuable human resource would lose whatever ethnic identity it possessed and be lost to the national cause. Could this immigration's ethnic
ties be transformed into a public, political expression of bonding to a
large community by language, culture, religion, and territory? Could the
immigration be inculcated with a patriotic national consciousness committed to Poland's independence? Could Polish nationalism, in the absence of an independent state, be transplanted across an ocean?[5]

Conditions in America were conducive to the spread of European nationalism among East European immigrants. The political repression
faced in the homeland was absent, while those forces advocating class
identification, such as labor union and socialists, lacked the power to
oppose the spread of European nationalism among East European immigrants, although sometimes embracing European patriotism. More important, various elements in the immigrant communities came to identify
with the homeland cause: the clergy, nationalist organizations, intellectuals, and the press.[6]

In the immigrant enclaves, the parish with its school, Polish pastor,
and teaching sisters was the primary institution where the immigrants
realized their Polishness. Already in the late 1870s the novelist Henryk
Sienkiewicz recognized that "the Church and the Polish priests" maintain
"some degree of moral unity among the Poles." The parish brought "together the Polish masses," creating "from them a social entity [and] does
not allow them to become scattered and to disappear unnoticed among
foreign elements."[7] Clerical leadership of the immigrants, however, did
not go unchallenged.

Two approaches emerged for organizing the immigrant community,
the "religionist" and the "nationalist," both traceable to the organization
of Chicago's first Polish parish, St. Stanislaus Kostka. When Kiołbassa
reorganized the St. Stanislaus Kostka Society in 1866, nationalist political
émigrés with contacts with Polish exiles in New York, Paris, and Geneva
organized the Gmina Polska (the Polish Commune). The two groups dif-

fered over the definition of a Pole and over the objectives of Polonia. The nationalists insisted that the restoration of the homeland was the community's primary goal. Recognizing the predominance of Roman Catholicism among Poles, the nationalists believed that nationality and faith were divisible, and they welcomed Protestants, Greek Catholics, Jews, as well as Roman Catholics to their organization. The more numerous religionists, led by dominating clerics such as Vincent Barzyński, insisted that a Pole could only be a Roman Catholic, and that the primary function of the community in America, organized around the Polish parish, was to maintain that identity. Although agreeing with the nationalists that an independent homeland was a desirable goal, to them that goal was secondary. The primary objective was to keep the Pole a Roman Catholic.[8]

The religionist-nationalist controversy in Chicago was projected onto a national stage in the 1870s, providing ideological rationales for the two leading nationwide Polish-American fraternals, the Polish Roman Catholic Union (1873) and the Polish National Alliance (1880), each vying to unify Polonia under its own leadership. Organized by influential priests, the PRCU focused upon Polonia's immediate religious and educational needs, creating institutions to elevate the immigrants' intellectual and material existence. Based upon a national network of parish societies, the PRCU was a Catholic organization and left the Polish question aside. For the nationalist elite, however, this was unacceptable.[9]

The impetus to mobilize the nationalists was provided in 1879 by a widely circulated letter from Agaton Giller, the Polish émigré leader in Switzerland. Giller argued for utilizing the immigration in America for "the [Polish] national cause" and preserving it for "the fatherland." Giller believed that the emigrating peasant or worker "without a consciousness of national duties" would acquire one "in a foreign country" as he recognized "the striking difference between his speech, his customs, his conceptions from those surrounding him." Therefore, "a national intellectual class" must be prepared to educate immigrants for "the national cause," to "unite the isolated individuals into . . . numerous associations and communities and to bind these together so that the resulting organization while serving the purposes of the Polish cause" will advance the "private interests of every one of its members." Anticipating the immigrant's eventual advancement in America, Giller believed that a unified and prosperous immigration "will render great services to Poland" when

the Poles begin to exercise an influence upon the public life of the United States, when they spread among Americans adequate conceptions about the Polish cause and . . . become intermediaries between Poland and the powerful republic so as to foster sympathy with our efforts for liberation and develop it into an enthusiasm that will express itself in action.[10]

Giller challenged the émigrés to unify the immigrants as a political force for Polish independence by nationalizing the Polish immigrant in America. The founders of the PNA meeting in Philadelphia in 1880 accepted the challenge. Although their ultimate objective was Polish independence, their initial efforts focused on the national enlightenment of the immigrants and the formulation of a political program. Wanting to establish a material and moral foundation for the "development of the Polish element in the United States," the founders of the PNA claimed "protection [*opieka*] over the Polish immigration." The new organization intended to effect, through its member societies and its own Polish-language organ, "the political establishment of the Polish immigration as citizens of the United States." It would provide mutual assistance for its members, organize "commemorations of notable anniversaries in honor of Poland," and fulfill "the obligations demanded by national honor."[11]

Achieving these objectives proved difficult. Though the PNA became the largest Polish-American fraternal, during its first fifteen years it remained small and the center of controversy. Catholic clergy objected to its secular definition of Polishness, attacking the PNA's failure to exclude church independents, atheists, Jews, anarchists, socialists, or Masons. Only near the end of the century did Polish fraternalism begin to measure up to the size of the immigration, and only then after insurance became integral elements in the fraternal programs.[12]

The fierce intra-fraternal polemics led to subsequent secessions and the fragmentation of Polish-American fraternalism, and to what Mieczysław Haiman termed the "partitioning of American Polonia." While the PNA-PRCU conflict divided the immigrant community, it also inspired the formation of new organizations. Kruszka averred that the "struggle which inspired American Polonia, gave it a sense of communion of patriotic love, a will to learn, a need for newspapers, libraries, celebrations, etc." It was, according to Haiman, "the main driving force of [Polonia's] social life."[13] Out of this turmoil came other patriotic organizations. The Polish Union of America (1889) formulated an ideological program that was a compromise between the PNA and the PRCU. The Polish Women's Alliance (1899) committed itself to "the maintenance of the national spirit" and to educating youth as "good Polish sons and daughters," while the Polish Falcons (1887) came to see themselves as "an immigrant academy of physical and military training, an emigrant school of citizenship and combat, an emigrant's preparation to active struggle for Poland's independence."[14] Other organizations espousing similar patriotic sentiments were the Polish Singers Alliance (1889), the Union of Polish Youth (1894), the Polish Alma Mater (1897), and local military marching societies and the Polish Troop Alliance. There was also the pro-independent Alliance of Polish Socialists, whose organization in 1900 signaled the emergence of class as a factor in national Polonia politics, and which Thomas and Znaniecki argued was "the only political organization for which Polish American society is not an entity, a self-sufficient object of activity."[15]

The self-partitioning of American Polonia was also evident in the abortive attempt to unify American Polonia in 1894–1895 in a PRCU-supported Liga Polska (Polish league); and in the ultimately abortive efforts of the PNA to arrogate to itself the role of Polonia's government and to subordinate nationalistic groups such as the Falcons, the Singers Alliance, and the Union to its jurisdiction as PNA departments. Even the 1910 dedication of the Kosciuszko and Pulaski monuments in Washington and the simultaneous convocation of a Polish National Congress under PNA auspices did not lead to a unification of American Polonia.[16] Fragmentation was also painfully apparent among the religionists, who fretted over the preservation of the putative national character of immigrant parishes and the question of Polish representation in the American Catholic hierarchy, and who ultimately were confronted with the formation of the schismatic Polish National Catholic Church (PNCC), which attempted to claim for itself the mantel of Polish nationalism.[17]

Fragmentation implied the dilution of the political potential. Nevertheless, the conflict aroused national consciousness and educated the immigrant for "new national tasks," thereby accelerating his nationalization. Equally significant was the struggle of Polish Catholics for *równouprawnienie* (equality) within the American Catholic Church and the rising challenge of the schismatic PNCC. When Paul Rhode became the first American bishop of Polish origin in 1908, he united the Catholicism of the Polish immigrant with the nationalist commitment to Polish independence, becoming the group's "major patriot priest." He united God and Country, doing much to resolve the aggravating tensions over Polishness and to elevate the ethnic consciousness of Polish immigrants. The elemental issue was the place of the immigrant and his national parish within American Catholicism. The Catholic Church, with Rhode's elevation to the episcopacy, sanctioned and stimulated Polish ethnic consciousness.[18]

While immigrant national consciousness evolved in this atmosphere of

:onflict, other factors contributed to the immigrants' nationalization. The mmigrant in America experienced "an entire school of Polish patrio-ism." The patriotic activities of organizations and institutions "broke down the regional identifications of "Galician," "Prussian," and "Rus-;ian" immigrants, fostering a common identification as a Pole.[19] The pa-:riot priest, the national parish, and parish schools (with curriculums em-phasizing Polish language, literature, history, and geography, and staffed by ethnically committed nuns) consolidated the consciousness of the im-migrants' Polish origins and faith in Poland's insurrection. In opting for the parish school, immigrant parents resisted efforts to "denationalize" their children and assured them an education in traditional and patriotic values.[20]

There were also the Polish-language press, patriotic commemorations, Polish-American theater, and fraternal, cultural, and educational activi-ties, all experienced most directly on the local level and endorsing a resur-rected Poland.[21] The institutions and organizations of the immigrant community constituted a formidable counterbalance to the assimilatory forces of urban industrial America. The peasant immigrant, politically passive in his homeland, in America was transformed into a reservoir of national strength. With awe and delight the nationalist *Prezgląd Emigra-cyjny*, after the visit of Professor Emil Dunikowski to the United States in 1891, proclaimed American Poles "the fourth sector" of Poland.[22]

The changing political situation in Poland likewise contributed to the nationalization of the Polish immigrant. The revolution of 1905 brought a new generation of political émigrés to the United States. There followed intense polemical competition within Polonia between adherents of Pol-ish political parties such as the nationalistic National Democratic Party and the Polish Socialist Party, each seeking influence in the PNA and the Falcons.[23] Interest in Polish independence was increased as the immigrant "turned from local disputes and questions to national programs and is-sues." It was, in the overall estimation of Henryk Wereszycki, thanks to the activities of political émigrés that "the national consciousness of the Polish people [*lud polski*] in emigration was at once significantly higher than in Poland."[24]

American factors also helped nationalize the immigrants. The host so-ciety's tendency to discriminate against and to identify the immigrants as Poles rather than Austrians, Prussians, or Russians, made regional loyalties less relevant, helping to consolidate a Polish national identity. The com-munity's institutional infrastructure reflected its national identity. On the eve of World War I, there were over seven hundred Polish Roman Catholic parishes and thirty-four National Catholic parishes. Furthermore, of the estimated 2 million or more first- and second-generation Polish immigrants, over 316,438 belonged to fourteen Polish-American fraternals.[25]

By 1914, immigrant leaders were accustomed to voicing collective demands for the restoration of Polish independence, often directing appeals and protests to federal and local officials. The resolution adopted at the Polish National Congress in 1910 asserted: "We the Poles, have a right to an independent national existence and consider it our sacred duty to strive towards political independence for Poland, our Fatherland." Tomasz Siemiradzki propagated a vision of American Polonia as the Fourth Partition of the Polish nation. In the absence of independence, the immigration's political organization was a surrogate state for the nation deprived of its statehood with an obligation to carry on the Polish political struggle.[26]

The rhetoric was grandiloquent; Thomas and Znaniecki conclude that, on the eve of World War I, the immigrant's Polish patriotism was superficial. Nevertheless, community activity during World War I confirmed the nationalization of a not inconsiderable number of immigrants. Polonia was initially organized and momentarily unified in the Committee of National Defense (Komitet Obrony Narodowy [KON]) just after the unification congress of the Polish Falcons in December 1912. KON was the American version of the "independent faction" centered around Józef Piłsudski in Austrian Poland. It was shortly eclipsed by the Polish Central Relief Committee and its political arm, the Wydział Narodowy (National Department), under the patronage of a PNA purged of its left wing and increasingly dominated ideologically and organizationally by the Polish National Democratic Party (endecja), a nationalistic Polish political party. The PRCU, which now tolerated secular nationalism, was aligned as well on Polonia's political right.[27]

American Polonia raised funds, rallying around and submitting to piano virtuoso Ignacy Jan Paderewski, who transmogrified the cause of Polish relief into the cause of Polish independence. Thanks in no small degree to Paderewski, President Woodrow Wilson was won over to the cause of Polish independence, and when America entered the war in 1917, the maestro led American Polonia on a national recruiting effort that eventually saw some twenty thousand volunteers sent to Gen. Józef Haller's army in France. According to M. B. Biskupski, "This was American Polonia's most dramatic success during the war," crowned, as it were, by Wilson's thirteenth of his famous Fourteen Points and the reemergence of independent Poland on November 11, 1918.[28]

During World War I, Polish immigrants and their children became what Giller had hoped for in 1879: "intermediaries between Poland and the powerful republic," fostering sympathy "with our efforts for liberation" with an "enthusiasm" that expressed itself "in action." The nationalized immigrants generally accepted the collective description of themselves as the Fourth Partition. Polonia declared itself a national minority, a "part of the Polish nation" committed to the homeland's liberation. Although the leadership articulated this vision, "this ethnic duty lay at the heart of local political consciousness."[29] The successful nationalization of the Polish immigrant and the results of the war even led to the erroneous assertion that Paderewski won Wilson to the Polish cause by promising him Polonia support in the 1916 election.[30] Thus within five decades Polonia arrived at the acme of political influence, capable of determining American foreign policy by flexing its political muscle.

But had Polonia really come that far politically? It was Paderewski, not Polonia, who determined what Polish interests were, and it was Wilson who determined what America's were. Paderewski's effectiveness as a spokesman for the Polish cause was a result of the authority he commanded in Polonia, but it was Paderewski "who made Polonia something significant in America." Paderewski found an American Polonia that in the course of a half-century had been to a considerable degree nationalized, momentarily unified in its acceptance of his leadership, and supportive of Polish independence; and he utilized it. It was during World War I that Polonia's national consciousness reached its zenith.[31] Polonia's nationalization, however, was achieved by its organizations, institutions, and leaders (especially political émigrés and Polish-born and -educated priests); and it was accomplished in America. Czechs, Slovaks, Lithuanians, Ukrainians, and others underwent similar national awakenings.[32] The question, therefore, is Did the immigrant acquire a Polish national identity or the ethnic consciousness of an American ethnic group?

Greene argues that "European" nationalism arose among Polish, Czech, and Slovak Americans as "an American experience" and that their allegiance to the Old Country and desire for its independence had little to do with Europe. It was an outgrowth of seeking a higher status and a more respected place in American society and a desire for the respect enjoyed by other American ethnic groups claiming their own independent homelands. More Polish Americans served in the U.S. armed forces during World War I than in Haller's Army, while the Polish-American purchase of liberty bonds exceeded what they donated to Polish relief. Furthermore, only an estimated 96,000 immigrants, just 3 percent of all Polish Americans, opted to return to independent Poland after the war.[33]

While others demur about aspects of this thesis, Polonia's Polish national consciousness declined after the war. The accompanying reorientation from Polish to domestic concerns was succinctly stated in 1926 by Mr. Lymanski from Hartford, Connecticut, when he addressed the Middletown Polish Republicans. As the minutes relate:

> [he] recalled the former times in which Polish Americans made sacrifices for our Poland just for the freedom of Poland, for the Polish Nation which sought freedom to be equal with other nations. Poles in America helped with everything, both materially and financially just so the dreams of Poles would be fulfilled. And now the Poles in the Fatherland have to decide about the good of Poland there in Europe. And we here in the United States have to care about the good of this country in which we live by becoming citizens of this country in order to care for our own good—which the law entitles us to—in order for us to sit down on an equal basis with other nationalities in this country—and which only citizenship decides—uniting Poles in the so-called citizens clubs.[34]

It was time for nationalism and homeland politics to give way to domestic priorities and local politics as immigrants could now come to terms with their place in America, free of the burden of Poland. The politics of Poland were, for the moment, over.

American Politics

The ground for immigrant participation in American politics was prepared well before World War I and corresponded to the changing identity of immigrants and their children. Kruszka and others, opposed to the immigrants' Anglicization, realized that they were evolving into "a distinct type of Pole in America," into "Americans of Polish descent." Sienkiewicz had observed earlier that "it would be dangerous to speak disparagingly of the States to any Pole residing here. He does not cease to love his former fatherland, but after Poland he loves most the United States."[35]

Whereas homeland politics generated broad community support, local politics—the politics of Polonia and American politics—responded to the immigrants' most immediate needs. Polonia's early political leaders not only wanted the immigrants to use their political and civil rights to advance the cause of Polish independence; they also wanted to root their countrymen in their new land and to assure their political representation and participation in civic affairs. The ongoing, day-to-day attachment of newcomers to American politics occurred on a quieter, more localized level, in neighborhoods, towns, and cities.[36]

Polonia politics were the politics of the parishes and the fraternals and were particularly intense. They contributed to the immigrant's nationalization but were also a prelude to American politics. Whereas the immigrant in the host society was just another inexpensive laborer, in the parish—as an officer in one of the numerous parish satellite societies, or as an officer in the local fraternal lodge—the immigrant found a sense of identity, self-worth, and social prestige denied him by the host society. Numerous internal parish and organizational conflicts shook Polish-American communities, confirming the seriousness of Polonia politics. These disputes—often pitting immigrants equipped with newly acquired organizational skills and self-confidence against autocratic-minded pastors—were likewise a gauge of the immigrants' increasing acculturation and Americanization. Additionally, participation in Polonia's religious and secular organizations exposed the peasant immigrant to the political process, from which he had been excluded in the Old Country. Such participation provided "useful lessons in the democratic process," ultimately schooling the immigrants for entry into American politics.[37]

Participation in American politics offered economic, occupational, and psychological advantages. For the sake of their votes, individuals and communities could benefit from access to boss-directed patronage. Furthermore, in a land where seemingly anyone could become a boss, political careers offered to ambitious and talented immigrants the control of patronage, increased influence in their own communities, personal gain, and eventually, social mobility. Immigrant politicians *(politykieri)* were "the new native aristocracy." Some were upstarts who made their fortunes at the expense of the passive mass of workers, while others were extraordinarily capable individuals who represented their communities well to American society. Participation in American politics, however, helped the entire community feel more secure in their new land. If they could vote as a bloc and influence elections, community leaders knew that the political establishment would heed them. There was also the easy political flattery of hearing politicians address them with a few words in their own language. Finally, "the inhabitants of Polonia felt an upsurge of pride in their growing importance in the new land" when their children entered American politics and began to hold public office. Political involvement meant recognition, a sense of pride that comes from wielding influence and being an insider.[38]

Despite the importance of politics for immigrants and the gatekeeper role of ethnic politicians as dispensers of favors to their constituents, we still lack a political history of Polonia and studies of Polonia politicians.[39] As late as 1970, Konstanty Symonolewicz-Symmons lamented the absence of significant studies on Polonia's participation in American political life.[40] Whereas community studies appeared in *Polish American Studies*, politics and political organizations received only marginal mention, if at all, with attention devoted to parishes, fraternals, and the sisterhoods.[41] Therefore, the handful of recent studies are important for our understanding of both how the immigrant used politics and of their successes and unfulfilled expectations.

Becoming an insider was slow. The early immigrants were concerned above all about establishing secure economic foundations. They did not know the language, lacked education, were politically inexperienced, were unfamiliar with American politics, and encountered prejudice, while many viewed their sojourn in the United States as temporary. Polish immigrants arrived later than the Irish, Germans, and Scandinavians, and both homeland and Polonia politics absorbed their early energies. Initially, Polish immigrants lacked an American political leadership, which emerged only with succeeding generations. Others attributed the slow progress in politics to the immigrants' social background and educational level, or to the preoccupation with homeland politics until 1918.[42]

The numbers taking out citizenship and registering as voters did not keep pace with the growing immigrant settlements. In 1920 only 28.8 percent (302,635) of first-generation Polish immigrant men and women over twenty-one years of age were naturalized, a figure that compared unfavorably with Germans (73.5%), Norwegians (68.2%), Swedes (69.9%), Czechoslovaks (44.2%), and Russians (42%), but favorably with Hungarians (30%), Italians (29%), South Slavs (24.8%), and Lithuanians (26%). The numbers subsequently rose. There were citizenship schools in cities like Chicago, and "getting papers" was a priority for local, ward-level political clubs.[43] Clubs were Democratic, Republican, or nonpartisan Polish-American political or citizens' clubs that decided which party to back during the election. The Polish-American political agenda was now naturalization, patronage in the form of appointments to municipal or county offices and commissions, and the elevation of the group's recognition and prestige through the election of candidates endorsed by Polish political clubs for local, state, and federal offices.[44]

Naturalization offered a key to political power as organizers grasped the equation between voters and clout. Political clubs invested in persuading immigrants to "take out papers," often requiring citizenship as a qualification for membership. The numbers of Polish voters did increase after World War I. Ironically, the PNA's efforts to politically mobilize the nationalized immigrants for Polish interests also accelerated their Americanization as political clubs integrated the immigrant into the host society. As Peter Kogut recalled the early days of the New York Mills, New York, Polish Democratic Club: "They knew they had to get into politics to be recognized and be part of the community—to be represented."[45]

Women recognized the importance of politics, but their participation was not motivated by militant political feminism. Having been prepared for American politics by their involvement in Polonia politics through fraternals like the Polish Women's Alliance, which supported the franchise for women, Polish-American women, because of community customs, values, and economics, found supportive roles in ladies' auxiliaries of the men's political clubs. In the 1930s the labor militancy of Polish women strengthened the Democratic Party as they followed their men into the unions such as the AFL and CIO.[46] Some middle-class women won election to municipal and state office, during and after World War II, including New York Lt. Governor Mary Ann Krupsak and Maryland's Senator Barbara Mikulski.[47] Nevertheless, the role of Polish immigrant women and of their daughters in politics remains to be written.

Political clubs and activity appear as early as the 1870s and 1880s in the Midwest in South Bend, Chicago, and Milwaukee, and in the 1880s in Wisconsin, Minnesota, Michigan, Buffalo, and later, nationally throughout other Polish communities, following chronologically the patterns of concentrated settlement, both large and small.[48] Polish immigrants were drawn to the Democratic Party. As Kantowicz notes in his study of Chicago, Poles arrived when the Republicans were the entrenched political establishment, anti-Catholic, Protestant, business oriented, and unresponsive to the needs of new groups. The Democratic Party drew immigrants, with its close association with the Catholic Church, its anti-prohibition platform and opposition to immigration restriction, and its sympathetic ear for the economic hardships of new arrivals. In municipal, state, and federal elections, Polish immigrants most often gave their votes to Democrats, although Republican and Socialist efforts to make inroads into Polish communities are forgotten and in need of further research.[49]

It is generally agreed that Al Smith's candidacy in 1928, the depression, and Roosevelt's social and economic New Deal all cemented Polish loyalty to the Democratic Party, and the Poles became part of the institutionalization of ethnicity within the party. The predominantly working-class social structure of the first and second generation reinforced the stereotype of the Polish-American Democrat. The Democratic Party platform was now the Polish-American political agenda, or from another view, the Polish-American "ethnic way of life was also a class way of life." In the 1920s it was estimated that 60 percent of Polish voters supported the Democrats, 35 percent voted Republican, with the remainder split among socialist and communist groups. Between 1932 and 1948, however, Polish-American support for Democratic presidential candidates ranged from 75 to 90 percent.[50]

The shift after World War I from homeland to American domestic politics reflected trends within Polonia. The prominence of the small, educated and Americanizing, second-generation professional middle class grew. Previously intent upon establishing its leadership within the immigrant community by invoking the ideology of Polish nationalism during the prewar period, it now gave priority to social and economic advancement in American society.[51] As a matter of course, a drive for political recognition and patronage accompanied these ambitions, and the symbols of these campaigns were postal stamps and dozens of monuments, streets, and bridges honoring Pulaski and Kosciuszko. In Chicago, the Chicago Society, the Polish Lawyers' Association, the Polish American Businessmen's Association, the Polish Firemen's Organization, and in 1933, the Polish Associated Federal Employees appeared. Similar associations, often second-generation organizations that pledged their loyalty to the United States in their bylaws, were to be found in other Polish communities.[52] Emblematic of the drive for recognition was Chicago's Polish American Democratic Organization, organized in 1932 "to arouse greater political interest among citizens of Polish extraction," to direct this interest to the Democratic Party, and to "obtain proper political representation and recognition" from the party. Concerned with patronage at the local and national level, PADO did not want to be left out of an anticipated Roosevelt victory. With contacts in other states, PADO was able to claim a Polish-American vote in excess of 90 percent for FDR, and in 1936 obtained official recognition from the Democratic National Committee as the official campaign body among Polish Americans. Similar voting percentages in Detroit brought Polish Americans congressional nominations. Polish Americans were moving into serious political brokerage and fulfilling the dreams of first-generation community leaders.[53]

The drive for recognition was not limited to Chicago. In Connecticut a statewide federation of Polish Republican clubs, the Connecticut Polish American Political Organization, was active in the 1920s; in 1931 the Pulaski Federation of Polish Democratic Clubs of Connecticut organized and in 1941 claimed thirty-two clubs representing fifty-two thousand Polish Democrats. There was also a New England Polish American Political Federation; and in upstate New York young activists successfully organized EC-POLE (Erie County Pole) after concluding that the only way to gain sufficient recognition from the major parties was through a third party.[54] Documenting the histories of similar state or regional political federations and professional associations elsewhere remains to be done.

Electoral victories and patronage are the benchmarks of political success, and early successes were few. In the late 1860s and 1870s, some political émigrés were elected to state legislatures, but not as ethnic candidates. In the 1880s and 1890s, primarily in the Midwest, Poles won scattered municipal and state offices. By 1895, thirteen candidates had managed at various times to win seats in the Minnesota, Illinois, Wisconsin, Michigan, and New York legislatures, and in 1892, Michael Kruszka became the first Pole to be elected to a state senate. Important municipal and statewide successes included Kiołbassa's election as Chicago treasurer in 1891, and Jan Smulski's election as Illinois treasurer in 1906. It was not until 1918, however, when John C. Kleczka was elected from Milwaukee to the House of Representatives and 1920 when Stanley Kunz was elected from Chicago, that Polish immigrants won federal elective office. Mieczysław Szalewski, a Polish consular official, nevertheless considered immigrant electoral successes before 1920s to be meager indeed when compared to other national groups, although he expected the situation to improve.[55]

In the 1920s and 1930s, Polish-American political presence became more noticeable. Between 1932 and 1938, the numbers elected to state legislatures rose from eleven to forty or more, including (in addition to the Midwestern states) New Jersey, New York, Connecticut, Pennsylvania, Ohio, Massachusetts, Nebraska, Indiana, Maryland, and New Hampshire. Four Polish Americans sat in Congress between 1920 and 1932, but in that year, reflecting FDR's New Deal Coalition, five Democrats were elected.[56] The appointment of Mieczysław (Matt) Szymczak to the Federal Reserve Board (1933–1961) was another victory for the politics of recognition. However, it was only after World War II, when Edward (Marciszewski) Muskie (the first Polish American to be elected governor) was elected from Maine, in 1958, that a Polish American reached the U.S. Senate. Muskie in 1968 became the only member of his group to receive his party's vice-presidential nomination, the penultimate prize for an insider.

Muskie's election and those of the only other Polish Americans to sit in the Senate—Barbara Mikulski (D-Md.) in 1986 and Frank Murkowski

(R-Ala.) in 1980—are anomalies. Whereas Muskie and Mikulski are Democrats (and Mikulski won with an ethnic, feminist, and liberal Democratic agenda), all three come from states with marginal Polish communities. None was elected with a Polish agenda, and their victories were individual rather than "Polish" triumphs.[57] Judging Polish success at the polls and with patronage is best analyzed at the municipal and state level, and in the U.S. House.

Polish immigrants settled largely in urban areas; and important cities (besides Chicago) included Milwaukee, Buffalo, Detroit, Gary, Cleveland, Pittsburgh, Erie, Philadelphia, Newark, New Britain, Boston, Toledo, and Jersey City. However, the cities most studied are Chicago, Milwaukee, Buffalo, and Detroit, the subjects of a work edited by Angela Pienkos, *Ethnic Politics in Urban America*. These were among the great cities of the American industrial revolution, attracting large immigrant populations, and the criteria for judging political success is the mayor's office. Whereas Poles scored early victories for council and other local offices, they won the mayoralty only in Detroit (1969) and Buffalo (1949, 1961, and 1973), and in each case only after World War II, almost as an anticlimax to the second-generation recognition drive. In Buffalo, Poles demonstrated ethnic solidarity in twice crossing over to vote for Republican mayoral candidates; in Detroit, Polish political activity was siphoned off to Hamtramck when "reform" in Detroit city government effectively limited the Poles' role in municipal politics until after World War II, while discrimination was reinforced by the stereotyping of Hamtramck Polish politics. It is argued that Poles were discriminated against in Detroit, whereas in Chicago, the failure to win the mayor's office is attributed to the absence of a Polish-American politician with the prerequisite leadership abilities and coalition-building skills necessary to capture control of the Democratic Party machine in such an ethnically competitive city. Furthermore, according to Kantowicz, group size fostered the myth of group solidarity as sufficient for citywide victory, while at the same time making other new arrivals consider the Polish community a threat.[58]

Unique conditions in each metropolis make it difficult to point to a single explanation for Polish-American success or failure in winning big-city mayoralties. Moreover, there are no studies of other cities, including smaller ones, to test these theses. Pienkos notes the remarkable success of Poles in winning elective office in Milwaukee, but were they stereotyped as unsuitable for the mayoralty? Louis Kostecki was Milwaukee's comptroller from 1912 to 1933 and was unofficially considered the "Polish mayor." In Meriden, Connecticut, Poles enjoyed a similar lock on the same office, but never won the mayoralty. Was the Polish place at the table already set? Was the denial of the brass ring the result of stereotyping or typecasting, a shortage of coalition builders or charismatic leaders, a lack of political skill and numbers or the requisite financial resources, or was it a tribute to the skill of the Irish Democrats in Chicago and elsewhere in playing off immigrant groups against each other? As for group solidarity, in New Britain, Poles mobilized through an effective voter registration drive to win the mayor's office in 1946. This victory opened the doors to city hall patronage and to subsequent victories by four other Polish candidates, including a Republican female. New Britain is an ethnically competitive city, yet group solidarity and a determined candidate won the laurel wreath.[59] And what were the reasons for Polish victories in Nanticoke, Pennsylvania, or Chicopee, Massachusetts, or Syracuse, New York?

The volume *Ethnic Politics in Urban America* forces reconsideration of the common lament about political underrepresentation. Beyond the mayoralty, Poles moved into the patronage system, electing candidates to city councils, state legislatures, and to the U.S. House of Representatives. Pienkos notes Polish successes in German-dominated Milwaukee; while Borowiec, acknowledging that Polonia did not take control of Buffalo's local political system, concludes that Buffalo Polonia scored "a remarkable record of electoral success."[60]

There is a need for more local study in order to arrive at a broader picture of Polonia's political history. Future research must include the years during and immediately following World War II, considered by some to be the peak of Polonia's political influence in local government.[61] At the same time, however, profound changes were in the making: outmigration to the suburbs, the Republicanization of Polish-American suburbanites, the political coming of age of other groups (such as blacks in Detroit and Chicago), the emergence of a more educated and professional second and third generation, and the further assimilation and acculturation of the immigrants' children and grandchildren.

The civil rights movement sparked tensions between blacks and the Poles, and abortive dialogues in the 1960s and 1970s, drawing Polish Americans into the whirlpool of racial politics. In Chicago in the 1950s and 1960s, Democratic Party strategy evolved from playing all ethnic groups off against each other toward creating accommodation and tensions between blacks and whites, polarizing racial tensions over issues such as housing. As cities declined and the Democratic Party came to be perceived as the representative of minority special interest groups, the number of Democrats among Polish Americans declined from nine in ten during Roosevelt's New Deal to five or six in ten in the 1980s, despite efforts to rally third-generation ethnic voters around the issues of neighborhood, ethnicity, class, and racial cooperation. John J. Bukowczyk, who associates being Polish American with being a liberal Democrat, explains the Polish political exodus from the Democratic Party in the 1980s in class and racial terms as the abandonment of a traditional ethnic identity for a "new," "white" ethnicity.[62] Polish-American Republicans would question whether one ceases to be a Polish American if one registers as a member of the GOP. Nevertheless, Polish Americans are no longer monolithically Democratic. This suggests the need to study both the relationship of postwar racial, economic, and urban social changes with changing Polish-American political affiliation and the impact of these changes upon Polish-American municipal politics. Although Polish Americans send mostly Democrats to Congress, the question is To what extent has the Republican Party platform become the Polish-American urban political agenda? To what extent did Polish Americans, together with other Catholic immigrant groups, become part of the emerging Republican majority envisioned by Kevin Phillips after Richard Nixon's victory in 1968?[63]

Municipal successes were a springboard to higher office. The precise number of Poles elected to state legislatures remains unknown, although they have been elected in at least nineteen states. A Polish study of 142 state legislators found that the numbers increased over time; that seven went on to the U.S. House and one (Muskie) to the U.S. Senate; that only a handful were women; and that over 85 percent were Democrats. The same study could find only one governor, two lieutenant governors, and two attorney generals. In terms of appointive positions, only four reached the high courts in their respective states; few were represented on state committees, while very few were appointed state commissioners, to gubernatorial cabinets, or to various public commissions and agencies. Therefore, Polonia participation in state politics was judged unsatisfactory, although modest gains denote political advancement. The Pienkoses caution, however, that these victories might be somewhat illusory. Polish candidates basically represented districts with heavy Polish constituencies and were proportionally underrepresented, with Milwaukee an exception.[64] Furthermore, while these legislators bore Polish names, did they view themselves as Polish representatives? Did they campaign on a "Polish" platform, or attend to constituents' interests through their party's socioeconomic platform? Did they care about "Polish interests," as Kruszka would have wished, or about their party's? Were they responsive to Polonia's interests, as in the 1970s, for example, when local communities successfully lobbied their legislatures for Polish Studies programs in higher education institutions in Wisconsin, Massachusetts, Michigan, and Connecticut? Were there Polish caucuses in state legislatures, and with what agendas?

These questions implicitly raise the issue as to whether local political strength can be transformed into political influence at higher levels of government. The question is particularly important to Polonia political leaders because of the voting strength of Polish Americans concentrated in influential electoral college states such as Illinois, Michigan, Pennsylvania, Connecticut, Wisconsin, Indiana, New Jersey, Ohio, New York, and Massachusetts. It is argued that, because these ten states, with the key metropolises, are politically competitive, any shift in voting patterns in groups as cohesive as the Poles, in close elections, could tip the results in favor of one or other of the candidates.[65] The thesis is provocative, although it abstracts Polish voters and voting patterns while not considering the impact of numerically larger groups like the Irish, Germans, and blacks.

Nevertheless, how has putative Polish-American voting power transferred itself to national politics? Polish Americans have been most visible in the U.S. House of Representatives. Between 1918, when Kleczka was elected, and 1982, forty-two men and one woman held congressional seats, thirty-five of them were Democrats. Over 90 percent of these delegates represented Chicago, Detroit, Milwaukee, Buffalo, and Connecticut. Furthermore, according to the 1970 census, of the eighty congressional districts with significant Polish-American populations, nine were represented by Polish Americans, a percentage (11.3%) that compared favorably with Italian-American (11.1%) representation.[66] Moreover, Clement Zablocki (International Relations), Daniel Rostenkowski (Ways and Means), and John Dingell (Energy and Commerce) chaired powerful committees.

Although this all suggests adequate representation, there are caveats. So far New York, Pittsburgh, Cleveland, and (until recently) Philadelphia have not elected Polish Americans to Congress. There has never been a "Polish Caucus," which may suggest ambivalence on the part of Polish-American congressmen about their responsibilities to their ethnic constituencies and a failure of Polish-American political representatives to formulate an agenda. Finally, the numbers of Polish-American congressional aides is minuscule.[67]

There are other caveats. Since the appointment of Matt Szymczak to the Federal Reserve Board (1933–1961), appointments in the executive branch have been few. John Gronouski was John F. Kennedy's postmaster general, an appointment that reflected the Kennedy use of ethnic politics. Zbigniew Brzezinski was Carter's national security advisor; Gen. Edwin Rowny, a Reagan aide on arms control; Edwin Derwinski, George Bush's secretary of veterans' affairs; and Gen. John Shalikashvili, William Clinton's chairman of the Joint Chiefs of Staff. Only the Gronouski and Derwinski appointments might be considered Polish-American appointments. Polish Americans, therefore, continue to complain that they receive few high-level appointments in the federal civil service and in the military, as well as at the state and municipal levels.[68] And whereas both parties at various times after World War II maintained nationality or ethnic divisions with designated liaisons with ethnic communities (Walter Zahariasiewicz and Mitchell Cieplinski), there are no studies to indicate if such activity went beyond the politics of paternalistic recognition and the pro forma mouthing of concern for the Captive Nations. Apart from serving as transmission belts for orchestrating campaigns in Polish-American communities, did participation in the nationality and ethnic divisions bring any federal appointments after a presidential election? The tentative evidence suggests not.[69]

This all further suggests that despite the well-documented Polish support for Democratic presidential candidates, and the shift to the Republicans when Eisenhower (1952), Nixon (1972), and Reagan (1984) triumphed, Polish-American leaders were unable to capitalize on the voting behavior of their ethnic confreres. It is also debatable as to whether Polish-American voters determined any presidential election. Rozmarek could not deliver the Polish vote for Republicans in 1946 and 1948. In the landslide victory of the popular Eisenhower in 1952, the shift in Polish votes contributed only marginally to the Republican victory. Polish Americans voted for Eisenhower because of dissatisfaction with Democratic foreign policy toward Poland under Roosevelt and Truman. Because Eisenhower (with reluctance and lack of sincerity) embraced "liberation," a surprising 50 percent voted Republican, raising questions about the future implications of this vote for the Democrats. The vote also convinced both Democratic and Republican analysts about the persistence of ethnic voting beyond the second generation, although in one observer's view fewer than actually expected voted for Eisenhower.[70] Eisenhower's embrace of "liberation" was nothing more than an election ploy for the ethnic Democratic vote, a point confirmed by Eisenhower's foreign policy.[71] This all suggests that community spokesmen mythologize about Polish-American political clout rather than engage in realpolitik and that they are manipulated by politicians, political parties, and the State Department. There is, therefore, a need to study the role and the caliber of ethnic leaders and the real influence of these leaders in American politics, both domestic and foreign.

Conversely, there are no systematic studies about the attitudes of the major parties toward East European Americans, to explain what commentators see as insufficient recognition and political reward. Were Polish Americans truly a part of the New Deal coalition, or merely runners in an Irish-dominated Democratic Party? Is the scarcity of political appointments related to their fund-raising inabilities and inadequate financial donations to political campaigns? Finally, has the putative "Polish interest" ever been seen in Washington since World War II as anything beyond Cold War anti-communism in domestic and foreign affairs? What is the Polish agenda? And who lobbies for it?

Homeland Politics Reprised

The Nazi and Soviet attacks on Poland in September 1939 and the establishment at the end of the war of a Soviet-controlled communist regime in Poland eclipsed the domestic Polish-American political agenda and linked the politics of recognition once again with the homeland. Polonia again was summoned to rally to Poland's assistance. A score of years had elapsed since Poland regained independence, and the numbers of earlier activists diminished, succeeded by a second, American-born generation reaching maturity. Could they be mobilized for homeland politics as they had two decades earlier? Did the national feelings of the immigrant generation survive within the new generation?

The self-identification of the Polish American evolved substantially during the interwar years. Emblematic of the changes was the refusal of the American delegation in 1934 at the organizational meeting of the World Union of Poles from Abroad to accede to the new organization, declaring: "Polonia in America is neither a Polish colony nor a national minority, but a component part of the great American nation, proud, however, of its Polish origin and careful to implant in the hearts of the younger generation a love for all that is Polish." This was the Polish-American declaration of independence. This was the point at which American Poles became Polish Americans or, "more correctly, Americans of Polish descent."[72]

The transformation was confirmed when efforts to renationalize American Polonia failed. While Polonia again mobilized to provide humanitarian assistance under the auspices of the Polish American Council (collecting some $20 million for Polish victims of the war), it ignored appeals to join the Polish army-in-exile.[73] However, the threat of an impending Soviet takeover of Poland and the loss of independence and Poland's eastern territories prompted Polonia leaders to abandon their apolitical stance. The establishment of an independent Poland helped legitimize Polonia in America in 1918, and Polonia's middle-class leadership sensed that the gains of the politics of recognition over the previous two decades were now jeopardized. The apprehensive leaders met in May 1944 in Buffalo and created the Polish American Congress (PAC). For the first time American Polonia united in a single nationwide umbrella organization with a mandate to exert pressure upon the Roosevelt administration to support Polish independence against Soviet advances and to promote the interests of Americans of Polish origin.[74] American Polonia had created a political lobby.

The politicization of American Polonia on Poland's behalf was remarkable. Feelings of protective paternalism toward the Old Country, the Soviet threat, and a perceived threat to Polonia's status in American society if independent Poland disappeared motivated Polonia's thinking. Politicization, however, occurred in an American context, as the PAC took pains to stress its members' loyalty to the United States.

The PAC was the result of the merging of Midwestern moderates gathered in the Polish American Council, with the National Committee of Americans of Polish Descent (1941), an organization influenced by the first arrivals of a new generation of émigrés. Like the pre–World War I émigrés, they believed that American Polonia still had political obligations toward Poland, asserting: "These great masses of *emigrants* . . . could become an active center on which fell the historical role of fighting for the Polish question in this tragic situation in which the Polish State found itself."[75] Brought together by Charles Rozmarek of the PNA, the new organization with its imposing name and organizational structure established itself as American Polonia's representative. In the process it eclipsed the small, pro-Soviet Polish-American left, which was prominent in the American Slav Congress established in 1942 and which competed for the attention of the Roosevelt administration. While the PAC's history is well known, the demise of Polonia's left awaits thorough and systematic research.[76]

It is ironic that, as a lobby, the PAC was initially unsuccessful. Roosevelt told Stalin at Yalta and Teheran of his concern for the Polish-American vote in explaining his unwillingness to publicly support Soviet demands upon Poland. Whereas Poland was for Stalin a question of boundaries and defense, and for Churchill a question of honor, it was for FDR a matter of domestic electoral and ethnic politics.[77] FDR accepted a postwar Europe divided into spheres of influence, and on July 5, 1945, the United States withdrew recognition from the Polish government-in-exile, transferring it to the newly constituted Polish Provisional Government of National Unity. Despite the Roosevelt administration's concern for the Polish vote, the October 1944 White House meeting and a similar episode with Truman in 1948 epitomized Polonia's power and powerlessness.[78]

The community, although consulted by the Roosevelt administration for domestic political reasons, lacked effective political pressure to influence the administration's actions. Whereas Polish Americans were large and important elements of the Roman Catholic Church, the Democratic Party, and the labor unions, they were all but absent from these organizations' high-level leadership positions. Furthermore, no Polish American except Szymczak held a high position in the federal administration or a U.S. Senate seat; and the ten or twelve Polish-American congressmen rarely spoke together, settling for politically valueless patriotic declamations for the *Congressional Record*.[79] The PAC, like other East European ethnic lobbies, did not achieve its minimal objectives: neither the prevention of the imposition of a communist government upon the homeland nor American recognition and the normalization of relations with the new authorities. And in the postwar years, no American administration seriously pursued the liberation of Eastern Europe from Soviet domination and the overthrow of the region's communist regimes.[80]

Despite early failure, it is not inaccurate to assert that the PAC became the "chief organization voicing the political interests of Americans of Polish descent in the United States," and an often eloquent advocate of the ideals contained in the Atlantic Charter. The PAC became a genuine American political interest or pressure group, not a political party, and remained true to its original goals, its convictions reinforced by the arrival of a new generation of political exiles after World War II. The PAC's most vital early years were between 1944 and 1952, a time that coincided with the onset of the Cold War, when it was successful in fund-raising and still had at its disposal a large Polish-American press. The PAC condemned Yalta, supported the Oder-Neisse Line, and refused to recognize the Soviet-controlled Warsaw regime (a policy it adhered to for forty-five years and attempted to impose upon Polonia).[81] In general, the PAC took upon itself the responsibility for presenting the case for Polish independence. The PAC attended the San Francisco Conference when the United Nations was founded and was successful in pressuring Congress to investigate the Katyn Massacre.[82] Until 1948 the PAC tried to be a stimulus upon American foreign policy. Later, however, the PAC supported whatever was in vogue in Washington, endorsing a conservative, anti-communist American foreign policy toward the Soviet Bloc and elsewhere on the globe. The PAC differed with American administrations only over the American unwillingness to recognize the Oder-Neisse Line as Poland's western border and over NATO's plan to lay down an atomic barrage "between the rivers Oder and Vistula" in the event of the outbreak of World War III.[83]

After 1956, with the emergence of a supposedly more liberal regime under Władysław Gomułka committed to a "Polish road to socialism," the United States recognized East European realities and pursued a policy of "differentiation," conditioning American economic support upon the degree of domestic liberalization in Soviet Bloc countries. Increasing numbers of Polish Americans traveled to Poland, implicitly challenging PAC efforts to isolate Poland from Polonia and its ostracism of communist diplomats. The PAC was demoralized, membership declined, and it accommodated itself to "differentiation." The PAC came to advocate the extension of Most Favored Nation trade status to Poland and supported economic assistance and individual contacts, distinguishing between the Warsaw regime (which it never recognized) and the nation (which could benefit from both American economic assistance and cultural exchanges). This approach, which enjoyed the general support of the Polish diaspora, was "unique among the Eastern European exiles."[84]

Active lobbying by any ethnic group either for or against its homeland's government traditionally raises questions about the group's primary loyalty, particularly in terms of the impact of ethnic-group voting upon the American system of government and upon American foreign policy. The matter arose during both world wars, and some scholars found the "hyphenate" in American politics and diplomacy a troubling problem. In the post–World War II era, communist penetration of the East European ethnic communities either as a result of visits to the homeland or by agents sent into local communities was a new fear. While evidence about manipulation from the homeland among East European Americans is circumstantial, the issue became contentious in the Polish-American community as contacts with Poland increased after 1956, contributing to a decline of PAC membership and raising questions about the group's role as representative for American Polonia.[85]

The fundamental issue was the proper relationship between American Polonia and the Warsaw regime and its diplomatic representatives. Although the PAC never recognized the regime and attempted, by and large successfully, to insulate Polonia from Warsaw's representatives, Warsaw looked for ways to penetrate Polonia. The Polonia Society was established in 1955, and, under Gierek, the society's president made a deputy foreign minister. Similarly, in the academic world, the Polonia Research Institute was inaugurated at the Jagiellonian University, with its own "five-year" plan for Polonia research, while summer programs of Polish language and culture were initiated in 1969. Such efforts responded to the cultural interests of third- and fourth-generation Polish Americans seeking their "roots," but they did not convert Polonia or its youth to communism. Nevertheless, the fear was that Polonia did not always clearly perceive the "distinction between cooperating with Warsaw or being used by it."[86] There is, therefore, a need to examine the postwar relationship between Polonia and Warsaw, Polonia's role in Polish foreign and cultural policy, and Polonia's role in the relationship between Washington and Warsaw, especially now that the archives are opening.

With the election in 1968 of Aloysius Mazewski as the PAC's second president, the organization was reanimated. Mazewski gave first priority to a Polonia domestic agenda: to upgrade the Polish-American image, fight defamation, teach Polish in schools, preserve ethnic parishes, protest the absence of Polish clergy in the hierarchy of the American Catholic Church, produce publications, gain government appointments, reverse discrimination and preferential hiring, and to improve relations with Jews. This agenda, at the least, suggested the Republicanization of Polish-American community leaders. In the 1970s, however, the issue of human rights in the Soviet Bloc reinvigorated the PAC's consistent anti-communism, while the election of John Paul II and the 1980 strikes demonstrated the authenticity of the PAC's policy of distinguishing between the communist regime and the Polish nation.[87]

The PAC genuinely articulated American Polonia's anti-communist sentiments, mirroring the attitudes of the vast majority of Polish Americans who belonged to Polonia organizations, as well as of those who did not belong. However, it was unable to transform this into popular votes and political pressure, a point exemplified by Rozmarek's endorsement of Dewey in 1948 as a protest against the Democrats' association with Yalta. Polish Americans voted from their pocketbooks; Rozmarek's failure to deliver the vote tarnished his and the PAC's prestige. It also raised questions that merit further research, about the marginality of postwar ethnic leaders in their communities. And although the PAC was also a vociferous exponent of domestic anti-communism, Polish-American voters did not succumb to the blandishments of McCarthyism, although some commentators later saw them as a building bloc in the Republican majority that Richard Nixon forged in 1972.[88] On the other hand, there is a need for research on the impact of McCarthyism on East European Americans. While the hyper-Americanism and anti-immigrant sentiment of the McCarthy era intensified the anti-communism of East European groups like the PAC, there is also reason to suspect that it drove many Polish Americans to abandon their ethnic identity and that it also destroyed the Polish-American left.[89]

Various factors account for the shortcomings of the PAC as a lobby until the 1980s, although Garrett considered it "undoubtedly the most sophisticated of the [East European] ethnic lobbying organizations." Polonia lacked a Polish caucus in Congress, which practically left the entire burden of Polish-American foreign policy initiatives with the PAC. Structurally, the PAC was ill-equipped, living in a symbiotic stepchild relationship with the Polish National Alliance (PNA). A permanently understaffed Washington office and the failure to create an effective media arm reflected the PAC's financial weakness and its need to rely on volunteers, which reduced its public relations activities to a kind of "ethnic fire-brigade."[90] The caliber of PAC leadership under Rozmarek (whom many found dictatorial) and Mazewski, as dedicated as they were, requires critical examination in assessing the PAC's effectiveness as a political lobby. The State Department's belief that it was better informed on Poland and better able to determine American interests in Poland also hampered the PAC, while the major parties paid only lip service to East European ethnic groups. These groups had to settle for recognition politics, such as proclamations and Captive Nations commemorations, which had the virtue of both keeping the issue alive and enabling East Europeans to identify the liberation of their homelands with American interests and ideals. Nevertheless, Stephen A. Garrett concluded in 1986 that the East European ethnic lobbies were failures, "manipulated more" by administrations and politicians "than manipulating as far as Washington's stance toward East Central Europe is concerned."[91] Others shared similar views. While believing that the Polish-American elite can serve as an interpreter of the United States to Poland and vice versa, Piotr S. Wandycz concluded in 1980:

> It is quite evident that the Polonia or its most articulate and active members constitute an important although thus far not decisive factor in Ameri-

can-Polish relations. Both Washington and Warsaw have on numerous occasions singled out this ethnic group as a special asset, but its potential is
not yet fully utilized, given the relatively narrow base of power of Polish
Americans and the low degree of political sophistication of the masses with
regard to Polish needs and problems.[92]

Such was the common scholarly wisdom about the PAC as Polonia's
lobby in 1980. The urgency of Polish developments, however, changed
that. As dissent developed in Poland in the last half of the 1970s, lobbying
on behalf of Poland was revitalized. In 1976 Professor Andrew Ehrenkreutz of the University of Michigan organized the North American Center for Polish Affairs (Studium) "to assist American and Canadian Polish
organizations professionally in their political activities on behalf of Poland's right of self-determination and independence."[93] Studium intended
to provide American opinion-makers with accurate information on Polish
conditions, and to serve as an intellectual policy resource for the PAC.

The election of John Paul II and Solidarity's leap onto the world stage
provided new opportunities for the PAC. With broad public knowledge
of and sympathy for events and developments in Poland, politicians from
both parties rediscovered how to court Polish Americans. The anti-Soviet
Reagan administration welcomed Mazewski to the White House, afford-
ing the PAC an opportunity to present its views to the administration.
The sophistication of this input was enriched by Studium and the naming
of the knowledgeable Jan Jezoranski-Nowak (retired director of Radio
Free Europe's Polish service) a PAC national vice-president. Nowak and
Kazimierz Łukomski—a thoughtful PAC policy analyst and, like Nowak,
a political émigré—articulated through the PAC's Polish Affairs Committee positions closely paralleling administration policy, ones calibrated to
ease the sanctions imposed after martial law in 1981. The normalization
of Polish-American relations was linked to expanded freedom for civil
rights and an incremental pluralization of political life.[94] For Garrett, the
PAC's difficult and dispassionate decision to support the administration's
lifting of sanctions was the culmination of a long process of its becoming
"a responsible and involved actor in the development of American policy
toward Poland." As in 1957 when the PAC, after considerable internal
debate, endorsed American economic assistance to Gomułka's Poland,
and as when it approved President Johnson's policy of "bridge-building"
to Eastern Europe, the PAC weighed its own policy concerns and reached
a position reflecting the complexities of its concern for Poland. More than

any other East European ethnic lobby, the PAC "approached a solution of the perennial problem facing the ethnic community: an appropriate melding of idealism and realism."[95]

There were challenges to the PAC as the primary Polish lobby. *Pomost* (Bridge), a small and intensely anti-Soviet group of newer political émigrés, considered the PAC politically too moderate and ineffective. American Polonia responded to martial law by organizing Solidarity support groups, and in 1982 and 1983 Solidarity exiles began reaching the United States. The support groups emerged because their organizers were unaware of the PAC, or dissatisfied with its response to Polish developments. However, these loosely confederated support groups joined the PAC as organizations or individuals. Solidarity exiles were generally welcomed by the PAC and Polonia, but tensions surfaced over who best could speak for Poland and many new arrivals bypassed the PAC and associated with their own generation. Solidarity's political impact and that of the Solidarity immigration, American Polonia's next generation, are fresh areas of research.[96]

Despite new challenges to its leadership, the PAC retained its preeminent role as Polonia's lobby. A stream of distinguished Solidarity émigrés and activists made political pilgrimages not only to Washington but also to Chicago. Individuals like Jerzy Milewski of the Solidarity Brussels office, in part because of PAC introductions, found the sympathetic ears of conservative and liberal senators and members of Congress, the State Department, and the AFL-CIO. Gorbachev was also a critical catalyst for change in Eastern Europe after 1985. Nevertheless, when the archives are opened on the past decade in both Washington and Warsaw, they will reveal that American Polonia, as during World War I, made its contribution to the restoration of Polish sovereignty. The Polish American Congress, as the community's long-established lobby, with its political objectives formulated by representatives of the post–World War II ideological emigration, actively pressed the Polish case with friendly administrations as well as engaging in an extensive program of humanitarian assistance. It is now time to reexamine postwar Polish-American relations, including Polonia's role in the relations between and the policies of Warsaw and Washington. The PAC merits both its own history and a place in the new histories of modern Poland.[97]

American Polonia's preoccupation with homeland politics over the past forty-five years culminated in October 1989 with the PAC's recognition of a postwar Warsaw government. Although the decision was arbitrary and unilateral, PAC president Edward Moskal took a delegation to

Poland and met with Wałęsa, Józef Cardinal Glemp, Prime Minister Tadeusz Mazowiecki, and also with the author of martial law, Gen. Wojciech Jaruzelski. The PAC came to Poland on its own terms, symbolically
restoring relations between American Polonia and a sovereign Poland.

Now that Poland is again among the ranks of independent nations,
American Polonia confronts the necessity of rethinking its position
toward Poland. It is time to redefine the "Polish" interest in American
politics and how and who is to articulate it. There is no longer a need for
a Cold War lobby, and the PAC may now resolve the permanent dualism
that has been the source of tension within the membership as to whether
homeland politics or the domestic agenda holds priority. The PAC might
transform itself into a "Polish lobby," supporting Polish economic, commercial, political, and cultural interests, such as Polish admission to
NATO and to the European Union. New lobbies might emerge to take
that task upon themselves in order to assure a Polish-American input on
American domestic and foreign policies. There may also be a shift away
from homeland politics as occurred after World War I for there is pressure
to formulate an "American agenda" for the next generation. The program
for the 1992 PAC convention includes nearly two days of discussion of an
"American agenda."[98]

Although it was frequently charged that the PAC, even under Mazewski, neglected a domestic agenda, the contrary view is that there always
was such an agenda, but that sufficient funds were never mobilized to
implement it. This raises the question as to whether there is any place to
conduct ethnic politics for third- and fourth-generation Polish Americans.
Many communities and their institutions and organizations were ener-
vated after World War II by migration to the suburbs; the educational,
social, and economic mobility of the third and fourth generations; and
the unfulfilled promises of the white ethnic renaissance of the 1960s and
1970s. While some continue to believe that a new ethnic "Polish" politics
might yet be possible for Polonia, this optimism and these theses remain
to be tested by Polonia's next generation.[99]

There has been a "Polish interest" in American politics going back to
the emergence of the early immigrant settlements. Prior to World War I,
as numerous studies indicate, the restoration of Polish independence was
the major preoccupation of immigrant leaders, who inculcated the peasant immigrants with a national consciousness. Scholars still dispute the
extent of this process, but World War I demonstrated that many immigrants were not, as had been feared earlier, lost for the cause of independence. Immigrant nationalists succeeded remarkably in transplanting Pol-

ish nationalism across the ocean. Victor Greene and others have suggested how this process occurred, but only recently has the substance of the "Polonia culture of nationalism" attracted scholarly study.[100]

Although this is an important area needing further research, immigrant nationalism was also forged within an American context, and related, as Greene suggests, to the immigrant's New World aspirations. World War I and the restoration of independent Poland compelled immigrants to decide where their future lay. A consequence of this was the growth of Polish-American citizen clubs and of regional political federations. Polish Americans now invested their energies in becoming political insiders. However, their participation in the electoral process, despite some recent studies, remains an unresearched area. Not only are the histories of political clubs and federations still to be written; so are the biographies of officeholders, ward bosses, and politicians. As Polish Americans used politics to come inside, they gave their loyalty in substantial numbers to the Democratic Party. Polish Americans came to think of themselves as members of the New Deal coalition, although Polish-American commentators argue that they did not reap political benefits in proportion to their loyalty and numbers. How the Democratic Party leadership viewed their Polish-American voters—whether they formed a group that could be taken for granted, whether they were really considered insiders—are questions that remain to be answered. Furthermore, the Polish-American political successes and failures at the municipal, state, and federal levels have to be placed in a comparative context with those of other ethnic groups, an approach rarely used. A comparative context will broaden our understanding of the place of Polish Americans in American politics and facilitate consideration of whether politics served Polish-American domestic concerns.

This brings us back to the question of defining the "Polish interest" in American politics. The outbreak of World War II, the remobilization of the community for active support of Polish independence, and the subsequent Cold War, altered the definition of "Polish interest" for the next four and a half decades. After the interwar period, during which the community focused upon its immediate local interests, Polish Americans were again (as was the case before and during World War I) preoccupied with a foreign policy question. From the organization of the Polish American Congress in 1944 until the first free, postwar Polish elections in 1989, the "Polish agenda" dominated the organizational life of American Polonia and Washington's and Polonia's relationship with Warsaw. At the same time, American cities underwent major socioeconomic transformations and immigrant and ethnic communities declined.

With the restoration of Polish sovereignty in 1989, the entire postwar history of Polonia politics becomes a new area for research and reevaluation. The postwar relationship between American Polonia, the Warsaw communist regime, and Washington needs to be documented and analyzed, utilizing materials from newly available Polish—as well as American—archives. Did McCarthyism and the Cold War drive the average Polish American from political involvement with American Polonia politics? What exactly was the role played by American Polonia in the triangular relationship between Warsaw, Washington, and the Polish diaspora in America? And, in the area of foreign policy, was Polonia a successful lobby? At the same time, did organized American Polonia, preoccupied with a "Polish agenda," sacrifice its "American agenda" precisely when its urban communities and power bases declined and needed assistance? Compared to the political successes of American Jews, African Americans, and Hispanics, was postwar American Polonia able to use American politics to serve its interests as an American ethnic group?

The history of American Polonia politics and of its political culture is rich and diverse, spanning as it does both Polish and American history. And it remains to be written.

7

Displaced Persons, Émigrés, Refugees, and Other Polish Immigrants

World War II Through the Solidarity Era

Anna D. Jaroszyńska-Kirchmann

EACH TIME AN IMMIGRANT WAVE REACHES THE SHORES OF THIS country, a multitude of personal histories are transformed according to the choices made by particular individuals. For the Poles, this process is defined by the specific time and historical context at work both in Poland and in the United States. Although the immigrant experience best can be explored on the individual level, immigration waves have usually some general characteristics that allow historians to identify particular groups of persons with particular migration experiences. Each wave arriving to settle in a foreign country is faced with the task of establishing its ethnic identity before the larger society as well as the previous immigrant waves within the same ethnic community. The inter-group dynamics of this difficult process are not free from conflict and social negotiation. Frequently, the history, degree of assimilation, life goals, education, relations to the homeland, and so on, stand in the way of the smooth transition between the old country and the immigrant community in the new one. Immigrants arriving within specific waves often feel the need to form their own separate organizations and social circles, based on the experiences and values that they hold in common.

Polish immigrant waves that appeared in the United States during and after World War II all displayed distinctive characteristics. In contrast to the "immigrants for bread" from the turn of the century, later immigrants often were described by—and themselves adopted—terminology directly indicating their different status as forced migrants. They were *exiles, refugees, displaced persons, émigrés,* or in Polish, *uchodźcy, wychodźcy, uciekinie-*

rzy, and *emigranci.* These terms are often used interchangeably in the common language, although their legal application may differ. All these terms came to designate political immigrants, who were forced to emigrate for political reasons or who fled their country to escape persecution.[1] Economic concerns working as additional motivations cannot be completely left out of the picture. In many cases, however, even this kind of stimulus was largely interpreted in political terms and justified by the prevailing political situation in Poland.

Each wave of immigrants coming to the United States since World War II entered Polish ethnic communities established by older immigrants from the turn of the century. The members of this so-called Old Polonia were proud of their many achievements in America: networks of Polish churches and parishes, Polish schools, press and publishing houses, various organizations, fraternals, and cultural associations, as well as certain defined sets of customs, traditions, and values formed and adapted throughout years of immigrant life in the United States. At the time of the outbreak of World War II, Old Polonia included a second generation of Polish Americans whose high degree of assimilation and acculturation within American society competed with a vivid sense of uniqueness and even isolation from the mainstream through the conscious retention of a Polish identity. This process of Americanization or acceptance of a double identity—Polish and American—was best illustrated in the declaration presented by the American Polonia's delegation to the World Union of Poles from Abroad (Światowy Związek Polaków z Zagranicy, or "Światopol"). "Światopol" was an international organization formed in Poland with an aim to unite and coordinate activities of Polish communities abroad in the interest of Poland and its government. In 1934, Światopol organized in Warsaw a congress attended by the representatives of Polonia from all over the world. The American delegation, led by F. X. Świetlik, declined the membership in Światopol and issued a statement justifying its position. "Regarding ourselves as an inseparable component of the great American nation," the statement announced, "we take an active and creative part in every walk of American life, thus contributing to boosting the name of Poland in our country." After returning to the United States, Świetlik further clarified his decision by saying, "Polonia in America is neither a Polish colony nor a national minority but a component part of the Great American nation, proud, however, of its Polish extraction and careful to make the young generation love everything Polish."[2] Miecislaus Haiman, a prominent Polish-American historian, summed up the controversy evoked by American Polonia's refusal to become a part of Światopol in a succinct and revealing statement: "In the eyes of the Poles in Poland and in other countries we are still only Poles while in fact we are already Americans of Polish extraction."[3]

The Americanization process of the 1930s obviously affected not only the intellectual leadership of Polonia but, first and foremost, the broad masses of working-class Polish Americans, whose "way of life was 'made in America,' just as the coal that they mined or the steel ingots that they rolled."[4] Thus transformed from "Polish" to "Polish-American," Old Polonia became a host community to the wave of Polish immigrants who entered the country as the first victims of World War II. Such a changed ethnic environment defined and influenced future relations among consecutive immigrant groups.

Poles who arrived in the United States during and after the war were an inseparable part of the larger influx of immigrants representing different ethnic groups: Jews, Ukrainians, Latvians, Lithuanians, Estonians, those described in governmental sources as Yugoslavs, as well as Greeks, Germans, Russians, Czechs, and Slovaks. Uprooted by the war and the political changes in Europe after its conclusion, the refugees of the Cold War era up to the most recent times have only lately gained more systematic scholarly attention. The recent increase of research is (among other reasons) related to the fall of communism in Eastern and Central Europe. The role of immigrant communities—vehemently anti-communist in the unfolding of the Cold War, or exerting political impact on East-West relations and on developments within the countries behind the Iron Curtain—has become an exciting topic for study. Other aspects of this newest chapter in immigration history, such as transformations within the ethnic communities in the United States, social interactions among the immigrant waves, assimilation into and participation in the life of the larger American society, also bring to light significant research questions.

Despite the abundance of available primary sources, broader general treatment of the postwar European refugee immigration to America thus far is missing. Few scholars have concentrated on the common experience of that group. Mark Wyman has studied the sojourn of the European displaced persons (DPs) in the DP camps in Europe between 1945 and 1951.[5] His work, although not free from too-far-reaching generalizations, is nevertheless important since it highlights the significance of the period spent by the refugees in Europe immediately prior to their emigration. Leonard Dinnerstein analyzed a different aspect of the DP experience, related to the legal battle over their admission to the United States. He concentrated on the efforts of the Jewish lobby to admit European refugees. The lobbying effort of many different ethnic groups in America had a profound impact on relationships between the DPs and established immigrant waves.[6] A few other studies treat the question of the postwar immigrants within the broader framework of world migrations and population movements, refugee populations, changes in the immigration legislation, resettlement programs, and their impact on ethnic life in America.[7]

Some of the ethnic groups represented in the postwar refugee waves began to sponsor research into the various areas of their refugee experience in America. The most noticeable example here are Ukrainian communities in the United States and Canada, which initiated systematic studies on Ukrainian displaced persons after World War II.[8] Jewish survivors of the Holocaust also received more attention.[9] Barbara Stern Burstin's comparative study of Polish Jews and Christians who resettled in the Pittsburgh area is a rare exception to the approach followed by most of these.[10] One also should note a few initiatives that brought together several ethnic groups interested in pursuing studies in the history of the newest immigration waves. An excellent example is a conference on the "Cold War Aftermath: Minnesota's Ethnic Communities and the Collapse of Soviet Hegemony," sponsored by the Friends of the Immigration History Research Center at the University of Minnesota in 1993.[11] In the future such initiatives ideally would result in an effective cooperation in research and systematic study of the postwar refugee immigration to the United States.

The United States was just one of the destinations for the European refugees since the end of World War II. Both displaced persons and subsequent immigrant waves were admitted in many European as well as some other countries on different continents. Poles established their communities in such European countries as Austria, Germany, Belgium, France, and Great Britain. Considerable numbers of Polish refugees settled in Canada, Argentina, Australia, and New Zealand.[12] The awareness of the world diaspora and ties to persons living in different parts of the globe played an important role in the construction of the community consciousness among Polish refugees. Studies conducted on new Polonias in various countries not only supplement our knowledge of the Polish-American community in recent times, but also offer fertile ground for comparative works.

Since studies on the postwar Polish immigration to the United States are still fragmentary, an overview such as this has to rely to a greater degree on the primary material. The majority of early Polish war refugees arrived here between 1939 and 1941. Some of them were caught by the outbreak of war while staying in the United States or in other countries, and some followed the thousands of war refugees who streamed out of Poland after September 1939, when Poland was attacked by Nazi forces from the west and by the Soviets from the east. Refugees arrived mainly through private channels, settling mainly in the New York and Chicago areas. Among them were numerous artists, scholars, writers, politicians, and representatives of the Polish governmental and social establishment.[13]

Shortly after their arrival, most refugees faced all the difficulties of immigrant existence: isolation, illness, lack of jobs, and decrease in social prestige. Looking for assistance from the Polonian organizations, especially Rada Polonii Amerykańskiej (Polish American Council, later renamed American Relief for Poland [ARP], the largest Polish-American wartime charitable agency), the refugees formed self-help organizations in order to alleviate the harsh economic conditions. Records of the ARP from the years 1940–1947 indicate the establishment of the Polish War Refugee Association in the United States (Zrzeszenie Uchodźców Wojennych z Polski w Stanach Zjednoczonych), based in New York and active between 1940–1947, and a smaller and short-lived Circle of Polish Refugees (Koło Uchodźców Polskich) working in Chicago.[14]

Some refugees quickly became involved in politics. Among them were such distinguished figures as General Bolesław Wieniawa Długoszewski, Polish ambassador in Rome and member of the governmental circles of interwar Poland, who came to the United States in the second half of 1940; Wacław Jędrzejewicz, ex–vice minister of education, and Henryk Florian Rajchman, ex–minister of industry and trade, both of whom arrived from England in the spring of 1941; and Ignacy Matuszewski, ex–minister of the treasury, who came via Portugal. These and other new arrivals from the Polish government's Piłsudski faction believed that American Polonia had moral obligations toward Poland and the political means to exert an impact on U.S. foreign policy. Shocked by the presumed lack of involvement and inaction of the Rada Polonii, they formed in 1942 the National Committee of Americans of Polish Descent (Komitet Narodowy Amerykanów Polskiego Pochodzenia [KNAPP]), one of the most influential and vocal Polish political organizations within American Polonia at that time. The high leadership of KNAPP also included representatives of the Polish-American press, editors Maksymilian F. Węgrzynek (*Nowy Świat*, New York) and Frank Januszewski (*Dziennik Polski*, Detroit).[15]

Although KNAPP's membership never surpassed three thousand, its impact on the increasing politicization of American Polonia at that time and on the creation of the Polish American Congress (PAC) in 1944 cannot be overestimated.[16] Its passionate interest in foreign politics and especially in the international position of Poland, as well as its leadership ambitions over the entire Polonia, quickly came to characterize this group of political émigrés and defined them in the eyes of the U.S. Polish-American community.

The remarkable achievements of this wave of immigrants included more than political activism. They also numbered among the founders of cultural institutions, such as the Polish Institute of Arts and Sciences in America, the Polish American Historical Association,[17] as well as the Józef Piłsudski Institute for Research in the Modern History of Poland, all designed to support and facilitate further development of Polish culture and scholarship and to represent them to the larger American society. The Józef Piłsudski Institute was established in 1943. Januszewski, Matuszewski, Jędrzejewicz, Rajchman, and Węgrzynek, as well as a few others, were among the founding fathers.[18] The Polish Institute of Arts and Sciences of America (PIASA) was established in New York in 1942 by a group of Polish scholars and members of the Polish Academy of Sciences who found themselves outside Poland at the outbreak of World War II. PIASA's goal became the continuation of scholarly activity disrupted by the war. It also aimed at providing adequate conditions for the presentation of its results to the larger American society. Among the first members and officers were world-renowned scholars such as Oskar Halecki, Rafał Taubeschlag, Bronisław Malinowski, Wacław Lednicki, and Wojciech Swiętosławski.[19]

The arrival of war refugees exerted its impact also in such areas of Polonian life as literature and theater. After the defeat of Poland, Julian Tuwim, one of the most prominent poets of the interwar period, found himself in New York, actively participating in the cultural life of the Polish community there. Kazimierz Wierzyński, a recognized poet and essayist, also settled in New York after wartime exile in France, Portugal, and Brazil. Jan Lechoń's odyssey followed the pattern of other refugee routes; after the fall of France, he arrived in New York via Brazil. He settled there and plunged into the social and cultural life of the émigré circles, also through the editorship of the New York–based weekly *Tygodnik Polski,* designed as a literary and intellectual periodical in the Polish language. Another renowned Polish writer and essayist, Józef Wittlin, found himself in New York in 1941. The group of writers, intellectuals, and other artists from the wartime refugee wave, together with similar groups of later arrivals, formed the basis of the postwar Polish intellectual diaspora.[20]

Their dramatic attempts to re-create a Polish intellectual and artistic community in New York brought mixed results. Some, like Wittlin and Wierzyński, supported activities of the Literary Section of the PIASA, participating in lectures and presentations organized there. Tuwim never really accepted the reality of the émigré existence and returned to Poland after the war. Lechoń committed suicide by jumping from a New York skyscraper in 1956. While many others continued their literary work and published both in Polish and English, some never fully recovered from the traumatic experiences of displacement and gave up writing altogether.

The story of Polish actors who found themselves among this first wave of war refugees represents another example of uneasy immigrant life in the United States. According to Emil Orzechowski who traces the history of Polonia theater in the United States, one of the most significant initiatives of the war years was the establishment in New York of the Polski Teatr Narodowy (Polish National Theater) with the support of Koło Artystów Sceny Polskiej (Polish Actors' Circle). Performances of the theater originally evoked much enthusiasm, especially among the most recent arrivals from Poland. By contrast, its artistic tours to other Old Polonia centers did not meet with a great deal of success. The high intellectual level of the repertoire did not appeal to the Polonian audience accustomed to a lighter kind of entertainment; frequent references to the war experiences could not be easily identified by the viewers, and high ticket prices and lack of energetic management and marketing further hurt the ambitious theater company.

In the fall of 1942, the Polish Actors' Circle announced the establishment of the Polski Teatr Artystów (Polish Artists' Theater), subsidized by the Sikorski government in London. The majority of actors who participated in the first undertaking of the Polish National Theater now transferred to the new company. Its nature was very different, however. From the beginning it was designed as an artistic enterprise that would cater mostly to the tastes of recent Polish refugees, without compromising the intellectual level. Perhaps it assumed a kind of temporary character and aimed to function only till the time when return to Poland became possible. The theater, despite some success, never achieved its goal of becoming the permanent center of the Polish performing arts in New York. When the governmental subsidies ended in 1945, the company ceased to exist. Most of the actors followed various career paths, including radio programs, individual tours to smaller communities in the country, or return to Poland.[21]

Although refugees were streaming into America throughout the war years, mostly following sojourns in other countries, the next large wave of

Polish immigrants appeared on American soil only in 1946. That year the so-called Truman directive, a presidential executive order issued in December 1945, allowed 39,000 refugees from American zones of occupation in Germany, Austria, and Italy to enter the country under existing quota regulations each year. Between March 31, 1946, and June 30, 1948, approximately 35,515 persons were issued visas under the Truman directive. Out of those, 25,594 were Jews. According to B. Burstin, although both Christian and Jewish resettlement agencies were already accredited and active at that time:

> There clearly was a difference in their effectiveness; the bulk of the agency assurances issued under the Truman directive came from Jewish agencies, despite the fact that less than 20 percent of the displaced persons population in Europe was Jewish. This poor showing on the part of the Catholic resettlement agencies was viewed with considerable consternation by Catholics and other interested parties.[22]

The enactment of the Truman directive was just one of the steps undertaken by the United States in the international effort to resolve the urgent problem of World War II refugees who in large numbers remained in the DP camps in Europe. They were former prisoners of Nazi concentration camps, forced laborers of the Third Reich, and civilian refugees scattered around the world, as well as political refugees from countries under Soviet domination. Several millions, representing a variety of ethnic groups, remained in Europe following the end of the war. By late 1946, the United Nations Relief and Rehabilitation Administration (UNRRA) repatriated about 8 million to their homelands.[23] About a million remained of those who considered a return either impossible or unwanted. Between 1945 and 1948, approximately 315,000 of the "last million" of "unrepatriables" were already resettled throughout the world. An increase in the number of those who still awaited resettlement was caused by a rising birth rate within the camps and the influx of refugees from behind the Iron Curtain.[24]

According to the UNRRA statistics, in December 1945, 438,643 Poles received UNRRA assistance in the territories of Germany and Austria. Statistics for December 31, 1946, after the major repatriation action was over, showed that 278,868 Polish displaced persons remained in the DP camps of Germany, Austria, and Italy. At that time, the total of 1,037,404 displaced persons of fifty-two nationalities lived in Germany, Austria, and Italy, both in and out of camps.[25]

Various countries admitted the displaced persons as part of the international resettlement effort. After the United States, it was Australia, Israel, Canada, Great Britain, France, and Belgium that accepted the largest numbers of refugees. According to IRO, between July 1, 1947, and December 31, 1951, the United States admitted 110,566 DPs whose principal nationality or last habitual residence was Poland. During the same period, Australia admitted 60,308 Poles, Israel 54,904, Canada 46,961, the United Kingdom 35,780, France 11,882, and Belgium 10,378. Other destinations included the Netherlands, and countries of South and Latin America.[26]

The American public, stimulated by the efforts of numerous ethnic groups, began to change its initially hostile attitude toward the proposals that America accept its share of war victims. As a result of ethnic lobbying efforts coordinated by the Citizens Committee for Displaced Persons (the PAC, led by Charles Rozmarek, also organized an effective lobbying campaign), the U.S. Congress passed the Displaced Persons Act in June 1948, which allowed 205,000 displaced persons to enter the country. The law included a number of conditions and limitations that made the process of immigration particularly complex. Another intense lobbying action succeeded in 1950, when amendments to the DP Act were accepted, prolonging the immigration deadline to June 1952 and increasing the number of eligible immigrants to 341,000. The 1950 amendments also included a provision under which 18,000 Polish veterans in Great Britain could enter the United States.[27] Rough estimates indicate that approximately a little over 140,000 Poles came to the United States under the Displaced Persons Act of 1948 and its 1950 amendments, including about eleven thousand Polish veterans and their families from Great Britain.[28]

American Polonia participated actively in the resettlement effort carried out primarily by the various religious and ethnic private agencies but coordinated by the governmental Displaced Persons Commission. The commission began its operations on August 27, 1948, and continued in existence until August 31, 1952. During this time, it resettled more than 339,000 DPs in the United States, aided by a number of social service agencies sponsored by religious and ethnic volunary organizations as well as state governments.[29] The Polish community was served mainly by three resettlement agencies: the Polish Immigration Committee (PIC) of New York, led by Father Colonel Felix Burant; American Relief for Poland, a major Polish charitable organization under the leadership of Francis X. Świetlik, both affiliated with the National Catholic Welfare Conference; and the American Committee for the Resettlement of Polish DPs (ACRPDP), formed by and affiliated to PAC.[30]

The DPs—called *wysiedleńcy* or *dipisi* in Polish—had many distinctive social characteristics. The available data for this group derives from the 1970s studies by Danuta Mostwin, based on the self-selective sample of 2,049 questionnaire respondents from thirty-five states. The majority of Mostwin's respondents arrived in the United States between January 1948 and December 31, 1952 (the closing date for the resettlement under the DP Act and its amendments), mostly from Great Britain. The next largest group, about 16.5 percent of the sample, arrived between 1957 and 1962, mostly from Poland. Mostwin's study indicates that of 920 respondents who were old enough at the time of leaving Poland to have acquired social status, 39 percent were upper class, 23 percent were upper middle class, and 9 percent were lower class. Data on the educational level demonstrated that 27 percent of the respondents had completed university training and received a degree, 20 percent had done some university work, and 23 percent had completed high school. Finally, attesting to the social mobility of the postwar immigrants was information on the current social status of the respondents that placed 25 percent of them in the upper class of the American society, 13 percent in the upper middle class, 27 percent in the middle class, 21 percent in the lower middle class, and 14 percent in the lower class. The obvious bias of the study (self-selection, connection to the Polish-American community and its press, where the study was advertised, inclusion of immigrants from Poland after 1957, and the overrepresentation of Polish veterans from Great Britain in the sample) limits the value of the study for the entire population. It does, however, confirm the visibility and activism of a group of *inteligencja* (intelligentsia, or professional middle class) within the postwar immigrant wave and their social and occupational mobility after the resettlement in America.[31]

Perhaps the most important characteristic was the political nature of this group of immigrants. They openly declared that the inability to accept the communist regime in Poland was the main reason for their emigration. Many immediately became involved in the political life of the Polish diaspora, supporting political parties organized around the émigré government in London and declaring their loyalty to the "constitutional authority" of that government. Although this involvement seemed more limited in the case of those who settled in the United States (as compared to Great Britain, for example), it still indicated the DPs' distinctively broad interest in world affairs and the foreign policy of the United States.[32] Some, at least in the first period after their arrival, still counted on their prompt return to Poland once the international situation changed. All felt a part of a larger Polish postwar diaspora and cultivated organizational as well as personal contacts with others resettled in different parts of the world.

The particular political character of the DP immigration was reinforced by the group of Polish ex-servicemen who arrived from Great Britain under the 1950 amendments to the DP act.[33] As those who came before them, the veterans carried a heavy burden of war sufferings and hardships and years of coping with the immigrant reality during their sojourn in Great Britain. Officers especially felt deprived of social prestige and hard-earned honor. While in America they frequently had to accept low-paying jobs involving manual labor and had to start building their lives anew in unfamiliar and uncooperative conditions. Their war memories, political views, relations to Poland, and close ties with the larger Polish diaspora often set them apart from other members of the U.S. Polish community, including the civilian portion of the DP group. Although some of the ex-soldiers did join existing Old Polonia veterans organizations, such as the Association of Veterans of the Polish Army (SWAP), most steered toward their own circles, mainly the Polish Veterans of World War II Association (Stowarzyszenie Polskich Kombatantów [SPK]) with existing branches in many countries of the world.[34] Some other newly established veterans organizations included the Polish Home Army Veterans Association (Armia Krajowa), the Polish Navy Veterans Association of America, the Polish Association of Former Political Prisoners of the Concentration Camps, the Association of War Invalids, the Association of Polish Parachutists in America, the First Polish Armoured Division Veteran Association, and the Association of Polish War Pilots.[35]

A good example of the distinctive attitudes of some soldier DPs, although unique in its turbulent course of events, is the case of Tadeusz Wyrwa, documented in the memoirs of his father, Józef Wyrwa. Both Wyrwas fought during the war in the Polish guerilla forces of the Home Army, earning high officer ranks. After their arrest upon the seizure of power by the communists, both Wyrwas managed to escape and crossed the border to the American occupation zone in Germany. They spent some time in the DP camps there and arrived in the United States with the DP transports of 1949. In 1950, Tadeusz Wyrwa received a draft order from the American army. He refused to join, justifying his decision with the argument that he was a Polish officer, obliged to follow orders of the legal Polish (that is, London government) authorities only. The case was quickly picked up by the American press, which interpreted it as an example of the DPs' ingratitude toward the country that had accepted them.

The incident was also broadly commented upon in the Polonian press, evoking discussion about the loyalty and allegiance of Poles in America, but mostly condemning Wyrwa's position. Personal attacks against him increased as the case lingered for two full years in various stages of the American legal system. Finally, in August 1952, a court decision freed Wyrwa from the obligation of military service in the American army. Discouraged and disappointed, Tadeusz Wyrwa nevertheless decided to leave the United States and, together with his father, emigrated to Spain and then settled in France.[36]

The soldiers were not the only ones who established their own organizations, separate from Old Polonia's fraternals. Shortly after the arrival of successive DP transports, Polish *wysiedleńcy* formed their first self-help organizations, designed to aid newcomers and provide them with the friendly support of persons who had also been through the horrors of war and the hardships of the DP camps. Gradually, these organizations also took over social and cultural functions, arranging artistic events, picnics, or money collections for those who, being unqualified for immigration, had to stay in Germany. Another organizational achievement of this wave of Polish immigrants was the re-creation of the Polish scouting organization for youth and children, Harcerstwo.[37]

Faced with the harsh reality of reestablishing their disrupted lives on foreign soil, Polish DPs also confronted the challenge of adjusting to the specific conditions of life in Polish-American communities in the United States. Sponsored in the initial process of DP immigration mainly by the members of Old Polonia, the *wysiedleńcy* found themselves instantly within the Polish-American world. Those who had originally traveled to destinations located farther from the Polonia centers were, sooner or later, naturally drawn back to those centers. Although both groups looked forward to the meeting, first encounters sometimes brought tension, disappointment, or even open conflict.

Reasons for these reactions are complex. The newcomers did not know much about American Polonia, its history, way of life, achievements, and level of assimilation. They tended to consider Polonia "the fourth province of Poland," according to popular nineteenth-century concepts.[38] The earlier immigrants, on the other hand, expected the newcomers to be their social replicas, whom they generously would introduce into the Polish-American world:

> While they [that is, "old" immigrants] welcomed the displaced persons with material assistance, "old Polonia" also adopted a patronizing attitude toward Poland and the new immigrants because of its earlier arrival, eco-

nomic success and assistance to the refugees. They expected to be looked
upon as benefactors and experienced older residents, assuming that the
displaced persons would be dependent upon them as they had been dependent upon family and friends. They also expected the displaced persons,
whom they sometimes referred to condescendingly as the "Biedaki" (poor
souls), to relive their early experiences, arriving poorly dressed and with no
knowledge of English.[39]

The greatest distinction lay perhaps in the specific working-class way of
life adopted by the majority of Polish Americans, which refugee Poles
found hard to accept. According to historian John J. Bukowczyk, "Polish
displaced persons with working-class, artisanal, and farming backgrounds
integrated easily into blue-collar America."[40] However, those coming
from middle-class backgrounds, despised and rejected the Polish-
American culture and way of life. Manual factory jobs, often the only
employment available for members of the émigré intelligentsia, were regarded as a degradation and a painful loss of social prestige.

Those displaced Poles detested the older immigrants' lack of Polish
language skills, their Americanization, low educational level, and "peasant" ways of life.[41]

These mutual misconceptions were sometimes reinforced by the unfavorable conditions of the complicated and often chaotic resettlement
process, which became a real challenge to entire Polonia. Despite the fact
that the obligations (or lack of them) between sponsors and DPs were in
some cases misinterpreted and served as a source of tensions, the resettlement effort brought also many examples of harmonious and friendly relationships, and, in its end result, can be justifiably considered a great success of the Polish-American community.[42]

The resettlement experience differed also depending on the place of
settlement itself. The great majority of the DPs settled in the urban centers of states with traditionally large Polish populations: New York, New
Jersey, Connecticut, Illinois, Michigan, Wisconsin, as well as California.
Agricultural provisions of the DP act, however, favored sponsorship for
work on farms, so a certain portion of DPs found themselves, at least
initially, in the countryside and far from any larger Polonia communities.
They usually felt their isolation severely and tried dramatically to find
jobs in the city.[43] Only a small percentage of DPs ended up in the South;
a well-publicized 1949 scandal which involved the slavelike labor of Slavic
DPs on the sugar plantations of Louisiana virtually ended the DP resettlement there.[44]

According to Mostwin's study, the DP arrivals infrequently joined old

Polish parishes in the cities, and after the initial settlement in Polish-American neighborhoods, often steered away from these and moved to the suburbs. Existing studies do not indicate what the exact level of the initial DP involvement was in the older Polonia fraternals and organizations, although it seems to have been relatively modest. Only after a certain period of adjustment, more Polonia institutions received support from the DP group of immigrants, whose representatives found themselves among the leaders of such national organizations as PAC. As it was with the earliest wave of war refugees, the Polish DPs also distinguished themselves in many areas of art and scholarship. The idea of the Polish theater was revived, and numerous representatives from the DP immigration worked their way to become members of American academia and cultural life.[45]

This account would not be complete without mentioning the substantial group of Polish Jews who immigrated to the United States under the same DP act. According to the sociological study by Barbara Stern Burstin, those refugees were sponsored mainly by Jewish resettlement agencies and after arrival in America usually chose to associate with Jewish communities. The memories of war as well as the interwar period in Poland held in common by both Polish Jews and Christians sometimes served as a bridge between them but more often divided their communities and reinforced mutual distrust and suspicion.[46]

Our knowledge of the history of the postwar immigration from Poland to the United States is fragmentary. Some periods and immigrant waves have attracted more scholarly attention or produced more source materials; others, usually smaller groups, have escaped scholarly scrutiny and have nearly disappeared in the rich mosaic of American society. The latter happened to the immigrants who came to America during the Cold War, which shaped not only the mentality of American society but also American immigration law at that time. The Refugee Relief Act of 1953 allowed another 205,000 persons to be admitted as non-quota immigrants. The impact of the Cold War was noticeable; refugees had to go through political screening, which was reinforced through the controversial Internal Security Act of 1950. The Immigration and Nationality Act of 1952 (the so-called McCarran-Walter Act), enacted over President Truman's veto, maintained the quota system (including the preferences for northern and western Europeans) but liberalized admittance policies for immigrants from Asian countries. Furthermore, it favored admission of persons with particular skills or "high education, technical training, specialized experiences, or exceptional ability."[47]

Additional acts of Congress went into effect in 1956, admitting Hungarians who were fleeing their country after the unsuccessful revolution of 1956, and in 1959, admitting anti-communist Cubans.[48] Only in 1965 did President Johnson sign the new law, finally abolishing the quota system and establishing immigration limits for the western and eastern hemispheres, which also reinforced the preference for skilled and educated persons (professionals, scientists, and artists) and relatives of U.S. citizens.[49] All these legal changes were significant for the Polish-American community and contributed to the "ebb and flow" character of Polish immigration into the United States in the 1950s and 1960s.

The main "push" factor influencing the emigration waves was the political situation in Poland. Already in the early 1950s stories of daring Polish pilots who defected from Poland on Soviet-built planes electrified the Polish-American community. In each case, the pilot received a hero's welcome and was sponsored to remain in America on the basis of political asylum.[50] There were also others who managed to escape from behind the Iron Curtain, for example stowaways and seamen from Polish ships entering American ports. The immigration laws also enabled some Polish intellectuals to come to the United States. Czesław Miłosz, the 1980 Nobel Prize winner in literature, left Poland in 1951 and after almost ten years spent in France, immigrated to the United States in 1960. Jerzy Kosiński, author of *The Painted Bird, Being There,* and many other works well known to the American public, arrived in the United States in 1957; and Stanisław Skrowaczewski, world-renowned conductor, came to America in 1958.[51]

The year 1956 and the collapse of the short-lived political thaw in Poland brought in a wave of so-called post-October immigrants (named after the October 1956 workers' revolt in Poznań). Their motivation for leaving the country was usually twofold. Some sought to escape increasing political oppression, and others took advantage of the liberalized passport laws in Poland and the possibilities for immigration under the program for reuniting families, which also offered a chance to better their economic conditions. It is hard to give this particular wave precise numbers, but the INS statistics show 130,576 quota and non-quota immigrants for the years 1953–1970, and 20,755 refugees for the same period.[52]

In 1968, a government-induced anti-Semitic campaign in Poland led to the emigration of about 20,000 Jews, persons of Jewish origin, and intellectuals.[53] Many of them immigrated to Israel or to other European countries, but a large group settled in the United States. Some of them never looked for any ties with the Polish communities in the United

States, but some joined various Polish cultural and social circles, which provided them with favorable conditions for maintaining dual Jewish and Polish identity.

The 1970s witnessed both the collapse of the Polish economy, which had been artificially inflated through foreign loans, and an increase in political repression and censorship.[54] This situation, coupled with the relaxation of U.S. immigration laws, brought in a new wave of Polish immigrants. It is impossible to classify all of them as political refugees, although even those whose first goal was the betterment of economic conditions were also, to a certain extent, victims of the prevailing political system in Poland. According to INS statistics, between 1971 and 1980 the United States admitted over 43,000 immigrants, including 5,882 refugees coming under the Refugee Act.[55] The mental anguish and confusion caused by the decision to emigrate is masterfully depicted in Sławomir Mrożek's famous play *The Emigrants,* constructed out of an extensive conversation between a Polish intellectual and a Polish worker under the conditions of the immigrant existence. They represent conflicting motivations for emigration and different perceptions of the immigrant experience, but both exemplify the complex character of the Polish immigration of that period.

We base part of our knowledge of the social structure of immigrants arriving between 1974 and 1984 on the results of yet another sociological study conducted by sociologist Danuta Mostwin in a form of a questionnaire. According to this study, 50.5 percent of respondents came to the United States invited by relatives, and 47 percent identified themselves as political immigrants. The majority of respondents came from big cities, almost one-third had a college education, and 90 percent had high school or vocational school diplomas. The average immigrant was 29–39 years old and married. According to Mostwin, her respondents had a strong Polish identity and ties to the Catholic Church. Reported friction between them and the established Polonia had their roots in mutual misconceptions and the inflated expectations of both groups not much different from the experiences of the earlier DP arrivals.[56]

The clearly economic character of the temporary migration to Chicago in the 1970s was best depicted in the ethnographical studies of cultural anthropologist Ryszard Kantor. Kantor focused on the history of the Zaborów parish clubs, existing in Chicago since the 1920s and designed to aid immigrants from this region of Poland in various ways as well as to collect money to help persons left in the home villages.[57] According to Kantor, the clubs went through a period of decline following World War

II. In the years 1960–1965, several dozen families left the Zaborów parish and settled permanently in Chicago. Later, they became "the new force," which revitalized and redirected the clubs' activities.[58] In the 1970s, groups of temporary immigrants from Zaborów parish arrived in Chicago and sometimes spent several years there while working and saving money for the return home. Their immigrant experience in America, opinions about American Polonia, as well as the impact of their travels on their home villages were studied by Kantor and others through oral history interviews after their return to Poland.[59] Kantor's works, however, show only a fraction of the many problems pertaining to the economic immigration to the United States at that time; the entire question needs further study and analysis.

The 1970s also became the period of ethnic revival and revitalization, in which American Polonia participated fully. The most noteworthy process included the building up of Polish pride, and fighting the prejudice and discrimination often expressed through the then-popular Polish jokes. Anti-defamation projects, carried out by various Polish-American agencies and most notably by PAC, involved many of the representatives of the "Nowa Emigracja," that is, persons from the DP and subsequent waves. According to sociologists Helena Znaniecka Lopata and Danuta Mostwin, the efforts to counteract the effects of the jokes strengthened the ranks of Polonia and unified them, providing a source of revitalization for the entire community.[60]

The cooperation among different immigrant waves was also conspicuous in other PAC activities, particularly the ones that had to do with formulation of foreign policy approaches by PAC leaders. The election of Kazimierz Łukomski as vice president of PAC and chairman of the PAC Polish Affairs Commission became the most significant symbol of the change in mutual relations between the Old Polonia and the "Nowa Emigracja." According to D. Pienkos, by 1978, eleven of the twenty-nine presidents of the PAC state divisions were from the post–World War II emigration. In her excellent study on the political action in Polonia on behalf of Poland, M. P. Erdmans also emphasizes that:

> Throughout the 1980s the PAC continued to express support for Solidarity and concern for the restrictions of freedom in Poland. PAC's work for Poland was done almost exclusively by members of the post–World War II emigration. The committees on Polish affairs were dominated by post–World War II, or second-cohort, Poles, the memoranda and statements were written by them, and PAC's political stance on U.S.-Poland relations was set by them.[61]

It seems that the result of this cooperation was that, in the eyes of the Polish newcomers to the United States in the 1970s, the sharp differences that divided Polonia after the war began to wane. From this period on they identified all who came to America earlier than the 1960s as "Stara Polonia."

Events in Poland in the 1980s—the birth of the Solidarity movement and the subsequent imposition of martial law with the suppression of the legal opposition—directly influenced emigration from Poland. In the first period after the creation of Solidarity, Polish passport laws were drastically relaxed. Although they were tightened again in the following years, the exodus from the country continued; as it was commonly said, persons were "choosing freedom" or "staying in the West." Some European governments considered increased immigration of Poles to be an economic exodus and tried to exert pressure on the refugees to return home. According to Marrus:

> During 1981 the flow of emigrants reached record levels, even before the imposition of martial law in December of that year. Four times as many Poles asked for refugee status in Austria in the first seven months of 1981 as in the whole of 1979. According to one UNHCR [United Nations High Commission for Refugees] official, as many as 500,000 Poles may have been outside their country as the crisis became evident: many sought to remain in the West, and 200,000 were still unsettled in Western Europe a year later. Although recognizing the refugee status of a minority among the Poles, international opinion has tended to consider them economic immigrants: European governments often urged the Poles to return home as soon as the crisis eased. But there is little doubt about the pressure these new arrivals brought to bear on the facilities in the various countries of reception and the UNHCR.[62]

Poles emigrated through different channels, usually involving prolonged sojourns in the European refugee camps. This phenomenon grew to such an extent that it came to be considered a social problem—both for the Polish government, which talked about "treason" and "escapes," and for the Catholic Church in Poland, which disapproved of young educated persons' leaving the country for good. Leaders of Solidarity active in the underground structures had divided opinions. Some openly condemned emigration as an exodus of the most talented and energetic activists; but some expressed more understanding and respect for the individual choices made under the pressure and persecution of the communist government.[63]

Although the precise numbers of these refugees and immigrants are hard to establish, it is estimated that between 1980 and 1987 about 600,000 Poles decided to emigrate for various reasons.[64] The INS reported that between 1981 and 1988, 61,800 Poles entered the United States permanently, including 26,144 immigrants admitted under the Refugee Act.[65] Numbers of return migrants, illegal immigrants, and those who stayed in connection with the granting of permanent-resident status to Polish refugees on the temporary Extended Voluntary Departure basis in December 1987 (termed "Reagan's visa") still need to be sorted out.

About two thousand Solidarity activists who were interned during the martial law were offered one-way passports out of Poland by the communist authorities in the first half of the 1980s. These exiles belonged to the most active and involved group of opposition leaders, and the U.S. government recognized their asylum requests without delay.

Adaptation to life in America for this particular group of Polish exiles became a difficult and trying experience. The complexities of the assimilation process overstep the boundaries of this article. It has to be said, however, that as the DP wave inspired American Polonia to greater involvement in Polish political affairs and support for Poland's interests in the international arena, the Solidarity exiles attempted to focus Polish-American as well as American attention on Polish matters. It turned out to be an arduous task, since many activists quickly found themselves in conflict with Polish Americans. As S. A. Blejwas reports, they regarded the oldest representatives of the economic immigration and their second generation as being too assimilated and could hardly find any common ground with them. As their postwar counterparts before them, the Solidarity refugees condemned the Americanization of the earlier immigrants and their detachment from political matters. It is ironic but ex-DPs did not become their instant allies, either. Mutual accusations and distrust about the level and methods of political activity, as well as competition for leadership, quickly disillusioned both groups about each other.[66]

H. Znaniecka Lopata also noted that "recent arrivals from Poland to Polonia form their own companionate circles." The older Polonia often considers them ignorant of American culture and democratic ways and unwilling to rely on the earlier immigrants' experience and leadership. The interviews conducted by both authors in some large Polish-American communities revealed:

The new arrivals feel comfortable only with each other, having obtained most of the help from Poles in the same situation and not from the established Polonia. They tell each other horror stories about life in central parts of Polonia. One respondent in New York called Chicago's Polonia "brutal." Those members of the third cohort who are able to do so, stay away from the main centers, living relatively dispersed, and returning only for church celebrations, foods, or services.[67]

Probably the most representative political organization formed by the Solidarity immigrants became POMOST Socio-Political Movement, established in January 1982 on the basis of the earlier quarterly *Pomost*. In its official informational materials POMOST formulated its goals as follows:

a. To give complete support to the government of the United States in its effort to win and maintain a just and durable peace, and to promote democratic principles throughout the world. b. To actively participate in the political life in the United States and to develop and forge close and direct contacts with democratic movements in other countries, especially in Poland and Eastern Europe. c. To perpetuate and to enrich the democratic ideals as reflected in the moral renewal of the Polish Solidarity Movement. d. To develop and coordinate work with other groups in the United States in order to promote principles of freedom, liberty and justice for all. e. To attract all men and women of good will who share concern for Human Rights in Poland, with the belief that such concern assists the pursuit and development of Human Rights generally, and peace throughout the world.[68]

About the current leadership within American Polonia POMOST wrote:

[It] lost its ideology. [It] does not understand Polish matters. [It] functions for financial and personal profit. [It] is unable to unite Polonia. [It] is infiltrated by the regime [that is the communist regime in Poland]. . . . Old Polonia can take care of American matters. The movement [PO-MOST] will take care of the Polish matters only.[69]

This kind of attitude evoked a negative response from Polonia circles and mainly from the PAC leadership, which aspired to represent the Polish-American community to the American public as well as to the American government.[70]

Mary P. Erdmans studied in detail Polonia's political action on behalf of Poland in the 1980s. According to her, different groups in Polonia had different perceptions of which actions would best help Poland. The types of political action undertaken between 1978 and 1990 included various strategies: symbolic and financial support for the opposition, humanitarian aid, protest activities against the communist regime, lobbying efforts to influence U.S. foreign policy, direct involvement in Poland's elections, as well as economic support for the free market. Erdmans distinguishes three main categories of migrants in the new Polish cohort: quota immigrants, nonimmigrants, and refugees. The migrants' status influenced the types of political action in which they were engaged. POMOST activists, who represented mostly Solidarity refugees, supported the Polish opposition movement both through financial aid and vigorous protest activity and through efforts to influence American foreign policy.[71]

Other political organizations designed to help the opposition in Poland emerged in 1984. Erdmans distinguishes two in particular that, together with POMOST, became most active: Freedom for Poland and the Brotherhood of Dispersed Solidarity Members. Although the newest immigrants and the established Polonia had different ways of approaching forms of help and protest, Erdmans notices some cooperation in the development of political action within Polonia. The activities of PAC and some other organizations set up by the World War II immigrants certainly played an important role, especially in supplying financial and humanitarian help and in lobbying the State Department and the White House. The political revitalization of Polonia in the 1980s affected in one way or another all ranks of the Polish-American community in the United States.[72]

Not all of the Solidarity exiles plunged into political work immediately after coming to the United States. Many experienced the usual hardships of immigrant existence in isolation from the political activities of the more active organizations. It is hard to provide much data about their daily lives and struggles to adjust to the new conditions. Journalistic accounts, social work reports, and scarce sociological studies do not furnish much information on this topic.[73] One could mention here, however, a short documentary (*After Solidarity*, directed by Gaylon Ross, with consultant Polonia historian Thaddeus Radzilowski), which included interviews with a few families of the Solidarity exiles in America. Given the lack of scholarly studies—and the abundance of possibilities for exploration, including oral history—historian M. B. Biskupski's appeal to concentrate scholarly efforts on this particular group of immigrants sounds both forceful and convincing.[74]

The large numbers of Polish immigrants coming to the United States in the 1980s clearly indicate that Solidarity activists and leaders exiled from Poland by the communist government constitute only a portion of the post-Solidarity immigration to America. Numerous artists, actors, writers, professionals, scholars, and intellectuals also left Poland at that time, arriving in the United States through different channels. Many of them have achieved success in American academia, business, theaters, or publishing. Although it would be difficult to call each and every immigrant a strictly political refugee, many decisions to "choose freedom" might have been dictated as much by political reasons as by the desire to gain intellectual freedom and improve economic conditions.[75]

The pressure of everyday life in Poland produced a substantial wave of economic immigrants, both temporary and permanent. We know next to nothing about their life in America. Many journalistic accounts that appeared in the Polish press in Poland had a misleading character because of censorship and the demands of propaganda. Systematic studies are scant and rare. One of the best attempts to explore this subject is historian Jarosław Rokicki's article on the economic emigrants in the Polish communities of Chicago. In 1986, their number in Chicago was estimated to fluctuate between 15,000 and 40,000. In Polish slang, they were commonly called *turyści* or *wakacjusze* (tourists or vacationers), since they came on tourist visas and extended their stay, working illegally in order to save money that would allow them a better life in Poland. Many of them eventually returned to Poland, some commuted several times as the need arose; many decided to stay permanently in the United States and legalized their status here. According to Rokicki, these immigrants, while in the United States, led an existence very similar to their turn-of-the-century counterparts'—remaining confined within the Polish communities and spending almost all their time working, sometimes up to several shifts a day. Their contact with the larger American society was limited, knowledge of English very narrow, and relationships with the rest of Polonia restricted to mostly economic connections.[76]

In her account of the wakacjusze, H. Znaniecka Lopata relies on Rokicki's findings, a popular novel *Wakacjuszka* by Mierzyńska, and personal interviews with members of Chicago's Polonia. She emphasizes a specific subculture of that group of immigrants. Their illegal status and their lack of English-language skills and of the experience required for many jobs make them prone to fraud and exploitation by job agencies, employers, dishonest lawyers, home owners, and so on. Many wakacjusze live in poor conditions, eat badly, and do not participate in any activities for entertainment, making the saving of money their main goal. Social arrangements—which include so-called Chicago marriages—aim at decreasing household expenses and fulfilling needs for companionship away from home. Wakacjusze tend to remain within their own circles, and relationships with the established Polonia can become even hostile. According to Znaniecka Lopata, "having to work hard to increase their social status and that of the community, many Polish Americans resent the ubiquitous presence of 'the Polish cleaning women.' " On the other hand, the author was often told during her interviews that "it is the 'Old Polonia' that cheats the new cohort," a circumstance that was met with great resentment and anger.[77]

The problem of intergroup relationships within the Polish-American community in contemporary Chicago became also the focus of sociologist Mary Patrice Erdmans in her article, "Immigrants and Ethnics: Conflict and Identity in Polish Chicago." The author effectively applied the dichotomy of immigrant versus ethnic to indicate the differences between the immigrant culture, embedded in the homeland, and ethnic culture, constructed over generations in the host country. The second source of conflict Erdmans identified with disparate needs and interests of the two groups. While the immigrants' need for jobs, housing, language, skills, and practical knowledge about American system and culture prevail (at least in the initial period after their arrival), ethnics concentrate on the maintenance of Polonia's cultural and organizational heritage.[78]

The history of the recent Polish immigration to the United States provides many more questions than answers. The inadequate state of the scholarship leaves space for extensive research and study by numerous students of this period. The significance of the postwar Polish immigrants to America has long been recognized; and current research agendas formulated both in the United States and in Poland put special emphasis on the problems of the recent immigrants.[79] The history of the postwar diaspora reveals much potential for the comparative study of the Polish experience in various countries of the world as well as for the comparative exploration of different ethnic groups coming to a certain country within the same immigrant wave (for example, displaced persons). Inter-ethnic relations (for example, Polish-Jewish or Polish-Ukrainian relations) seem to be a fruitful ground for research, too. It is to be hoped that this approach will have the chance to develop into larger multi-ethnic projects whose significance and potential cannot be overestimated.

The very definition of immigrants as refugees, exiles, émigrés, or political (versus economic) immigrants needs further attention. Do these terms—as adopted by the immigrants themselves for the purposes of self-definition—mean the same to them as to society at large or to the rest of the same ethnic group? When does the change from "refugees" or "émigrés" to just "immigrants" take place? Is it when a new immigrant group arrives and applies its own classification to the old immigrants? What significance lies in the formulation of such terms as "Nowa Emigracja," "Stara Polonia," or "turyści," from the perspective of intergroup dynamics?

Similarly, our understanding of the immigrant wave as such can be further elaborated, for example, through the determination of the individual's self-identification with one or more specific waves. Many DPs with working-class backgrounds have fitted in better with Old Polonia than with the highly political elements within the intelligentsia of the DP wave. War veterans formed their own community, although, from a legal standpoint, they were all a part of the immigration coming under the DP act. How does belonging to a specific "wave" influence the assimilation process of individual immigrants? There are many examples of persons who suffered discrimination because they were labeled by previous immigrants as dehumanized and criminal *"wysiedleńcy,"* or as "communists" when coming from the country under communist government.

The Polish immigrant waves as identified in this essay each had their particular characteristics, therefore specific questions about their history need to be addressed. The early Polish refugees of World War II (many of whom still can be reached for oral history projects) left us mixed sources. The activities of their most successful institutions—for example KNAPP, PIASA, PAHA, and the Piłsudski Institute—are relatively well documented. However, the story of the literary and other cultural circles as well as self-help organizations is less known. Although biographies of some famous representatives of this wave do exist, we need to answer the question To what extent were these refugees just a group of exceptional individuals and to what extent did they form a specific community? How much did they have in common? How did they fit into the larger Polonia and American society? How did relationships between them and the older Polonia take shape? Coming from conditions of war in Europe, they obviously needed help. Was adequate care and aid provided by the older Polish-American organizations? What was the reality of their everyday existence in the environs of New York or Chicago?

More questions can be posed in connection with the next immigrant wave, consisting of Polish DPs and including the war veterans. Polish displaced persons influenced ethnic consciousness of Polonia in America in many significant ways. Probably the most important was the increased politicization of the entire group resulting from the DPs' intense involvement in the political parties in exile and their ardently hostile attitude toward the communist government in Poland. The political situation in Poland as well as the international circumstances that conditioned it became the focus brought to the constant attention of the entire Polish-American community. This new mass of immigrants also exerted an impact on Polish organizational life in the United States through the creation of new, and the reinforcement of old, Polish-American organizations. The presence of Polish DPs in the United States became a reminder of the existence of the broader Polish diaspora in the world, and consequently contacts with Polonias in other countries increased. Last but not least, the new arrivals visibly influenced the development of Polish cultural and artistic life in America and Polish participation in American arts and sciences.

Many aspects of which we know little include life and organizations of Poles in European DP camps; Polonia's lobbying effort to change the immigration law; various resettlement programs (for example, group resettlement, special projects for Polish orphans, and resettlement in specific geographical regions); adjustment—success or failure—of displaced Poles in America; DPs' influence on Polish-American ethnic life; participation in older associations and fraternals and separate DP organizations. Many questions about older Polonia also await examination: for example, the role of ethnic organizations and parishes in facilitating the DPs' adjustment, Old Polonia's involvement in the resettlement process on the grassroots level, competition between major Polonia resettlement organizations, the struggle for the leadership of Polonia between newcomers and older Polish Americans, and many other problems.[80]

It also seems that the DP wave is most suitable for comparative studies in the direction suggested above. Study of the similarity or contrast with experiences of Poles resettled in other countries or of displaced persons from other ethnic groups who also arrived in America under the Displaced Persons Act could suggest valuable conclusions. Polish-Jewish relations in America cannot be forgotten in this context. Another aspect that needs exploration is the assimilationist impact of the American society as well as the broadly defined culture of the 1950s. Living apart from the Polish-American communities, the DPs were exposed to and participated in specific social processes taking place within American society as a whole. Identification of such experience and influence could shed more light on the total immigrant experience of the Polish displaced persons in the United States at that time.

Immigration during the late 1950s and the 1960s yields even less easily to historical exploration. Thus far, we can see it more in terms of the scarce testimonies offered by individuals than as a group experience of the larger community. Can a broad picture of this wave of immigration be constructed at all? Will it always remain only a part of the personal experience of individuals, many of whom received or will receive extra attention because of their exceptional status as artists, writers, and other creative individuals? The story of the Polish Jews who arrived to America from Poland after 1968 is also long overdue. How many of them joined the Polish-American or Jewish-American communities? What was the influence of these newcomers on relations between the two? The Polish American Congress initiated dialogue with some Jewish organizations in the 1970s and 1980s.[81] Did the presence of the 1968 immigrants play a role in the entrance of both sides into this cooperation?

The problem of economic versus political motivation for immigration pertains directly to those who came to the United States in the 1970s. We do not know much about their specific experiences of everyday life and even less about their relationships with other immigrant waves. How different was the community of the *wakacjusze* from the older Polonia population? How did they participate in the life of that community? Did their presence within the urban ethnic enclaves in any way transform traditional Polish-American neighborhoods? Did they aspire to create their own parishes, schools, press, or other institutions? How large is the phenomenon of return or multiple migration? Each of the previous postwar waves increased in a specific way the politicization of American Polonia. Did these newcomers exert any influence of that type? How did they fit into the ethnic revival? How did they respond to the efforts to change the unfavorable Polish image in American society at that time?

Many of the above questions can be asked also about the Polish immigrants of the 1980s. This wave may need to be divided into particular groups, such as Solidarity activists expelled by the Polish government, political and intellectual refugees, and economic immigrants. How did they influence transformations within the Old Polonia communities? What new communities (organizations, press, culture, schools, and so forth) did they form? The relation of these immigrants to the previous immigration waves remains one of the major problems to be studied. The political involvement of a large part of the post-Solidarity newcomers competed with and challenged the political programs of Polish Americans, especially those from the DP generation. How did this struggle for leadership affect the ethnic consciousness of American Polonia? How did it affect relationships on the grassroots level, for instance, within a single parish or organization? This wave of immigration was characterized by enormous social mobility and success, but at the same time it provided evidence for the existence of profound social problems, such as crime, homelessness, prostitution, oppression, and violence. Some of these problems were addressed in rare journalistic accounts, but they all await scholarly treatment and analysis.

The study of the latest trends in Polish immigration to the United States is probably the most difficult. The completely changed situation in Poland reduces chances for a large political immigration, and the stable relation of the dollar to the zloty makes economic migration much less profitable than in the past. It is hard to predict what shape this immigration will take in the future in terms of numbers as well as overall social character. It is certain, however, that recent changes in Poland did affect those who were already here in many concrete ways. The tourist movement on both sides increased, the political activity of some groups waned, and many economic migrants ready to go back suddenly discovered that their hard-earned American money would not secure them a worry-free future in Poland anymore. All these transformations need careful examination.

In addition to focusing on the history of each specific immigrant wave as a whole, one can think of a multitude of other problems that would cut across chronological frameworks. Gender and family relations among the postwar Polish immigrants would be an important area of study. The community-building processes and the quest for leadership within these communities deserve a closer look from social scientists. The role of religion, parish organizations, or the influential activity of the priests from the Society of Christ form a whole new set of questions that need to be addressed.

The transformation of organizational life, which is so visible within Polonia (and more specifically the decline of the fraternals and the increase in cultural and professional association membership), may need to be examined in the broader context of social mobility, as well as the assimilation and acculturation processes. The immigrant press remains one of the most important sources for information on the transformations within ethnic communities. As in the past, it can be used effectively to explore complex relations and inter-group dynamics. The political involvement of the postwar immigrant waves and changes in the political attitudes and forms of activity continue to be among the most crucial aspects that tie together different facets of the recent Polish immigrant experience in America. Finally, both Polish contributions to the cultural, intellectual, and professional life of American society and the acute social problems of American Polonia need to be addressed in a systematic way.

The study of the Polish immigrant experience in America after World

War II is promising and rich in intellectual rewards. Above all, it will contribute to our knowledge of the times and persons who have been and are shaping the reality of contemporary Polish America that we and our children call home.

8

Post–World War II Polish

Historiography on Emigration

Andrzej Brożek

IT IS ESTIMATED THAT POLISH TERRITORIES REMAINING UNDER Russian, Austrian, and Prussian partition and inhabited by more than 27 million persons produced a total emigration of about 5 million (Poles as well as Jews, Ukrainians, Germans, Lithuanians, Byelorussians) before 1914. Of the figure, net emigration (excluding re-migration) reached approximately 3.5 million persons. World War I forced some additional mass migration; according to some estimates the emigration of 1914–1918 corresponds to that of 1870–1913. During the interwar period more than 2.1 million persons emigrated from the Republic of Poland producing a net emigration of approximately 950,000 persons. The six-year period of 1939–1945 was characterized by a significant geographical scattering of Poles, unknown in other periods of the nation's history. It is estimated that, while even discounting shifts of population within the occupied territory, migrations and deportations (both to the West and to the East) covered 5 million persons, such that, during World War II, every seventh resident of prewar Poland (as defined by its 1938 borders), or every sixth resident of Polish nationality, found himself or herself outside the country. The postwar period accordingly was marked by a recovery of Poles from the territories annexed by the USSR or deported there, their repatriation from the western countries, and the simultaneous displacement of German population. These movements were completed about 1950.[1]

The major emigration movements occurring throughout the period of 1950–1990 were those directed toward the Federal Republic of Germany.[2] They had been initiated on the *family reunion* basis but soon included a growing number of persons that were of Polish origin, or those with a fluctuating and unsettled national consciousness or identity. Throughout the period 1955–1980, nearly 600,000 persons moved to Germany; in the 1980s the number reached about 1 million (that is, emigration from Poland during the last decade exceeded that of the twenty-year-long interwar period). As this was basically a one-way movement, the figures may be considered net values. However, if we consider that, by the end of the 1950s, 300,000 persons moved to Poland from the former USSR, it appears that the net loss for the so-called Polish People's Republic through emigration reaches 1.3 million persons.

A look at Polish population abroad should not ignore the centers of Polish and Polish-origin population resident for centuries in the Polish borderlands now consisting of the neighboring countries of Lithuania, Byelorussia, Ukraine, the Czech Republic, or Slovakia, as well as persons previously inhabiting territories controlled by the former USSR and at different times subjected to deportation inside the Russian Empire or Soviet Union. This dispersion, together with more recent migrations as well as some geopolitical changes occurring throughout the last 130 years, resulted in centers of Polish and Polish-ancestry population outside present-day Poland; in descending order (by size of Polish population): the United States, Germany, Brazil, Byelorussia, Lithuania, Ukraine, Canada, France, Great Britain, Australia, and the Czech Republic. Prior to its dissolution, the former USSR had constituted the second-largest such center.

The Polish social sciences manifested some interest in emigration as early as the nineteenth century. Before World War I numerous contributions were published to analyze the emigration to the Americas (basically to the United States) and to Germany; those were the two major destinations of the migration movements. Emigration was viewed mainly in terms of its current effect on the country, but some original historical investigations also appeared. Restoring Polish independence in 1918 brought new life to the extensive analysis of emigration, now more frequently carried out by historians. Topics they looked into usually concerned the questions of emigration to the United States. Due to the restrictive immigration policy of the United States, the emigration process from Poland to the States was considered terminated; at the same time the phenomenon of American emigration gained more historical perspective. The interest in Polish population in Germany focused on the Polish minority that stayed behind the new Polish-German border, rather than centers that actually originated from emigration—the more so because the latter either re-emigrated farther away (mainly from the Ruhr Basin to France) or returned to Poland. At the same time emigration to other European and overseas countries was increasing. New investigations featured some tendencies that correspond to those before 1914, but historians still tended to devote less effort to European emigration, which remained the domain of other social science disciplines.

Research on pre-1939 themes was hampered by the war as well as by the political situation Poland had to face after 1945. The early postwar years left no place for emigration in Polish historiography. There are two reasons for this. First, historiography at that time reflected the struggle of Marxism against other approaches. A number of scholars representing research schools other than the Marxist either had to accept the Marxist approach or were forced to leave the universities. The second reason, even more important, is that wartime and postwar Polish emigrants who did not accept the communist changes in Poland and appeared hostile toward the regime were not considered worthy of any scientific investigations. Such a situation remained till the late 1950s.[3]

Some temporary liberalization of political relations in Poland after 1956 and some consequent contacts with the West allowed Polish historians to undertake some studies on certain aspects of emigration. Several university centers began to specialize in emigration studies, including the Jagiellonian University (Cracow), Adam Mickiewicz University (Poznań), the Catholic University of Lublin, Maria Curie-Skłodowska University (Lublin), and others. The social scientists of these universities were not the only scholars to manifest some interest in questions concerning the Polish ethnic group, Polonia. Some early contributions presenting project results also were published.[4] In 1960 a yearly *Problemy Polonii Zagranicznej* (Problems of foreign Polonia) was established in Warsaw. After nine issues it appeared as a semi-annual and later as a quarterly under the title *Przegląd Polonijny* (Polonia review); the editorial office was located at the Jagiellonian University in Cracow. *Przegląd Zachodni* (Western review), a publication of the Western Institute in Poznań, devoted one out of six issues published throughout the year to the question of emigration. *Studia Polonijne* (Polonia studies) was published by the Catholic University of Lublin and *Rocznik Polonijny* (Polonia annual) by Maria Curie-Skłodowska University in Lublin. The question of emigration history also started to appear in other periodicals. Reports on the developing studies were published in the form of volumes and monographs.

It should be clear that the present review has been devoted only to the most important titles; these obviously were supplemented by numerous papers, theses, and contributions recorded in the bibliographical compendia cited below. Initially the topic was dominated by the question of European continental emigration, which also loomed large in postwar Polish studies. However, more and more attention was devoted to American topics, principally concerning emigration to the United States.

The problem of Polish emigration in France was discussed relatively early. The first of these studies is the book by Halina Janowska.[5] One also should note two important titles devoted to two significant aspects of life of the Polish population in France: pastoral care and the press.[6] Both left the Marxist methodology far behind and their interdisciplinary approach marks a pioneering effort in historiography. Rev. Roman Dzwonkowski, the author of the first title, is a leader among social scientists at the Catholic University of Lublin studying the Polish ethnic group. He also was a forerunner in studying the history of Poles in the former USSR, publishing under a pen name in *Kultura* in Paris. His book successfully unites historical methodology with that developed by pastoral theology. Andrzej Paczkowski, the author of the second title, is one of the top figures among Polish historians and his historical skills merge well with that of the press expert. It was for him to present the model for studies on the Polish ethnic press in all countries of Polish settlement abroad. The last title worth citing in this series is a nearly 400-page book by Wiesław Śladkowski, a historian investigating these problems and presenting his work in numerous theses and contributions.[7] It appears as the state-of-the-art report on Polish emigration in France, meeting all requirements of contemporary historiographical methods.

Two groups of Poles living in Germany were analyzed: the population inhabiting the western outskirts of the Polish ethnic territory that had remained under German rule until 1945 (when this area was reincorporated into Poland) and those who emigrated into purely German provinces. The studies of the first population were initiated by Bogusław Drewniak, the author of a book on the migrations of Polish seasonal agricultural workers to Western Pomerania. The other side of the issue, that is, departure of workers from this region, also was studied.[8] A corresponding topic has been analyzed by Kazimierz Wajda for neighboring Eastern Pomerania.[9]

Somewhat earlier I had undertaken studies on migration, focusing on the migration of Polish workers from territories under Russian and Austrian partition to Upper Silesia, remaining under Prussian (German) rule, and later some questions concerning emigration from Silesia.[10] This began my investigations on population movements as well as analyses of the history of Polish ethnic communities in different parts of the world, the first of which to be analyzed was emigration from Silesia.[11]

Meanwhile, studies on Polish emigration to Germany were becoming more extensive. In the first instance, the efforts of B. Drewniak, concerning the interwar period, were continued by Anna Poniatowska. Later both authors turned to the question of Poles in Szczecin. Eventually A. Poniatowska undertook the difficult task of analyzing the history of Poles in Berlin from 1918 through 1945.[12] On the other hand, the history of Poles settling in Berlin at the end of the nineteenth century still awaits investigation, for example, through the rich files of the Brandenburgisches Landesarchiv in Potsdam. Significant contribution to the recognition of Polish emigration in Germany before World War I comes from Krystyna Murzynowska; her book on Poles in the Ruhr Basin was published both in Polish and in German.[13] Jerzy Kozłowski likewise provided a synthetic approach toward the social and national activity of Polish immigrant communities in Germany.[14] Wojciech Wrzesiński also has studied these topics among the Poles who remained outside pre-1939 Western Poland.[15] One should note here the contribution of Henryk Chałupczak who analyzed the relations of the interwar Polish Republic and the Polish minority in Germany; the value of the study could have been greater if the author had used the records of the Politisches Archiv des Auswörtigen Amts in Bonn, where dozens of files reportedly concern this topic.[16]

As the result of World War II many Poles found themselves in the territory of occupied Germany; some had performed forced labor during the war, some had been imprisoned in concentration camps, and some had been otherwise displaced. This element of the national history has not been analyzed in a satisfactory manner yet. The only exception is the question of religious ministry provided for these exiles.[17] For political reasons the research on the latest phase of the life of Poles in Germany was not easy. The more so we should appreciate the studies of Urszula Kaczmarek who managed to hide her true research intentions from the surveillance of the former East German communist regime (as well as of like regimes in other countries of East-Central Europe).[18] The general outlook on Polish movements in Germany from 1922 through 1982 was provided in the book by A. Poniatowska, Stefan Liman, and Iwona Krężałek; unfortunately, uneven scholarship characterizes this work.[19]

The interest of researchers also focused on some minor Polish communities in Western Europe. Irena Kościelecka wrote a book on Poles in Denmark. A Polish-Austrian symposium was held in Cracow on the questions of Poles in Austria.[20] The influence of Polish political emigration on some Polish communities has been analyzed; for instance, the actions of Agaton Giller, one of the leaders of the January 1863 uprising in Poland, who, while living in exile in Western Europe, intended to create some organizational framework for the Polish movement, both in Europe and in the United States. An analysis of these issues is found in the book by Halina Florkowska-Francić. The policy of the Polish government-in-exile toward Polish communities in Western Europe during World War II has also been investigated.[21]

Polish emigration in Great Britain has not been a topic frequently recognized by Polish historiography; we can mention here only the study by Tadeusz Radzik on Polish schools.[22] The studies on Polish communities in Europe found their recapitulation in a 750-page volume edited by Barbara Szydłowska-Ceglowa, for many years head of the Department of Studies on Polonia, at the Polish Academy of Sciences in Poznań. After martial law was imposed in Poland, she presented a letter of resignation, which was eagerly accepted by academy authorities at that time. In the case of those countries to which systematic research has been devoted throughout recent decades, we have been provided with a complete image of the development of Polish communities abroad and those of Polish origin.[23]

Before 1990, not all investigations on the communities in question could be revealed. Political changes that started in Poland in 1989 (as in the former communist countries) normalized political, social, and other conditions and brought full freedom of research into the academic field. In particular, this change concerned investigation of the history of Poles in Russia and the former USSR, topics that had been studied earlier but only to a limited degree. It became possible to publish Zygmunt Łukawski's book on Polish communities in Russia before World War I.[24] However, the same series was not ready to bring out Elżbieta Trela's contribution on Polish children in the Soviet Union during World War II: after some time the author succeeded in finding another, more courageous publisher.[25]

Intentions to perform such projects were labeled as "interfering in domestic affairs of the neighbor countries" (this was the case, for instance, during the meeting of the Committee for Polonia Studies at the Polish Academy of Sciences in Warsaw, 1983). On May 18, 1984, a symposium was held at the Jagiellonian University of Cracow to analyze the Polish peasant communities in Socialist countries. The valuable proceedings could have been published as an interesting volume of *Przegląd Polonijny,* an issue focused exclusively on this topic. Such a suggestion came to naught and the contributions were scattered in different numbers of the periodical. One of my own articles, "The Closest Polonia," which was not actually intended as a scientific study, was confiscated by the state censors, leaving only two traces: one a short note about confiscation in *Tygodnik Powszechny,* the other the published article itself in the underground periodical *Vacat.*[26]

The existence of such research was proved, for example, because the study by Mikołaj Iwanow from Wrocław University (in the framework of a project I had been leading) appeared in 1990 in a symbolic number of copies actually not intended for distribution: M. Iwanow could present the full version of his research—more than 400 pages in length (as well as a more popular version of about 170 pages)—only in 1991.[27] Studies by Piotr Żaroń, on Poles in the Soviet Union during World War II, were advanced well enough to appear as a book as early as 1990.[28] At that time the Polonia Research Institute at the Jagiellonian University was headed by a person who had borne political responsibility for such studies (and Polish science as a whole) in the 1980s and was also a former member of the Political Bureau and secretary of the Central Committee of the Polish United Workers' Party.[29] In early December 1990, following some quick preparations, a conference on Polish communities in the USSR was organized there. The proceedings appeared as a volume, obviously including some valuable material as well as contributions that brought to mind some ambiguous associations.[30]

Research on Polish ethnic population and population of Polish national origin in the United States developed so as to bring out several publications in the early 1970s. The first to appear were the contributions by Hieronim Kubiak and Józef Miąso; twelve years later, the book by Kubiak on the Polish National Catholic Church was published in English.[31] The historical aspects of Kubiak's sociological study (especially in the original Polish version) meet significant reproach. Some incorrect historical information contained therein, incorrect bibliographical data and so on, fortunately are eliminated in the English version. The contribution by Józef Miąso on Polonia education—published in Poland and, without alteration, by the Kosciuszko Foundation in the United States— appears based on primary sources, yet some basic sources have not been considered by this primitive publication.[32]

Two years later I published a book based on my own studies on the origins of Polish settlements with a special focus on the earliest Polish settlements in Texas; it was in fact a set of reports from these settlements, supplemented with an extensive introduction. A year later Florian Stasik presented his book on Polish political emigration between the November uprising of 1830–1831 and the January uprising of 1863–1864. At the same time Bogdan Grzeloński published a book focusing on the end of the eighteenth century (the author also cooperated with Izabella Rusinowa on these issues).[33]

Several monographs were devoted to different aspects of life of the Polish ethnic group. Historians managed to fill a significant and long-standing gap in the historiography on the everyday life of Polish immigrants in the United States, their work and living conditions, that is to say, the group's "history from the bottom." These problems were dealt with in the fundamental and competent work by Adam Walaszek, which embraced the modern methodology of historical studies. Similar questions are discussed in the book by Danuta Piątkowska-Koźlik, analyzing the Polish Socialist Alliance in America. Another aspect discussed frequently, yet in a fragmentary manner, was cultural life. The valuable contribution by Emil Orzechowski focused on one important aspect of culture, namely the ethnic theater; his interdisciplinary work successfully merges the efforts of the theater and literature expert, as well as the historian. When discussing culture of some foreign Polish communities one also should note the book by Andrzej Kłossowski, which concerns not only the United States.[34]

Some steps were taken to research relations between the Polish group and other ethnic communities in the United States, basically from a sociological standpoint. As far as Polish-Jewish relations are concerned, we should note two publications devoted to the short, yet signal period immediately after World War I; the questions are discussed in a brief contribution by Tadeusz Radzik as well as in the publication of important source material by Andrzej Kapiszewski.[35] Attention of Polish historians has been drawn to World War I as well as to the postwar years. Fifty years after Poland regained its independence, the Jagiellonian University organized a conference, which contributed not only to classification of the problems but also to recognition of the phenomena taking place within different Polish immigrant communities during World War I.[36] What had been happening among American Poles (mainly among one of the political groups, the Committee of National Defense) was described by Mirosław Francić.[37]

Subsequent developments formed the subject of research by Adam Walaszek and Tadeusz Radzik. Walaszek focused on re-migration, revealing some of the dilemmas faced by those Poles who decided to return from America to the Old Country. Radzik showed how the approach toward

Poland in the interwar years changed, both for the majority of immigrants and for the new generation remaining in the United States. Radzik supplemented his analysis with some broader studies on the interwar period.[38] Polish ethnic organizations were dealt with largely only by sociologists, and none of the organizations was examined by Polish historians active in Poland (note that the book on Little Poland Clubs was written by a nonprofessional author).[39] This state of affairs in the Polish historical science became evident in the proceedings of the conference organized at the Jagiellonian University in October 1984.[40] The situation appears similar in the case of scholarship on Polish ethnic participation in the political life of the United States; a book by Andrzej Ławrowski is a compilation of information rather than an attempt to establish how the Polish ethnic group had been represented in American political life.[41]

Investigation of the history of Polish emigration to the United States resulted in the publication of a number of source documents. The first to mention is the publication of American letters from the years 1890–1891, which had been sequestered by tsarist censorship; the edition was prepared by Witold Kula, Nina Assorodobraj-Kula, and Marcin Kula. This monumental volume appears as another example of the role letters have played as a source in Polish social science since William I. Thomas and Florian Znaniecki. The somewhat weak English translation (owing to the insufficient competence of the translator) was also published in the United States.[42] Next in importance are the various memoirs, which had been submitted in manuscript form in response to a competition announced before World War II by the Institute of Social Economy in Warsaw. The material managed to survive the war years; however, its postwar publication, comprising two volumes, cannot be mentioned here without criticism concerning the way the editors handled the material, which mainly involved presenting misinformation in the introductions and explanatory notes. Some personal sources originating in the United States also may be found in the earlier anthology by Kazimierz Koźniewski.[43] Several anthologies, memoirs, and press records also should be noted and finally also some political documents. One title in particular might be noted here. It is a selection by Marian Marek Drozdowski and Eugeniusz Kusielewicz.[44] Apart from that, many source records concerning the history of Polish emigration in the United States are included in a four-volume edition of materials from the archives of pianist-statesman Ignacy Jan Paderewski, who, of course, was deeply involved in Polish-American issues.[45]

As far as North America is concerned, Polish research on Canadian topics proved less frequent. Only some titles from among the few produced can be cited here. The first is a monograph on Polish emigration for Canada by Anna Reczyńska; the study of Polish settlements in Ontario, by Izabella Jost, was published in Poland, yet its author did not live there. Additional titles include the edition of Canadian memoirs, which also followed the previously mentioned prewar competition by the Institute of Social Economy cited above, as well as two volumes of memoirs by Józef Samulski, a peasant immigrant from Prussian Poland to Canada.[46]

Much more scholarly effort has been devoted to the subject of emigration to South America. The first attempt to present the issue was a comprehensive volume published to commemorate the centenary of Polish settlement in Brazil. We must note, however, that the scholarship of the contributions included in this volume is uneven and often not professional and that among the contents are reprints of prewar texts. The next year brought the turning point of the work by Krzysztof Groniowski, the first scholarly approach toward this emigration in the Polish postwar historiography, followed by a contribution from Izabella Klarner. Marcin Kula also devoted one of his books to the Polish ethnic group in Brazil.[47] Meanwhile two separate teams were preparing collective publications on Polish communities in South America. The first was edited by Zbigniew Dobosiewicz. The second, edited by Marcin Kula, emerged from an extensive research project developed for many years in order to elaborate a synthetic history of the Polish ethnic group in Latin America. In the meantime, the topic was discussed by Maria Paradowska; however, her books concern the development of material culture rather than historical issues. Finally, one should note the documentary effort of Rev. Tadeusz Dworecki. The four volumes delivered comprise the activities of the convent Societas Verbi Divini, a leader in social and religious activity among the Polish ethnic group in Brazil. Not all materials included are of high scholarly value, but the publication also cannot be ignored when investigating Polish emigration to Brazil.[48]

The books discussed were, of course, supplemented with parallel publications of informational materials as required by a historian investigating the question of emigration. The basic volume is the bibliography prepared by the team headed by Andrzej Pilch and Irena Paczyńska; 6,700 entries are specified throughout 525 pages.[49] Bibliographies by Wojciech Chojnacki appear of great significance. They include the yearly issues, published regularly since 1977 (the first edition concerns the year 1976), first by the Jagiellonian University and now by the Department of National Studies (formerly Department of Studies on Foreign Polonia) of the Polish Academy of Sciences in Poznań. One also should note here two bibliographies of almanacs, prepared by Władysław and Wojciech Chojnacki.[50]

Some other informational materials also have been published. The most significant title, although compiled in California, was published in Poland, namely the bibliography by Jan Kowalik. Some other publications of this type are, for example, the directories of Polish libraries; the series was initiated with the publication of the catalogue by Kazimiera Tatarowicz concerning the holdings of the Jagiellonian Library in Cracow. Similar directories for other Polish libraries are published on the basis of an extensive project, headed by Andrzej Kłossowski; the series includes the National Library in Warsaw, the Adam Mickiewicz Museum of Literature in Warsaw, and others.[51] A number of publications present information about Polish archives with holdings pertaining to the history of Polonia (including the file catalogues of Polish diplomatic and consular offices in Germany).[52]

Thanks to these publications the groundwork was laid for several attempts at writing a synthesis of the history of Polish emigration. One pioneering volume was prepared by the Catholic University of Lublin and published in 1976 as an initial stage of research about Polish groups abroad. Apart from the investigations cited, some authors attempted to present their own comprehensive studies on certain geographical or chronological topics. In 1977, for example, I published a 300-page outline of the history of the Polish ethnic group in the United States (an English version was published in 1985). Halina Janowska attempted a comprehensive study on Polish employment-seeking emigration from 1918 through 1939; a similar contribution came from Edward Kołodziej. The team headed by Wojciech Wrzesiński undertook the task of elaborating the Atlas of Polonia; however the project thus far has presented only the statistical records compiled.[53]

Meanwhile, some initial results of research were being presented during symposia and conferences. In June 1976, a bicentennial conference was held on the role of Poles in the history and culture of the United States. Conferences devoted to the culture of Polonia communities were held in Radziejowice (April 1980) and in Warsaw (June 1984 and May 1988), to mention only some examples.[54]

The project headed by Andrzej Pilch on the historical synthesis of Polish emigration between the close of the eighteenth century and the twentieth century resulted in a fundamental work of more than 500 pages, which presented such research results as could be achieved in Poland under the conditions of the early 1980s.[55] The Polish-American synthesis project on the history and present conditions of the Polish ethnic group in the United States (including twelve Americans and nineteen Poles) was intended to follow the pattern of the expansive and well-known Uppsala project. Unfortunately, the 850-page volume features little coherence and follows different patterns and methodologies. Instead of an ambitious synthesis following the Uppsala model, the result was a volume of mere study reports. The manuscript was ready in the late 1970s (also an English translation for foreign publication was ready at that time) and represented the level of scholarship possible at that point. Due to reasons beyond the control of the authors, publication of the Polish version was put off for a period of ten years and the English version not published at all. This was quite fortunate as the work, though intended as comprehensive, appeared incoherent and many fragments were outdated when the book did appear.[56]

Some interesting historical material occasionally may be found in publications on other aspects of Polish community life, for example, the book *Język polski w świecie* (Polish language in the world). At the same time there appeared a few synthetic volumes whose intent exceeded the actual capabilities of the authors (for example, Edward Kołodziej's outline of worldwide Polonia history throughout the interwar period). Only a few publications are found in the field of biography. The most comprehensive collection of well-elaborated pieces may be found in the subsequent volumes of the monumental all-Polish biographical dictionary, *Polski słownik biograficzny:* these biographies currently are recorded in the yearly *Bibliografia . . .* by W. Chojnacki cited above. The only biographic publication is the book *Polacy w historii i kulturze krajów Europy Zachodniej;* this pioneering effort gathered authors of different experience and therefore could not be free of the disadvantages characteristic of such enterprises. One also should note a set of biographical essays on Polish Americans by Bogdan Grzeloński.[57]

As stated above, consolidation of the communist government in Poland produced, in the 1950s, practically a historiographical gap concerning research on Polish emigration. Therefore, Marxist methodology could not be reflected in a field of research that did not exist. It is a paradox that Soviet-style Marxism, so careful about the attitudes of human masses, eliminated from the scientific spectrum such great movements as emigration, which actually appears as the function of social pauperization. When circumstances allowed, some investigations of the history of emigration, which produced the first contributions (J. Miąso, A. Ławrowski), clearly were marked by the Marxist pattern, ignoring many important sources and subordinating themselves to an accepted methodological framework.

It was as late as the mid-1950s when Polish historiography became attracted to the French *Annales* School. Young Polish historians, fascinated with the methodological guidelines of the school, tried to employ them for their own studies on emigration. The *Annales* School since has dominated the historiography of Polish emigration.[58]

Polish historians studying Polish emigration after World War II seized upon scholarly opportunities as soon as the situation allowed (restricted, however, by some taboo issues such as Polish communities in neighboring countries, Polish political exiles after World War II in the West, and so on). Polish historians first investigated European emigration; however, American emigration frequently attracted the scholars' attention. In this way, by the end of the 1980s, Polish historiography reached a state of equilibrium in recognizing the position of Polish and Polish-ancestry communities in Europe, on one hand, and in the Americas (principally the United States), on the other. Studies of Polish ethnic communities in the former USSR were left far behind, which does not necessarily mean that no other areas were also somehow neglected.

Polish historiography is now looking forward to some cognitive tasks on both topics: territories behind the eastern border of the Republic of Poland as well as those in the West—in Europe, America, and Australia.[59] Considering the desperate financial situation of scholarly research in Poland, we may fear that Polish historiography may soon lose some of its vigor in recognizing phenomena of emigration and settlements abroad.

Notes

Preface

1. *Brak* may be translated as "absence" or "deficiency." It is a word that recurred during the commodity scarcities in Poland during the 1980s.

2. It should be noted that any net royalties from this volume will be directed to the Polish American Historical Association, a 501(c)(3) Illinois nonprofit corporation.

1. Polish Americans, History Writing, and the Organization of Memory

Among the bibliographical sources that facilitated the writing of this essay, I found Irene Paczyński and Andrzej Pilch, ed., *Materiały do bibliografjii dziejów emigracji oraz skupisk polonijnych w ameryce północnej i południowej w XIX i XX wieku* (Warsaw and Cracow: Państwowe Wydawnictwo Naukowe, 1979) especially helpful. I would like to thank Stanislaus Blejwas, Bill Falkowski, Donna Gabaccia, Joseph Parot, and especially Nora Faires for their keen comments, and also research assistant David Smith for help in gathering sources. Any errors are my responsibility. The epigraph is taken from Alexander Syski, "The Nestor of Polish Historians in America: Reverend Waclaw Kruszka," *Polish-American Studies* 1 (1944): 67 (hereafter cited as *PAS*).

1. *Echo z Polski* cited in Wacław Kruszka, *A History of the Poles in America to 1908, Part 1*, ed. James S. Pula et al., trans. Krystyna Jankowski (1905–1908; Washington, D.C.: Catholic University Press of America, 1993), 258. Early attempts at writing a Polish-American history are described in Kruszka's multivolume work (ibid., 4–6).

2. Syski, "The Nestor of Polish Historians in America," 62; Kruszka, *History of the Poles in America, Part 1*, 6 (human being), 7, 20 (Fredro), 21 (young Pole).

3. This phrase comes from the title of a recent history of America's Polish seminary, Frank Renkiewicz, *For God, Country, and Polonia: One Hundred Years of the Orchard Lake Schools* (Orchard Lake, Mich.: Center for Polish Studies and Culture, Orchard Lake Schools, 1985).

4. For a history of partitioned Poland, see Piotr S. Wandycz, *The Lands of Partitioned Poland, 1795–1918: A History of East Central Europe,* vol. 7, ed. Peter F. Sugar and Donald W. Treadgold (Seattle and London: University of Washington Press, 1974). The journals included *Przegląd Emigracyjny* (1892–1894) in Lwów; *Polski Przegląd Emigracyjny* (1907–1914), headquartered in Lwów and later Cracow; and, also in Cracow, the short-lived *Biuletyn Polskiego Towarzystwa Emigracyjnego* (1910). See Paczyński and Pilch, *Materiały do bibliografjii dziejów emigracji,* 81–83.

5. Leopold Caro, "Die Statistik der österreichisch-ungarischen und polnischen Auswanderung nach den Vereinigten Staaten von Nordamerika," *Zeitschrift für Volkswirtschaft, Socialpolitik, und Verwaltung* 16 (1907): 68–113; Caro, *Auswanderung und Auswanderungspolitik in Österreich* (Leipzig: Duncker und Humbold, 1909); Caro, *Emigracya i polityka emigracyjna ze szczególnym uwzględnieniem stosunków Polskich* (Poznań: Księg. Św. Wojciecha, 1914); Franciszek Bujak, *Wieś zachodnio-galicyjska u schyłku XIX w. Wieś polska* (Lwów: Druk. Ludowa, 1905), 53–111; and Bujak, "Maszkienice, wieś powiatu brzeskiego: Rozwój od r. 1900–1911," *Rozsprawy Akademii Umiejętności: Wydział Historyczno-Filozoficzny,* ser. 2, v. 58 (Cracow, 1915): 1–164; Józef Okołowicz, *Wychodźtwo i osadnictwo polskie przed wojną światową* (Warsaw: Urząd Emigr., 1920). Also see Bolesław Koskowski, *Wychodźtwo zarobkowe włościan w królestwie* (Warsaw: Sadowski, 1901). Stanisław Kłobukowski, "Dzień Polski w Chicago," *Przegląd Emigracyjny* (Lwów) 2 (1893): 223–26; and Kłobukowski, "Kolonizacya Polska w Wisconsinie i Michiganie," *Przegląd Emigracyjny* (Lwów) 2, no. 2 (1908): 6–7; 2, no. 3 (1908): 5–7.

6. See R. Dmowski, *Wychodźtwo i osadnictwo* (Lwów: Tow. Wydawn. A. Sadowski, A. Cybulski, 1900). From a pan-national perspective, when Poles abroad helped themselves, they also helped world Polonia. For an exploration of these debates and positions, see Benjamin P. Murdzek, *Emigration in Polish Social-Political Thought, 1870–1914,* East European Monographs, vol. 33 (Boulder, Colo.: East European Quarterly, 1977).

7. The journals included the Warsaw-based *Kwartalnik Instytutu do Badań Emigracji i Kolonizacji* (1926–1931), *Przegląd Emigracyjny* (1926–1927), and *Polacy Zagranica* (1930–1939); and Poznań's Roman Catholic *Annales Missiologicae* (1928–1937). See *Materiały do bibliografjii dziejów emigracji,* 81–83. For the studies see, for example, Mieczysław Szawleski, *Kwestja emigracji w polsce* (Warsaw: Pol. Tow. Emigr., 1927); Józef Chałasiński, "Parafia i szkoła parafialna wśród emigracji polskiej w ameryce: Studium dzielnicy polskiej w pół[nocnym] Chicago," *Przegląd Socjologiczny* 3, nos. 3–4 (1935): 631–711; Krystyna Duda-Dziewierz, *Wieś małopolska a emigracja amerykańska: Studium wsi babica powiatu rzesowskiego* (Warsaw and Poznań: Pol. Inst. Socjologiczny, 1938); Frank Renkiewicz, *The Poles in America, 1608–1972: A Chronology and Fact Book,* Ethnic Chronology Series, no. 9 (Dobbs Ferry, N.Y.: Oceana Publications, 1973), 23.

8. Emily Greene Balch, "Emigration from Galicia," *Charities and the Commons* 16, no. 5 (1906); Peter Roberts, *Anthracite Coal Communities: A Study of the Demography, the Social, Educational, and Moral Life of the Anthracite Regions* (1904; New York: Arno Press, 1970); Roberts, *Immigrant Races in North America* (1912; New York: Associated Press, 1970); Roberts, *The New Immigration: A Study of the Industrial and Social Life of Southeastern Europeans in America* (New York: Macmillan, 1912); Robert E. Park and Herbert A. Miller, *Old World Traits Transplanted* (New York: Harper and Brothers, 1921).

9. See W. I. Thomas and F. Znaniecki, *The Polish Peasant in Europe and America: Monograph of an Immigrant Group,* 5 vols. (Boston: Richard G. Badger, 1918–1919). See also Thomas and Znaniecki, *The Polish Peasant in Europe and America,* ed. Eli Zaretsky, abridged ed. (Urbana and Chicago: University of Illinois Press, 1984), "Edi-

tor's Introduction," 1–53; Zygmunt Dulczewski, *Florian Znaniecki: Life and Work* (Poznań: NAKOM, 1992); Herbert Blumer, *Critique of Research in the Social Sciences: An Appraisal of Thomas and Znaniecki's "The Polish Peasant in Europe and America"* (New Brunswick, N.J.: Transaction Books, 1979).

10. John Dewey, *Conditions Among the Poles in the United States: A Confidential Report* (n.p.: 1918); Robert E. Park, *The Immigrant Press and Its Control* (New York: Harper and Row, 1922); Paul Fox, *The Poles in America* (New York: George H. Doran, 1922); and Fox, *The Polish National Catholic Church* (Scranton, Pa.: n.p., 1937).

11. Woodrow Wilson, *A History of the American People* (1901; New York: Wm. H. Wise, 1931), vol. 5, 212–13, quoted in Edward R. Kantowicz, *Polish-American Politics in Chicago, 1888–1940* (Chicago and London: University of Chicago Press, 1975), 104.

12. Thereafter, textbooks reproduced what writer Frances FitzGerald has referred to as the "new orthodoxy," that "We are a nation of immigrants." See Frances Fitz-Gerald, *America Revised: History Schoolbooks in the Twentieth Century* (Boston and Toronto: Atlantic Monthly Press, Little Brown, 1979), 79–82. Also see John F. Kennedy, *A Nation of Immigrants,* revised and enlarged ed. (1957; New York: Harper and Row, 1964).

13. [Jan Słomka], *From Serfdom to Self-Government: Memoirs of a Polish Village Mayor, 1842–1927,* trans. William John Rose (London: Minerva Publishing, 1941). It might be speculated that the oral tradition also preserved stories about peasant uprisings.

14. Some of these issues are discussed in John J. Bukowczyk, "Mary the Messiah: Polish Immigrant Heresy and the Malleable Ideology of the Roman Catholic Church, 1880–1930," *Journal of American Ethnic History* 4 (Spring 1985): 5–32.

15. On the trusteeism problem, see Msgr. Peter Keenan Guilday, *Trusteeism, 1814–1821* (New York: 1928); David Gerber, "Trusteeism and the Survival of European Communal Traditions? The Case for a New Perspective: Notes Based on the Experience of Buffalo's St. Louis Church, 1829–1856," *American Catholic Studies Newsletter* 6 (Spring 1980); Patrick Carey, "Two Episcopal Views of Lay-Clerical Conflicts, 1785–1860," *Records of the American Catholic Historical Society* 87 (March–December 1976): 85–98; Carey, "The Laity's Understanding of the Trustee System, 1785–1855," *Catholic Historical Review* 64 (1977): 357–76 (hereafter cited as *CHR*); Carey, *A National Church: American Catholic Search for Identity, 1820–1829,* Working Paper Series, no. 3 (Notre Dame, Ind.: Center for the Study of American Catholicism, Fall 1977); Carey, "Trusteeism: American Catholic Search for Identity, 1785–1860," *American Catholic Studies Newsletter* 3 (Fall 1977); Timothy L. Smith, "Lay Initiative in the Religious Life of American Immigrants, 1880–1950," in *Anonymous Americans,* ed. Tamara Hareven (Englewood Cliffs, N.J.: Prentice-Hall, 1971), 214–49. On the broader issue of immigrant representation in the hierarchy, see Colman J. Barry, O.S.B., *The Catholic Church and the German Americans* (Milwaukee: Catholic University of America Press, 1953); John Meng, "Cahenslyism: The First Stage, 1883–1891," *CHR* 31 (January 1946): 389–413; Meng, "Cahenslyism: The Second Chapter, 1891–1910," *CHR* 32 (October 1946): 302–40.

16. See William J. Galush, "Faith and Fatherland: Dimensions of Polish-Ameri-

can Ethnoreligion, 1875–1975," in *Immigrants and Religion in Urban America*, ed. Randall M. Miller and Thomas D. Marzik (Philadelphia: Temple University Press, 1977), 84–102; John J. Bukowczyk, "The Immigrant 'Community' Re-examined: Political and Economic Tensions in a Brooklyn Polish Settlement, 1888–1894," *PAS* 37 (Autumn 1980): 5–16.

17. Rev. Wacław Kruszka, "Polyglot Bishops for Polyglot Dioceses," *Freeman's Journal* (July 29, 1901); Wacław Kruszka, *Historya Polska w Ameryce*, 13 vols. (Milwaukee: Wydawn. "Kur. Pol.," 1905–1908). See also the first installment of a Kruszka translation project, Kruszka, *A History of the Poles in America, Part 1*; and Kruszka, *Siedem siedmioleci czyli pół wieku zycia: Pamiętnik i przyczynek do historii polskiej w Ameryce* (Poznań and Milwaukee: Nakł. aut., 1924).

18. See Anthony J. Kuzniewski, *Faith and Fatherland: The Polish Church War in Wisconsin, 1896–1918* (Notre Dame, Ind., and London: University of Notre Dame Press, 1980).

19. See Kruszka, *A History of the Poles in America, Part 1*, 250–300; Edmund G. Olszyk, *The Polish Press in America* (Milwaukee: Marquette University Press, 1940); Alphonse S. Wolanin, *The Polish Press*, a study prepared at the Graduate Library School, University of Chicago (Chicago: University of Chicago Press, 1952); A. J. Kuzniewski, "The Polish-American Press," in *The Ethnic Press in the United States: A Historical Analysis*, ed. Sally M. Miller (New York: Greenwood Press, 1987), 275–90.

20. See Helena Chrzanowska, "Polish Book Publishing in Chicago," *PAS* 4 (1947): 37–39; Bernard Pacyniak, "An Historical Outline of the Polish Press in America," in *Poles in America: Bicentennial Essays*, ed. Frank Mocha (Stevens Point, Wis.: Worzalla Publishing, 1978), 518 (quotation); also Kruszka, *A History of the Poles in America, Part 1*, 283.

21. See Ks. Aleksander Syski, *Ks. Józef Dąbrowski: Monografia historyczna* (Orchard Lake, Mich.: Polish Seminary, 1942); Rev. Joseph Swastek, *The Formative Years of the Polish Seminary in the United States* (1959; Orchard Lake, Mich.: Center for Polish Studies and Culture, Orchard Lake Schools, 1985); Renkiewicz, *For God, Country, and Polonia*.

22. Stanisław Osada, *Sokolstwo Polskie, jego dzieje, cele i ideały w czterech odczytach* (Chicago: Wydz. Zw. Sokolów w Amer. Półn., 1900); Osada, *Liga narodowa a polacy w Ameryce* (Chicago: Nakł. aut., 1905); Osada, *Sześć odczytów o stronnictwie demokratyczno-narodowym i lidze narodowej* (Chicago: Nakł. aut., 1905); Osada, *Historia związku narodowego polskiego i rozwój ruchu narodowego w Ameryce północnej* (Chicago: Zw. Nar. Pol., 1905); Osada, *Na rok grunwaldzki: Ludowi polskiemu w Ameryce i jego wodzom pod rozwage* (Chicago: W. Dyniewicz, 1910); and Osada, *Jak się kształtowała polska dusza wychodźtwa w Ameryce* (Pittsburgh: "Sokół Pol.," 1930). Osada criticized Polonia's clericalist and socialist camps. On Osada, see Stanislaus A. Blejwas, "Stanislaw Osada: Immigrant Nationalist," *PAS* 50, no. 1 (Spring 1993): 23–50.

23. For opposing political camps, see Karol H. Wachtel, *Z.P.R.K. Dzieje zjednoczenia polskiego rzymsko-katolickiego w Ameryce* (Chicago: L. J. Winiecki, 1913). For Polonia's central ideological issue, see Victor Greene, *For God and Country: The Rise of Polish and Lithuanian Ethnic Consciousness in America, 1860–1910* (Madison: State Historical Society of Wisconsin, 1975). For the identification of Polish nationality

with Roman Catholic religion, see John J. Bukowczyk, *And My Children Did Not Know Me: A History of the Polish-Americans* (Bloomington and Indianapolis: Indiana University Press, 1987), 46–48.

24. For "ethno-religion," see Timothy Smith, "Religion and Ethnicity in America," *American Historical Review* 83 (December 1978): 1155–85. On Jewish emigration from Poland, see Raphael Mahler, "The Economic Background of Jewish Emigration from Galicia to the United States," in *YIVO Annual of Jewish Social Science,* ed. Koppel S. Pinson, vol. 7 (New York: Yiddish Scientific Institute, 1952).

25. On Polish messianism, see Peter Brock, "The Socialists of the Polish 'Great Emigration'," in *Essays in Labour History in Memory of G. D. H. Cole, 25 September 1889–14 January 1959,* ed. Asa Briggs and John Saville (New York and London: St. Martin's Press and Macmillan, 1960), 140–73; Nikolai Onufrïevich Losskii, *Three Chapters from the History of Polish Messianism,* International Philosophical Library Periodical Publication, vol. 2, no. 9 (Prague: 1936); Monica Gardner, "The Great Emigration and Polish Romanticism," in *The Cambridge History of Poland, 1697–1935,* ed. William F. Reddaway et al. (New York and London: Cambridge University Press, 1951), vol. 2, 324–35. For the Battle of Grünwald, see Osada, *Na rok grunwaldzki.*

26. See Adam Walaszek, *Reemigracja ze stanów zjednoczonych do polski po I wojnie swiatowej, 1919–1924* (Warsaw and Cracow: Państwowe Wydawnictwo Naukowe, 1983).

27. Henryk Sienkiewicz, *Portrait of America: Letters of Henry Sienkiewicz* (1876–1878), quoted in Bukowczyk, *And My Children Did Not Know Me,* 105. It is interesting that Sienkiewicz apparently believed that women—more specifically, mothers—acted as the bearers of culture.

28. For an excellent annotated bibliography treating the sociological studies on the "community studies" model, see Irwin T. Sanders and Ewa T. Morawska, *Polish-American Community Life: A Survey of Research,* Community Sociology Monograph Series, vol. 2 (n.p.: Community Sociology Training Program, Department of Sociology, Boston University and Polish Institute of Arts and Sciences in America, June 1975); Theodore F. Abel, "Sunderland: A Study of Changes in the Group Life of Poles in a New England Farming Community," in *Immigrant Farmers and Their Children,* ed. Edmund Brunner (New York: Doubleday, 1929), 213–43; Niles Carpenter and Daniel Katz, *A Study of Acculturation in the Polish Group in Buffalo, 1926–1928,* University of Buffalo Studies, vol. 7, no. 3 (June 1929), Monographs in Sociology, no. 3.

29. See Pacyniak, "An Historical Outline of the Polish Press in America," 520.

30. Clarence A. Manning, *A History of Slavic Studies in the United States* (Milwaukee, Wis.: Marquette University Press, 1957), vii (quotation), 19, 21, 26, 28, 40.

31. Ibid., 29, 31, 47–49, 52, 60. Mitana later moved to Alliance College, thwarting efforts to establish a Polish chair in Ann Arbor. On the holdings of the Hoover Institution, see Charles G. Palm and Dale Reed, *Guide to the Hoover Institution Archives* (Stanford, Calif.: Hoover Institution Press, Stanford University, 1980), esp. 5–9. For the Nationality Rooms in Pittsburgh, see E. Maxine Bruhns, *The Nationality Rooms* (Pittsburgh, Pa.: The Nationality Rooms Program, University of Pittsburgh, n.d.), 3, 32.

32. Manning, *A History of Slavic Studies,* 51–52 (quotation). See Arthur Prudden Coleman and Marion Moore Coleman, *The Polish Insurrection of 1863 in the Light of New York Editorial Opinion* (Williamsport, Pa.: Bayard Press, 1934); Arthur Prudden Coleman, *A New England City and the November Uprising: A Study of Editorial Opinion in New Haven, Connecticut, Concerning the Polish Insurrection of 1830–1831,* in *Annals of the Polish Roman Catholic Union Archive and Museum* (Chicago: PRCU of America, 1939), vol. 4; Coleman and Coleman, *Wanderers Twain, Modjeska and Sienkiewicz: Their Influence on and How They Were Influenced by the American Scene* (Cheshire, Conn.: Cherry Hill Books, 1963); Coleman and Coleman, *Wanderers Twain, Modjeska and Sienkiewicz: A View of California* (Cheshire, Conn.: Cherry Hill Books, 1964); and Marion Moore Coleman, *Fair Rosalind: The American Career of Helena Modjeska* (Cheshire, Conn.: Cherry Hill Books, 1969).

33. For a discussion of this sensitive issue, see Piotr Taras, Angela T. Pienkos, and Thaddeus Radzialowski, "Paul Wrobel's *Our Way*—Three Views," *PAS* 37, no. 1 (Spring 1980): 42–51; Charles Keil, "Class and Ethnicity in Polish-America," *Journal of Ethnic Studies* 7, no. 2 (Summer 1979): 37–45; William G. Falkowski Jr., "Polka History 101," in *History for the Public,* ed. G. David Brumberg, Margaret M. John, and William Ziesel (Ithaca, N.Y.: New York Historical Resources Center, Cornell University, and the Institute for Research in History, 1983).

34. Manning, *A History of Slavic Studies,* 50 (first quotation). The Foundation extended the work of the Polish American Scholarship Committee, organized in 1924. See Eugene Kusielewicz, "The Kosciuszko Foundation: A Half Century of Progress," in Mocha, ed., *Poles in America,* 672 (second quotation). See also [Stefan P. Mierzwa], *Dziesięciolecie Fundacji Kościuszkiego, 1926–1936: Czyn polonji amerikańskiej* (New York: Kosciuszko Foundation, 1936); Stephen P. Mizwa, "The Kosciuszko Foundation Plans," *Bulletin of the Polish Institute of Arts and Sciences in America* 2 (1943–1944): 626–29; Mizwa, *The Story of the Kosciuszko Foundation: How It Came About* (New York: Kosciuszko Foundation, 1972); Eugene Kusielewicz, "In Memoriam: Stephen Mierzwa (1892–1971)," *Polish Review* 16 (1971): 116 (hereafter cited as *PR*); Eugene Kusielewicz, ed., *A Tribute to Stephen P. Mizwa* (New York: Czas Publishing, 1972). Although based in New York, the Foundation's organizational meeting took place in the Philadelphia offices of Samuel Vauclain, president of the Baldwin Locomotive Works. Its other founders, besides Mizwa and Vauclain, included an investment counselor and banker; two American professors; an airforce colonel who had commanded the Kosciuszko Squadron, "which defended Lwów against the Bolsheviks in 1920"; and Henry Noble MacCracken, president of Vassar College and later president of the Kosciuszko Foundation for thirty years. See Kusielewicz, "The Kosciuszko Foundation," 671, 673 (quotation). Baldwin Locomotive also inspired the founding of the magazine *Poland* by the Polish legation in Washington, D.C. According to Slavicist Clarence A. Manning, "Baldwin Locomotive Works had taken a prominent part in the rehabilitation of the Polish railroads after World War I" (Manning, *A History of Slavic Studies,* 56).

35. Manning, *A History of Slavic Studies,* 50. Among the publications the Foundation supported were William John Rose's biography of Poland's Queen Jadwiga, a biography of Polish pianist-statesman Ignatz Jan Paderewski, and Mizwa's own *Great Men and Women of Poland.* See Kusielewicz, "The Kosciuszko Foundation," 677.

36. Manning, *A History of Slavic Studies,* 58. See Miecislaus Haiman, "Polish Scholarship in the United States: 1929–1947," *PAS* 4, nos. 3–4 (July–December 1947): 65–87.

37. For Polish Day, see Greene, *For God and Country,* 137. For July 1910, see Renkiewicz, *The Poles in America,* 15–16. On ethnic recognition, see John Bodnar, *Remaking America: Public Memory, Commemoration, and Patriotism in the Twentieth Century* (Princeton, N.J.: Princeton University Press, 1992).

38. *Who Is Who in Polish America,* ed. Francis Bolek (Sharon, Pa.: Sharon Herald Co., 1939), and Francis Bolek, ed., *Who's Who in Polish America,* 3d ed. (New York: Harbinger House, 1943), 48–49.

39. For an assessment of Haiman, see Robert Szymczak, "The Pioneer Days: Mieczysław Haiman and Polish American Historiography," *PAS* 50, no. 1 (Spring 1993): 7–22. See also LeRoy H. Fischer, "Mieczysław Haiman: Historian of Polish America," in Miecislaus (Mieczysław) Haiman, *Polish Past in America, 1608–1865* (1939; Chicago: Polish Museum of America, 1974), 1n. See Mieczysław Haiman, *Z przeszłości polskiej w Ameryce: Szkice historyczne* (Buffalo: Druk. "Telegramu," 1927); and Haiman, *The Fall of Poland in Contemporary American Opinion* (Chicago: PRCU of America, 1935).

40. For the Civil War, see Mieczysław Haiman, *Historia udziału polaków w amerykańskiej wojnie domowiej* (Chicago: "Dzien. Zjedn.," 1928). For pioneers on the western frontier, see Mieczysław Haiman, *Polacy wśród pionierów ameryki: Szkice historyczne* (Chicago: "Dzien. Zjedn.," 1930), and also (all subtitled *Annals of the Polish Roman Catholic Union Archive and Museum)* Miecislaus Haiman, *The Poles in the Early History of Texas* (Chicago: PRCU of America, 1936), vol. 1; Haiman, *Polish Pioneers of Virginia and Kentucky* (Chicago: PRCU of America, 1937), vol. 2; Haiman, *Polish Pioneers of California* (Chicago: PRCU of America, 1940), vol. 5; Haiman, *Polish Pioneers of Pennsylvania* (Chicago: PRCU of America, 1940), vol. 6. For the colonial period, see Miecislaus Haiman, *Poles in New York in the Seventeenth and Eighteenth Centuries* (Chicago: PRCU of America, 1938), vol. 3; and Haiman, *Polish Past in America, 1608–1865* (Chicago: PRCU of America, 1939). For the American Revolution, see Mieczysław Haiman, *Polacy w walce o niepodległość ameryki: Szkice historyczne* (Chicago: Pol. Katol. S-ka Wydawn., 1931); and Miecislaus Haiman, *Poland and the American Revolutionary War* (Chicago: PRCU of America for the Two Hundred [sic] Anniversary of the Birth of George Washington, 1932).

41. See John J. Bukowczyk, "The Transformation of Working-Class Ethnicity: Corporate Control, Americanization, and the Polish Immigrant Middle Class in Bayonne, N.J., 1915–1925," *Labor History* 25 (Winter 1984): 53–82; Bukowczyk, *And My Children Did Not Know Me,* 65–75; also Haiman, *Polish Past in America,* p. III.

42. See Stephen S. Grabowski, "P.R.C.U. Archives and Museum in Chicago," *PAS* 18, no. 1 (1961): 37–40. For an insider's discussion of the museum under Haiman's tutelage, see the memoir by his secretary, Sabina Logisz, "First Curator of the Polish Museum in America," *PAS* 18, no. 2 (1961): 87–92.

43. Manning, *A History of Slavic Studies,* 65–67, 63, 64.

44. See Michael Budny, "Józef Piłsudski Institute of America for Research in the Modern History of Poland," in Mocha, *Poles in America,* 687–708; A. K. [krypt.],

"The Józef Piłsudski Institute of America for Research in Modern History of Po-land," *PR* 4, nos. 1–2 (1959): 158–59.

45. I rely here extensively on *Polish American Historical Association, 1942–1951, Including Program of the Eighth Annual Meeting* (Orchard Lake, Mich.: Polish American Historical Association [PAHA], 1951); and Frank Mocha, "The Polish Institute of Arts and Sciences in America, Its Contributions to the Study of Polonia: The Origins of the Polish American Historical Association (PAHA)," in Mocha, ed., *Poles in America*, 709–24. Also see Paul Best, "Polish-American Scholarly Organizations," in *Pastor of the Poles: Polish American Essays Presented to Right Reverend Monsignor John P. Wodarski in Honor of the Fiftieth Anniversary of His Ordination*, ed. Stanislaus A. Blejwas and Mieczysław B. Biskupski, Polish Studies Program Monographs, no. 1 (New Britain: Central Connecticut State College, 1982), 153–65; Stanisław Strzetelski, *The Polish Institute of Arts and Sciences in America: Origin and Development* (New York: Polish Institute of Arts and Sciences in America, 1960). Also see John J. Bukow-czyk, " 'Harness for Posterity the Values of a Nation': Fifty Years of the Polish Ameri-can Historical Association and *Polish American Studies*," *PAS* 50, no. 2 (Autumn 1993): 5–100.

46. The conference papers were assembled and published in PIASA's new journal, the *Bulletin of the Polish Institute of Arts and Sciences in America*. See Mocha, "The Polish Institute of Arts and Sciences in America," 709–10, 720 n. 2.

47. Ibid., 711–12.

48. For a review of the organization's early years, see *Polish American Historical Association, 1942–1951* (I am indebted to Thaddeus Gromada for providing a photo-copy of this document); Mocha, "The Polish Institute of Arts and Sciences," 713 (first quotation), 722 n. 29, 713; *PAS* 1 (1944): iii; "Foreword," *PAS* 2, nos. 1–2 (Janu-ary–June 1945): 3 (second quotation). Symonolewicz (whose first name also appears variously as Constantin and Konstantin) co-edited *Polish American Studies* from 1944–1974. For an example of his historical works, see Constantin Symonolewicz, "Polish Travelers and Observers in the U.S.A., 1918–1939," *PAS* 2 (1945): 43–45; Konstantin Symmons-Symonolewicz, "The Polish-American Community, Half a Century After 'The Polish Peasant'," *PR* 11, no. 3 (1966): 67–73; Konstanty Symonolewicz, "Polonia amerykańska," *Kultura* 20, nos. 7–8 (1966): 105–35; Mocha, "The Polish Institute of Arts and Sciences," 713–14.

49. It is not clear whether by "cultural vacuity" he meant to suggest the condition of "anomie" or social "disorganization," as diagnosed by Thomas and Znaniecki. See Stefan Wloszczewski, "The Polish 'Sociological Group' in America," *American Slavic and East European Review* 4, nos. 8–9 (1945): 156–57 (hereafter cited as *ASEER*). Also see Horace M. Kallen, *Culture and Democracy in the United States: Studies in the Group Psychology of the American Peoples* (New York: Boni and Liveright, 1924). For a critique of Wloszczewski, see Rev. Francis Bolek, "Integration of the Polish American Group" (address delivered at the PAHA annual conference, December 29, 1949), 3.

50. *PAS* 3, nos. 3–4 (1946): inside back cover (quotations); Bukowczyk, *And My Children Did Not Know Me*, 91. For a comparative look at ethnic historical societies, see John J. Appel, *Immigrant Historical Societies in the United States, 1880–1950* (New York: Arno Press, 1980), and the forum on the topic in the *Journal of American Ethnic History* 13, no. 2 (Winter 1994): 30–75.

51. See Bolek, "Integration of the Polish American Group," 2 (Bolek), 3 (Swietlik); Bolek, *Who's Who*, 3d ed., 441.

52. See *PAS* 4, nos. 3–4 (July–December 1947): 112–17. On these statistical trends, see Bukowczyk, " 'Harness for Posterity the Values of a Nation,' " 16, 18. See *Polish American Historical Association, 1942–1951*, 9, 10.

53. Among the hobbyists and such were, for example, Celia Wong and Edward Pinkowski. See Victor R. Greene, "E. Pinkowski, Lay Collector: A Neglected Historical Resource," *Journal of American Ethnic History* 8, no. 1 (Fall 1988); 10–20. Charles [Karol] H. Wachtl, "Historical Research of Poles in America," *PAS* 1 (1944): 10–14; and Karol [H.] Wachtl, *Polonia w Ameryce: Dzieje i dorobek* (Philadelphia: Nakł aut., 1944); Artur L. Waldo, *Sokolstwo przednia straż narodu: Dzieje idei i organizacji w Ameryce*, 5 vols. (Pittsburgh: Sokolstwo Pol. w Amer., 1953–1974); Waldo, *First Poles in America, 1608–1958: In Commemoration of the 350th Anniversary of Their Landing at Jamestown, Virginia, October 1, 1608* (Pittsburgh: Polish Falcons of America, 1957); Waldo, "Searching for Polish Jamestown Sources," *PAS* 17, nos. 3–4 (1960): 105–14; Arthur L. Waldo, *The Origin and Roles of the Falcons: An Outline of Their Mission of Yesterday and Today* (Pittsburgh: Falcons Inst. of Historical Research, 1965).
Wolanin also served as associate director of the PRCU Archives and Museum in Chicago (and assistant to Haiman), in which capacity he produced a guide to the holdings, Alphonse S. Wolanin, *Polonica in English: Annotated Catalogue of the Archives and Museum of the Polish Roman Catholic Union* (Chicago: PRCU of America Archives and Museum, 1945), and *Polonica Americana: Annotated Catalogue of the Archives and Museum of the Polish Roman Catholic Union* (Chicago: PRCU of America Archives and Museum, 1950); *Who's Who*, 3d ed., 501–2.

54. Mocha, "The Polish Institute of Arts and Sciences," 714 (quotations), 715.

55. "What and How We Should Know About the Poles in Jamestown: St. Mary's College Symposium," *PAS* 15 (1958): 30–43; Joseph A. Wytrwal, "Pulaskiana in America," *PAS* 14 (1957): 1–11; Wytrwal, "Lincoln's Friend—Captain A. Bielaski," *PAS* 14, nos. 3–4 (1957): 65–67; Bronislas A. Jezierski, "Modjeska in Virginia City and Cambridge," *PAS* 14, nos. 3–4 (1957): 68–77. One genealogical piece considered how to fashion a family coat of arms. See Frank R. Walczyk, "The Walczyk Family in America," *PAS* 18, no. 1 (1961): 45–46; Iza Mikusiewicz, "University of Buffalo's Polish Room," *PAS* 18, no. 1 (1961): 40–42.

56. See Rev. Francis Bolek, "A Project for a 'Polish-American Encyclopedia': A Summary," *PAS* 1 (1944): 32–33; *Polish American Historical Association, 1942–1951*, 5, 10; Franciszek Bolek and Władysław Siekaniec, ed., *Polish-American Encyclopedia*, vol. 1 (Buffalo, N.Y.: Polish American Encyclopedia Committee, 1954). See also Syski, *Ks. Józef Dąbrowski*.

57. See, for example, Sr. Mary Remigia Napolska, *The Polish Immigrant in Detroit to 1914: Annals of the Polish Roman Catholic Union Archives and Museum*, vol. 10 (Chicago: PRCU of America, 1946); and Swastek, *The Formative Years of the Polish Seminary in the United States*.

58. Msgr. John Tracy Ellis, *American Catholicism* (Chicago and London: University of Chicago Press, 1956), 129–30. See Helena Znaniecki Lopata, *Polish Americans: Status Competition in an Ethnic Community* (Englewood Cliffs, N.J.: Prentice-Hall,

1976), 88–89; Hieronim Kubiak, *The Polish National Catholic Church in the United States of America from 1897 to 1980: Its Social Conditioning and Social Functions,* trans. M. Budka, B. Leś, and M. Teutsch-Dwyer (Warsaw and Cracow: Jagiellonian University, 1982), 121; Will Herberg, *Protestant-Catholic-Jew* (1955; Garden City, N.Y.: Doubleday, 1960), 153.

59. See *PAS* 4, nos. 3–4 (1947): 112–17.

60. On parochial education in Polish America, see Józef Miąso, *The History of the Education of Polish Immigrants in the United States,* trans. Ludwik Krzyżanowski (1970; New York and Warsaw: The Kosciuszko Foundation and PWN—Polish Scientific Publishers, 1977). For parochial enrollment and staff statistics, see Francis Bolek, *The Polish American School System* (New York: Columbia Press, 1948).

61. See Marina Warner, *Alone of All Her Sex: The Myth and the Cult of the Virgin Mary* (New York: Alfred A. Knopf, 1976); Renkiewicz, *Poles in America,* 29–31.

62. The organ of the American Association of Teachers of Slavic and East European Languages was the *Slavic and East European Journal;* see Manning, *A History of Slavic Studies,* 70. For Haiman, see Szymczak, "The Pioneer Days," 12, 24–25 n. 20. For Halecki, see Renkiewicz, *The Poles in America,* 29. For the Kosciuszko Foundation, see Stefan P. Mizwa, "A Clarification of Policy," *The Kosciuszko Foundation Monthly News Letter* 3, no. 5 (25) (January 1949): 1–2, quoted in Stanislaus A. Blejwas, "The Adam Mickiewicz Chair of Polish Culture: Columbia University and the Cold War, 1948–1954 (Part 1)," *PR* 36, no. 3 (1991): 336. See also Blejwas, "The Adam Mickiewicz Chair (Part 1)," 323, 326, 327, 332, and "The Adam Mickiewicz Chair (Part 2)," *PR* 36, no. 4 (1991): 442, 444, 446, 449.

63. Blejwas, "The Adam Mickiewicz Chair (Part 2)," 448 (quotation); Stanislaus A. Blejwas, ed., *East Central European Studies: A Handbook for Graduate Students, a Preliminary Edition* (New York: American Association for the Advancement of Slavic Studies, 1973), vii (quotation); and Harold H. Fisher, "Growing Pains of Slavic and East European Area Training," *ASEER* 17, no. 3 (1958): 346–50. For an annotated listing of postwar courses offered, see Arthur P. Coleman, "American Area and Language Courses in Slavic and East European Studies, 1946–1947," *ASEER* 5 (1946): 162–92.

In 1958, six American universities and two Canadian universities already had Eastern European area programs. See Jacob Ornstein, "The Development and Status of Slavic and East European Studies in America Since World War II," *ASEER* 16, no. 3 (1957): 382–83; Cyril E. Black, "The Development of Slavic and East European Studies in the United States," and James F. Clarke, "Some Problems in East European Area Studies," in *Area Study Programs: The Soviet Union and Eastern Europe,* ed. Royden Dangerfield (Urbana: Institute of Government and Public Affairs, University of Illinois, 1955), 15–33, 34–62, respectively. Also see J. F. Wellemeyer Jr. and M. H. North, *American Personnel in Asian, African, and Eastern European Studies* (Washington, D.C.: American Council of Learned Societies, 1953), mimeograph.

64. Manning, *A History of Slavic Studies,* 67; Waclaw Lednicki, "The State of Slavic Studies in America," *ASEER* 13, no. 1 (1954): 102; Charles Jelavich, ed., *Language and Area Studies: East Central and Southeastern Europe* (Chicago and London: University of Chicago Press, 1969), 4–6, 32 (quotation).

65. Lednicki, "The State of Slavic Studies," 108, 113 (quotations). In some measure this helps to explain the preoccupation of Polish-American writers such as Haiman with documenting Polish-American contributions and achievements, as if to show that members of the Polish "race" possessed worth.

66. Lednicki, "The State of Slavic Studies," 105–6. The outline to which Lednicki referred was *An Outline of Ancient, Medieval, and Modern History,* revised by J. A. Rickard and Albert Hyma (New York: Barnes and Noble, 1942). See also Piotr S. Wandycz, "The Treatment of East Central Europe in History Textbooks," *ASEER* 16, no. 4 (1957): 515–23.

67. See Jelavich, ed., *Language and Area Studies,* xii, 6, 40 (survey results). The Jelavich study also contains a still useful review of the scholarly literature on Poland in various disciplines. For an update on Polish history, see Piotr S. Wandycz, "Historiography of the Countries of Eastern Europe: Poland," *American Historical Review* 97, no. 4 (October 1992): 1011–25.

68. Sluszka study cited in Ornstein, "Development and Status of Slavic and East European Studies," 376 n. 5. For a review of language offerings on the eve of the NDEA's passage, see ibid., 369–81. *United States Code: Congressional and Administrative News, Eighty-Fifth Congress, Second Session, Convened January 3, 1958, Adjourned August 24, 1958* (St. Paul, Minn. and Brooklyn, N.Y.: West Publishing and Edward Thompson, 1958–1959), vol. 1, 1894–1924; L. G. Derthick, "Purpose and Legislative History of the Foreign Languages Titles in the National Defense Education Act, 1958," *Publications of the Modern Language Association of America* 74 (May 1959): 48–51.

69. For foundations and nonprofit organizations, see Ornstein, "Development and Status of Slavic and East European Studies," 385; Jelavich, ed., *Language and Area Studies,* 23. For the ACS and AAASS, see Deborah M. Burek, ed., *Encyclopedia of Associations, 1992: National Organizations of the U.S., Part 1 (Sections 1–6),* 26th ed. (Detroit and London: Gale Research, 1991), vol. 1, 1122; also see *Organizations Involved in Soviet-American Relations* (Washington, D.C.: Institute for Soviet-American Relations, 1986), 4–5; Manning, *A History of Slavic Studies,* 68, 70. See also Ornstein, "Development and Status of Slavic and East European Studies," 385.

70. Journals included the *American Slavic and East European Review* (published by the AAASS), which later became the *Slavic Review; the Journal of Central European Affairs* (1939–1964); and the *Journal of East European History* at the University of Chicago. Others were the *East European Quarterly* at the University of Colorado (1967); *Canadian Slavic Studies* (1967); and *Central European History* (1968), published by the Group on Central European History of the American Historical Association. See Jelavich, ed., *Language and Area Studies,* 10, 12–13; Manning, *A History of Slavic Studies,* 68–69, 74.

71. See Jelavich, ed., *Language and Area Studies,* 18–19 (quotations), 40; Blejwas, ed., *East Central European Studies,* vii. See also Franklin D. Murphy, "Languages and the National Interest," *Publications of the Modern Language Association of America* 75 (May 1960): 27.

72. On the rise of cultural pluralism in the postwar years, see Nathan Glazer, *Ethnic Dilemmas, 1964–1982* (Cambridge, Mass., and London: Harvard University

Press, 1983), 103–10. Also see George Lerski, *A Polish Chapter in Jacksonian America: The United States and the Polish Exiles of 1831* (Madison: University of Wisconsin Press, 1958); Victor R. Greene, "Pre–World War I Polish Emigration to the United States: Motives and Statistics," *PR* 6, no. 3 (1961): 45–68 (although Greene has focused principally upon Christian Poles, interestingly he himself is Jewish); Wytrwal, "Lincoln's Friend—Captain A. Bielaski," 65–67; Wytrwal, "The PAHA in Perspective," *PAS* 16 (1959): 95–98; and Wytrwal, *America's Polish Heritage: A Social History of the Poles in America* (Detroit: Endurance Press, 1961); Roman L. Haremski, *The Unattached, Aged Immigrant: A Descriptive Analysis of the Problems Experienced in Old Age by Three Groups of Poles Living Apart from Their Families in Baltimore* (Washington, D.C.: Catholic University of America Press, 1940); Helena Znaniecki, *The Function of Voluntary Associations in an Ethnic Community "Polonia"* (Chicago: University of Chicago Press, 1964) (Znaniecka Łopata is Florian Znaniecki's daughter); Harriet Pawlowska, "The Questionnaire as an Aid to Community Studies," *PAS* 7, nos. 3–4 (1950): 88–95; 11, nos. 1–2 (1954): 49–50; 11, nos. 3–4 (1954): 103–11; 12, nos. 1–2 (1955): 50–52; 12, nos. 3–4 (1955): 101–4; and Harriet M. Pawlowska, ed., *Merrily We Sing: 105 Polish Folksongs* (Detroit: Wayne State University Press, 1961). Helen Stankiewicz Zand's numerous short articles, which also appeared between the late 1940s and early 1960s, are gathered together in Eugene E. Obidinski and Helen Stankiewicz Zand, ed., *Polish Folkways in America: Community and Family* (Lanham, Md., New York, and London: University Press of America, 1987).

73. See Nicholas Bethell, *Gomułka: His Poland and His Communism,* rev. ed. (1969; Harmondsworth, England: Pelican Books, 1972), 231–35. In 1960, the Polish Academy of Sciences created a commission for the study of emigration, which began publication of the journal, *Problemy polonii zagranicznej.* See Stanley B. Kimball, "East Central European Ethnic Studies in the United States," in Blejwas, ed., *East Central European Studies,* 96. On this subject, also see the essay by Andrzej Brożek in this volume.

74. "PAHA Members and Studies Recipients," *PAS* 20, no. 1 (January–June 1963): 58–64; 20, no. 2 (June–December 1963): 117–25; Joseph W. Wieczerzak, *A Polish Chapter in Civil War America: The Effects of the January Insurrection on American Opinion and Diplomacy* (New York: Twayne Publishing, 1967); Richard Kolm, "The Identity Crisis of Polish-Americans," *Quarterly Review* 21, no. 2 (1969): 1–4; Danuta Mostwin, "Post–World War II Polish Immigrants in the United States," *PAS* 26, no. 2 (1969): 5–14.

75. "PAHA Members and Studies Recipients," *PAS* 20, no. 1 (January–June 1963): 58–64; 20, no. 2 (June–December 1963): 117–25.

76. "Poland's Millennium Observances in the U.S.A. in Review: St. Mary's College Symposium," *PAS* 25, no. 1 (1968): 20–50. The observance also recalled Poland's (and Polonia's) resistance to Soviet control and communism. See O. Halecki, *A History of Poland,* trans. Monica M. Gardner and Mary Corbridge-Patkaniowska (1942; New York: David McKay, 1976), 354–55. For religious events, see Charles E. Wisniewski Jr., "Religious Millennial Observances," and Thomas S. Chrzanowski, "Polish Seminary Observance," in "Poland's Millennium Observances," 20–23, 47–50. For civic commemorations, see Norman Malinowski, "Political Observances," in

"Poland's Millennium Observances," 35–39. For contests and publications, see James A. Holtz, "Artistic Observances," Joseph Tomecsko Jr., "Millennium Contests," and Richard Bigos, "Millennium Publications," in "Poland's Millennium Observances," 28–34, 39–43, 43–46.

77. Renkiewicz, *The Poles in America,* 34, 39; Blejwas, "The Adam Mickiewicz Chair (Part 2)," 446; Bernard Wielewinski, ed., *Polish National Catholic Church, Independent Movements, Old Catholic Church, and Related Items: An Annotated Bibliography* (Boulder, Colo.: East European Monographs, 1990), 196. See Michael Novak, *The Rise of the Unmeltable Ethnics: Politics and Culture in the Seventies* (New York: Macmillan, 1971, 1972).

78. "Hansen's Law" derives from a remark by historian Marcus Lee Hansen: "What the son wishes to forget, the grandson wishes to remember." Whereas references to the Hansen model sometimes have anticipated a return to ethnicity, Hansen actually referred not to return but to recollection. See Marcus Lee Hansen, *The Problem of the Third Generation Immigrant* (Rock Island, Ill.: Augustana Historical Society, 1938). For a critical look at Hansen's Law in relation to the historiography, see Peter Kivisto and Dag Blanck, ed., *American Immigrants and Their Generations: Studies and Commentaries on the Hansen Thesis After Fifty Years* (Urbana and Chicago: University of Illinois Press, 1990).

79. Alex Haley, *Roots* (New York: Doubleday, 1976); in 1974, *Reader's Digest* published a condensed edition of a portion of the book. See Novak, *The Rise of the Unmeltable Ethnics;* Rev. Leonard Chrobot, *Ethnic Awareness and Self-Identity,* Monograph no. 6 (Orchard Lake, Mich.: Orchard Lake Center for Polish Studies and Culture, St. Mary's College, April 1971), 8. See also Chrobot, *Who Am I? Reflections of a Young Polish American on the Search for Identity,* Monograph no. 4 (Orchard Lake, Mich.: Orchard Lake Center for Polish Studies and Culture, St. Mary's College, February 1971). The intellectual sources for Chrobot's critique included Erik Erikson and Charles Reich. Other noted proponents of the "new ethnicity" included author Rev. Andrew Greeley; Wayne State University social scientist Otto Feinstein; and Monsignor Geno Baroni, director of the National Center for Urban Ethnic Affairs.

80. *Ethnic Heritage Studies Program: Assessment of the First Year* (Washington, D.C.: National Education Association, 1977), 11; "Ethnic Heritage Studies Program," in *Harvard Encyclopedia of American Ethnic Groups,* ed. Stephan Thernstrom (Cambridge, Mass., and London: Harvard University Press, Belknap Press, 1980), 343–44. Pucinski cited in *Congressional Record: Proceedings and Debates of the 92nd Congress, First Session* (Washington, D.C.: United States Government Printing Office, 1971), vol. 117, pt. 30, 39278 (quotation), 39279, 39280.

81. *Congressional Record: Proceedings and Debates of the 92nd Congress, First Session,* 39277. Echoing a conclusion reached by many Polish-American scholars who had examined American school curricula, Pucinski observed that many parents simply did not teach their offspring about their own ethnic heritage. For 1974–1976, see *Ethnic Studies at the Federal Level,* 37–75; *Ethnic Heritage Studies Program: Assessment,* 41, 43–44, 45, 52. For one state legislature as an example, see *Ethnic Studies in Michigan* (Detroit: Michigan Ethnic Heritage Studies Center and Ethnic Studies Division, Center for Urban Studies, Wayne State University, 1977), 29–33. For the Smithsonian Institution, see *Ethnic Heritage Studies Program: Assessment,* 9.

82. Stanley B. Kimball, "East Central European Studies in the United States," in Blejwas, ed., *East Central European Studies,* 93–100; *University of Minnesota Immigration History Research Center Guide to Manuscript Holdings, April 1975* (n.p., n.d.); Monica Bourque and R. Joseph Anderson, comp. and ed., *A Guide to Manuscript and Microfilm Collections of the Research Library of the Balch Institute for Ethnic Studies* (Philadelphia: The Balch Institute for Ethnic Studies, 1992). For the funding of the microfilm project, see *Spectrum* 1, no. 1 (January 1975): 2; "Polish Microfilm Project," *PR* 16, no. 4 (1971): 93–94; and also Edward V. Kolyszko, "Preserving the Polish Heritage in America: The Polish Microfilm Project," *PAS* 32, no. 1 (Spring 1975): 59–63.

83. Historian Mary Cygan directed both projects; the latter received partial funding from the National Endowment for the Humanities. See *Passage: Oral History Archives of Chicago Polonia* (n.p., n.d.), pamphlet; *Master Index for the Oral History Archives of Chicago Polonia* (n.p., December 1977); Ronald Zaraza, *Teacher's Guide for Using Oral History Materials on the Immigrant Experience* (Chicago: Chicago Historical Society, December 1977); Mark A. Vargas, ed., *Guide to the Polish-American Holdings in the Milwaukee Urban Archives* (Milwaukee: Golda Meir Library, University of Wisconsin–Milwaukee, 1991). The widespread public legitimization of ethnicity also took other forms. In the late 1970s, for example, Wayne State University in Detroit planned a Polish Room, patterned after the ethnic rooms at the University of Pittsburgh's Cathedral of Learning. See *Ethnic Heritage Center,* pamphlet published by the Division of Community Relations, Wayne State University (n.d.).

84. National conferences included an April 1972 meeting on "The Forgotten Ethnic Americans," held at Jersey City State College, and a June 1972 conclave, held in Washington, D.C., and sponsored by the American Council of Polish Cultural Clubs, which discussed "Polish studies programs" and "Ethnic studies legislation." See Winnie Bengelsdorf, ed., *Ethnic Studies in Higher Education: State of the Art and Bibliography* (Washington, D.C.: American Association of State Colleges and Universities, 1972), 9, 10. For a guide to Polish-American serials, see Jan Wepsiec, *Polish American Serial Publications, 1842–1966: An Annotated Bibliography* (Chicago: n.p., 1968). For a guide to archival sources, see Theodore Lebiedzik Zawistowski, *The Zawistowski Collection: The Library and Papers of the Reverend Senior Józef Lebiedzik Zawistowski of the Polish National Catholic Church* (Storrs: University of Connecticut, 1972). For a guide to historical literature, see Joseph W. Zurawski, *Polish American History and Culture: A Classified Bibliography* (Chicago: Polish Museum of America, 1975), and John J. Grabowski et al., *Polish Americans and Their Communities of Cleveland* (Cleveland: Cleveland Ethnic Heritage Studies, Cleveland State University, 1976). For a guide to sociological literature, see Sanders and Morawska, *Polish-American Community Life.*

85. For essay collections, see *PR* 21, no. 3 (1976), bicentennial issue; Mocha, ed., *Poles in America;* Frank Renkiewicz, ed., *The Polish Presence in Canada and America* (Toronto: Multicultural History Society of Ontario, 1982); and Blejwas and Biskupski, eds., *Pastor of the Poles.* For subsequent scholarship, see Joseph A. Wytrwal, *Poles in American History and Tradition* (Detroit: Endurance Press, 1969); Theresita Polzin, *The Polish Americans: Whence and Whither* (Pulaski, Wis.: Franciscan Publishers,

1973); Renkiewicz, *The Poles in America;* Lopata, *Polish Americans;* W. S. Kuniczak, *My Name Is Million: An Illustrated History of the Poles in America* (Garden City, N.Y.: Doubleday, 1978). See also Greene, "Poles," in Thernstrom, *Harvard Encyclopedia of American Ethnic Groups,* 787–803.

86. See Konstantin Symmons-Symonolewicz, "Polish American Studies, 1942– 1970: An Overview," *PAS* 27, nos. 1–2 (Spring–Autumn 1970): 5–19. Symmons-Symonolewicz's works have been collected and reprinted in *Ze studiów nad Polonia amerykańska* (Warsaw: Ludowa Spółdzielnia Wydawnicza, 1979). For a precursor of the "new social history," see, for example, Wytrwal, *America's Polish Heritage,* which actually was not a "social" history as historians have come to use the term; also see Victor R. Greene, *The Slavic Community on Strike: Immigrant Labor in Pennsylvania Anthracite* (Notre Dame, Ind., and London: University of Notre Dame Press, 1968).

87. For the Polish nationalist movement, see, for example, Mieczysław B. Biskupski, " 'Kościuszko, We Are Here?': American Volunteers for Poland and the Polish-Russian War, 1918–1920," in Blejwas and Biskupski, eds., *Pastor of the Poles,* 182–204; as well as the work of Joseph Hapak and Louis J. Zake.

For Polish associational life, see Frank Renkiewicz, "The Profits of Nonprofit Capitalism: Polish Fraternalism and Beneficial Insurance in America," in *Self-Help in Urban America: Patterns of Minority Business Enterprise,* ed. Scott Cummings (Port Washington, N.Y., and London: Kennikat Press, National University Publications, 1980), 113–29; Donald Pienkos, "The Secular Organizations of Polish Americans: The Fraternals Role in Polonia," in Renkiewicz, *The Polish Presence,* 287–304.

For Polish electoral politics, see Edward R. Kantowicz, *Polish-American Politics in Chicago, 1888–1940* (Chicago and London: University of Chicago Press, 1975); Donald Pienkos, "Politics, Religion, and Change in Polish Milwaukee," *Wisconsin Magazine of History* 61 (Spring 1978): 141–82; Pienkos, "Polish-American Ethnicity in the Political Life of the United States," in *America's Ethnic Politics,* ed. Joseph S. Roucek and Bernard Eisenberg (Westport, Conn., and London: Greenwood Press, 1982), 273–305; Angela T. Pienkos, *Ethnic Politics in Urban America: The Polish Experience in Four Cities* (Chicago: Polish American Historical Association, 1978); Stanislaus A. Blejwas, "The Local Ethnic Lobby: The Polish American Congress in Connecticut, 1944–1974," in Renkiewicz, *The Polish Presence,* 305–26.

For immigrant military and government service, see James S. Pula, "Krzyżanowski's Civil War Brigade," *PAS* 28, no. 2 (1971): 22–49; and LeRoy H. Fischer, *Lincoln's Gadfly: Adam Gurowski* (Norman: University of Oklahoma Press, 1964). For Poland–United States foreign relations, see Robert Szymczak, "A Matter of Honor: Polonia and the Congressional Investigation of the Katyn Forest Massacre," *PAS* 41, no. 1 (Spring 1984): 25–65.

88. For Polish-American trusteeism and independentism, see Daniel S. Buczek, *Immigrant Pastor: The Life of the Right Reverend Monsignor Lucyan Bójnowski of New Britain, Connecticut* (Waterbury, Conn.: Heminway Corp., 1974); Greene, *For God and Country;* Galush, "Faith and Fatherland"; Kuzniewski, *Faith and Fatherland;* Bukowczyk, "The Immigrant 'Community' Re-examined," 5–16; Bukowczyk, "Factionalism and the Composition of the Polish Immigrant Clergy," in Blejwas and Biskupski, eds., *Pastor of the Poles,* 37–47; Joseph John Parot, *Polish Catholics in*

Chicago, 1850–1920: A Religious History (DeKalb: Northern Illinois University Press, 1981); Lawrence D. Orton, *Polish Detroit and the Kolasiński Affair* (Detroit: Wayne State University Press, 1981).

89. Lednicki, "The State of Slavic Studies in America," 107–8. For work, families, strikes, and unions, see Caroline Golab, *Immigrant Destinations* (Philadelphia: Temple University Press, 1977); John Bodnar, Roger Simon, and Michael P. Weber, *Lives of Their Own: Blacks, Italians, and Poles in Pittsburgh, 1900–1960* (Urbana, Chicago, and London: University of Illinois Press, 1982); Frank Renkiewicz, "Polish American Workers, 1880–1980," in Blejwas and Biskupski, eds., *Pastor of the Poles*, 116–36; Dominic A. Pacyga, "Villages of Steel Mills and Packinghouses: The Polish Worker on Chicago's South Side, 1880–1921," in Renkiewicz, *The Polish Presence*, 19–27; John J. Bukowczyk, "Polish Rural Culture and Immigrant Working Class Formation, 1880–1914," *PAS* 41 (Autumn 1984): 23–44; Bukowczyk, "The Transformation of Working-Class Ethnicity: Corporate Control, Americanization, and the Polish Immigrant Middle Class in Bayonne, N.J., 1915–1925," *Labor History* 25 (Winter 1984): 53–82; Ewa Morawska, *For Bread with Butter: Life-Worlds of East Central Europeans in Johnstown, Pennsylvania, 1890–1940* (Cambridge: Cambridge University Press, 1985); James R. Barrett, *Work and Community in the Jungle: Chicago's Packinghouse Workers, 1894–1922* (Urbana and Chicago: University of Illinois Press, 1987).

For community life, see Neil C. Sandberg, *Ethnic Identity and Assimilation: The Polish-American Community: Case Study of Metropolitan Los Angeles* (New York: Praeger, 1974); T. Lindsay Baker, *The First Polish Americans: Silesian Settlements in Texas* (College Station and London: Texas A&M University Press, 1979); Leonard F. Chrobot, "The Pilgrimage from *Gemeinschaft* to *Gesellschaft:* Sociological Functions of Religion in the Polish American Community," and Eugene Obidinski, "Urban Location: A Necessary or Sufficient Basis for Polonian Ethnic Persistence," both in Renkiewicz, ed., *The Polish Presence*, 81–96, 243–67, respectively.

For popular culture, see Angeliki and Charles Keil, "In Pursuit of Polka Happiness," *Cultural Correspondence* 5 (Summer–Fall 1977): 4–11, 74; and Bill Falkowski, "Polka History 101." For popular religion, see Bukowczyk, "Mary the Messiah"; Bukowczyk, "The Transforming Power of the Machine: Popular Religion, Ideology, and Secularization Among Polish Immigrant Workers in the United States, 1880–1940," *International Labor and Working-Class History* 34 (Fall 1988): 22–38.

90. See Richard Kolm, quoted in the *Polish American Journal* (Buffalo, N.Y.), October 11, 1969.

91. Paul Wrobel, *Our Way: Family, Parish, and Neighborhood in a Polish-American Community* (Notre Dame, Ind., and London: University of Notre Dame Press, 1979), esp. 155–72. See Taras, Pienkos, and Radzialowski, "Paul Wrobel's *Our Way*—Three Views," 42–51. Among scholars of the so-called Detroit School, Radzilowski cited Leonard Chrobot, John Gutowski, Thomas Napierkowski, Dominic Pacyga, Joseph Parot, and himself. Several of the contributors to this volume, many of them already active scholars in the 1970s, also deserve the designation, including John Bukowczyk, William Falkowski, and probably also William Galush and Stanislaus Blejwas. Radzilowski also might have mentioned Dennis Koliński, James S. Pula, and Mary Cygan. (Incidentally, the discrepancy in the spelling of Radzilowski's surname results from a

change of name in the 1980s, which restored the correct, pre-migration spelling of the family name. The spelling of Radzilowski's name as it appeared in his earlier articles is retained in the notes here.)

92. Taras, Pienkos, and Radzialowski, "Paul Wrobel's *Our Way*—Three Views," 44–45.

93. Essay collections: "The Polish Americans," *PR* 21, no. 3 (1976), bicentennial issue; Mocha, ed., *Poles in America;* Blejwas and Biskupski, eds., *Pastor of the Poles;* Renkiewicz, ed., *The Polish Presence.* The Polish American is Bukowczyk, *And My Children Did Not Know Me;* the Pole, Andrzej Brożek, *Polish Americans, 1854–1939,* trans. Wojciech Worsztynowicz (1977; Warsaw: Interpress, 1985).

94. For a brief description of the "Poles in North America" conference, see Renkiewicz, ed., *The Polish Presence,* ix–x. The Polonia Research Institute is discussed in Andrzej Brożek's contribution to this volume. For the Ecclesiastical Institutions Project: conversation with Daniel Buczek, Cambridge, Mass. (October 10, 1977); Daniel Buczek, "The Atlas of the Socio-Religious History of East Central Europe: A Project of the Catholic University of Lublin," paper presented at the PAHA annual meeting, New York City (December 29, 1990); "Methodology for the Study of Polish-American Ecclesiastical Institutions: A Historical Geography, 1854–1976," (n.p., n.d.), mimeographed flyer in author's files. For the Labor Migration and Labor Newspaper Preservation, see Dirk Hoerder, with Christiane Harzig, *"Why Did You Come?" The Proletarian Mass Migration: Research Report, 1980–1985* (Bremen, Federal Republic of Germany: Labor Migration Project and Labor Newspaper Preservation Project, University of Bremen, 1986).

95. See John Bukowczyk, "Anniversaries, Academics, and Ideas," *Polish American Journal* (Buffalo, N.Y.) (October 1992), 3. A detailed review of the secularization trends appears in Bukowczyk, " 'Harness for Posterity the Values of a Nation'," 55, 70, 70–71. Throughout this discussion, statistics have been calculated from lists of PAHA board members published in *PAS.*

96. Bukowczyk, " 'Harness for Posterity the Values of a Nation'," 55, 71.

97. See Chrobot, *Ethnic Awareness and Self-Identity,* 8. On the development of immigration and ethnic history since the 1960s, see John J. Bukowczyk and Nora Faires, "Immigration History in the United States, 1965–1990: A Selective Critical Appraisal," *Canadian Ethnic Studies/Études Ethniques au Canada* 33, no. 2 (1991): 1–23.

98. See Sara M. Evans, *Personal Politics: The Roots of Women's Liberation in the Civil Rights Movement and the New Left* (New York: Knopf, 1979), esp. 43.

99. The questions Where do we come from? What are we? Where are we going? come from the title of Paul Gauguin's monumental 1897 painting. The question What is a Polish American? has recurred in Polish-American scholarly writing across the generations. Kruszka himself addressed it in the first chapter of his magnum opus, "The Distinct Type of Pole in America," and the question thereafter has been asked again and again. See Kruszka, *A History of the Poles in America, Part 1,* 13–22; Rev. Joseph Swastek, "What Is a Polish-American?" *PAS* 1 (1944): 34–44; Leonard F. Chrobot, "Polish American Identity: How Can This Be Defined?" in *American Polonia: The Cultural Issues,* ed. Alfred F. Bochenek (Detroit: American Council of

Polish Cultural Clubs, 1981), 34–38; Bukowczyk, *And My Children Did Not Know Me*, Epilogue, 143–46; and, most recent, James S. Pula, *Polish Americans: An Ethnic Community* (New York: Twayne Publishers, 1995).

100. See Jake Ryan and Charles Sackrey, *Strangers in Paradise: Academics from the Working Class* (Boston: South End Press, 1984).

101. Thomas S. Gladsky, *Princes, Peasants, and Other Polish Selves: Ethnicity in American Literature* (Amherst: University of Massachusetts Press, 1992), 3–4, 8. Gladsky builds upon the distinction between "descent" and "consent" as developed in Werner Sollors, *Beyond Ethnicity: Consent and Descent in American Culture* (New York and Oxford: Oxford University Press, 1986).

102. See John J. Bukowczyk, "Movie Reviews: *God Bless America and Poland Too*," *Journal of American History* 78 (December 1991): 1171–72.

2. *Labor, Radicalism, and the Polish-American Worker*

A version of this article was presented on December 28, 1991, at the Fiftieth Anniversary Conference Program of the Polish American Historical Association (PAHA) in Chicago. The author wishes to thank James Barrett, John J. Bukowczyk, Nora Faires, and Christiane Harzig for their useful insights and comments on this paper. The epigraph is taken from John R. Commons, *Races and Immigrants in America* (New York: Macmillan, 1924), 11–12.

1. Scholarship in the field has progressed beyond earlier mechanical "push-pull" models of migration toward more dynamic notions concerning world capitalist development, as discussed in John J. Bukowczyk, "Migration and Capitalism: A Review Essay," *International Labor and Working Class History* 36 (Fall 1989): 61–75 (hereafter cited as *ILWCH*); and Dominic A. Pacyga, "Polish Emigration to the United States Before World War One and Capitalist Development," *Polish American Studies* 46:1 (Spring 1989): 10–18 (hereafter cited as *PAS*).

The political dimensions of the Polish emigrant experience remain a relatively neglected issue. The following works provide essential background information: Richard Blanke, *Prussian Poland and the German Empire, 1871–1900*, East European Monographs, no. 86 (Boulder, Colo.: East European Quarterly, 1970); Stanislaus A. Blejwas, *Realism in Polish Politics: Warsaw Positivism and National Survival in Nineteenth Century Poland* (New Haven, Conn.: Yale Concilium in International and Area Studies, 1984); Lucjan Blit, *The Origins of Polish Socialism: The History and Ideas of the First Polish Socialist Party, 1878–1886* (New York: Cambridge University Press, 1971); Robert Blobaum, *Feliks Dzierżyński and the SDKPiL: A Study of the Origins of Polish Communism*, East European Monographs, no. 154 (Boulder, Colo.: East European Quarterly, 1984); Adam Bromke, *Poland's Politics: Idealism Versus Realism* (Cambridge, Mass.: Harvard University Press, 1967); Kazimiera Janina Cottam, *Bolesław Limanowski: A Study in Socialism and Nationalism*, East European Monographs, no. 41 (Boulder, Colo.: East European Quarterly, 1978); Alvin Marcus Fountain II, *Roman Dmowski: Party, Tactics, Ideology, 1897–1907*, East European Monographs, no. 60 (Boulder, Colo.: East European Quarterly, 1983); Paul Frolich, *Rosa Luxemburg* (New York: Monthly Review Press, 1972); Dyzma Galaj, "The Polish Peasant Movement in Politics: 1895–1969," in *Rural Protest: Peasant Movements and Social Change,* ed. Harry Landsberger (New York: Harper and Row, 1973), 316–50; William W. Hagen, *Germans, Poles, and Jews: The Nationality Conflict in the Prussian East, 1772– 1914* (Chicago: University of Chicago Press, 1980); John-Paul Himka, *Socialism in Galicia: The Emergence of Polish Social Democracy and Ukrainian Nationalism, 1860– 1890* (Cambridge, Mass.: Harvard Ukrainian Research Institute, 1983); Stanisław Kalabinski, ed., *Polska klasa robotnicza: Zarys dziejów* (The Polish working class: A historical outline), 3 vols. (Warsaw, Poland: Państwowe Wydawnictwo Naukowe, 1978); Stefan Kieniewicz, *The Emancipation of the Polish Peasantry* (Chicago: University of Chicago Press, 1969); Norman Naimark, *The History of the "Proletariat" and the Emergence of Marxism in the Congress Kingdom of Poland, 1870–1887,* East European Monographs, no. 54 (Boulder, Colo.: East European Quarterly, 1979); Olga A. Narkiewicz, *The Green Flag: Polish Populist Politics, 1867–1970* (Totowa, N.J.: Rowman and Littlefield, 1976); Peter Nettl, *Rosa Luxemburg* (New York: Oxford University Press, 1966); Harry K. Rosenthal, *German and Pole: National Conflict and Modern Myth* (Gainesville, Fla.: University of Florida Presses, 1976); Lawrence Schofer, *The Formation of a Modern Labor Force, Upper Silesia, 1865–1975* (Berkeley and Los Angeles: University of California Press, 1975); Jan Słomka, *From Serfdom to Self-Government: Memoirs of a Polish Village Mayor, 1842–1927* (London: Minerva Publishing, 1941); Jan B. de Weydenthal, *The Communists of Poland* (Stanford, Calif.: Stanford University Press, 1978); and Anna Zarnowska, "Determinants of the Political Activity of the Working Class at the Turn of the Nineteenth Century," *Acta Poloniae Historica* 42 (1980): 97–110.

2. For more on the Atlantic economy, see Caroline Golab, *Immigrant Destinations* (Philadelphia: Temple University Press, 1977); Ewa Morawska, *For Bread with Butter: The Life-Worlds of East Central Europeans in Johnstown, Pennsylvania, 1890–1940* (New York: Cambridge University Press, 1985); William G. Falkowski Jr., "Accommodation and Conflict: Patterns of Polish Immigrant Adaptation to Industrial Capitalism and American Political Pluralism in Buffalo, New York, 1873–1901" (Ph.D. diss., State University of New York at Buffalo, 1990); John J. Bukowczyk, *And My Children Did Not Know Me: A History of the Polish-Americans* (Bloomington and Indianapolis: Indiana University Press, 1987).

3. Works that devote considerable attention to East European immigrants include David Brody, *Steelworkers in America: The Non-Union Era* (Cambridge, Mass.: Harper and Row, 1960); Brody, *Labor in Crisis: The Steel Strike of 1919* (Philadelphia, New York, Toronto: J. B. Lippincott, 1965); Brody, *The Butcher Workmen: A Study of Unionism* (Cambridge, Mass.: Harvard University Press, 1963); Herbert G. Gutman, *Work, Culture, and Society in Industrializing America* (New York: Vintage Books, Random House, 1977); Victor R. Greene, *The Slavic Community on Strike: Immigrant Labor in Pennsylvania Anthracite* (Notre Dame, Ind.: University of Notre Dame Press, 1968); David Montgomery, *Workers' Control in America: Studies in the History of Work, Technology, and Labor Struggles* (New York: Cambridge University Press, 1979); Montgomery, *The Fall of the House of Labor: The Workplace, the State, and American Labor Activism, 1865–1925* (Cambridge: Cambridge University Press, 1987); Montgomery, "Nationalism, American Patriotism, and Class Consciousness Among

Immigrant Workers in the United States in the Epoch of World War One," in *"Struggle a Hard Battle": Essays on Working Class Immigrants,* ed. Dirk Hoerder (DeKalb: Northern Illinois Press, 1986), 327–51; and Montgomery, " 'The New Unionism' and the Transformation of Workers' Consciousness in America, 1909–1922," *Journal of Social History* 7:4 (Summer 1974): 509–29.

4. Victor R. Greene, "The Polish American Worker to 1930: The 'Hunky' Image in Transition," *Polish Review* 11:3 (1976): 63–78; and Frank Renkiewicz, "Polish American Workers, 1880–1890," in *Pastor of the Poles: Polish American Essays Presented to Right Reverend John P. Wodarski in Honor of the Fiftieth Anniversary of His Ordination,* ed. Stanislaus A. Blejwas and Mieczysław B. Biskupski (New Britain: Central Connecticut State College, 1982), 37–47.

5. Adam Walaszek is a notable exception in this regard and has also published excerpts of his work in English. See his *Polscy robotnicy, praca i związki zawodowe w Stanach Zjednoczonych Ameryki, 1880–1922* (Polish workers, labor, and trade unions in the United States of America, 1880–1922) (Wrocław: Zakład Narodowy im. Ossolińskich Wydawnictwo, 1988) and "Emigranci polscy wśród robotników przemysłowych swiata, 1905–1917" (Polish emigrants among the industrial workers of the world) *Przegląd Polonijny* (Polonia review) 14:2 (1988): 41–45. His English-language articles are Walaszek, "Was the Polish Worker Asleep? Immigrants, Unions, and Workers' Control in America, 1900–1922," *PAS* 46:1 (Spring 1989): 74–96, and " 'For in America Poles Work Like Cattle': Polish Peasant Immigrants and Work in America," in *In the Shadow of the Statue of Liberty: Immigrants, Workers, and Citizens in the American Republic, 1880–1920,* ed. Marianne Debouzy (1988; Urbana and Chicago: University of Illinois Press, 1992), 83–93.

A sampling of articles in Polish by Polish scholars include Krzysztof Groniowski, "Socjalistyczna emigracja polska w Stanach Zjednoczonych, 1883–1914" (The Polish socialist emigration in the United States, 1883–1914), *Z pola walki* (From the field of battle) 77:1 (1976): 3–35; Groniowski, "Korespondenci 'Przyjaciel Ludu' w Stanach Zjednoczonych, 1896–1932" (The correspondents of 'Friend of the People' in the United States), *Przegląd Polonijny* 13:2 (1987): 5–21; Groniowski, "Polski ruch zawodowy w Chicago, 1918–1942" (Polish workers' movement in Chicago), *Kwartalnik historii ruchu zawodowego* (Trade union history quarterly) 3 (1987): 21–36; and Groniowski, "Struktura społeczno-zawodowa Polonii amerykańska" (The socio-occupational structure of American Polonia), in *Polonia amerykańska: Przeszłość i współczesność* (American Polonia: The past and present), ed. Hieronim Kubiak, Eugene Kusielewicz, and Thaddeus Gromada (Wrocław: Zakład Narodowy im. Ossolińskich, Wydawnictwo Polskiej Akademii Nauk, 1988), 99–122; Danuta Piątkowski, "Polscy socjaliści w USA wobec rewolucji 1905 roku" (Polish socialists in the USA during the 1905 revolution), *Przegląd Polonijny* 12:2 (1986): 37–48; Zygmunt Piotrowski, "Ruch socalistyczny w Ameryce" (The socialist movement in America), in *Księga pamiątkowa PPS* (Commemorative book of the Polish Socialist Party) (Warsaw: Robotnik, 1923), 256–65; Wiktor Tylewski, "Materiały do dziejów polskiego socjalizmu w Stanach Zjednoczonych" (Materials toward the history of Polish socialism in the United States), *Problemy Polonii zagranicznej* (Problems of Polonia abroad) 2 (1961): 210–16. See also Andrzej Brożek, *Polish Americans, 1854–1939* (Warsaw: Interpress, 1985).

6. Aronowitz, *False Promises: The Shaping of American Working Class Consciousness* (New York: McGraw-Hill, 1973), 164. The classic portrayal of the passive immigrant is Oscar Handlin's *The Uprooted* (Boston: Little, Brown, 1951), a work powerfully influenced by William I. Thomas and Florian Znaniecki's massive sociological study, *The Polish Peasant in Europe and America*, 5 vols. (Boston: Richard G. Badger, 1918–1919). Other works that proceed from the John Commons school of labor historiography, which tended to portray immigrants as impediments to unionization, include Gabriel Kolko, *Main Currents in Modern American History* (New York: Harper and Row, 1976), and Gerald Rosenblum, *Immigrant Workers: Their Impact on American Labor Radicalism* (New York: Basic Books, 1973). It is curious that scholars working in the Commons tradition made few specific references to Poles or other groups that comprised the so-called new immigration or, at best, lumped them together as "Slavs" or "Eastern Europeans." For a trailblazing and influential corrective to this approach, albeit one dealing with South Italians, see Rudolph J. Vecoli, "*Contadini* in Chicago: A Critique of *The Uprooted*," *Journal of American History* 51 (December 1964): 404–17.

7. For important critiques of modernization theory, see Dean Tipps, "Modernization Theory and the Comparative Study of Societies: A Critical Perspective," *Comparative Studies in Society and History* 15:2 (April 1973): 199–226, and Joseph R. Gusfield, "Tradition and Modernity: Misplaced Polarities in the Study of Social Change," *American Journal of Sociology* 72:4 (January 1967): 351–62.

8. John Bodnar, Roger Simon, and Michael P. Weber, *Lives of Their Own: Blacks, Italians, and Poles in Pittsburgh, 1900–1980* (Urbana: University of Illinois Press, 1982); and John Bodnar, *Immigration and Industrialization: Ethnicity in an American Mill Town, 1870–1940* (Pittsburgh: University of Pittsburgh Press, 1977); Bodnar, *Workers' World: Kinship, Community, and Protest in an Industrial Society, 1900–1940* (Baltimore: Johns Hopkins University Press, 1982); Bodnar, *The Transplanted: A History of Immigrants in Urban America* (Bloomington: Indiana University Press, 1985); Bodnar, "Immigration and Modernization: The Case of Slavic Peasants in Industrial America," *Journal of Social History* 10:1 (Fall 1975): 44–71; Bodnar, "Immigration, Kinship, and the Rise of Working Class Realism in Industrial America," *Journal of Social History* 14:1 (Fall 1980): 23–47; and Bodnar, "Materialism and Morality: Slavic American Immigrants and Education," *Journal of Ethnic Studies* 3:4 (Winter 1976): 1–21.

9. Bodnar, *The Transplanted*, 100. Similar views are presented in James S. Pula, "American Immigration Policy and the Dillingham Commission," *PAS* 37:1 (Spring 1980): 5–31; Robert Asher, "Union Nativism and the Immigrant Response," *Labor History* 23:3 (Summer 1983): 325–48; A. T. Lane, *Solidarity or Survival: American Labor and European Immigrants, 1830–1924* (New York: Greenwood Press, 1987); and Gwendolyn Mink, *Old Labor and New Immigrants in American Political Development: Union, Party, and State* (Ithaca, N.Y.: Cornell University Press, 1986). Selig Perlman also outlined this view in *A History of Trade Unionism in the United States* (New York: Macmillan, 1923), 179.

10. Morawska, *For Bread with Butter*, 4, 8, 22; see also chaps. 1–2.

11. Ibid., 23, 183, and chap. 8.

12. See John Bukowczyk, *And My Children Did Not Know Me*; Bukowczyk,

"Steeples and Smokestacks: Class, Religion, and Ideology in the Polish Immigrant Settlements in Greenpoint and Williamsburg, Brooklyn, 1880–1929" (Ph.D. diss., Harvard University, 1980); Bukowczyk, "Factionalism and the Composition of the Polish Immigrant Clergy," in *Pastor of the Poles*, 37–47; Bukowczyk, "The Immigrant 'Community' Re-Examined: Political and Economic Tensions in a Brooklyn Polish Settlement, 1888–1894," *PAS* 37:2 (Autumn 1980): 5–16; Bukowczyk, "Mary the Messiah: Polish Immigrant Heresy and the Malleable Ideology of the Roman Catholic Church, 1880–1930," *Journal of American Ethnic History* 4:2 (Spring 1985): 5–32; and Bukowczyk, "The Transforming Power of the Machine: Popular Religion, Ideology, and Secularization Among Polish Immigrant Workers in the United States, 1880–1940," *ILWCH* 34 (Fall 1988): 22–38.

13. Bukowczyk, "Polish Rural Culture and Immigrant Working Class Formation, 1890–1914," *PAS* 41:2 (Autumn 1984), 23–44.

14. Ibid., 36.

15. Bukowczyk, "The Transformation of Working-Class Ethnicity: Corporate Control, Americanization, and the Polish Immigrant Middle Class in Bayonne, New Jersey, 1915–1925," *Labor History* 25:1 (Winter 1984): 53–82.

16. Bukowczyk, "Immigrants and Their Communities: A Review Essay," *ILWCH* 25 (Spring 1984): 47–57.

17. Falkowski, "Accommodation and Conflict," 275–99, 420–50.

18. Ibid., 241–58, 391–407.

19. Leon Fink, *Workingmen's Democracy: The Knights of Labor and American Politics* (Urbana and Chicago: University of Chicago Press, 1983), 186.

20. Ibid., 178–212.

21. See Mink, *Old Labor and New Immigrants*.

22. Richard Jules Oestreicher, *Solidarity and Fragmentation: Working People and Class Consciousness in Detroit, 1875–1900* (Urbana and Chicago: University of Illinois Press, 1989), 13–25, 52–60, 161.

23. James R. Barrett, *Work and Community in the Jungle: Chicago's Packinghouse Workers, 1894–1922* (Urbana and Chicago: University of Illinois Press, 1987); Dominic A. Pacyga, *Polish Immigrants and Industrial Chicago: Workers on the South Side, 1880–1922* (Columbus: Ohio State University Press, 1991); Robert A. Slayton, *Back of the Yards: The Making of a Local Democracy* (Chicago: University of Chicago Press, 1986).

24. Barrett, *Work and Community in the Jungle*, 36–38, 42–44, 54–57, 79–83, 131–34, 138–46, 181. Similar conceptualizations of Americanization are found in Neil Betten, "Polish American Steelworkers: Americanization Through Industry and Labor," *PAS* 33:2 (Autumn 1976): 31–42; George Dorsey, "The Bayonne Refinery Strikes, 1915–1916," *PAS* 33:2 (Autumn 1976): 19–30; and Bukowczyk, "The Transformation of Working-Class Ethnicity."

25. Barrett, *Work and Community in the Jungle*, 203–4. Barrett also disputes contentions that the union organizing campaign precipitated the riot. See also Eric Bryan Halpern, "Black and White Unite and Fight: Race and Labor in Meatpacking" (Ph.D. diss., University of Pennsylvania, 1989); Barrett, *Work and Community in the Jungle*, 176, 256–68.

26. Pacyga also deals with Polish steelworkers in *Polish Immigrants and Industrial Chicago*, esp. 82–110.

27. Ibid., 13 (quotation), 176–78, 225–28, 255.

28. Ibid., esp. 5–10; Slayton, *Back of the Yards,* 129–50.

29. James S. Pula and Eugene E. Dziedzic, *United We Stand: The Role of Polish Workers in the New York Mills Textile Strikes, 1912 and 1916,* East European Monographs, no. 286 (Boulder, Colo.: East European Quarterly, 1990), 230.

30. Ibid., 46–122, 147–215.

31. David J. Goldberg, *A Tale of Three Cities: Labor Organization and Protest in Patterson, Passaic, and Lawrence, 1916–1921* (New Brunswick, N.J.: Rutgers University Press, 1989), 4–5, 14, 51–52, 82, 144, 166, 170–72, 206.

32. Ibid., 39, 96 (quotations). On the relationship between socialists and the Polish National Catholic Church, see Joseph W. Wieczerzak, "Bishop Hodor and the Socialists: Some Associations and Disassociations," *PAS* 40:2 (Autumn 1983): 5–35, and Lawrence Orzell, "A Minority Within a Minority," *PAS* 36:1 (Spring 1979): 53–58. Goldberg, *A Tale of Three Cities,* 83–122, 140–85. On Polish radicalism in Lawrence, see also Lucille O'Connell, "The Lawrence Textile Strike of 1912: The Testimony of Two Polish Women," *PAS* 36:2 (Autumn 1979): 44–61.

33. Goldberg, *A Tale of Three Cities,* 51–52, 60–62.

34. Ibid., 69, 82 (quotation), 171, 172. See also Morton Siegal, "The Passaic Strike of 1926" (Ph.D. diss., Columbia University, 1953).

35. Mary Eleanor Cygan, "Political and Cultural Leadership in an Immigrant Community: Polish American Socialism, 1880–1950" (Ph.D. diss., Northwestern University, 1989).

36. Ibid., 65–66. See also Paul Buhle, "Debsian Socialism and the 'New Immigrant' Workers," in *Insights and Parallels: Problems and Issues of American Social History,* ed. William L. O'Neill (Minneapolis: Burgess, 1973). Cygan, "Political and Cultural Leadership in an Immigrant Community," 67–68, 66–67, 55–56. For an account of Polish-American radio theater, see Mary E. Cygan, "A 'New Art' for Polonia: Polish American Radio Comedy During the 1930s," *PAS* 45:2 (Autumn 1988): 5–22.

37. Cygan, "Political and Cultural Leadership in an Immigrant Community," 27–32, 73–97, 105–16. On the complicated politics in Polonia engendered by World War I, see also Mieczysław B. Biskupski, "Paderewski as Leader of American Polonia, 1914–1916," *PAS* 43:1 (Spring 1986): 37–56; William J. Galush, "Polish Americans and the New Poland: An Example of Change in Ethnic Orientations," *Ethnicity* 1:1 (October 1974): 209–23; and Louis J. Zake, "The National Department and the Polish American Community, 1916–1923," *PAS* 38:2 (Autumn 1981): 16–25.

38. Cygan, "Political and Cultural Leadership in an Immigrant Community," 98–104.

39. Ibid., 133, 134–40, 139 (quotation).

40. Ibid., 140–49. On Polonia's competing political agendas during World War II, see Peter Irons, "The Test Is Poland: Polish Americans and the Origins of the Cold War," *PAS* 30:2 (Autumn 1973): 5–63, and Charles Sadler, "Pro-Soviet Polish Americans: Oscar Lange and Russia's Friends in the Polonia," *Polish Review* 22:4 (Winter 1977): 25–39.

41. Margaret Collingwood Nowak, *Two Who Were There: A Biography of Stanley Nowak* (Detroit: Wayne State University Press, 1989).

42. Collingwood Nowak, *Two Who Were There*, 42–74. For what is probably the only other extended biographical account in English of a Polish-American leftist, see Eugene Miller, "Leo Krzycki—Polish American Labor Leader," *PAS* 33:2 (Autumn 1976): 52–64.

43. Nowak, *Two Who Were There*, 65. See also Roger Keeran, *The Communist Party and the Auto Workers Union* (Bloomington: Indiana University Press, 1980); Keeran, "The International Workers Order and the Origins of the CIO," *Labor History* 30:3 (Summer 1989): 385–408; Thomas Gobel, "Becoming American: Ethnic Workers and the Rise of the CIO," *Labor History* 29:3 (Summer 1988): 173–98; and Gary Gerstle, "The Politics of Patriotism: Americanization and the Formation of the CIO," *Dissent* 33:1 (Winter 1986): 84–92.

44. Collingwood Nowak, *Two Who Were There*, 28–41. On the role of women in the rise of the CIO, see also Stella Nowicki, "Back of the Yards," in *Rank and File, Personal Histories by Working-Class Organizers*, ed. Alice and Staughton Lynd (Boston: Beacon Press, 1973), 67–88, and Georg Schrode, "Mary Zuk and the Detroit Meat Strike of 1935," *PAS* 43:2 (Autumn 1986): 5–39.

45. Collingwood Nowak, *Two Who Were There*, 75–128.

46. Ibid., 129–262. Radzilowski in ibid., 14. On Cold War–era persecutions of Eastern European Americans, see Robert Jeffrey Ryan, "The Conspiracy That Never Was: U.S. Government Surveillance of East European Leftists, 1942–1959" (Ph.D. diss., Boston College, 1990).

47. Steven Fraser, *Labor Will Rise: Sidney Hillman and the Rise of American Labor* (New York: The Free Press, Macmillan, 1991), 106. For a similar analysis, see Peter Friedlander, *The Emergence of a UAW Local, 1936–1939: A Study in Class and Culture* (Pittsburgh: University of Pittsburgh Press, 1975).

48. Fraser, *Labor Will Rise*, 106–8, 155–57, 337–43, 423–26.

49. Lizabeth Cohen, *Making a New Deal: Industrial Workers in Chicago, 1919–1939* (New York: Cambridge University Press, 1990), esp. 5–7, 13.

50. Ibid., esp. 11–13, 28, 38, 99–158, 213–38. For "moral capitalism," see esp. 209, 253, 286, 289, 291–92, 315, 366, 301 (quotation).

51. Ronald W. Schatz, *The Electrical Workers: A History of Labor at GE and Westinghouse, 1923–1960* (Urbana and Chicago: University of Illinois Press, 1983), xiii, 66, 81, 176.

52. Paul John Nyden, "Miners for Democracy: A Struggle in the Coal Fields" (Ph.D. diss., Columbia University, 1979), esp. 60–61, 90–91, 324–25, 474–528.

53. Philip W. Nyden, *Steelworkers Rank and File: The Political Economy of a Union Reform Movement* (New York: Praeger Press, 1984), esp. 69–89. William G. Falkowski, David A. Franczyk, and Russell Pawlak, "An Interview with Ed Sadlowski," oral history interview conducted in Buffalo, New York, in 1979 (manuscript at East Side Historical Association Archives, Polish Community Center of Buffalo); Nora Faires, "Immigrants and Industry: Peopling the 'Iron City'," in *City at the Point: Essays on the Social History of Pittsburgh,* ed. Samuel P. Hays (Pittsburgh: University of Pittsburgh Press, 1989), 23; and Staughton Lynd, "The Genesis of the Idea of a Community Right to Industrial Property in Youngstown and Pittsburgh, 1977–1987," *Journal of American History* 74:3 (December 1987): 926–58.

54. See J. Carroll Moody, "Introduction," in *Perspectives on American Labor History: The Problem of Synthesis,* ed. J. Carroll Moody and Alice Kessler-Harris (DeKalb: Northern Illinois University Press, 1989), ix.

55. George S. Pabis, "The Polish Press in Chicago and American Labor Strikes, 1892–1912," *PAS* 48:1 (Spring 1991): 7–22. The most extensive listing of such sources can be found in Groniowski, "Socjalistyczna emigracja Polska w Stanach Zjednoczonych, 1883–1914." There are also several valuable memoirs by Polish activists, which include Feliks Cienciara, "Wspomnienie" (Reminiscences) (manuscript at Polish Museum of Chicago, c. 1935); Boleslaw J. Gebert, *Za Tykocina za Ocean* (From Tykocina across the ocean) (Warsaw: Czytelnik, 1982); Gebert, "35 Lat w USA," *Z pola walki* (From the field of battle) 2:3 (1959): 140–82; Gebert, "Polska prasa robotnicza w USA" (The Polish workers' press in the USA), *Prasa Polska* (The Polish press) 13:6 (1960): 16–19; Gebert, "Polska lewica w USA w latach drugiej wojny światowej" (The Polish left in the USA in the years of World War II), *Z pola walki* 11:3 (1968): 199–221; Gebert, "Akcja komunistów polskich w USA w obronie Polski przed inwazją Hitlera" (Actions of Polish communists in the USA in defense of Poland against the invasion of Hitler), *Z pola walki* 12:3 (1969): 159–65; Gebert, "Amerykańsko-Polsko rada pracy, 1944–1948" (The Polish-American labor council, 1944–1948), *Kwartalnik historii ruchu zawodowego* 16:1 (1977): 44–55; Gebert, "Polacy w Amerykańskich związkach zawodowych" (Poles in American labor unions), *Przegląd Polonijny* 2:1 (1976): 158–76; Zofia Mazurowa and Leonild Wyszomirska, *Wspomnienia o Jędrzeju Cierniaku* (Reminiscences about Jedrzej Czerniak) (Warsaw: Ludowa Spółdzielnia Wydawnicza, 1982); and Stanley Nowak, "Udział Polaków w organizowaniu związku zawodowego robotników automobilowych w USA" (The participation of Poles in organizing the Automobile Workers Trade Union in the USA), *Problemy polonii Zagranicznej* (Problems of Polonia abroad) 6 (1971): 165–89.

56. On the history of the American left, see, for example, James Weinstein, *The Decline of Socialism in America* (New York: Monthly Review Press, 1967), and Christopher Lasch, *The Agony of the American Left* (New York: Vintage Books, 1969). Falkowski, "Accommodation and Conflict," 430.

57. Sean Wilentz, "Against Exceptionalism: Class Consciousness and the American Labor Movement, 1790–1920," *ILWCH* 26 (Fall 1984): 1–24.

58. See Jean-Yves Calves and Jacques Perrin, *The Church and Social Justice: The Social Teaching of the Popes from Leo XIII to Pius XII, 1878–1958* (Chicago: Henry Regnery, 1961).

59. Articles specifically focusing attention upon Polish-American workers up through the World War I era include Laura Anker, "Women, Work, and Family: Polish, Italian, Eastern European Immigrants in Industrial Connecticut," *PAS* 45:2 (Autumn 1988): 23–51; George Dorsey, "The Bayonne Refinery Strikes, 1915–1916," *PAS* 33:2 (Autumn 1976): 19–30; Tadeusz Z. Gasinski, "Polish Contract Labor in Hawaii, 1896–1899," *PAS* 39:1 (Spring 1982): 14–27; Edward F. Keuchel, "The Polish American Migrant Worker: The New York Canning Industry, 1900–1935," *PAS* 33:2 (Autumn 1976): 43–51; Joseph J. Parot, "The 'Serdeczna Matko' of the Sweatshops: Marital and Family Crises of Immigrant Working-Class Women in Late Nineteenth-Century Chicago," in *The Polish Presence in Canada and America,* ed. Frank Renkie-

wicz (Toronto: Multicultural History Society of Ontario, 1982), 19–28; Thaddeus Radzialowski, "A View from the Polish Ghetto: Some Observations on the First One Hundred Years in Detroit," *Ethnicity* 1:2 (July 1974): 125–50; Radzialowski, "The Competition for Jobs and Racial Stereotypes: Poles and Blacks in Chicago," *PAS* 33:2 (Autumn 1976): 5–18; Richard S. Sorrell, "Life, Work, and Acculturation Patterns of Eastern European Immigrants in Lackawanna, New York: 1900–1922," *Polish Review* 14:4 (Autumn 1969): 65–91.

Recent dissertations dealing with the subject of Polish-American workers include Laura Anker Schwartz, "Immigrant Voices, Home, Work, Community: Women/ Family in the Migration Process" (Ph.D. diss., State University of New York at Stony Brook, 1984); Mildred A. Beik, "The Miners of Windber: Class, Ethnicity, and the Labor Movement in a Pennsylvania Coal Town, 1890s–1930s" (Ph.D. diss., Northern Illinois University, 1989); Ewa Krystyna Hauser, "Ethnicity and Class Consciousness in a Polish American Community" (Ph.D. diss., Johns Hopkins University, 1982); Jeffrey David Kleiman, "Great Strike: Religion, Labor, and Reform in Grand Rapids, Michigan, 1890–1910" (Ph.D. diss., Michigan State University, 1985); Leslie Patricia Pilling, "A Case Study of Skilled Polish-American Auto Workers in Hamtramck, Michigan" (Ph.D. diss., Wayne State University, 1987); and Ron Isaac Rothbart, "Work, Family, and Protest: Immigrant Labor in the Steel, Meatpacking, and Anthracite Industries" (Ph.D. diss., University of California at Berkeley, 1988).

On the recognized need for studies on successive generations of working-class Polish Americans, see, for example, Thaddeus Radzilowski, "The Second Generation: The Unknown Polonia," *PAS* 43:1 (Spring 1986): 5–13.

On latter generations' conceptions of working-class ethnicity, see Richard D. Alba, *Ethnic Identity: The Transformation of Ethnicity in the Lives of Americans of European Ancestry* (New Haven: Yale University Press, 1991); Mary C. Waters, *Ethnic Options: Choosing Identities in America* (Berkeley and Los Angeles: University of California Press, 1990); and Bukowczyk, *And My Children Did Not Know Me,* 104–46.

60. Previously cited works by Cygan, Bukowczyk, and Falkowski have considered assimilation in terms of the process of capitalist hegemony.

61. A general treatment of the ACTU is found in Douglas P. Seaton, *Catholics and Radicals: The Association of Catholic Trade Unionists and the American Labor Movement, from Depression to Cold War* (East Brunswick, N.J.: Associated University Presses, 1981). For a more localized account, see Gerald R. Forton, "History of the Diocesan Labor College of Buffalo, N.Y., 1939–1959" (master's thesis, Niagara University, 1960).

3. Family, Women, and Gender: The Polish Experience

1. *Okolica* according to Florian Znaniecki is " 'the country around' both in the topographic and social sense." Helena Znaniecki Lopata calls it "the area within which a person's reputation is contained, the social area in which a person lives and interacts, the social life space which contains his identities." In Europe the *okolica* usually included the village, the parish, and the commune. See William I. Thomas and Florian Znaniecki, *The Polish Peasant in Europe and America* (New York: Dover,

1958), vol. 1, 144–56; and Helena Znaniecki Lopata and Mary P. Erdmans, *Polish Americans: Status Competition in an Ethnic Community* (New Brunswick, N.J.: Transaction, 1993), 19. The *okolica* is a key element of Thomas and Znaniecki's analysis of the problem of the Polish family in Europe and America. As the peasant had developed few internalized controls, in their view, the external control exercised by the *okolica* was the major source of social peace and order in Polish peasant society.

There have been no modern studies of the Polish-American family comparable to the excellent historical monographs that have appeared on the Italian-American family such as Virginia Yans-McLaughlin, *Family and Community: Italian Immigrants in Buffalo, 1880–1930* (Ithaca, N.Y.: Cornell University Press, 1977).

2. Lois Kalloway, "An Analysis of Polish-American Research, 1967–1977" (typescript in the author's possession).

3. See Caroline Golab, "The Impact of the Industrial Experience on the Immigrant Family: The Huddled Masses Reconsidered," in *Immigrants in Industrial America, 1850–1920,* ed. Richard Erlich (Charlotteville, Va.: University Press of America, 1977), 1–32, and Helena Z. Lopata, "The Polish American Family," in *Ethnic Family in America: Patterns and Variations,* ed. C. H. Mindel and R. W. Habenstein (New York: Elsevier, 1976), 15–40. For a more extended version, see H. Znaniecka Lopata, "Rodziny polonijne" (Polish-American families), in *Polonia amerykańska przeszłość i współczesność* (American Polonia past and present), ed. H. Kubiak, G. Kusielewicz, and T. Gromada (Wrocław: Ossolineum, 1988). See also John Bodnar, Roger Simon, and Michael P. Weber, *Lives of Their Own: Blacks, Italians, and Poles in Pittsburgh, 1900–1960* (Urbana: University of Illinois Press, 1982); Ewa Morawska, *For Bread with Butter: Life-Worlds of East Central Europeans in Johnstown, Pennsylvania, 1890–1940* (New York: Cambridge, 1985); and Adam Walaszek, *Światy imigrantów: Tworzenie polonijnego Cleveland, 1880–1930* (Immigrant worlds: The making of Polish Cleveland) (Cracow: Nomos, 1994).

4. The classic example is Thomas and Znaniecki's *The Polish Peasant in Europe and America.* See also Niles Carpenter and Daniel Katz, *A Study of Acculturation in the Polish Group of Buffalo, 1926–1928,* University of Buffalo Studies, vol. 7, no. 4 (June 1929); Peter Ostafin, "The Polish Peasant in Transition: A Study of Group Integration as a Function of Symbioses and Common Defunction" (Ph.D. diss., University of Michigan, 1948); Arthur E. Wood, *Hamtramck: A Sociological Study of a Polish American Community* (New Haven, Conn.: College and University Press, 1955); Theodore F. Abel, "Sunderland: A Study of Changes in the Group Life of Poles in a New England Farming Community," in *Immigrant Farmers and Their Children,* ed. Edmund de Brunner (New York: Doubleday, 1929), 213–43; Eugene Obidinski, "Ethnic Group to Status Group: A Study of Polish Americans in Buffalo" (Ph.D. diss., State University of New York at Buffalo, 1968); Harold Pederson, "Acculturation Among Danish and Polish Ethnic Groups in Wisconsin" (Ph.D. diss., State University of Wisconsin, 1949); Theresita Polzin, *The Polish Americans: Whence and Whither* (Pulaski, Wis.: Franciscan Publishers, 1973); Ewa Krystyna Hauser, "Ethnicity and Class Consciousness in Polish American Community" (Ph.D. diss., Johns Hopkins University, 1981); Lopata and Erdmans, *Polish Americans;* Elizabeth Rooney, "Polish Americans and Family Disorganization," *American Catholic Sociolog-*

ical Review (March 1957): 47–51; W. Lloyd Warner and Leo Srole, *The Social Systems of American Ethnic Groups* (New Haven: Yale University Press, 1945); and William C. McCready "The Persistence of Ethnic Variation in American Families," in Andrew Greeley, *Ethnicity in the United States: A Preliminary Reconnaissance* (New York: John Wiley and Sons, 1974). For a brief survey of some of these studies, see Irwin T. Sanders and Ewa T. Morawska, *Polish-American Community Life: A Survey of Research* (New York: Polish Institute of Arts and Sciences, 1975), 139–84.

5. Thomas and Znaniecki, *The Polish Peasant*, vol. 2, 1647–830. See also Robert E. Park, "The City: Suggestions for the Investigation of Human Behavior in the Urban Environment," *American Journal of Sociology* 20 (1916): 577–612.

6. Thomas and Znaniecki, *The Polish Peasant*, vol. 2, 1743, 1751–52.

7. The new view draws its inspiration from the work of E. P. Thompson, especially his classic, *The Making of the English Working Class* (New York: Pantheon, 1963); and Herbert Gutman, "Work, Culture, and Society in Industrializing America, 1819–1918," *American Historical Review* 78 (1973): 531–88. On immigrant families, see Tamara K. Hareven, "Family and Work Patterns of Immigrant Laborers in a Planned Industrial Town, 1900–1930," in Erlich, *Immigrants in Industrial America*, 46–66; Virginia Yans-McLaughlin, "A Flexible Tradition: South Italian Immigrants Confront a New Work Experience," in Erlich, *Immigrants in Industrial America*, 67–84; and Yans-McLaughlin, "Patterns of Work and Family Organization: Buffalo's Italians," *Journal of Interdisciplinary History* 2 (1971): 299–314.

8. Morawska, *For Bread with Butter*, 144–50, 206–8; Bodnar, Simon, and Weber, *Lives of Their Own*, 153–82; Olivier Zunz, *The Changing Face of Inequality: Urbanization, Industrial Development, and Immigrants in Detroit* (Chicago: University of Chicago Press, 1982), 170–76; John Bodnar, "Immigration and Modernization: The Case of Slavic Peasants in Industrial America," *Journal of Social History* 10 (1976): 49–50; Robert Barrows, "Beyond the Tenement: Patterns of American Urban Housing, 1870–1930," *Journal of Urban History* 9 (August 1983): 415–16; Margaret F. Byington, *Homestead: The Households of a Mill Town*, ed. Paul Kellogg (New York: Charities Publications, 1910), 153–56; Edith Abbott, *The Tenements of Chicago, 1908–1935* (Chicago: University of Chicago Press, 1936), 379–82; Thomas and Znaniecki, *The Polish Peasant*, vol. 1, 162; David Hogan, "Education and the Making of the Chicago Working Class, 1880–1930," *History of Education Quarterly* 18 (Fall 1978): 236–45.

9. Hogan, "Education," 246–48. Hogan notes that "high levels of home ownership were associated with high rates of child labor and low rates of school attendance" (246). See also Morawska, *For Bread with Butter*, 127–29.

10. Zunz, *The Changing Face*, 173–76; Roger D. Simon, "Housing and Services in an Immigrant Neighborhood: Milwaukee's Ward 14," *Journal of Urban History* 2 (August 1976): 450–53.

11. Golab, "The Impact of the Industrial Experience on the Immigrant Family," 32. Golab also notes that "America was merely another alternative . . . available to some one desperately in need of work to preserve a way of life that was slipping through his fingers" (ibid., 6).

12. Morawska, *For Bread with Butter*, 22–78.

13. Golab, "The Impact of the Industrial Experience on the Immigrant Family,"

17–18; Bodnar, Simon, and Weber, *Lives of Their Own*, 56–57. See also interview with Joseph Debski in Tamara Hareven and Randolph L. Langenbach, *Amoskeag: Life and Work in an American Factory-City* (New York: Pantheon, 1978), 135–36.

14. Figures compiled by the U.S. Bureau of Immigration and Naturalization for 1909–1914 are probably accurate for most of the 1880–1914 period. They indicate that only 38 percent of Polish immigrants aged between fourteen and forty-four were married. See Tamara Hareven and John Modell, "Family Patterns," in the *Harvard Encyclopedia of American Ethnic Groups*, ed. Stephan Thernstrom (Cambridge: Harvard University Press, 1980), table 1, p. 347. Golab, *The Impact of the Industrial Experience on the Immigrant Family*, 18.

15. Zand, *Polish Folkways in America*, 28. Hareven and Modell, in "Family Patterns," table 1, p. 347, give the ratio of unmarried women to men to be 1:1.8. This is the ratio for immigration between 1909 and 1914. The endogamy rate for the large Polish community in New York City was 91 percent for the first generation and 83 percent for the second generation on the eve of World War I, according to a 1921 study noted in Hareven and Modell, "Family Patterns," table 2, p. 348. A more recent study gives out-group marriage rates for Poles in Wisconsin in 1910 as 10.7 percent in the first generation and 19.1 percent for the second generation. See Richard M. Barnard, *The Melting Pot and the Altar: Marital Assimilation in Early Twentieth-Century Wisconsin* (Minneapolis: University of Minnesota Press, 1980), 66. The out-group marriage rates may, however, be even lower than Bernard indicates. His one example of a Polish-German intermarriage is of a Rose Robakowski, a Polish immigrant leather cutter, marrying Paul Poczoch, a mariner and the son of a "German" West Prussian immigrant. His name and the fact that they met at St. Stanislaus Church casts doubt on his Germanness. Bernard seems to have confused nationality with ethnicity in this case. Given the West Prussian origin of his family, the spelling of his name, and his occupation, Paul Poczoch was probably a Kaszub who, following family tradition or his own decision, identified as a Pole, as evidenced by his attendance at the Polish church. For a summary of all major intermarriage studies, see Sanders and Morawska, *Polish American Community Life*, 178–84.

16. Zand, *Polish Folkways in America*, 28. In Wisconsin in 1910 about 35 percent of Polish immigrant males married second-generation Polish-American women. Only 8 percent of Polish immigrant women married second-generation men. See Bernard, *The Melting Pot and the Altar*, 56. Interview with Mary Stojak (from Chicago), STO-136, *Oral History Archive of Chicago Polonia* (OHACP) (Chicago Historical Society, Chicago, Illinois), 103. Woman from Detroit cited in *Dziennik Polski* (Detroit), November 1, 1924. Zand, *Polish Folkways in America*, 28.

17. Sophia Nadrowska, Chicago, Illinois, to Reynold Nadrowski, Rypin District 2/XII/1890, #270, cited in Witold Kula, Nina Assordobraj-Kula, and Marcin Kula, *Writing Home: Immigrants in Brazil and the United States, 1890–1891*, trans. Josephine Wtulich (Boulder, Colo.: East European Monographs, 1986). See also Adam Raczkowski letter in Thomas and Znaniecki, *Polish Peasant*, vol. 1, 729.

18. Zand, *Polish Folkways in America*, 28.

19. Tamara Hareven notes that some of the new studies of the family have created a "neo-romantic interpretation" of it that not only refutes the notion of social break-

down but exaggerates the family's strength and autonomy. See Tamara Hareven, "Family and Work Patterns of Immigrant Laborers in a Planned Industrial Town," 48–49.

20. Thomas and Znaniecki, *The Polish Peasant,* vol. 2, 1773. It should be noted that Thomas and Znaniecki themselves do not adduce much statistical support for their contentions. Herbert Blumer in his now classic critique of *The Polish Peasant in Europe and America* argued that Thomas and Znaniecki "have shown surprising liberty in making generalizations . . . for which there are few if any data in the materials." See Herbert Blumer, *An Appraisal of Thomas and Znaniecki's "The Polish Peasant in Europe and America"* (New York: Social Science Research Council, 1939), 10.

21. For the idea of disorganization, see, for example, the 1929 Carpenter and Katz monograph, "A Study of the Acculturation of the Polish Group in Buffalo." Nelson Algren, *Never Come Morning* (New York: Harper and Row, 1942); Clifford Shaw, *The Jack Roller* (Chicago: University of Chicago Press, 1966). On Clifford Shaw and his work with Polish-American youth of Chicago, see Dominic Pacyga, "The Russell Square Community Committee: An Ethnic Response to Urban Problems," *Journal of Urban History* 15, no. 2 (February 1989): 159–84. For the pre-1940 period, see, for example, the editorial in *Głos Polek* (Chicago), November 17, 1910, in response to a report indicating that Poles in Chicago had the highest number of juvenile offenders and children wards of court.

22. Thomas and Znaniecki, *The Polish Peasant,* vol. 2, 1651. On gangs and juvenile crime in Cleveland, see Walaszek, *Światy imigrantów,* 143–44, who notes that 60 percent of the juvenile shoplifters arrested in a major Cleveland department store in the last decade of the nineteenth century were Polish. Frederick M. Thrasher, *The Gang* (Chicago: University of Chicago Press, 1927). Thrasher notes that along Milwaukee Avenue in the heart of the Polish community "there is a gang in almost every block" (ibid., 9–10). Dr. Anna Wrzezokowska to Jane Addams, Feb. 23, 1912, in the Jane Addams Correspondence, roll 3 (December 1911–July/August 1913), Swarthmore College Peace Collection, Swarthmore, Pa.

23. Carolyn Golab asserts in passing that the problem of crime and juvenile delinquency was "very low" for Polish Americans and that they "have always been less likely to form gangs." This directly contradicts Thrasher as well as Thomas and Znaniecki. Golab, however, does not indicate the period for which she feels this is true, nor any details of her survey. As documentation she cites the following: "Statements on gangs and juvenile delinquency are based on a study of crime statistics in Polish sections of Philadelphia, Baltimore, Chicago, Scranton and Wilkes-Barre, and interviews of parish priests, school principals, civic leaders, social workers and police captains in predominantly Polish wards of these cities." See Golab, "The Impact of the Industrial Experience on the Immigrant Family," 30. My own survey of data on juvenile delinquency in the Polish neighborhoods of Detroit in the late 1930s show it to be considerably higher than the city average. See *City of Detroit, City Plan Commission, Master Plan Reports: The People of Detroit* (Detroit, 1946), 33–34.

24. Joseph John Parot, " 'The Serdeczna Matko' of the Sweatshops: Marital and Family Crises of Immigrant Working Class Women in Late Nineteenth Century Chicago," in *The Polish Presence in Canada and America,* ed. Frank Renkiewicz (Toronto: Multicultural History Society of Ontario, 1982), 175.

25. McCreedy, "The Persistence of Ethnic Variation in American Families," 168.

26. John L. Thomas, S.J., *The American Catholic Family* (Englewood Cliffs, N.J.: Prentice Hall, 1956), 251–58; Charles T. O'Reilly and Margaret M. Pembroke, *Older People in a Chicago Community* (Ann Arbor, Mich.: Braun-Brumfield, 1957), 28–29.

27. Helen Wendell, "Conditions in Hamtramck," *Pipps Weekly* 2:23 (September 24, 1921): 10–11.

28. City of Detroit, *Annual Report of the Departments of Public Welfare, 1929.* This report and others from the period are on file at the Burton Historical Collection of the Detroit Public Library.

29. For additional data on social and economic conditions of Detroit's Polonia, see Thaddeus C. Radzialowski, "Ethnic Conflict and the Polish Americans of Detroit, 1921–1942," in Renkiewicz, *The Polish Presence,* 199–203. Today infant mortality rates of 15–20 per 1,000 births, which occur in drug-ravaged inner-city areas and the poorest Indian reservations, are considered shocking. See Judith Rosenblatt, ed., *Indians of Minnesota* (Minneapolis: University of Minnesota Press, 1985), 202.

30. Mary E. Cygan, "Mothers as Managers: A Revolution in Polish Agriculture?" (paper delivered at the Conference on Conflict and Cooperation: Comparative Research on East European Migratory Experience, 1880–1930, University of Bremen, Bremen, Germany, April 1990).

31. Thomas and Znaniecki, *The Polish Peasant,* vol. 1, 180.

32. Cygan, "Mothers as Managers," 12–13. For an excellent study of an area of Russia in which women assumed the majority of the agricultural tasks in many households while the men migrated for wages, see Barbara Alpern Engel, "The Woman's Side: Male Out-Migration and the Family Economy in Kostroma Province," *Slavic Review* 45, no. 2 (Summer 1986): 257–71. Engel notes that a young man who was not the householder often married prior to migration in order to leave behind a worker in the family. The males who returned regularly for part of the year to the villages in Kostroma did not resume agricultural tasks (see ibid., 257–58, 262–63). We have no evidence that this was true for Polish migrants who returned from America since it appears that most of their duties had been assumed by other male relatives rather than by their wives.

33. Cygan, "Mothers as Managers," 5–6.

34. *Merrily We Sing: 106 Polish Folksongs,* collected and edited by Harriet M. Pawlowska (Detroit: Wayne State University Press, 1961), 154–55.

35. See case histories cited by Krystyna Duda-Dziewierz, *Wieś małopolska a emigracja amerykańska* (A village in Little Poland and the American emigration) (Warsaw-Poznań: Polski Institut Socjologiczny, 1938), 34–36. See also Kula et al., *Writing Home* (letters #787, #276); and Thomas and Znaniecki, *The Polish Peasant,* vol. 1, 494 (letters #494, #495), 840–41 (#516, #517), and 851–52 (#527). For perceptive analyses of the dilemmas faced by the women left behind, see Cygan, "Mothers as Managers," 3–12.

36. J. A. Perkins, "The Agricultural Revolution in Germany, 1850–1914," *Journal of European Economic History* 10 (1981): 107–8.

37. A surprising number of the interviews in the OHACP are with single women who came alone or with a small group of peers. See OHACP interviews CIS-049,

LEN-014, JED-070, SIW-097. One young woman for example left her home to escape a cruel sister-in-law (see OHACP interview LEN-014). See also Carol Williams, "The Life History of a Polish Immigrant," *Polish American Studies* 25, no. 2 (July–December 1968): 87–89 (hereafter cited as *PAS*).

38. Interview STO-020 OHACP; Interview CIS-049 OHACP.

39. See Kula et al., *Writing Home,* letters #148, #166, #174, #212, #276. See OHACP interviews MAK-106, MON-024. On the other hand, some husbands gave quite detailed advice on the trip. One husband even advised his wife on her hair style and dress so that she would not look out of place. In particular, he advised her not to wear a shawl. See Marja Gliwicowna, "Droga emigracji" (The emigration road), *Przegląd Socjologiczny* 4, no. 34 (1936): 512.

40. See "Protection of Immigrant Girls on Arrival at Interior Point," from the "First Annual Report of the Immigrants Protective League of Chicago," in *The Ordeal of Assimilation,* ed. Stanley Feldstein and Lawrence Costello (Garden City, N.Y.: Anchor Press, 1974), 86–89; also George K. Turner, "The Daughters of the Poor," *McClure's* (November 1909): 45–58, and Lucille O'Connell, "Travelers' Aid for Polish Immigrant Women," *PAS* 31, no. 1 (Spring 1974): 15–19. O'Connell notes that, during its first year in operation in New York (1909), Travelers' Aid helped more Polish girls than girls of any other ethnic group.

41. "Steerage Conditions," from *Reports of the United States Immigration Commission,* vol. 37 (1911).

42. Edith Abbott, "Grace Abbott and Hull House, 1908–1921," *Social Service Review* (September 1950): 384–85.

43. Kula et al., *Writing Home,* letter #220, and OHACP interviews SIW-097, JED-070, STO-136, BOG-093, MAJ-080, CHR-021; Louise Lamphere, *From Working Daughters to Working Mothers: Immigrant Women in a New England Industrial Community* (Ithaca, N.Y.: Cornell University Press, 1987), 81–82, 159–65; Leslie Woodcock Tentler, *Wage Earning Women; Industrial Work and Family Life in the United States, 1900–1930* (Oxford: Oxford University Press, 1979), 80–81.

44. On clashes over marriage choices, leisure activities, tastes, ideas, and so on, see OHACP interviews ORK-115, MON-024; "The Foreign Born in Our Midst," a speech by M. McDowell, 1929, in *McDowell Papers* (folder 12, Chicago Historical Society Archives, Chicago, Illinois); for a case of a sixteen-year-old Polish girl who refused to return to Europe with her parents, see OHACP interview ARE-055.

45. See OHACP interviews BLA-144, MAR-028. For an example of a young immigrant woman who did not know how to care for her child until taught by an aunt, see interview ORK-115. Lamphere, *From Working Daughters to Working Mothers,* 77–81; see also Thaddeus C. Radzilowski, "The Second Generation: The Unknown Polonia," *PAS* 43, no. 1 (Spring 1986): 5–12.

46. Thomas and Znaniecki, *The Polish Peasant,* vol. 2, 1750–51.

47. On this topic, see Suzanne Sinke, "A Historiography of Immigrant Women in the Nineteenth and the Early Twentieth Centuries," *Ethnic Forum* 9, nos. 1–2 (1989): 123–28, and Sidney S. Weinberg, "The Treatment of Women in Immigration History: A Call for a Change," in *Seeking Common Ground: Multidisciplinary Studies of Immigrant Women in the United States,* ed. Donna Gabaccia (Westport, Conn.: Praeger, 1992), 3–22.

48. Miceala di Leonardo, "The Female World of Cards and Holidays: Women, Families, and the Work of Kinship," *SIGNS* 12 (Spring 1987): 440–53.

49. Donna Gabaccia, "Immigrant Women: Nowhere at Home?" *Journal of American Ethnic History* 10, no. 4 (Summer 1991): 70–71. For a study that sees recent Polish immigrant women as isolated and unsupported in a family that has, in immigration, turned from cooperation to competitiveness, see Harriet Block, "Changing Domestic Roles Among Polish Women," *Anthropological Quarterly* 49 (1976): 3–10.

50. Obidinski and Zand, *Polish Folkways in America*, 5–18.

51. Thomas and Znaniecki, *The Polish Peasant*, vol. 2, 1511–66. See also Radzilowski, "The Unknown Polonia," 7–10.

52. The history of the Polish Women's Alliance has unfortunately been little studied. There is a two-volume official history in Polish: Jadwiga Karlowiczowna, *Historia Związku Polek w Ameryce*, vol. 1 (Chicago: ZPA Press, 1938), and Maria Lorys, *Historia Związek Polek w Ameryce*, vol. 2 (Chicago: ZPA Press, 1980). The second volume takes the story up through 1959. For the early history, see Thaddeus C. Radzialowski, "Immigrant Nationalism and Feminism: *Głos Polek* and the Polish Women Alliance in America, 1898–1920," *Review Journal of Philosophy and Social Science* 2, no. 2 (Winter 1977): 183–203, reprinted in abridged form as "Let Us Join Hands: The Polish Women's Alliance," in *Immigrant Women*, ed. Maxine Seller (Philadelphia: Temple University Press, 1981), 174–80. See also William Galush, "Purity and Power: Chicago Polonia Feminists, 1880–1914," *PAS* 47, no. 1 (Spring 1990): 5–24; and Adam Walaszek, "The Polish Women's Alliance in America: Between Feminism and Patriotism" (paper read at Conference on Ethnic Fraternals in America, Maribor, Slovenia, May 1994).

53. Radzialowski, "Immigrant Nationalism and Feminism," 186–88, 193–97.

54. *Głos Polek*, November 24, 1910 (quotation). The failure to know and understand the history of ethnic women's organizations like the ZPA or the First Catholic Slovak Ladies Union (FCSLU) has impoverished our understanding of women's experience in America. In 1975, for example, the establishment of a Women's Bank capitalized at 3 million dollars was heralded as a breakthrough for women. At that time, the ZPA was capitalized at over 30 million dollars and the FCSLU at more than 45 million dollars, and each represented more than three-quarters of a century of experience by women in investing, making loans, writing insurance, and running a complex financial institution. The Women's Bank failed within a few years, but the ZPA, FCSLU, and other such institutions founded by immigrant women are still going strong. On the Women's Bank, see *New York Times*, October 17, 1978.

55. The material on the Polish-American sisterhoods is vast. For an overview with an excellent bibliography that carries the story through 1960, see Sister Mary Julia Doman, CSSF, "Polish American Sisterhoods and Their Contributions to the Catholic Church in the U.S.," *Sacrum Poloniae Millenium* (Rome: Gregorian University Press, 1962), vol. 6, 371–612. For some recent histories, see Sister Anne Marie Knawa, OSF, *As God Shall Ordain: A History of the Franciscan Sisters of Chicago, 1894–1987* (Lemont, Ill.: Franciscan Sisters, 1989); Sister Mary Janice Ziolkowski, CSSF, *The Felician Sisters of Livonia, Michigan: The First Province in America* (Detroit: Harlo Press, 1984); Sister Josephine Marie Peplinski, SSJ-TOSF, *A Fitting Response: The*

History of the Sisters of St. Joseph of the Third Order of St. Frances (South Bend, Ind.: Sisters of St. Joseph, 1982). For a preliminary attempt to put the experience of the Polish-American sisterhoods in the context of the social history of the Polish-American community, see Thaddeus C. Radzialowski, "Reflections on the History of the Felicians in America," *PAS* 32, no. 1 (Spring 1976): 19–28.

56. For a general discussion of this new religious outlook, see Timothy L. Smith, "Lay Initiative in the Religious Life of American Immigrants, 1880–1950," in *Anonymous Americans: Explorations in Nineteenth Century Social History,* ed. Tamara Hareven (Englewood Cliffs, N.J.: Prentice-Hall, 1971), 214–49.

57. For further discussion of these themes, see Thaddeus Radzilowski, *Immigrant Women and Their Daughters: The Polish Experience,* Annual Fedorczyk Lecture, Central Connecticut State University, 1989 (New Britain, Conn.: Polish Studies Program, 1992), and Radzilowski, "Reflections on the History of the Felicians," 22–25. See also John J. Bukowczyk, "The Immigrant 'Community' Re-examined: Political and Economic Tensions in a Brooklyn Polish Settlement, 1888–1894," *PAS* 37, no. 2 (Autumn 1980): 5–16. These topics—especially questions of investment and patronage—will be the subject of a future study. On the role of French-Canadian nuns in stimulating migration of family members, see Lamphere, *Working Daughters to Working Mothers,* 72.

58. Doman, "Polish American Sisterhoods," 362–71; Sister Ellen Marie Kuznicki, CSSF, "The Polish Parochial Schools," in *Poles in America: Bicentennial Essays,* ed. Frank Mocha (Stevens Point, Wis.: Worzalla Publishing, 1978), 435–60. See also Thaddeus Radzilowski, "Inventing Polonia: Polish American Parochial Schools and the Creation of Polish American Ethnicity" (paper delivered at the joint meeting of the international conference on Research in Education and the Society for the History of Education, October 23, 1992, Cambridge, Mass.).

59. For an important early study of wages and conditions, see Caroline Manning, *The Immigrant Woman and Her Job* (Washington, D.C.: Government Printing Office, 1930). A study that draws on and summarizes census and labor surveys and confines itself to Polish Americans is Edward Pinkowski, "The Great Influx of Polish Immigrants and the Industries They Entered," in Mocha, *Poles in America,* 435–60. See also Barbara Klaczynska, "Why Women Work: A Comparison of Various Groups—Philadelphia, 1910–1930," *Labor History* 17 (Winter 1976): 73–87; Corrine Agen Krause, "Urbanization Without Breakdown: Italian, Jewish, and Slavic Immigrant Women in Pittsburgh, 1900–1945," *Journal of Urban History* (May 1978): 291–306; Susan Davis, "Women's Roles in a Company Town: New York Mills, 1900–1951," *New York Folklore* 4, nos. 1–4 (1978): 35–47; Virginia Yans-McLaughlin, "Patterns of Work and Family Organization: Buffalo's Italians," *Journal of Interdisciplinary History* (Autumn 1971): 298–314; Tamara K. Hareven, "The Laborers of Manchester, New Hampshire, 1912–1922: The Role of the Family and Ethnicity in Adjustment to Industrial Life," *Labor History* (Spring 1975): 248–65; and *Family Time and Industrial Time* (Cambridge: Cambridge University Press, 1982), 228–40; Doris Weatherford, *Foreign and Female: Immigrant Women in America, 1840–1930* (New York: Schoeken, 1986), 106–8, 120–23; Laura Anker, "Women, Work, and Family: Polish, Italian, and East European Immigrants in Industrial Connecticut, 1890–

1940," *PAS* 45, no. 2 (Autumn 1988): 32–46; Lamphere, *From Working Daughters to Working Mothers*, 77–82, 159–68; Lamphere with Ewa Hauser, Dee Rubin, Sonya Michel, and Christina Simmons, "The Economic Struggle of Female Factory Workers: A Comparison of French, Polish, and Portuguese Immigrants," in *Conference on the Educational and Occupational Needs of White Ethnic Women* (Washington, D.C.: National Institute of Education, 1980), 129–52; Morawska, *For Bread with Butter*, 123–24, 195–96, 217–18, 288–89. The account that follows is drawn from the above sources.

60. Edward Kantowicz, *Polish American Politics in Chicago* (Chicago: University of Chicago Press, 1975), 30. Kantowicz estimates that, at the beginning of the century, 3 percent of Poles in Chicago ran saloons.

61. Mary McDowell, "The Standard of Living: Civic Frontiers Men" (1914) in McDowell Papers, box 3, folder 13, 1–5. For 1915, see Anker, "Women, Work, and Family," 37.

62. See Lawrence Orton, *Polish Detroit and the Kolasiński Affair* (Detroit: Wayne State University Press, 1981).

63. For Pennsylvania, see Victor Greene, *The Slavic Community on Strike* (South Bend, Ind.: Notre Dame University Press, 1965), 143–45. For Brooklyn, see Frank Renkiewicz, "Polish-American Workers, 1880–1980," in *Pastor of the Poles: Polish American Essays,* ed. Stanislaus Blejwas and M. Biskupski (New Britain, Conn.: Polish Studies Monographs, 1982), 121.

64. Samuel Yellin, *American Labor Struggles* (New York: Monad Press, 1974), 176. See also Lucille O'Connell, "The Lawrence Strike of 1912: The Testimony of Two Polish Women," *PAS* 36, no. 2 (Autumn 1979): 44–62. On the role of Polish-American women in other textile strikes, see James S. Pula and Eugene E. Dziedzic, *United We Stand: The Role of Polish Workers in the New York Mills Textile Strikes, 1912 and 1916* (New York: East European Monographs, 1990).

65. See, for example, *Dziennik Chicagoski* (The Chicago daily news), December 8, 9, 1921. The most intense participation by the women was in the street demonstrations and battles and in the community relief committees. See also *Dziennik Chicagoski*, December 21, 1921, and January 23, 1992. Some women were members of the union and played a role in it. See James R. Barrett, *Work and Community in the Jungle: Chicago's Packing House Workers, 1894–1922* (Urbana: University of Illinois Press, 1987), 136–37, 176. Barrett notes that the "wives and mothers played an extremely important role in holding the strike together." On immigrant women unionists in the 1903–1904 strike, see "Labor—The Great Strike," in McDowell Papers, box 3, folder 15, 7–14.

66. For an account of the meat strike and Mary Zuk's subsequent career, see George Schrode, "Mary Zuk and the Detroit Meat Strike of 1935," *PAS* 43, no. 2 (Autumn 1986). Although useful, the article should be used with some caution. The author, unable to read Polish, could not use a number of important sources. He also made several errors that weaken his argument at points. For a critique of the article, see my comments in *PAS* 44, no. 1 (Spring 1987): 96–97.

67. On these activities, see my paper "Class, Ethnicity, and Gender: Polish American Women and the Organization of CIO Unions in Detroit," delivered at the

Missouri Valley Historical Conference, Omaha, Nebraska, on March 9, 1989. See also Steve Babson, *Working Detroit* (New York: Adama Books, 1984), 71–78; Jane Dobija, "Women on Strike: Polish Solidarity in Detroit," *Monthly Detroit* (April 1982): 60–63; Margaret C. Nowak, *Two Who Were There* (Detroit: Wayne State University, 1988), 28–42.

68. Nowak, *Two Who Were There,* 103–19; Ruth Meyerowitz, "Organizing the United Automobile Workers: Women Workers at the Ternstedt General Motors Parts Plant," in *Women Work and Protest,* ed. Ruth Milkman (Boston: Routledge and Kegan Paul, 1984), 245–58; Patricia Pilling, "The Response of Skilled Polish American Automobile Workers to Job Challenges in Hamtramck, Michigan, in the Early 80's," *PAS* 47, no. 1 (Spring 1990): 51; Nowak, *Two Who Were There,* 124–25. Nowak notes that the whole Polish neighborhood turned out to battle police with eggs, rocks, sticks, and stones.

69. See, for example, John J. Bukowczyk and Peter D. Slavcheff, "Metropolitan Detroit Polish Americans: A Statistical Profile," *PAS* 48, no. 1 (Spring 1991): 23–62.

4. Polish Americans and Religion

1. The best expression of Smith's views is his 1978 essay, now dated as to sources but still provocative in perspective, Timothy L. Smith, "Religion and Ethnicity," *American Historical Review* 83 (December 1978): 1155–85. Dolan, while confining his study to Catholics, has introduced a concern for the laity and a sensitivity to ethnicity and class seldom found earlier among students of his faith community. Most representative is Jay P. Dolan, *The American Catholic Experience: A History from Colonial Times to the Present* (Garden City, N.Y.: Doubleday, 1985).

Examples of overviews of religion among Poles are in John Bukowczyk, *And My Children Did Not Know Me: A History of the Polish-Americans* (Bloomington: Indiana University Press, 1987); and Dolores Liptak, R.S.M., *Immigrants and Their Church* (New York: Macmillan, 1989), 114–30. Older but still useful is Daniel S. Buczek, "Polish Americans and the Roman Catholic Church," *Polish Review* 21 (1976): 39–61. A sociological perspective with some useful observations, though in dated typology, is Rev. Leonard F. Chrobot, "The Pilgrimage from *Gemeinschaft* to *Gesellschaft:* Sociological Functions of Religion in the Polish American Community," in *The Polish Presence in Canada and America,* ed. Frank Renkiewicz (Toronto: The Multicultural History Society of Ontario, 1982).

2. M. Torosiewicz, "Pierwszy ksiądz Polak w Stanach Zjednoczonych," *Przegląd Kościelny* 2 (1924): 567–71; Mieceslaus Haiman, *Polish Past in America, 1608–1865* (Chicago; PRCU, 1939). For a reverential survey with references to clergy, see Joseph Wytrwal, *Poles in American History and Tradition* (Detroit: Endurance Press, 1969).

3. Anthony Kuzniewski, S.J., "Francis Dzierożynski and the Jesuit Restoration in the United States," *Catholic Historical Review* 78 (January 1992): 51–73 (henceforth referred to as *CHR*).

4. Rev. Wacław Kruszka, *Historya polska w Ameryce* (Milwaukee: Kuryer Publishing, 1905–1908). A recent fine English translation under the editorship of James S. Pula has printed half in two volumes, and the remainder will follow. See *A History of*

Poles in America (Washington, D.C.: Catholic University Press, 1993, 1994). Kruszka was also one of the few priests to publish an autobiographical work, *Siedm siedmioleci czyli pół wieku życia: Pamiętnik i przyczynek do historii w Ameryce,* 2 vols. (Milwaukee: Author's imprint, 1924).

5. Rev. Alexander Syski, *Ks. Józef Dąbrowski: Monografia historyczna* (Orchard Lake, Mich.: Seminarium Polski, 1942); Rev. Joseph Swastek, *Polish Priest and Pioneer* (Detroit: n.p., 1951). Filiopietistic articles are common in *Polish American Studies* (hereafter referred to as *PAS*) before 1960, but they are useful sources of factual data. Examples include Sr. M. Edwin, O.P., "The Founder of the Polish Seminary," *PAS* 8 (January–June 1951): 21–28; Sr. M. Benedicta, C.S.S.F., "Father Joseph Dąbrowski—Educator," *PAS* 9 (January–June 1952–1953): 11–16; Sr. M. Donata Slominska, "Rev. John Pitass, Pioneer Priest of Buffalo," *PAS* 17 (1960): 28–41. A more recent uncritical study is T. Lindsay Baker, "The Early Years of Rev. Wincenty Barzyński," *PAS* 32 (Spring 1975): 29–52. A more popularly written but still fertile source for brief lives of clerics is *Sodalis,* especially in the 1950s: for example, Rev. Joseph Swastek, "Pierwszy kapłan polski w Michigan," *Sodalis* 32 (February 1951): 21–24, and "Ks. Moczygemba a Ks. Dąbrowski," *Sodalis* 33 (February 1952): 19–21. Capsule biographies of clerics and laypersons in this vein appear in Rev. Francis Bolek, *Who's Who in Polish America* (New York: Harbinger House, 1943).

6. The Polish Museum of America in Chicago has a large collection of these works, with more at the Immigration History Research Center at the University of Minnesota. There are also sizable holdings at the Central Archives of Polonia at Orchard Lake, Michigan; see Roman Nir, "The Central Archives of Polonia," *PAS* 51 (Spring 1994), esp. 67–68. Parishes typically have copies of works concerning their own congregation.

7. Daniel S. Buczek, *Immigrant Pastor: The Life of the Right Reverend Monsignor Lucyan Bójnowski of New Britain, Connecticut* (Waterbury, Conn.: Heminway, 1974). Stanislaus Blejwas is less complimentary in his characterization of Bójnowski. See Stanislaus Blejwas, "A Polish Community in Transition: The Origins of Holy Cross Parish, New Britain, Connecticut," *PAS* 34 (Spring 1977): esp. 33–34.

8. Andrzej Brożek, *Ślązacy w teksasie: Relacje o najstarszych osadach polskich w Ameryce* (Warsaw: Państwowe Wydawnictwo Naukowe, 1972); Anthony J. Kuzniewski, S.J., *Faith and Fatherland: The Polish Church War in Wisconsin, 1896–1918* (Notre Dame: University of Notre Dame Press, 1980). See also his "Wenceslaus Kruszka and the Origins of Polish Roman Catholic Separatism in the United States," in *The Polish Presence in Canada and America,* ed. Renkiewicz; Victor Greene, *For God and Country: The Rise of Polish and Lithuanian Ethnic Consciousness in America, 1860–1910* (Madison: State Historical Society of Wisconsin, 1975); Joseph John Parot, *Polish Catholics in Chicago, 1850–1920* (DeKalb: Northern Illinois University Press, 1981); John Bukowczyk, "Steeples and Smokestacks: Class, Religion, and Ideology in the Polish Immigrant Settlements in Greenpoint and Williamsburg, Brooklyn, 1880–1929" (Ph.D. diss., Harvard University, 1980); see also Bukowczyk, "The Immigrant Community Re-examined: Political and Economic Tensions in a Brooklyn Polish Settlement, 1888–1894," *PAS* 37 (Autumn 1980): 5–16.

9. John Iwicki, C.R., *The First Hundred Years: A Study of the Apostolate of the*

Congregation of the Resurrection in the United States, 1866–1966 (Rome: Gregorian University Press, 1966). His ambitious multivolume general history of the congregation has the first tome in publication. See John Iwicki, C.R., with James Wahl, C.R., *Resurrectionist Charism: A History of the Congregation of the Resurrection, 1836–1886* 1 (Rome: n.p., 1986); Parot, *Polish Catholics,* esp. 47–94.

10. A more reverential work is Rev. Franciszek Domański, S.J., "Patriarcha amerykańskich Jezuitów O. Franciszek Dzierożynski, T.J.—Szkic życia i działalności," *Sacrum poloniae millenium* (Rome: Gregorian University Press, 1960), vol. 1, 459–530. A brief but professional study is Kuzniewski, "Francis Dzierożynski."

11. Ludwik Grzebień, S.J., *Burzliwe lata polonii amerykańskiej: Wspomnienia i listy misjonarzy jezuickich, 1864–1913* (Cracow: Wydawnictwo Apostolstwa Modlitwy, 1983). Letters sent to the Galician Jesuit internal publication *Nasze Wiadomości* in this period are good sources of information.

12. Descriptive essays with historical background and statistics on numerous congregations serving Polonia worldwide appear in Rev. Józef Bakalarz et al., *Działalność męskich zgromadzeń wśród Polonii* (Lublin: Katolicki Uniwersytet Lubelski, 1982).

13. Victor Greene, *The Slavic Community on Strike: Immigrant Labor in Pennsylvania Anthracite* (Notre Dame: Notre Dame University Press, 1968), esp. 35–39. For Chicago, see Greene, *For God and Country,* and Parot, *Polish Catholics.* Other colonies in the Midwest are examined in Kuzniewski, *Faith and Fatherland;* Frank Renkiewicz, "The Poles," in *They Chose Minnesota: A Survey of the State's Ethnic Groups,* ed. June Drenning Holmquist (St. Paul: Minnesota Historical Society Press, 1981); Galush, "Forming Polonia." John Bukowczyk discusses Brooklyn in "Steeples and Smokestacks"; while Stanislaus Blejwas, *St. Stanislaus B. and M. Parish, Meriden, Connecticut: A Century of Connecticut Polonia, 1891–1991* (New Britain, Conn.: Polish Studies Program Monographs, 1991), and Buczek, *Immigrant Pastor,* look at New England communities.

14. A fine survey of the multiple purposes of fraternalism is Frank Renkiewicz, "The Profits of Non-Profit Capitalism: Polish Fraternalism and Beneficial Insurance in America," in *Self-Help in Urban America: Patterns of Minority Economic Development,* ed. Scott Cummings (Port Washington, N.Y.: Kennikat Press, 1980); see also William J. Galush, "Forming Polonia: A Study of Four Polish-American Communities, 1890–1940" (Ph.D. diss., University of Minnesota, 1975), esp. 47–54, 137–54.

15. Parot, *Polish Catholics,* esp. 3–46; Greene, *For God and Country.* Dominic Pacyga describes, the role of fraternals in the later-developing South Side of Chicago. See Dominic A. Pacyga, *Polish Immigrants and Industrial Chicago: Workers on the South Side, 1880–1922* (Columbus: Ohio State University Press, 1991), esp. 128–36.

16. Mieczysław Haiman, *Zjednoczenie polskie rzymsko-katolickie w Ameryce, 1873–1948* (Chicago: PRCU, 1948).

17. Greene, *For God and Country,* esp. 85–99, is the best exponent of this perspective. Parot, *Polish Catholics,* basically agrees; and the most recent history of the PNA follows this line. See Donald E. Pienkos, *PNA: A Centennial History of the Polish National Alliance of the United States of North America* (Boulder, Colo.: East European Monographs, 1984), esp. 50–66.

18. See William J. Galush, "Forming Polonia," esp. 82–105, which describes the

supportive stance of the PNA lodges in Minneapolis and Utica, N.Y. Examples of instances of conflict between "clericals" and "nationalists" in smaller communities such as Rochester, New York, and Meriden, Connecticut, appear in Kathleen Urbanic, *Shoulder to Shoulder: Polish Americans in Rochester, N.Y., 1890–1990* (Rochester: Monroe Reprographics, 1991), esp. 38–40; and Blejwas, *St. Stanislaus,* esp. 23–26.

19. Timothy L. Smith, "Religious Denominations as Ethnic Communities: A Regional Case Study," *Church History* 35 (June 1966): 207–26; Josef J. Barton, *Peasants and Strangers: Italians, Rumanians, and Slovaks in an American City, 1890–1950* (Cambridge: Harvard University Press, 1975); Jay P. Dolan, *The Immigrant Church: New York's Irish and German Catholics, 1815–1865* (Baltimore: Johns Hopkins University Press, 1975).

Polity in the antebellum period is best covered in Patrick Carey, *People, Priests, and Prelates: Ecclesiastical Democracy and the Tensions of Trusteeism* (Notre Dame: University of Notre Dame Press, 1987). This includes astute observations on the postbellum era in his "Epilog." An older clericalist work offers useful legal information; see Patrick Dignan, *A History of the Legal Incorporation of Catholic Church Property in the United States, 1784–1932* (Washington, D.C.: 1932).

20. An older general description of the process is Karol Wachtl, *Polonja w Ameryce: Dzieje i dorobek* (Philadelphia: Author's imprint, 1944), esp. 85–88. Examples in Minnesota, Ohio, and New York are in Galush, "Forming Polonia," 82–100; for Buffalo, see William Falkowski, "Accommodation and Conflict: Patterns of Polish Immigrant Adaptation to Industrial Capitalism and American Political Pluralism in Buffalo, N.Y., 1873–1901" (Ph.D. diss., State University of New York at Buffalo, 1990), 111–25. For examples of laity forming Roman Catholic parishes in defiance of episcopal wishes, see Gallagher, *Century of History,* esp. 161–71.

For listing of Roman Catholic parishes, see Joseph E. Ciesluk, *National Parishes in the United States* (Washington, D.C.: Catholic University Press, 1947); for the presence of Polish National as well as Roman Catholic congregations (with unsubstantiated population figures), see F. Niklewicz, *Polacy w Stanach Zjednoczonych* (Green Bay, Wisc.: n.p., 1937).

21. Older Roman Catholic historians deplored departures from the Roman obedience as examples of personal vindictiveness, lay arrogance, or infatuation with American democratic structures. Their counterparts in the Polish National Catholic orientation usually described the dissenters as democratic and patriotic heroes standing up to an authoritarian church run by non-Poles. A representative Roman Catholic interpretation is Kruszka, *History of the Poles,* vol. 1, 78, 95–98; on Polish National Catholics, see Paul Fox, *The Polish National Catholic Church* (Scranton, Penn.: School of Christian Living, 1957), and Theodore Andrews, *The Polish National Catholic Church in America and Poland* (London: SPCK, 1953).

Recent students have examined Detroit most fully, with numerous studies on the Kolasiński conflict at St. Albertus in the late 1880s. See Lawrence D. Orton, *Polish Detroit and the Kolasiński Affair* (Detroit: Wayne State University Press, 1981); Leslie Woodcock Tentler, "Who Is the Church?" *Comparative Studies in Society and History* 25 (April 1983); Earl Boyea, "Father Kolasiński and the Church of Detroit," *CHR* 74 (July 1988): 420–39. For Chicago, see Parot, *Polish Catholics,* esp. 95–132. For an unusual example of an abortive attempt in Winona, Minnesota, see William Crosier, "A Social History of Winona, Minnesota, 1880–1905" (Ph.D. diss., University of Nebraska, 1975). *PNCC Studies*—an annual of the Polish National Catholic Church, founded in 1980—has occasional articles on early separatists.

22. Examples of early pro-Polish National Catholic publications are Fox, *Polish National Catholic Church; Po drodze życia* (Scranton: Straż Printery, 1922); *Księga pamiątkowa "33" w trzydziestą trzecią rocznice powstania polsko narodowego kościoła w Ameryce i dwudziestą rocznicę pierwszego sejmu polsko narodowej spójni, 1897–1930* (Scranton: Straż Printery, 1930). Less polemical but still in the older tradition is Rev. Stephan Wlodarski, *The Origin and Growth of the Polish National Catholic Church* (Scranton, Pa.: PNCC, 1974).

23. Kruszka, *History of the Poles,* vol. 1, esp. 95–100. A history of the Scranton Roman Catholic diocese treats the origins extensively, portraying Father Hodur as duplicitous in his secret efforts to arrange a reconciliation on his own terms while publicly portraying his opposition to the old church. See John Gallagher, *A Century of History: The Diocese of Scranton, 1868–1968* (Scranton, Pa.: Haddon Craftsmen, 1968), 210–43.

24. In addition to this publication focusing exclusively on independentism in its various forms, *Polish American Studies* and *Acta Polonia Historia* have some articles on dissent.

25. Hieronim Kubiak, *The Polish National Catholic Church in the United States of American from 1897 to 1980* (Cracow: Państwowe Wydawnictwo Naukowe, 1982). There is a Polish version dated 1970; the English version is not revised but notes some new publications. Barbara Strassberg, "The Origins of the Polish National Catholic Church: The 'Polish National' Catholic Factor Reconsidered," *PNCC Studies* 7 (1986): 25–38; John Bukowczyk, "The Transforming Power of the Machine: Popular Religion, Ideology, and Secularization Among Polish Immigrant Workers in the United States, 1880–1940," *International Labor and Working Class History* 34 (Fall 1988): 28–30.

26. Along with the Lutheran majority, there were scatterings of Polish Baptists, Methodists, Presbyterians, and others. See Mirosław Boruta, "Przegląd źródeł do badań nad Polonia nierzymskokatolicka ze szczególnm uwzględnieniem polonijnych skupisk protestanskich," *Przegląd Polonijny* 14 (1988): 3, 73–84 (henceforth referred to as *PP*); Barbara Leś, "Funkcje polskich zborów bapystycznych w środowisku polonii amerykańskiej," *PP* 6 (1980): 1, 19–32; W. Borkenhagen, *Zarys historii lutersko-polskich zborów synodu Missouri* (Chicago: n.p., 1956). A brief summary appears in Andrzej Brożek, *Polish Americans, 1854–1939* (Warsaw: Interpress, 1977), 53–55.

27. Protestant evangelism up to World War I is summarized in Joel Hayden, "Religious Work Among the Poles" (New York: n.p., 1916); see also Paul Fox, *The Poles in America* (1922; New York: Arno Press, 1970), esp. 115–34.

28. Kruszka, *History of the Poles,* vol. 1, 89–90, 100–106; see also his autobiography, *Siedm siedmioleci.* There are numerous articles on Bishop Hodur and his episcopal rivals in other dissenting denominations in *PNCC Studies.*

29. Greene, *For God and Country,* esp. 122–42; Kuzniewski, *Faith and Fatherland,* esp. 45–69; Galush, "Both Polish and Catholic."

30. Edward Kantowicz, *Corporation Sole: Cardinal Mundelein and Chicago Catholicism* (Notre Dame, Ind.: University of Notre Dame Press, 1983), esp. 71–72. For other references to Rhode's national role, see Kuzniewski, *Faith and Fatherland,* 75–76; Buczek, *Immigrant Pastor,* 72. Since Edward Kozlowski, appointed in 1914, died soon after, Rhode for many years was the sole Polish-American bishop.

31. Tentler, "Who Is the Church?" 241–76; William J. Galush, "Purity and Power: Chicago Polonian Feminist Leaders, 1880–1914," *PAS* 47 (Spring 1990): 5–24.

32. Jadwiga Karlowiczowa, *Historia związku polek w Ameryce* (Chicago: Związek Polek, 1938); there are two later volumes in the same format of amateur narrative. See also Donald Pienkos, *One Hundred Years Young: A History of the Polish Falcons in America, 1887–1987* (Boulder, Colo.: East European Monographs, 1987).

33. Margaret Thompson, "Women, Feminism, and the New Religious History: Catholic Sisters as a Case Study," in *Belief and Behavior: Essays in the New Religious History,* ed. Philip R. Vandemeer and Robert P. Swierenga (New Brunswick, N.J.: Rutgers University Press, 1991). More explicit references to Polish nuns are in her "Sisterhood and Power: Class, Culture, and Ethnicity in the American Convent," *Colby Library Quarterly* 25 (September 1989): 149–75. See also Barbara Misner, "A Comparative Social Study of the First Eight Permanent Communities of Women Religious Within the Original Boundaries of the United States, 1790–1850" (Ph.D. diss., Catholic University, 1981).

34. For example, Sr. Mary Jeremiah Studniewska, C.S.S.F., "The Educational Work of the Felician Sisters of the Province of Detroit in the United States, 1874–1948" (Ph.D. diss., Catholic University, 1948); Sr. Mary Theophania Kalinowski, C.S.S.F., "First Decade of the Sisters of St. Felix in America, 1874–1884" (master's thesis, Loyola University of Chicago, 1956); N.a., *Magnificat: A Centennial Record of the Congregation of St. Felix* (Buffalo: Privately printed, 1955); Artur Górski, *Angela Truszkowska* (Poznań: Pallottinum, 1959). Even the recent work by Ziolkowski is essentially an uncritical narrative: Sr. Mary Janice Ziolkowski, C.S.S.F., *The Felician Sisters of Livonia, Michigan: First Province in America* (Detroit: Harlo Press, 1984).

35. Sr. Mary Jane Kadyszewski, C.S.S.F., *One of the Family: History of the Felician Sisters Our Lady of Sacred Heart Province, Corapolis, Pennsylvania, 1920–1977* (Pittsburgh: Wolfson Publishing, 1982). For a rare work by an outsider, see the insightful article by Thaddeus Radzialowski, "Reflections on the History of the Felicians in America," *PAS* 32 (Spring 1975): 19–28.

36. Older works are sometimes strong narratives and well researched, but frequently reverential. Catholic universities often have theses on local institutions: for example, Sr. M. Dulcissima Malolepszy, C.S.S.F., "A Historical Study of St. Hedwig's Home, an Institution for the Care of Dependent Children, Archdiocese of Chicago" (master's thesis, Loyola University of Chicago, 1945); Sr. Mary Bonaventura Kalinowska, "History and Development of Villa Maria Academy" (master's thesis, Canisius College, 1949); Mary Celestine, "A Historical and Developmental Study of the Immaculate Heart of Mary Home for Children" (master's thesis, University of Buffalo, 1945); Raymond A. Punda, "History of St. Joseph's Orphanage in Milwaukee" (master's thesis, St. Francis Seminary, 1939).

37. Sr. Anne Marie Knawa, O.S.F., *As God Shall Ordain: A History of the Francis-*

can Sisters of Chicago, 1894–1987 (Lemont, Ill.: League of the Servant of God Mother Mary Theresa, 1989); also "Jane Addams and Josephine Dudzik: Social Service Pioneers," *PAS* 35 (Spring/Autumn 1978): 13, 22; Sr. M. DeChantal, C.S.F.N., *Out of Nazareth: A Centenary of the Sisters of the Holy Family of Nazareth in the Service of the Church* (New York: Exposition Press, 1974); Sr. Antonia Pisarska, C.R., "Powstanie i rozwój Zgromadzenia Sióstr Zmartwychstania Pańskiego" in *Sacrum poloniae millenium* (Rome: Gregorian University Press, 1960), vol. 7, 145–380.

38. For examples of communities born of division, see Sr. Josephine Marie Peplinski, S.S.J., T.O.S.F., *A Fitting Response: The History of the Sisters of St. Joseph of the Third Order of St. Francis,* vol. 1 (South Bend, Ind.: The Sisters of St. Joseph of the Third Order of St. Francis, 1982); Srs. M. Edwina Bogel and Jane Marie Blach, *In All Things Charity: A Biography of Mother M. Collette Hilbert, Franciscan Sisters of St. Joseph* (Hamburg, N.Y.: n.p., 1983); Sr. Mary Dunstan Klewicki, O.S.F., *Ventures for the Lord: The History of the Sisters of St. Francis Sylvania, Ohio* (Sylvania, Ohio: n.p., 1990). A recent work on Duluth Benedictines describes a secession by Polish nuns. See Sr. Mary Richard Boo, O.S.B., *House of Stone: The Duluth Benedictines* (Duluth, Minn.: St. Scholastica Priory Books, 1991), esp. 57–68.

39. Rev. Dacian Bluma, O.F.M., *A History of the Province of the Assumption of the Blessed Virgin Mary* (Pulaski, Wisc.: Franciscan Publishers, 1967) has many useful citations. A massive jubilee book by Rev. Eugene Hagedorn, O.F.M., on *Franciscans in Nebraska* (n.p., 1931) has numerous biographies and descriptive essays with sources noted in the introduction. More scholarly is Rev. Antoni Zwiecan, O.F.M., "Działalność franciskanów wśród polonii, 1772–1976," *Studia Polonije* 3 (1979): esp. 120–42.

40. William Galush, "Both Polish and Catholic: Immigrant Clergy in the American Church," *CHR* 70 (July 1984): 407–27; John Bukowczyk, "Factionalism and the Composition of the Polish Immigrant Clergy," in *Pastor of the Poles: Polish-American Essays Presented to the Right Reverend John P. Wodarski in Honor of the Fiftieth Anniversary of his Ordination,* ed. Stanislaus Blejwas and M. B. Biskupski (New Britain: Central Connecticut State College, 1982).

41. Daniel O'Neill, "St. Paul Priests, 1851–1930: Recruitment, Formation, and Mobility" (Ph.D. diss., University of Minnesota, 1979); see also Marvin O'Connell, *John Ireland and the American Catholic Church* (St. Paul: Minnesota Historical Society Press, 1988), esp. 378–80, 411–12. Recent studies reiterate this in other dioceses. See Leslie Woodcock Tentler, *Seasons of Grace: A History of the Catholic Archdiocese of Detroit* (Detroit: Wayne State University Press, 1990), 305; Kantowicz, *Corporation Sole,* 60–61.

42. Early works were more reverent tributes: for example, Rev. Joseph Swastek, "The Formative Years of the Polish Seminary in the United States," in *Sacrum poloniae millenium* (Rome: Gregorian University Press, 1959), vol. 6, 39–150. The most complete and professional survey is Frank Renkiewicz, *For God, Country, and Polonia: One Hundred Years of the Orchard Lake Schools* (Orchard Lake, Mich.: Center for Polish Studies and Culture, 1985).

43. References are most common in studies of major organizations, but only in a descriptive manner: for example, Pienkos, *PNA,* 91–93; Renkiewicz, "The Profits of Non-Profit Capitalism," in *Self-Help in Urban America: Patterns of Minority Business Enterprise,* ed. Scott Cummings (Port Washington, N.Y., 1980).

44. Joseph Hapak, "The Polish Military Commission, 1917–1919," *PAS* 38 (Autumn 1981): 26–38; John Bukowczyk, "Mary the Messiah: Polish Immigrant Heresy and the Malleable Ideology of the Roman Catholic Church, 1880–1930," *Journal of American Ethnic History* 4 (Spring 1985): 5–32. On the change in Polonian orientation, in which religious leaders played a significant role, see William J. Galush, "American Poles and the New Poland: An Example of Change in Ethnic Orientation," *Ethnicity* 1 (1974): 209–21.

45. William I. Thomas and Florian Znaniecki, *The Polish Peasant in Europe and America* (New York: Dover, 1958); Jan Perkowski, *Vampires of the Slavs* (Cambridge, Mass.: Slavica, 1976).

46. John Bodnar, *Workers' World: Kinship, Community, and Protest in an Industrial Society, 1900–1940* (Baltimore and London: Johns Hopkins University Press, 1982); Herbert Gutman, *Work, Culture, and Society in Industrializing America* (New York: Vintage, 1977), 3–78; John Bukowczyk, "The Transforming Power of the Machine," 22–38.

47. Helen Stankiewicz Zand and Eugene Obidinski, *Polish Folkways in America: Community and Family* (Lanham, Mass.: University Press of America, 1987); Aleksander Posern-Zielinski, *Tradycja a etniczność: Przemiany kultury Polonii amerykańskiej* (Wrocław: Ossolineum, 1982). More general observations, which include Poles, are in Colleen McDannell, "Catholic Domesticity, 1860–1960," in *American Catholic Women: A Historical Exploration,* ed. Karen Kennelly, C.S.J. (New York: Macmillan, 1989). For Chicago Polonia, see Pagyga, *Polish Immigrants,* esp. 111–19. For Detroit Polonia, see Sr. Mary Remigia Napolska, C.S.S.F., *The Polish Immigrant in Detroit to 1914* (Chicago: PRCU, 1946), esp. 63–71, and Arthur E. Wood, *Hamtramck, Then and Now: A Sociological Study of an American Community* (New Haven: College and University Press, 1955), esp. 40–42. For San Antonio Polonia, see Sr. Jan Maria Wozniak, "St. Michael's Church: The Polish National Catholic [actually Roman Catholic] Church in San Antonio, Texas, 1855–1950" (master's thesis, University of Texas, 1964), esp. 57–62.
Occasionally parish anniversary books include sections on local customs: for example, Rev. Michael R. Dylag, "Seventy-Five Years of an Ethnic Parish, 1900–1975: St. Francis of Paola Church (Polish), Ford City, Pennsylvania" (Ford City, Pa.: Privately printed, 1975), esp. 18–27. On the tradition of living pictures, see Emil Orzechowski, "Polonijne widowska parateatralne w Stanach Zjednoczonych (opisy kilku żywych obrazów)," *PP* 14 (1988): 2, 131–45. Suggestive general comments on Polish religious sensibilities are in Joseph Swastek, "The Contributions of the Catholic Church in Poland to the Catholic Church in the United States of America," *PAS* 24 (January–June 1967): 15–26.

48. Several writers have offered multigenerational or comparative studies. See Stanislaus Blejwas, "Nowa i stara Polonia: Napięcie w społeczność," in *Polonia amerykańska: Przeszłość i współczesność,* ed. Hieronim Kubiak (Wrocław: Ossolineum, 1988), and Helena Lopata Znaniecka, *Polish Americans: Status Competition in an Ethnic Community* (Englewood Cliffs, N.J.: Prentice-Hall, 1976).

49. On changes in the content of instruction in Polish schools, see Józef Miąso, *The History of the Education of Polish Immigrants in the United States,* trans. Ludwik

Krzyżanowski (Warsaw: Polish Scientific Publishers, 1977). For examples of changes in nuns' ministry and the effect of declining numbers, see Knawa, *As God Shall Ordain,* esp. 764–66, 832–34; also Peplinski, *A Fitting Response: The Growth, 1902–1962,* vol. 2; Sr. M. Charles Szymanska, "History and Work of the Ave Maria Guild of Felician Sisters of Buffalo" (master's thesis, Canisius College, N.Y., 1949). A new history of the Buffalo Felicians by Sr. Ellen Kuznicki should be available about 1996.

50. Daniel Buczek, *Last of the Titans: Monsignor-Colonel Alphonse A. Skoniecki of Massachusetts* (Sterling Heights, Mich.: The Society of Christ in America, 1986); and Buczek, "Three Generations of the Polish Immigrant Church: Changing Styles of Pastoral Leadership," in Blejwas and Biskupski, *Pastor of the Poles,* 20–36. For a homeland perspective, see Piotr Taras, S.A.C., "Problemy duszpasterstwa polonijnego na przykładzie sytuacji w USA," *Studia Polonijne* 2 (1977): 181–205.

51. Rev. Leonard Chrobot, ed., "Seventy-Five Years of the Orchard Lake Seminary" (Orchard Lake, Mich., 1960); Renkiewicz, *For God, Country, and Polonia.*

52. Rev. Jacek Przygoda, "Szkic historyczny polskiej katolickiej literatury homiletycznej w Stanach Zjednoczonych," *Sacrum poloniae millenium,* vol. 4 (1957); Rev. Aleksander Syski, *Pamiętnik pierwszego zjazd homiletycznego w Ameryce* (Detroit: n.p., 1941), and *Pamiętnik drugiego zjazd homiletycznego w Ameryce* (Pittsburgh: n.p., 1946). For examples of sermons printed for clerical use, see Rev. T. Misicki, *Siedem krótkich kazan* (Chicago: Dziennik Zjednoczenia Press, 1922); Rev. Casimir Smogor, *Nauki wielkopostne na niedziele wielko postu* (Niles, Ill.: n.p., 1925); Rev. Justyn Figas, *Mówy radiowe* (Milwaukee: Nowiny Polskie Press, 1932–1945); Rev. Józef Bakalarz, TChr., "Polskie modlitewniki na emigracji," *Studia Polonijne* 4 (1981): 213–27.

For a biography of Figas, see Clement R. Jarnot, "The Very Reverend Justyn M. Figas, O.F.M. Conv., His Life and Accomplishments" (master's thesis, St. Bonaventure University, 1971).

53. Blejwas, *St. Stanislaus,* and "A Polish Community in Transition," *PAS* 34 (Spring 1977): 26–69. Less analytical but well described is Urbanic, *Shoulder to Shoulder.* Two works on aspects of recent Detroit Polonia are Thaddeus Radzialowski, "The View from the Polish Ghetto," *Ethnicity* 1 (July 1974): 125–50, and Jeannie Wylie, *Poletown: Community Betrayed* (Urbana: University of Illinois Press, 1989). A sociologist has examined Buffalo Polonia in Eugene E. Obidinski, "Ethnic to Status Group: A Study of Polish Americans in Buffalo" (Ph.D. diss., State University of New York at Buffalo, 1968). For a listing of Polish congregations, see Rev. Zdzisław Peszkowski, "A List of Polish Roman Catholic Parishes in the United States," in *Sacrum poloniae millenium,* vol. 6 (1959): 255–71.

54. Mary Cygan, "Ethnic Parish as Compromise: The Spheres of Clerical and Lay Authority in a Polish American Parish, 1911–1930" (Working Paper Series, Notre Dame University, 1983); Jarosław Rokicki, "Obrzęd religijny jako symbol grupy etnicznej: Konflikt o pasterkę w diecezji Scranton, Pa., w latach 1935–1936," *PP* 12 (1986): 4, 39–52. Quarrels did not disappear entirely, however; for an example from the 1970s, see Blejwas, *St. Stanislaus,* 131–40.

55. See Wachtl, *Polonja w Ameryce,* esp. 90–92; Rev. Francis Bolek, "Catholic Priests of Polish Descent in the United States to 1957: A Tentative List," in *Sacrum poloniae millenium,* vol. 6 (1959): 151–253. Renkiewicz addresses the matter more ana-

lytically in the context of his study of the Polish Seminary. See Renkiewicz, *For God, Country, and Polonia,* esp. 66–70.

56. George G. Gargasz, "St. John Cantius Seminary, 1918–1964," *PAS* 24 (July–December 1967): 84–87.

57. Edward Kulik, "Polish-American Catholic Bishops," *PAS* 24 (January–June 1967): 27–31; on Krol, see James F. Connelly, *The History of the Diocese of Philadelphia* (Wynnewood, Pa.: Unigraphics, 1976), 473–572.

58. Pienkos, *PNA,* esp. 190–94; Haiman, *Zjednoczenie,* esp. 371–75.

59. Barbara Leś, *Kościół w procesie asymilacji polonii amerykańskiej* (Wrocław: Ossolineum, 1981); Paul Wrobel, *Our Way: Parish and Neighborhood in a Polish-American Community* (Notre Dame: University of Notre Dame Press, 1979); Posern-Zielinski, *Tradycja a etniczność;* Walter J. Slowiak, "A Comparative Study of the Social Organizations of the Family in Poland and the Polish Immigrant Family in Chicago" (master's thesis, Loyola University of Chicago, 1950); Walter Duda, "A Study of the Polish Welfare Association of Chicago" (master's thesis, Loyola University of Chicago, 1951).

60. Kubiak, *Polish National Catholic Church,* 121–24, 150–204; Eugene E. Obidinski, "Ethnic Conflict to Ethnic Conservation: Changing Functions of Polish National Catholic Congregations," *PNCC Studies* 7 (1986): 53–66; Adam Lenarczyk, "Threats to and Chances for the Development of the Polish National Catholic Church: Psychological and Legal Aspects," *PNCC Studies* 3 (1982): 31–46.

5. Jewish Emigration from Poland Before World War II

1. Sholem Ash [Asch], *Kiddush Ha-Shem: An Epic of 1648* (1926; New York: Arno Press, 1975), 63–64. Alternate versions appear in *The Shtetl Book,* ed. Diane K. Roskies and David G. Roskies (n.p.: Ktav, 1975), xii–xiii. Bernard D. Weinryb, *The Jews of Poland* (Philadelphia: Jewish Publication Society, 1973), 156–76, discusses Jewish identification with Poland.

2. Timothy L. Smith puts religious definitions of national identity in perspective in "Religion and Ethnicity in America," *American Historical Review* 83:5 (December 1978): 1155–85.

3. Wiktor Weintraub, "Tolerance and Intolerance in Old Poland," *Canadian Slavonic Papers* 13:1 (1971): 21–43. Gershon David Hundert and Gershon C. Bacon survey the scholarly literature in *The Jews in Poland and Russia: Bibliographical Essays* (Bloomington: Indiana University Press, 1984). There is no modern survey of Jewish history in Poland; still valuable, though dated and incomplete, is *Żydzi w Polsce odrodzonej,* 2 vols. (Warsaw: 1933). The 1980s witnessed a remarkable growth of Polish Jewish studies, including Chimen Abramsky et al., ed., *The Jews in Poland* (Oxford: Blackwell, 1986); the ongoing series *Polin: A Journal of Polish-Jewish Studies* (Oxford: Blackwell); and Magdalena Opalski and Israel Bartal, *Poles and Jews: A Failed Brotherhood* (Hanover: University Press of New England, 1992). For the interwar period, see Ezra Mendelsohn, *The Jews of East Central Europe Between the World Wars* (Bloomington: Indiana University Press, 1983), 11–83. Two recent books exploring complementarity between Poles and Jews are M. J. Rosman, *The Lords' Jews: Magnate*

Jewish Relations in the Polish-Lithuanian Commonwealth During the Eighteenth Century (Cambridge, Mass.: Harvard University Press, 1990), and Gershon David Hundert, *The Jews in a Polish Private Town: The Case of Opatów in the Eighteenth Century* (Baltimore: Johns Hopkins University Press, 1992).

4. Yisrael Gutman et al., ed., *The Jews of Poland Between Two World Wars* (Hanover: University Press of New England, 1989), 223–537.

5. Stephen D. Corrsin, *Warsaw Before the First World War: Poles and Jews in the Third City of the Russian Empire, 1880–1914* (Boulder, Colo.: East European Monographs, 1989), 33–34. For disagreements as to the accuracy of census figures, compare Antony Polonsky, *Politics in Independent Poland, 1921–1939* (Oxford: Clarendon Press, 1972), 40, and Joseph Lichten, "Notes on the Assimilation and Acculturation of Jews in Poland, 1863–1943," in Abramsky et al., *The Jews in Poland*, 106–29. See also *Żydzi w polsce odrodzonej*, vol. 1, 395–401, 531–32, Celia S. Heller, *On the Edge of Destruction: Jews of Poland Between the Two World Wars* (New York: Columbia University Press, 1977), 143–248, and Aleksander Hertz, *The Jews in Polish Culture*, trans. Richard Lourie (Evanston, Ill.: Northwestern University Press, 1988), for assimilated and traditional Jews in Poland.

6. Two excellent new surveys of American Jewish history, with bibliographies, are Howard M. Sachar, *A History of the Jews in America* (New York: Knopf, 1992); and Henry L. Feingold, *The History of the Jewish People in America*, a five-volume series in which the relevant volumes are Gerald Sorin, *A Time for Building: The Third Migration, 1880–1920*, and Henry L. Feingold, *A Time for Searching: Entering the Mainstream, 1920–1945*. All three works provide extensive bibliographies. Louis Finkelstein, ed., *The Jews: Their History, Culture, and Religion*, 3d ed. (New York: Harper and Brothers, 1960), includes significant chapters by noted specialists on Jewish immigration and life in America. Gerald Tulchinsky, *Taking Root: The Origins of the Canadian Jewish Community* (Toronto: Lester, 1992) covers Canadian Jewish history to 1914; and Tulchinsky's article "Recent Developments in Canadian Jewish Historiography," *Canadian Ethnic Studies* 14:2 (1982): 114–25, provides a bibliography for the interwar period. See also Jonathan D. Sarna, "Jewish Immigration to North America: The Canadian Experience," *Jewish Journal of Sociology* 18:1 (June 1976): 31–41. Irving Howe, *The World of Our Fathers* (New York: Harcourt, Brace, Jovanovich, 1976), offers a vivid account of New York City's East European Jewish community emphasizing proletarian and socialist culture.

7. Simon Kuznets, "Immigration of Russian Jews to the United States: Background and Structure," *Perspectives in American History* 9 (1975): 36–41.

8. Ibid., 39, 117–18; Andrzej Kapiszewski, "Stosunki polsko-zydowskie w Stanach Zjednoczonych," *Przegląd Polonijny* 4 (1978): 16–18. Jacob Lestschinsky, "Jewish Migrations, 1840–1956," in Finkelstein, *The Jews*, vol. 2, 1563; *Polish Encyclopaedia* (Geneva: Polish National Committee of America, 1924), vol. 2, 934–37; Milton Doroshkin, *Yiddish in America: Social and Cultural Foundations* (Rutherford, N.J.: Fairleigh Dickinson University Press, 1969), 192.

9. Moses Rischin, *The Promised City* (New York: Corinth, 1964), 70; Lestschinsky, "Jewish Migrations," 1559–60; Nathan Glazer, "Social Characteristics of American Jews," in Finkelstein, *The Jews*, vol. 2, 1702; Jacob R. Marcus, *The Colonial*

American Jew, 1492–1776 (Detroit: Wayne State University Press, 1970), 259–61, 1073, 1128, 1316; Jacob Rader Marcus, *Early American Jewry* (Philadelphia: Jewish Publication Society, 1953), vol. 2, 132–64.

10. Abraham G. Duker, "Polish Political Émigrés in the United States and the Jews, 1833–1865," *Publications of the American Jewish Historical Society* 39:2 (December 1949): 149; Norton Stern and William Kramer, "The Major Role of Polish Jews in the Pioneer West," *Western States Jewish Historical Quarterly* 8:4 (July 1976): 326–44.

11. Kuznets, "Immigration of Russian Jews," 121; Lestschinsky, "Jewish Migrations," 1545–53. Fresh research on the pogroms shows that the tsarist government did not sponsor the pogroms. See I. Michael Aronson, *Troubled Waters: The Origins of the 1881 Anti-Jewish Pogroms in Russia* (Pittsburgh: University of Pittsburgh Press, 1990); see also John D. Klier and Shlomo Lambroza, ed., *Pogroms: Anti-Jewish Violence in Modern Russian History* (Cambridge, England: Cambridge University Press, 1992).

12. Sheldon Thomas Neuringer, "American Jewry and the United States Immigration Policy, 1881–1953" (New York: Arno Press, 1980), 6–7, 21–22, 368–69; Selma Berrol, "When Uptown Met Downtown: Julia Richman's Work in the Jewish Community," *American Jewish History* 70:1 (September 1980): 33–51. Differences between these two major branches of the American Jewish community have proved controversial. See Selma Berrol, "Germans Versus Russians: An Update," *American Jewish History* 73:2 (December 1983): 143–56, and Harold Silver, "The Russian Jew Looks at Organized Charity," *Trends and Issues in Jewish Social Welfare in the United States, 1899–1952*, ed. Robert Morris and Michael Freund (Philadelphia: Jewish Publication Society, 1966), 57–60.

13. Kuznets, "Immigration of Russian Jews," 98–100; Samuel Joseph, *Immigration to the United States from 1881 to 1910* (New York: Columbia University, 1914), 165, 171, 185; Lestschinsky, "Jewish Migrations," 1563–67. Jonathan B. Sarna disputes the standard account in "The Myth of No Return: Jewish Return Migration to Eastern Europe, 1881–1914," *American Jewish History* 65:3 (December 1981): 256–68.

14. Kuznets, "Immigration of Russian Jews," 73–74, 101–7. "Personal services" included diverse jobs such as innkeeping, domestic employ, and military duty. Lestschinsky, "Jewish Migrations," 1568–69, provides similar statistics.

15. Joseph, *Jewish Immigration to the United States*, 187–88.

16. Ibid., 190–94.

17. Ibid., 195.

18. Gerald Sorin, *A Time for Building: The Third Migration, 1880–1920*, 137.

19. Howe, *The World of Our Fathers*, 88; Rischin, *The Promised City*, 76–94.

20. Selma C. Berrol, "Education and Economic Mobility: The Jewish Experience in New York City, 1880–1920," *American Jewish Historical Quarterly* 65:3 (March 1976): 257–71; Sherry Gorelick, *City College and the Jewish Poor* (New Brunswick, N.J.: Rutgers University Press, 1981), 85, 90; Deborah Dash Moore, *At Home in America: Second Generation New York Jews* (New York: Columbia University Press, 1981), 100–103.

21. Jenna Weissman Joselit, *Our Gang* (Bloomington: Indiana University Press, 1983), 23–53, 157–58; Albert Fried, *The Rise and Fall of the Jewish Gangster in America*

(New York: Holt, Rinehart and Winston, 1980), 8–9; Edward J. Bristow, *Prostitution and Prejudice* (Oxford: Clarendon, 1982).

22. Howe, *The World of Our Fathers*, 287–324; Susan A. Glenn, *Daughters of the Shtetl: Life and Labor in the Immigrant Generation* (Ithaca, N.Y.: Cornell University Press, 1990), 170; Lizabeth Cohen, *Making a New Deal: Industrial Workers in Chicago, 1919–1939* (New York: Cambridge University Press, 1990), 47–48.

23. Glenn, *Daughters of the Shtetl*, 8–49, 207–42.

24. Howe, *The World of Our Fathers*, 190–204; Marshall Sklare, "Aspects of Religious Worship in the Contemporary Conservative Synagogue," in *The Jews: Social Patterns of an American Group*, ed. Marshall Sklare (New York: The Free Press, 1958), 357–76; David Rudavsky, *Modern Jewish Religious Movements* (New York: Behrman House, 1967).

25. Howe, *The World of Our Fathers*, 460–98; Hannah Kliger, ed., *Jewish Hometown Associations and Family Circles in New York: The WPA Yiddish Writers' Group Study* (Bloomington: Indiana University Press, 1992), 39.

26. Gorelick, *City College and the Jewish Poor*, 115; Sachar, *A History of Jews in the United States*, 340–46; Nathan Glazer, "Social Characteristics of American Jews," 1711–18; Simon Kuznets, "Economic Structure and Life of the Jews," in Finkelstein, *The Jews*, vol. 2, 1628–29.

27. Joel Perlmann, "Beyond New York: The Occupations of Russian Jewish Immigrants in Providence, R.I., and in Other Small Jewish Communities, 1900–1915," *American Jewish History* 76, no. 3, 388–89.

28. Louis J. Swichkow and Lloyd P. Gartner, *The History of the Jews of Milwaukee* (Philadelphia: Jewish Publication Society, 1963), 160–66.

29. Robert A. Rockaway, *The Jews of Detroit* (Detroit: Wayne State University Press, 1986), 55–57, 61–66, 144.

30. W. Lloyd Warner and Leo Srole, *The Social Systems of American Ethnic Groups* (New Haven: Yale University Press, 1945), 31–32, 58, 73–74. With some overlap, Warner and Srole's scale is as follows: "lower lower class" involves unskilled and semi-skilled factory work; "upper lower class" involves skilled factory work and skilled craft work; "lower middle class" involves skilled craft work and management-aid occupations; "upper middle class" involves management operation and professional occupations.

31. Ibid., 150, see also 2301–32; Nathan Glazer, "The American Jew and the Attainment of Middle-Class Rank: Some Trends and Explanations," in Sklare, *The Jews*, 144.

32. Rockaway, *The Jews of Detroit*, 65; Shelly Tenenbaum, "Immigrants and Capital: Jewish Loan Societies in the United States, 1880–1945," *American Jewish History* 76:1 (September 1986): 67–77.

33. Warner and Srole, *The Social Systems of American Ethnic Groups*, 113.

34. Sachar, *A History of the Jews in America*, 324–34, 340; Abraham K. Korman, *The Outsiders: Jews and Corporate America* (Lexington, Mass.: Lexington Books, 1988), 43–56, 108–11; Moore, *At Home in America*, 129–46.

35. Robert Shosteck, *Small-Town Jewry Tell Their Story* (Washington, D.C.: B'nai B'rith, 1953); see also Joseph Greenblum and Marshall Sklare, "The Attitude of the Small-Town Jew Toward His Community," in Skare, *The Jews*, 288–303.

36. Fredelle Bruser Maynard, *The Tree of Life* (Markham, Ont.: Penguin, 1989), xiv, and Maynard, *Raisins and Almonds* (Markham, Ont.: Paperjacks, 1973), 27–28.

37. Doroshkin, *Yiddish in America*, 142–43. See also William C. Glicksman, *Jewish Social Welfare Institutions in Poland* (Philadelphia: M. E. Kalish Folkshul, 1976).

38. Nathan M. Kaganoff, "The Jewish Landsmanshaftn in New York City in the Period Preceding World War I," *American Jewish History* 76:1 (September 1986): 60.

39. I. E. Rontch, "The Present State of the Landsmanschaften," *Jewish Social Service Quarterly* 15 (June 1939): 360–78; Sidney Sorkin, *Bridges to an American City: A Guide to Chicago's Landsmanshaften, 1870 to 1990* (New York: Peter Lang, 1993); *American Jewish Year Book 5687, September 9, 1926, to September 26, 1927* (Philadelphia: Jewish Publication Society, 1926): 28, 196.

40. Doroshkin, *Yiddish in America*, 63, 144.

41. Ibid., 154, 156–57.

42. Ibid., 160–65.

43. Kliger, ed., 67–70; Daniel Soyer, "Between Two Worlds: The Jewish Landsmanshaftn and Questions of Immigrant Identity," *American Jewish History* 76:1 (September 1986): 5–24.

44. Kliger, ed., 41.

45. Susan Milamed, "Proskurover Landsmanshaftn: A Case Study of Jewish Communal Development," *American Jewish History* 76:1 (September 1986): 40–55.

46. Harry S. Linfield, *The Communal Organization of the United States, 1927* (New York: American Jewish Committee, 1930), 176.

47. Yehuda Bauer, *My Brother's Keeper* (Philadelphia: Jewish Publication Society, 1974), 103, 127, 190, 306; Linfield, *The Communal Organization of the United States, 1927*, 109; Michael R. Weisser, *A Brotherhood of Memory: Jewish Landsmanshaftn in the New World* (New York: Basic Books, 1985), 112–40.

48. Norman Salsitz (as told to Richard Skolnik), *A Jewish Boyhood in Poland: Remembering Kolbuszowa* (Syracuse: Syracuse University Press, 1992), 206–07.

49. Jewish historians have bitterly criticized fellow Jews and others for failing to prevent, or reduce, the immense losses of the Holocaust. See Feingold, *A Time for Searching: Entering the Mainstream, 1920–1945,* 219, for a guide to the controversy.

50. Feingold, *A Time for Searching,* 249; Melvin I. Urofsky, *A Voice That Spoke for Justice: The Life and Times of Stephen S. Wise* (Albany: State University of New York Press, 1982), 256–330; Sachar, *A History of the Jews in America,* 549–53.

51. David S. Wyman, *The Abandonment of the Jews* (New York: Pantheon, 1983), 25–26, 87–90, 209–87; Yehuda Bauer, *American Jewry and the Holocaust* (Detroit: Wayne State University Press, 1981), 73, 80, 94, 97, 298; Martin Gilbert, *Auschwitz and the Allies* (London: Mandarin, 1981), 299–312.

52. Sachar, *A History of the Jews in America,* 553–79.

53. Donald E. Pienkos, *PNA: A Centennial History of the Polish National Alliance of the United States of North America* (Boulder, Colo.: East European Monographs, 1984), 54–56, 75–76; John J. Bukowczyk, *And My Children Did Not Know Me: A History of the Polish-Americans* (Bloomington: Indiana University Press, 1987), 45–47; Edward R. Kantowicz, *Polish-American Politics in Chicago, 1888–1940* (Chicago: University of Chicago Press, 1975), 118.

54. Marian Fuks, *Prasa żydowska w Warszawie, 1823–1939* (Warsaw: PWN, 1979).

55. William I. Thomas and Florian Znaniecki, *The Polish Peasant in Europe and America* (New York: Dover, 1958), 1, 138–39, 292–93; Ewa Morawska, "A Replica of the 'Old-Country' Relationship in the Ethnic Niche: East European Jews and Gentiles in Small-Town Western Pennsylvania, 1880s–1930s," *American Jewish History* 77 (1987): 38–49. See also the English translation of a 1946 study, Aleksander Hertz, *The Jews in Polish Culture* (Evanston, Ill.: Northwestern University Press, 1988).

56. Salsitz, *A Jewish Boyhood in Poland,* 241, 242, 244; Thomas and Znaniecki, *The Polish Peasant in Europe and America,* 1, 138; see also 186–87.

57. Swichkow and Gertner, *The History of the Jews of Milwaukee,* 161; Rockaway, *The Jews of Detroit,* 90.

58. Morawska, "A Replica of the 'Old-Country' Relationship in the Ethnic Niche," 55–66. Some Polish Jews may have claimed Polish nationality to protect their businesses. The Perlowski Brothers (a Jewish-sounding name) appealed to Poles to buy from "their own" at their furniture store in Chicago. See Melvin G. Holli and Peter d'A. Jones, ed., *The Ethnic Frontier* (Grand Rapids, Mich.: William B. Eerdmans, 1977), 206.

59. Louis Wirth, *The Ghetto* (Chicago: University of Chicago Press, 1956), 229; Thomas and Znaniecki, *The Polish Peasant in Europe and America,* 1, 138.

60. Cohen, *Making a New Deal,* 29, 54–61, 147; Bukowczyk, *And My Children Did Not Know Me,* 70–71; Rockaway, *The Jews of Detroit,* 64–65.

61. George J. Lerski, "Dmowski, Paderewski, and American Jews, a Documentary Compilation," *Polin* 2 (1987): 95–116.

62. Tadeusz Radzik, *Stosunki polsko-żydowskie w Stanach Zjednoczonych Ameryki w latach 1918–1921* (Lublin: Uniwersytet Marii Curie-Składowskiej, 1988). See also Józef Lewandowski, "History and Myth: Pińsk, April 1919," *Polin* 2 (1987): 50–72; Andrzej Kapiszewski, "Stosunki polsko-żydowskie w Stanach Zjednoczonych Ameryki," in *Polonia amerykańska: Przeszłość i współczesność,* ed. Hieronim Kubiak et al. (Wrocław: Ossolineum, 1988), 618–32; Ezra Mendelsohn, *The Jews of East Central Europe Between the World Wars* (Bloomington: Indiana University Press, 1983), 40; Jerzy Tomaszewski, "Pińsk, Saturday 5 April 1919," *Polin* 1 (1986): 227–51; Piotr S. Wandycz, *The United States and Poland* (Cambridge, Mass.: Harvard University Press, 1980), 157–69; Bogusław W. Winid, *W cieniu Kapitolu: Dyplomacja polska wobec Stanów Zjednoczonych Ameryki, 1919–1939* (Warsaw: PoMost, 1991), 21–22, 37–40, 61–62.

63. *The American Jewish Year Book 5680, September 25, 1919, to September 12, 1920* (Philadelphia: Jewish Publication Society, 1919), 177–81; Joseph John Parot, *Polish Catholics in Chicago, 1850–1920* (DeKalb: Northern Illinois University Press, 1981), 175–76.

64. Morawska, "A Replica of the 'Old-Country' Relationship in the Ethnic Niche," 72–84; Kapiszewski, "Stosunki polsko-żydowskie," in *Polonia amerykańska,* 614–18.

65. Daniel Stone, "Winnipeg's Polish Language Newspapers and Their Attitude Towards Jews and Ukrainians Between the Two World Wars," *Canadian Ethnic Studies* 21, no. 2 (1989): 27–37.

66. Daniel Stone, "Polish Diplomacy and the American-Jewish Community Between the Wars," *Polin* 2 (1986): 73–94; Kapiszewski, "Stosunki polsko-żydowskie," in *Polonia amerykańska,* 634.

67. Steven Fraser, *Labor Will Rule: Sidney Hillman and the Rise of American Labor* (New York: Free Press, 1991), 417–26; Moore, *At Home in America,* 201–30; Kantowicz, *Polish-American Politics in Chicago,* 123; Edward Herbert Mazur, *Minyans for a Prairie City: The Politics of Chicago Jewry, 1850–1940* (New York: Garland, 1990), 301–19; Mazur, "Jewish Chicago," *Ethnic Chicago,* 63–65.

6. Polonia and Politics

1. *Swoboda,* September 6, October 8, 9, 1872, cited in Wacław Kruszka, *Historya polska w Ameryce* (Milwaukee, Wisc.: Społka Wydawniczej Kuryera, 1905), vol. 3, 29–31. On Kiołbassa, see Helen Busyn, "The Political Career of Peter Kiolbassa," *Polish American Studies* 7, nos. 1–2 (January–June 1950): 8–22 (hereafter cited as *PAS*), and "Peter Kiolbassa—Maker of Polish America," *PAS* 8, nos. 3–4 (July–December 1951): 65–84. Unless otherwise noted, all translations are by the author.

2. Kruszka, *Historya polska w Ameryce,* 130.

3. Edward R. Kantowicz, *Polish American Politics in Chicago, 1888–1940* (Chicago: University of Chicago Press, 1975), 38–42.

4. William I. Thomas and Florian Znaniecki, *The Polish Peasant in Europe and America,* 2d ed. (1918–1920; New York: Dover Publications, Inc., 1958), vol. 2, 1581.

5. Stanisław Osada, *Jak się kształtowała polska dusza Wychodźtwa w Ameryce* (Pittsburgh, Pa.: Sokół Polski, 1930), 10 quotation). See also Jan Molenda, "The Formation of National Consciousness of the Polish Peasants and the Part They Played in the Regaining of Independence by Poland," *Acta Poloniae Historica* 63–64 (1991): 121–48. On Polish nationalism, see Peter Brock, "Polish Nationalism," in *Nationalism in Eastern Europe,* ed. Peter F. Sugar (Seattle: University of Washington Press, 1969), 310–72.

6. Robert A. Slayton, *Back of the Yards: The Making of Local Democracy* (Chicago: University of Chicago Press, 1986), esp. 131.

7. Andrzej Brożek, *Polish Americans, 1954–1939* (Warsaw: Interpress, 1985), 52. Sienkiewicz cited from Charles Morley, ed. and trans., *Portrait of America: Letters of Henry Sienkiewicz* (New York: Columbia University Press, 1959), 282. Sienkiewicz was also pessimistic about the immigrant's eventual denationalization, which was only "a matter of time" (290).

8. Victor Greene, *For God and Country; The Rise of Polish and Lithuanian Ethnic Consciousness in America, 1860–1910* (Madison: State Historical Society of Wisconsin, 1975), 66–75.

9. Ibid., 85. Mieczysław Haiman, *Zjednoczenie Polskie Rzymsko-Katolickie w Ameryce, 1873–1948* (Chicago: Zjednoczenie Polskie Rzymsko-Katolickie w Ameryce, 1948), 27, 33–55. Outside Chicago, local internal politics resulted in fraternal allegiances that were at variance with national trends. Minneapolis PNA lodges were consistently proclerical, while some in Cleveland were quite anti-clerical. See William John Galush,

"Forming Polonia: A Study of Four Polish-American Communities, 1890–1940" (Ph.D. diss., University of Minnesota, 1975), 137–48.

10. For Giller, see Halina Florkowska-Frančić, *Emigracyjna dzialalność agatona Giller po powstaniu styczyniowym,* Biblioteka Polonijna, no. 13 (Wrocław: Ossolineum, 1985), 152–70. Quotations are excerpted from Stanisław Osada, *Historya związku narodowego polskiego i rozwój ruchu narodowego polskiego w Ameryce północne: W dwudziesta piąta rocznice założenia związku* (Chicago: Związek Narodowe Polskie, 1905), 104.

11. Grzegorz Babiński, "Przemiany stosunku do polski w programach dzialalności organizacji polonijnych w Stanach Zjednoczonych," in *Studia nad organizacjami polonijnymi w Ameryce północnej,* ed. Grzegorz Babiński, Biblioteka Polonijna, no. 19 (Wrocław: Ossolineum, 1988), 151 (quotations), 157–58.

12. Frank Renkiewicz, "The Profits of Nonprofit Capitalism: Polish Fraternalism and Beneficial Insurance in America," in *Self-Help in Urban America: Patterns of Minority Business Enterprise,* ed. Scott Cummings (Port Washington, N.Y.: Kennikat Press, 1980), 119–20, 121; and Haiman, *Zjednoczenie Polskie Rzymsko-Katolickie,* 152. On the economic and social aspects of Polish immigrant fraternalism, see another excellent study by Renkiewicz, "An Economy of Self-Help: Fraternal Capitalism and the Evolution of Polish America," in *Studies in Ethnicity: The East European Experience in America,* ed. Charles A. Ward et al. (Boulder, Colo.: East European Monographs, 1980), 71–79. On the PNA's early years and growth, see Donald E. Pienkos, *A Centennial History of the Polish National Alliance of the United States of North America* (Boulder, Colo.: East European Monographs, 1984), 3–98.

13. Haiman, *Zjednoczenie polskie Rzymsko-Katolickie,* 149–56, and Kruszka cited in Brożek, *Polish Americans,* 67.

14. For the Polish Union of America, see Jadwiga Karlowiczowa, *Historia związku polek w Ameryce: Przycznki do poznania Duszy Wychodźtwa Polskiego w Stanach Zjednoczonych Ameryki północnej* (Chicago: Związek Polek w Ameryce, 1938), 26–27; for the Polish Women's alliance, see Thaddeus C. Radzialowski, "Immigrant Nationalism and Feminism: *Glos Polek* and the Polish Women's Alliance in America, 1898–1917," *Review Journal of Philosophy and Social Science* 2, no. 2 (Winter 1977): 183–203; for the Falcons, see Donald E. Pienkos, *One Hundred Years Young: A History of the Polish Falcons of America, 1877–1987* (Boulder, Colo.: East European Monographs, 1987), 39.

15. Thomas and Znaniecki, *Polish Peasant,* 1609. On these and other organizations, see Brożek, *Polish Americans,* 221–25. On the Socialists, see Mary E. Cygan, "Political and Cultural Leadership in an Immigrant Community: Polish American Socialism, 1880–1950" (Ph.D. diss., Northwestern University, 1989), 26–72. On the marching societies, today largely forgotten, see Stanley Bruno Stephan, "The Preparation of American Poles for Polish Independence, 1880–1918" (master's thesis, University of Detroit, 1939), 88–96.

16. See Renkiewicz, "The Profits of Nonprofit Capitalism," 120–23; Osada, 387–94; Osada, *Jak się kształtowała polska dusza;* and Romuald Piątkowski, ed., *Pamiętnik wzniesienia i odsłonięcia pomników Tadeusza Kościuszki i Kazimierza Pułaski* (Chicago, Ill.: Związek Narodowy Polski, 1911), 604–16; and Pienkos, *Polish National Alliance,* 89–91.

17. See Paul Fox, *The Polish National Catholic Church* (Scranton, Pa.: School of Christian Living, 1957), 69–73; Stephen Wlodarski, *The Origin and Growth of the Polish National Catholic Church* (Scranton, Pa.: PNCC, 1974), 52–56, 66–67, 72–73, 81–98, 197–205; Hieronim Kubiak, *The Polish National Church in the United States of America from 1897 to 1980* (Warsaw and Crakow: PWN, 1982), 130–33; and Lawrence J. Orzell, "The 'National Catholic' Response: Franciszek Hodur and His Followers, 1897–1907," in *The Polish Presence in Canada and America,* ed. Frank Renkiewicz (Toronto: Multicultural History Society of Ontario, 1982), 117–35.

18. Mieczysław Szalewski, *Wychodźtwo polskie w Stanach Zjednoczonych Ameryki* (Lwów: Ossolineum, 1924), 100 (quotation); Greene, *For God and Country,* 10, 13, 168–70. See also Anthony J. Kuzniewski, *Faith and Fatherland: The Polish Church War in Wisconsin, 1896–1918* (Notre Dame, Ind.: University of Notre Dame Press, 1980); and Joseph John Parot, *Polish Catholics in Chicago, 1850–1920* (DeKalb: Northern Illinois University Press, 1981).

19. Andrzej Brożek, "The National Consciousness of the Polish Ethnic Group in the United States, 1854–1939: Proposed Model," *Acta Poloniae Historica* 37 (1978): 100–101. Quotations are from Tomasz Siemiradzki, "O politycznem znaczeniu wychodźtwa," in Piątkowski, *Pamiętnik,* 207.

20. Józef Miąso, "Polonia's Contribution to the Development of Education in the United States," in *Poles in History and Culture of the United States of America,* ed. Grzegorz Babiński and Mirosław Frančić, Biblioteka Polonijna, no. 4 (Wrocław: Ossolineum, 1979), 74; Anthony Kuzniewski, "Boot Straps and Book Learning: Reflections on the Education of Polish Americans," *PAS* 32, no. 2 (1975): 7; and Ellen Marie Kuznicki, "A Historical Perspective on the Polish American Parochial School," *PAS* 35, nos. 1–2 (1978): 6.

21. Szalewski, *Wychodźtwo polskie,* 105, 107, 173–74; A. J. Kuzniewski, "The Polish American Press," in *The Ethnic Press in the United States: A Historical Analysis and Handbook,* ed. Sally M. Miller (New York: Greenwood Press, 1987), 275–90; Joseph A. Wytrwal, *America's Polish Heritage; A Social History of the Poles in America* (Detroit: Endurance Press, 1961), 148–235; Mary Cygan, "Secular Popular Culture" (paper delivered Annual Meeting of Polish American Historical Association, Chicago, December 28, 1991); and the works on the fraternals previously cited.

22. Benjamin P. Murdzek, *Emigration in Polish Social-Political Thought, 1870–1914* (Boulder, Colo.: East European Monographs, 1977), 169, 269; *Przegląd Emigracyjny* 1, no. 6 (1892): 51–52, and no. 12 (December 15, 1892): 117–18. For an early but informed analysis of the immigrant's nationalization, see Stephan, "The Preparation of American Poles for Polish Independence," 31–49.

23. Cygan, "Political and Cultural Leadership in an Immigrant Community," 35–54; and Krzysztof Groniowski, "Socjalistyczna emigracja polska w Stanach Zjednoczonych, 1883–1914," *Z Polą Walki* 20, no. 1 (1977): 3–35. On the activities of Polish socialists in Buffalo before 1901, see William G. Falkowski, "Accommodation and Conflict: Patterns of Polish Immigrant Adaptation to Industrial Capitalism and American Political Pluralism in Buffalo, New York, 1873–1901" (Ph.D. diss., State University of New York at Buffalo, 1990), 250–58, 267–74, 295–99, 418. On the National Democrats, see Osada, *Jak się kształtowała polska dusza,* 18–42; and Krzysz-

tof Groniowski, "Polonia amerykańska a narodowa demokracja, 1893–1914," *Kwartalnik Historyczny* 79, no. 1 (1972): 24–55.

24. Szalewski, *Wychodźtwo polskie*, 174; Henryk Wereszycki, *Historia polityczna polski w dobie popowstaniowej, 1864–1918* (Warsaw: Wiedzą, 1948), 13.

25. Galush, "Forming Polonia," 200; Pienkos, *Polish National Alliance*, 332; Kubiak, *The Polish National Church*, 123; Brożek, *Polish Americans*, 45. On Polish Protestants and Jews, see Brożek, *Polish Americans*, 53–59.

26. Polish National Congress cited in Donald E. Pienkos, *For Your Freedom Through Ours: Polish American Efforts on Poland's Behalf, 1863–1991* (Boulder, Colo.: East European Monographs, 1991), 257. For Siemiradzki, see Piątkowski, *Pamiętnik*, 34, 199–213. See also Szalewski, *Wychodźtwo polskie*, 105; Pienkos, *Polish National Alliance*, 91, 396.

27. Thomas and Znaniecki, *Polish Peasant*, 1582. Mirosław Frančić, *Komitet Obrony Narodowej w Ameryce, 1912–1918*, Biblioteka Polonijna, no. 11 (Wrocław: Ossolineum, 1983); M. B. Biskupski and Joseph T. Hapak, "The Polish National Defense Committee in America, 1912–1918: A Dual Review Essay," *PAS* 44, no. 2 (Autumn 1987): 70–75. See also Louis J. Zake, "The National Department and the Polish American Community," *PAS* 38, no. 2 (Autumn 1981): 16–25.

28. Mieczysław B. Biskupski, "American Polonia and the Resurrection of Independent Poland, 1914–1919," *The Fiedorczyk Lecture in Polish American Studies* (New Britain: Central Connecticut State University, April 6, 1989), 4–5. See also Biskupski, "The United States and the Rebirth of Poland, 1914–1918" (Ph.D. diss., Yale University, 1981), and Biskupski, "Paderewski as Leader of American Polonia, 1914–1918," *PAS* 43, no. 1 (Spring 1986): 37–56.

29. Giller cited in Osada, *Historya związku narodowego*, 104; Tadeusz Paleczny, *Ewolucja ideologii i przemiany tozsamości narodowej polonii w Stanach Zjednoczonych w latach 1870–1970* (Cracow: PWN, 1989), 210; Galush, "Forming Polonia," 200.

30. Louis L. Gerson, *Woodrow Wilson and the Rebirth of Poland, 1914–1920* (New Haven: Yale University Press, 1953). On the historical reliability of Gerson's work, see Zygmunt J. Gasiorowski, "A Note on Louis L. Gerson's 'Woodrow Wilson and the Rebirth of Poland, 1914–1920,'" *Polish Review* 2, no. 4 (Autumn 1957): 89–94. See also Piotr S. Wandycz, *The United States and Poland* (Cambridge, Mass.: Harvard University Press, 1980), 111–12.

31. Biskupski, "Paderewski as Leader of American Polonia," 53 (quotation); Paleczny, *Ewolucja ideologii*, 162–75.

32. On the Lithuanians, see David Fainhauz, *Lithuanians in the USA: Aspects of Ethnic Identity* (Chicago: Lithuanian Library Press, 1991), 87–135.

33. Victor R. Greene, "Slavic American Nationalism," in *American Contribution to the Seventh International Congress of Slavists, Warsaw, August 1973*, vol. 3, *History*, ed. Anna Cienciala (The Hague: Mouton, 1973), 197–215.

34. Lymanski cited in minutes of the Polish American Club of Middletown, Connecticut, February 28, 1926 (Connecticut Polish American Archives and Manuscript Collection, Central Connecticut State University, New Britain, Conn.). See also Brożek, "The National Consciousness," 111; and Paleczny, *Ewolucja ideologii*, 175–88. For a broader systematic treatment of the changes, see William John Galush, "American

Poles and the New Poland," *Ethnicity* 1 (October 1974): 209–21; Szalewski, *Wychodź-two polskie*, 181–94; and Hieronim Kubiak, "Położenie społeczne i ewolucja świado-mości narodowej ludności polskiej w USA w latach 1910–1918," in *Polonia wobec niepodległości polski w czasie i wojny swiatowej*, ed. Halina Florkowska-Frančić, Miro-sław Frančić, and Hieronim Kubiak, Biblioteka Polonijna, no. 6 (Wrocław: Ossoli-neum, 1979), 49–61.

35. Kruszka, *Historya polska w Ameryce*, vol. 1, 39, and vol. 2, 58–59. Sienkiewicz cited in Morley, *Portrait of America*, 276.

36. Victor R. Greene, *American Immigrant Leaders, 1800–1910: Marginality and Identity* (Baltimore: Johns Hopkins University Press, 1987), 105–21; John Bodnar, *The Transplanted: A History of Immigrants in Urban America* (Bloomington: Indiana University Press, 1985), 203–4.

37. Stanislaus A. Blejwas, *A Polish Community in Transition: The Origins and Evolution of Holy Cross Parish, New Britain, Connecticut* (Chicago: Polish American Historical Association), reprinted from *PAS* 34, no. 1 (Spring 1977), and 35, nos. 1–2 (Spring–Autumn 1978). More broadly, also see Brożek, *Polish Americans*, 43–59. Kantowicz, *Polish American Politics*, 40 (quotation). See also the battles for control of PNA *sejms* (parliaments) in the 1920s and 1930s. Pienkos, *Polish National Alliance*, 127–50.

38. Szalewski, *Wychodźtwo polskie*, 220; Kantowicz, *Polish American Politics*, 42; see also pp. 165–72, 174.

39. Walter A. Borowiec, "Persistence and Change in the Gatekeeper Role of Eth-nic Leaders: The Case of Polish Americans," *Political Anthropology* 1, no. 1 (1975): 19–44. See also Greene, *American Immigrant Leaders*, 105–21. There is no chapter on the Poles in John Higham, ed., *Ethnic Leadership in America* (Baltimore: Johns Hop-kins University Press, 1978).

40. Konstanty Symonolewicz-Symmons also appears as Konstantyn Symmons-Symonolewicz. See Konstanty Symonolewicz-Symmons, "Polish American Studies, 1942–1970: An Overview," *PAS* 27, nos. 1–2 (Spring–Autumn 1970): 16. At the inau-gural meeting of the Commission for Research on Polish Immigration (the forerun-ner of the Polish American Historical Association) on December 29–30, 1943, there were no papers on politics. Rev. Francis Bolek listed Political Organizations as a category for his project for a Polish-American encyclopedia. In his famous essay "What Is a Polish American?" Rev. Joseph Swastek noted laconically that he "with a certain measure of success ran for minor city, county and state political offices, more often on the Democratic than on the Republican ballot" (*Bulletin of the Polish Insti-tute of Arts and Sciences in America* 3, no. 1 [October 1944]: 71, 79).

41. The identification of the parish, the school, and the fraternals with the com-munity is reflected in Galush, "Forming Polonia," which bypasses politics. For scat-tered references, see M. Remigia, O.S.F., "The Polish Immigrant in Detroit to 1914," *PAS* 2, nos. 1–2 (January–June 1945): 7–8; Joseph Swastek, "The Poles in South Bend to 1914," *PAS* 2, nos. 3–4 (July–December 1945): 87–88; M. Theresa, O.S.F., "Polish Settlements in Minnesota, 1860–1900," *PAS* 5, nos. 3–4 (July–December 1948): 72–73; M. Accursia Bern, "Poles in Shenandoah, Pennsylvania," *PAS* 6, nos. 1–2 (January–June 1949): 12; Ladislas J. Siekaniec, O.F.M., "The Poles of Northern Wis-

consin," *PAS* 14, nos. 1–2 (January–June 1957): 15; Edward A. Chmielewski, "Polish Settlement in East Minneapolis, Minnesota," *PAS* 17, nos. 1–2 (January–June 1960): 26; Edward Symanski, "Polish Settlers in Grand Rapids, Michigan," *PAS* 21, no. 2 (July–December 1964): 101–2.

42. See Angela T. Pienkos, "Comparing, Contrasting, and Generalizing About the Polish American Political Experience: Some Introductory Observations," in *Ethnic Politics in Urban America: The Polish Experience in Four Cities,* ed. Angela T. Pienkos (Chicago: Polish American Historical Association, 1978), 13–14; Jan Piekoszewski, *Problemy polonii amerykańskiej* (Warsaw: PAX, 1981), 113; and Eugene J. Pawlowski, "The Polish Element in the Politics of Chicago, Ill." (master's thesis, Northwestern University, 1940), 59.

43. Naturalization figures are from Szalewski, *Wychodźtwo polskie,* 224–25. Karol Wachtl, *Polonja w Ameryce* (Philadelphia: Author's imprint, 1944), 191–97.

44. Jonathan Shea and Christine Stoj, "The Pulaski Democratic Club of New Britain, Connecticut," in *Pastor of the Poles: Polish American Essays Presented to Right Reverend Monsignor John P. Wodarski,* ed. Stanislaus A. Blejwas and Mieczyslaw B. Biskupski (New Britain, Conn.: Polish Studies Program Monographs, 1992), 138–41; Szalewski, *Wychodźtwo polskie,* 228; and Pawlowski, "The Polish Element in the Politics of Chicago," 61–70. Ethnic political clubs are not systematically studied or analyzed. Most recently, see Slayton, *Back of the Yards,* 161–71.

45. Arthur W. Thurner, "Polish Americans in Chicago Politics, 1890–1930," *PAS* 38, no. 1 (Spring 1971): 22–23. The Pulaski Democratic Club in New Britain, founded in 1931, is believed to have helped as many as four thousand Poles acquire citizenship. See Shea and Stoj, "The Pulaski Democratic Club of New Britain," 141. Kogut quoted in James S. Pula and Eugene E. Dziedzic, *United We Stand: The Role of Polish Workers in the New York Mills Textile Strikes, 1912 and 1916* (Boulder, Colo.: East European Monographs, 1990), 220.

46. Thaddeus Radzilowski, "Immigrant Women and Their Daughters," *Fiedorczyk Lecture in Polish American Studies,* April 19, 1990 (New Britain, Conn.: Polish Studies Program, 1992), 18–26. See also the brief but informative discussion of the Women's Auxiliary of the Polish Regular Democratic Club in Chicago's Fourteenth Ward (the Back of the Yards) in Slayton, *Back of the Yards,* 164–66.

47. In 1944 there were thirty-nine women in the Connecticut general assembly, including four Polish Americans. See Stanislaus A. Blejwas, *St. Stanislaus B. & M. Parish, Meriden, Connecticut: A Centennial of Polish in Connecticut* (New Britain and Meriden, Conn.: Polish Studies Program Monographs, 1982), 102. See Stanisława Olbrycht-Tillson, "Walka amerykanów polskiego pochodzenia o zdobycie uznanie w swiecie politycznym Buffalo i okręgu Erie," *Studia Polonijne* 9 (1985): 240–44, 249–51, for women in Buffalo area politics.

48. See Frank A. Renkiewicz, "The Polish Settlement of St. Joseph County, Indiana, 1855–1935" (Ph.D. diss., University of Notre Dame, 1967), 47–102; and Falkowski, "Accommodation and Conflict," 194–96, 233–34, 408–41. For two recent community studies giving passing mention to politics, see Kathleen Urbanic, *Shoulder to Shoulder: Polish Americans in Rochester, N.Y., 1890–1990* (Rochester, N.Y.: Polonia Civic Center, 1991), 97; and Blejwas, *St. Stanislaus B. & M. Parish,* 80, 98, 116, 174.

49. Kantowicz, *Polish American Politics*, 49–52. See also John Myers Allswang, "The Political Behavior of Chicago's Ethnic Groups, 1918–1932" (Ph.D. diss., University of Pittsburgh, 1967). On the socialists, see Donald Pienkos, "Politics, Religion, and Change in Polish Milwaukee, 1900–1930," *Wisconsin Magazine of History* 61, no. 3 (Spring 1978): 179–209; Frank Renkiewicz, "Polish American Workers, 1880–1980," in *Pastor of the Poles*, 123–25; Falkowski, "Accommodation and Conflict," 250–58, 267–74, 295–99, 418; and Cygan, "Politics and Cultural Leadership." A very recent work is Danuta Piątkowska-Koźlik, *Związek socjalistów Polskich w Ameryce (1900–1914)* (Opole: Wyższa Szkoła Pedagogiczna, 1992). Falkowski found that early political affiliation was linked to Buffalo's fraternal politics (PNA equaled Republican; and PRCU equaled Democrat), an assessment that Bukowczyk projects nationally. See John J. Bukowczyk, *And My Children Did Not Know Me: A History of the Polish-Americans* (Bloomington: Indiana University Press, 1987), 69. Borowiec asserts that Buffalo Polonia in its early years aligned itself with neither party. See Walter A. Borowiec, "Politics and Buffalo's Polish Americans," in Pienkos, *Ethnic Politics in Urban America*, 19.

50. For the Democratic Party, see, for example, Louis Harris, *Is There a Republican Majority? Political Trends, 1952–1956* (New York: Harper and Brothers, 1954), 94–95. For the Polish-American political agenda, see Irwin T. Sanders and Ewa T. Morawska, *Polish-American Community Life: A Survey of Research*, Community Sociology Monograph Series, no. 2 (Boston and New York: Department of Sociology, Boston University, and the Polish Institute of Arts and Sciences, 1975), 62–66; and Bukowczyk, *And My Children Did Not Know Me*, 83 (quote). Estimated percentages are from Szalewski, *Wychodźtwo polskie*, 226. For 1932–1948, see Donald Pienkos, "Polish-American Ethnicity in the Political Life of the United States," in *America's Ethnic Politics*, ed. Joseph S. Roucek and Bernard Eisenberg (Westport, Conn.: Greenwood Press, 1982), 288. Only Jews were more Democratic. See Lawrence H. Fuchs, "Political Aspects of Immigration," in *American Ethnic Politics*, ed. Lawrence H. Fuchs (New York: Harper and Row, 1968), 23.

51. See John J. Bukowczyk, "The Transformation of Working-Class Ethnicity: Corporate Control, Americanization, and the Polish Immigrant Middle Class in Bayonne, New Jersey, 1915–1925," *Labor History* 25, no. 1 (Winter 1984): 58–61, 69–72. On the Buffalo middle class, see Falkowski, "Accommodation and Conflict," 156–57, 180–258; and Olbrycht-Tillson, "Walka amerykánów polskiego pochodzenia," 221.

52. See *Poles in Chicago; Their Contribution to a Century of Progress* (Chicago: Polish Day Association, 1933); and Kantowicz, *Polish American Politics*, 165–82. On organizational changes in a local community (New Britain, Connecticut) during the interwar period, see David G. Januszewski, "Organizational Evolution in a Polish American Community," *PAS* 42, no. 1 (Spring 1985): 43–58. Study of the second generation, along with its values and organizations, is neglected. Thaddeus Radzilowski, "The Second Generation: The Unknown Polonia," *PAS* 43, no. 1 (Spring 1986): 5–12.

53. Kantowicz, *Polish American Politics*, 171–72, 189–91. For an earlier remark, see Pawlowski, "The Polish Element in the Politics of Chicago," 61–66. See also Siemiradzki, "O politycznem znaczeniu wychodźtwa," 203.

54. Stanislaus A. Blejwas, "The 'Polish Tradition' in Connecticut Politics," *Connecticut History* 33 (November 1992): 61–98; Borowiec, "Politics and Buffalo's Polish Americans," 24; and Olbrycht-Tillson, "Walka amerykanów polskiego pochodzenia," 225–26.

55. Andrzej Ławrowski, *Reprezentacia polskiej grupy etnicznej w życiu politycznym Stanów Zjednoczonych* (Warsaw: PWN, 1979), 102–4; Pienkos, "Politics, Religion, and Change in Polish Milwaukee," 183–84; Szalewski, *Wychodźtwo polskie,* 228–30. On the colorful Kunz, who won six terms to the U.S. House, see Pawlowski, "The Polish Element in the Politics of Chicago," 72–81.

56. Ławrowski, *Reprezentacia polskiej grupy etnicznej,* 117–23. These figures are most likely incomplete. "Polish-American Congressmen in Review: St. Mary's College Symposium," *PAS* 21, no. 1 (January–June 1964): 23–42.

57. On Muskie's special case, see Perry Weed, *The White Ethnic Movement and Politics* (New York: Praeger, 1973), 211–14.

58. For Detroit, see Thaddeus C. Radzialowski with Donald Binkowski, "Polish Americans in Detroit Politics," in *Ethnic Politics in Urban America,* 47, 49–50, 64–65. See also Arthur Evans Wood, *Hamtramck: A Sociological Study of a Polish-American Community* (New Haven: College and University Press, 1955), chaps. 3, 4. For Chicago, see "The Limitations of Ethnic Politics: Polish Americans in Chicago," in *Ethnic Politics in Urban America,* 92–104. Kantowicz's article is excerpted from Kantowicz, *Polish American Politics.*

59. Pienkos, "Politics, Religion, and Change in Polish Milwaukee," 184. For Meriden, see Blejwas, *St. Stanislaus B. & M. Parish,* 80, 98, 116. For Chicago, see Slayton, *Back of the Yards,* 151–71. For New Britain, see Kazuhiro Ebuchi, "The Ethnicity of Polish Americans and Its Political Mobilization," in *Ethnicity and Cultural Pluralism in the USA,* ed. Tsuneo Ayabe (Fukuoka, Japan: Research Institute of Comparative Education and Culture, 1978), 9–49.

60. Borowiec, "Politics and Buffalo's Polish Americans," and Pienkos, "The Polish Americans in Milwaukee Politics," in *Ethnic Politics,* 36; see also 78–85.

61. Longin Pastusiak, Stanisław Przywarski, and Bohdan Bielewicz, "Polonia w organach władzy politycznej Stanów Zjednoczonych Ameryki (na szczeblu federalnym, stanowym i lokalnym)," in *Polonia amerykańska: Przeszłość i współczesność,* ed. Hieronim Kubiak, Eugeniusz Kusielewicz, and Tadeusz Gromada (Wrocław: Ossolineum, 1988), 536. For a recent community history, which integrates politics into the broader story, see Adam Walaszek, *Światy imigrantów: Tworzenie polonijnego Cleveland, 1880–1930* (Cracow: "Nomos," 1994).

62. Quintard Taylor, "The Chicago Political Machine and Black-Ethnic Conflict and Accommodation," *PAS* 29, nos. 1–2 (Spring–Autumn 1972): 40–66. See also Joseph Parot, "Ethnic Versus Black Metropolis: The Origins of Polish-Black Housing Tensions in Chicago, *PAS* 29, nos. 1–2 (Spring–Autumn 1972): 5–33. Bukowczyk, *And My Children Did Not Know Me,* 136–37. Olbrycht-Tillson lists Polish political successes in Buffalo while complaining of Irish influence and about federal laws favoring racial minorities that she believes to be discriminatory. See Olbrycht-Tillson, "Walka amerykanów polskiego pochodzenia," 255–56.

63. Kevin Phillips, *The Emerging Republican Majority* (New Rochelle, N.Y.: Arlington House, 1969), 123–75, 330–57.

64. Pastusiak et al., "Polonia w organach władzy," 526–28. Angela Pienkos and Donald Pienkos, "Badania nad zachowaniami politycznymi amerykanów polskiego pochodzenia: Przegląd literatury przedmiotu, cześć 1," *Przegląd Polonijny* 6, no. 4 (18) (1980): 43–44. This is an expanded version of D. Pienkos, "Research on Ethnic Political Behavior Among the Polish Americans: A Review of the Literature," *Polish Review* 21, no. 3 (1976): 123–48.

65. Pienkos, "Polish-American Ethnicity," 278.

66. For the House, see ibid., 291–92; and Blejwas, "The 'Polish Tradition' in Connecticut Politics." For 1970 census, see Pienkos, "Polish American Ethnicity," 292.

67. Pienkos, "Polish-American Ethnicity," 291–93; and Pastusiak et al., "Polonia w organach władzy," 508–9.

68. For Gronouski, see Weed, *The White Ethnic Movement*, 144–48. For complaints, see Pastusiak et al., "Polonia w organach władzy," 509–10; Charles Allan Baretski, "How Polonia Reacts to Inadequate Political Recognition in the Political Arena," *PAS* 28, no. 1 (Spring 1971): 43–53.

69. For the Captive Nations, see George H. Glinka-Janczewski, "American Policy Toward Poland Under the Truman Administration, 1945–1952" (Ph.D. diss., Georgetown University, 1966), 296–309. Baretski, "How Polonia Reacts to Inadequate Political Recognition," 46–50. Weed's discussion is basically descriptive, avoiding the question of political returns. Weed, *The White Ethnic Movement*, 148–55.

70. Stanley P. Wagner, "The Polish-American Vote in 1960," *PAS* 21, no. 1 (1964): 6; Harris, *Is There a Republican Majority?* 99–101. See Lewis L. Gerson, *The Hyphenated in Recent American Politics and Diplomacy* (Lawrence: University of Kansas Press, 1964), 178–99.

71. Robert Szymczak, "Hopes and Promises: Arthur Bliss Lane, the Republican Party, and the Slavic-American Vote, 1952," *PAS* 45, no. 1 (Spring 1988): 12–27. See also Glinka-Janczewski, 349–63.

72. For the World Union of Poles, see Wachtl, *Polonja w Ameryce*, 396. The declaration of independence is from Swastek, cited in Brożek, "The National Consciousness," 121. Quotation from Konstanty Symonolewicz-Symmons, "The Polish American Community—Half a Century After 'The Polish Peasant,' " *Polish Review* 11, no. 3 (Summer 1966): 71.

73. Helena Znaniecki Lopata, "The Function of Voluntary Associations in an Ethnic Community: 'Polonia' " (Ph.D. diss., University of Chicago, 1954), 80–102. On the activities of the Polish American Council, see Pienkos, *For Your Freedom Through Ours*, 79–104.

74. On the events leading up to the formation of the PAC, see Richard C. Lukas, *The Strange Allies: The United States and Poland, 1941–1945* (Knoxville: University of Tennessee Press, 1978), 107–20. See also Stanislaus A. Blejwas, " 'Equals with Equals': The Polish National Catholic Church and the Founding of the Polish American Congress," *PAS* 44, no. 2 (Autumn 1987): 5–23.

75. Wacław Jędrzejewicz, *Polonia amerykańska w polityce polskiej: Historia Komitetu Narodowego Amerykanów Polskiego Pochodzenia* (New York: National Committee of Americans of Polish Descent, 1954), 11; see also 14–17.

76. Lukas, *The Strange Allies,* 115–18; Cygan, "Politics and Cultural Leadership," 141–49; and Charles Sandler, " 'Pro-Soviet Polish Americans': Oskar Lange and Russia's Friends in Polonia, 1941–1945," *Polish Review* 22, no. 4 (1977): 26–39. For the voices of the left, see Boleslaw Gebert, "Progressive Traditions Among Polish-Americans During World War II," in *Poles in History and Culture of the United States of America,* ed. Grzegorz Babiński and Mirosław Francić, Biblioteka Polonijna, no. 4 (Wrocław: Ossolineum, 1979), 99–115; Gebert, *Z Tykocina za ocean* (Warsaw: Czytelnik, 1982); and Margaret Collingwood Nowak, *Two Who Were There: A Biography of Stanley Nowak* (Detroit: Wayne State University Press, 1989). See also Stanislaus A. Blejwas, "A Polish American Fellow Traveller," *Polish Review* 36, no. 2 (1991): 169–77. An interesting but very unevenly researched work on the fate of the East European left is Jeffrey Robert Ryan, "The Conspiracy That Never Was: United States Government Surveillance of Eastern European American Leftists, 1942–1959" (Ph.D. diss., Boston College, 1990), 41–157. A briefer and unsatisfactory study attributes Polonia's anti-Soviet sentiment to the Catholic Church and the "machiavellian forces of reaction of the [London] Polish Government." The discussion of the Polish-American left, however, is based upon interviews with both the right and the left and on the press. See F. F. Wasell, "Attitudes of the Various Polish-American Organizations Toward American Foreign Policy, 1939–1945" (master's thesis, Columbia University, 1946), 26–36, 58–66.

77. See Lukas, *The Strange Allies,* 46–47, 124–25; Charles Sandler, " 'Political Dynamite': The Chicago Polonia and President Roosevelt in 1944," *Journal of the Illinois State Historical Society* 71, no. 1 (February 1978): 119–32.

78. On 1948, see Glinka-Janczewski, "American Policy Toward Poland Under the Truman Administration, 1945–1952," 296–309; and David McCullogh, *Truman* (New York: Simon & Schuster, 1992), 683–84.

79. Peter Irons, " 'The Test Is Poland': Polish Americans and the Origins of the Cold War," *PAS* 30, no. 2 (Autumn 1973): 5–63. KNAPP's association with the PAC also made it suspect in Washington. See also Wandycz, *The United States and Poland,* 283–84, 290–91.

80. Stephen A. Garrett, *From Potsdam to Poland: American Policy Toward Eastern Europe* (New York: Praeger, 1986), 10–16.

81. Donald E. Pienkos, "The Polish American Congress—An Appraisal," *PAS* 36, no. 2 (Fall 1979): 7. For the immediate postwar years, see Richard C. Lukas, *Bitter Legacy: Polish-American Relations in the Wake of World War II* (Lexington: University of Kentucky Press, 1982), 119–34. Wasell in 1946 recognized the lack of influence of the Polonia left ("Attitudes of the Various Polish-American Organizations Toward American Foreign Policy," 26–32).

82. Robert Szymczak, "A Matter of Honor: Polonia and the Congressional Investigation of the Katyn Forest Massacre," *PAS* 41, no. 1 (Spring 1984): 25–65.

83. Z. A. Kruszewski, "The Polish American Congress, East-West Issues, and the Formulation of American Foreign Policy," in *Ethnic Groups and U.S. Foreign Policy,* ed. Mohammed E. Ahrari (New York: Greenwood Press, 1987), 89–90.

84. Kruszewski, "The Polish American Congress," 92; and Bennett Kovrig, *Of Walls and Bridges: The United States and Eastern Europe* (New York: New York Uni-

versity Press, 1991), 106. For PAC activities at the local level, see Stanislaus A. Blejwas, "The Local Ethnic Lobby: The Polish American Congress in Connecticut, 1944–1974," in Renkiewicz, *The Polish Presence in Canada and America*, 305–25.

85. See Gerson, *The Hyphenate in Recent American Politics and Diplomacy*, 223–60. Garrett, *From Potsdam to Poland*, 53.

86. Wandycz, *The United States and Poland*, 411 (quotation). See also "Proby rozkładania Polonii," *Kultura* 9, no. 324 (September 1974): 121–22; A. Z., "Zamki dla 'Polonii,' " *Kultura* 11, no. 326 (November 1974): 116–21; Benedykt Heydenkorn, "Międzynarodowa konferencja etniczna w Krakowie," *Kultura* 12, no. 339 (December 1975): 90–95; "Działalność twa. Polonia—dokumenty," *Kultura* 1, no. 340 (January–February 1976): 181–91.

87. Pienkos, "The Polish American Congress—An Appraisal," 5–43.

88. George Janczewski, "The Significance of the Polish Vote in 1948," *Polish Review* 13, no. 4 (1969): 101–9; Gerson, *The Hyphenate*, 161; and Garrett, *From Potsdam to Poland*, 42–44. Polish American Catholics voted overwhelmingly against McCarthy in his 1952 election. See Donald F. Crosby, S.J., *God, Church, and Flag: Senator Joseph R. McCarthy and the Catholic Church, 1950–1957* (Chapel Hill: University of North Carolina Press, 1978), 70–71, 96–97, 242–43; also Phillips, *The Emerging Republican Majority*, 123–75, 330–56.

89. Blejwas, "A Polish American Fellow Traveller," 173–74. See also Ryan, "The Conspiracy That Never Was," 41–157, 299–367.

90. Garrett, *From Potsdam to Poland*, 32 (quotation), and Kruszewski, "The Polish American Congress," 97.

91. Garrett, *From Potsdam to Poland*, vii. The only surveys of the first two PAC leaders are in Pienkos, *Polish National Alliance*, 151–206, and Pienkos, *For Your Freedom Through Ours*, 105–95. Stephen A. Garrett, "Eastern European Ethnic Groups and American Foreign Policy," *Political Science Quarterly* 93, no. 2 (Summer 1978): 301–23.

92. Wandycz, *The United States and Poland*, 412–13.

93. Studium Membership circular (n.d.).

94. Kovrig, *Of Walls and Bridges*, 149–51. Also Kruszewski, "The Polish American Congress," 93.

95. Garrett, *From Potsdam to Poland*, 62.

96. See *Region USA: Działacze "Solidarności" o kraju, o emigracji, o sobie* (London: ANEKS, 1989); Mary Erdmans, "Ethnics and Emigrés: Patterns of Cooperation in the Polish Community in Chicago, 1976–1990" (Ph.D. diss., Northwestern University, 1992); the chapter by Erdmans in Helena Znaniecka Lopata, *Polish Americans* (New Brunswick, N.J.: Transaction Publishers, 1994), 213–42; and Stanislaus A. Blejwas, "American Polonia: The Next Generation," *PAS* 49, no. 1 (1992).

97. For a recent overview, see Pienkos, *For Your Freedom Through Ours*, 105–244. Forthcoming is Stanislaus A. Blejwas, "Polska Ludowa i Polonia Amerykańska, 1944–1956," *Przegląd Polonijny*.

98. Agitation for an "American agenda" emanates from the PAC's Washington Metropolitan Division, whose American Agenda Committee is headed by Alfred F. Bochenek. In the PAC divisions there is considerable interest in an American agenda.

99. Pienkos, "The Polish American Congress," 21. For the 1970s, see Michael Novak, *The Rise of the Unmeltable Ethnics: The New Political Force of the Seventies* (New York: Macmillan, 1971). For "Polish" politics, see A. and D. Pienkos, "Badania nad zachowaniami politycznymi," *Przegląd Polonijny* 7, no. 1 (19) (1981): 32–41; and Pienkos, "Polish American Ethnicity," 197–99.

100. See Matthew Frye Jacobson, "Martial Art: Literature and Romantic Militarism in Turn-of-the-Century Polonia," *PAS* 51, no. 1 (Spring 1994): 5–19.

7. Displaced Persons, Émigrés, Refugees, and Other Polish Immigrants: World War II Through the Solidarity Era

1. Similar status was claimed by the early Polish arrivals to the United States who arrived from partitioned Poland in the mid–nineteenth century. See Joseph A. Wytrwal, *America's Polish Heritage: A Social History of Poles in America* (Detroit: Endurance Press, 1961), 36–76; Joseph Wieczerzak, "Pre- and Proto-Ethnics: Poles in the United States Before the Immigration 'After Bread'," *Polish Review* 21, no. 3 (1976): 7–38. In 1852 the Democratic Society of Polish Refugees in America (Towarzystwo Demokratyczne Wygnańców Polskich w Ameryce) was formed. See J. A. Wytrwal, *America's Polish Heritage*, 59; Donald E. Pienkos, *PNA: A Centennial History of the Polish National Alliance of the United States of North America* (New York: Columbia University Press, 1984), 46–48. See also Maria J. E. Copson-Niećko, "The Poles in America from the 1830s to 1870s: Some Reflections on the Possibilities of Research," in *Poles in America: Bicentennial Essays,* ed. Frank Mocha (Stevens Point, Wisc.: Worzalla Publishing, 1978), 45–302.

2. Karol Wachtl, *Polonja w Ameryce. Dzieje i Dorobek* (Philadelphia: By the author, 1944), 397, 396. The quotations appear here as translated in Brożek, 190, 191.

3. M. Haiman, *Dziennik Zjednoczenia,* September 25, 1934, cited in Brożek, 190. See also Stanislaus A. Blejwas, "Old and New Polonias: Tensions Within an Ethnic Community," *Polish American Studies* 38, no. 2 (Autumn 1981): 55–57; Pula, *Polish Americans,* 72–73.

4. John J. Bukowczyk, *And My Children Did Not Know Me: A History of the Polish-Americans* (Bloomington: Indiana University Press, 1987), 83.

5. Mark Wyman, *DP: Europe's Displaced Persons, 1945–1951* (Philadelphia: Balch Institute Press, 1989). See also reviews by R. Breitman, *Journal of American Ethnic History* 10, no. 2 (1990): 131–32; J. H. M. Laslett, *International Migration Review* 24 (1990): 839–40; M. R. Marrus, *American Historical Review* 95, no. 3 (1990): 814; and, for a special insight into everyday life in the DP camps, the firsthand account by the United Nations Relief and Rehabilitation Administration (UNRRA) and then the International Refugee Organization (IRO) employee Kathryn Hulme in *The Wild Place* (Boston: Little, Brown, 1953).

6. Leonard Dinnerstein, *America and the Survivors of the Holocaust* (New York: Columbia University Press, 1982). See also Anna D. Jaroszyńska-Kirchmann, " 'Knocking on the Polish Hearts': American Polonia's Effort for the Change of Immigration Laws After World War II" (unpublished paper presented at the fifty-

second annual meeting of the Polish Institute of Arts and Sciences of America at the American University, Washington, D.C., in 1994).

7. Malcolm J. Proudfoot, *European Refugees, 1939–1952: A Study in Forced Population Movement* (Evanston, Ill.: Northwestern University Press, 1956); John George Stoessinger, *The Refugee and the World Community* (Minneapolis: University of Minnesota Press, 1956); Jacques Vernant, *The Refugee in the Post-War World* (London: Allen and Unwin, 1953); Gil Loescher and John A. Scanlan, *Calculated Kindness: Refugees and America's Half-Open Door, 1945 to the Present* (New York: Free Press, 1986); Michael R. Marrus, *The Unwanted: European Refugees in the Twentieth Century* (New York: Oxford University Press, 1985); Haim Genizi, *America's Fair Share: The Admission and Resettlement of Displaced Persons, 1945–1952* (Detroit: Wayne State University Press, 1993); Leonard Dinnerstein and David M. Reimers, *Ethnic Americans: A History of Immigration and Assimilation* (New York: Harper and Row, 1975).

8. Yuri Boshyk, *Political Refugees and "Displaced Persons," 1945–1954: A Selected Bibliography and Guide to Research with Special Reference to Ukrainians* (Edmonton: Canadian Institute of Ukrainian Studies, University of Alberta, 1982); Yuri Boshyk and Wlodzimierz Kiebalo, ed., "Publications by Ukrainian 'Displaced Persons' and Political Refugees, 1945–1954," in *The John Luczkiw Collection, Thomas Fisher Rare Books Library, University of Toronto: A Bibliography* (Edmonton: Canadian Institute of Ukrainian Studies, University of Alberta, 1988); Wsewolod W. Isajiw, Yuri Boshyk, and Roman Senkus, ed., *The Refugee Experience: Ukrainian Displaced Persons After World War II* (Edmonton: Canadian Institute of Ukrainian Studies, University of Alberta, 1992).

9. See, for example, David S. Wyman, *Paper Walls* (Boston: University of Massachusetts Press, 1968), and *The Abandonment of the Jews* (New York: Pantheon, 1984); Dinnerstein, *America and the Survivors;* Sharon R. Lowenstein, *Token Refugee: The Story of the Jewish Shelter at Oswego, 1944–1946* (Bloomington: Indiana University Press, 1986); Jacob Biber, *Risen from the Ashes: A Story of the Jewish Displaced Persons in the Aftermath of World War II, Being a Sequel to Survivors* (San Bernardino: Borgo Press, 1990). For the Lithuanian group, see Milda Danys, *DP: Lithuanian Immigration to Canada After the Second World War* (Toronto: Multicultural History Society of Ontario, 1986); Anastas J. Van Reenan, *Lithuanian Diaspora: Königsberg to Chicago* (Lanham: University Press of America, 1990); Alfred Erich Senn, "Emigrés and Immigrants: Problem of National Consciousness," *Spectrum* 6 (published by the Immigration History Research Center of the University of Minnesota).

10. Barbara Stern Burstin, *After the Holocaust: The Migration of Polish Jews and Christians to Pittsburgh* (Pittsburgh: University of Pittsburgh Press, 1989). See also reviews by Frederick B. Lindstrom, *The Annals of the American Academy of Political and Social Science* 511 (1990): 191–92; Thomas Szendrey, *International Migration Review* 25 (1991): 416–17.

11. The proceedings of the conference are being published in volume 6 of *Spectrum.*

12. See, for example, Czesław Łuczak, "Przemieszczenia ludności z Polski podczas drugiej wojny światowej," in *Emigracja z ziem polskich w czasach nowożytnych i najnowszych (XVIII–XX w.),* ed. Andrzej Pilch (Warsaw: PWN, 1984), 451–83; Andrzej

Pilch and Marian Zgórniak, "Emigracja po drugiej wojnie światowej," in ibid., 484–511; Grzegorz Janusz, "Stowarzyszenie naczelne polskich ośrodków wysiedleńczych w Niemczech Zachodnich w latach 1945–1980," in *Organizacje polonijne w Europie zachodniej: współczesność i tradycje,* ed. Barbara Szydłowska-Ceglowa and Jerzy Kozłowski (Poznań: PAN, Zakład Badań Nad Polonią Zagraniczną, 1991), 149–69; Władysław Stanisław Kucharski, *Polacy i Polonia w rdzennej Austrii w XIX i XX wieku* (Lublin: Uniwersytet Marii Curie-Skłodowskiej, 1994); Keith Sword, with Norman Davies and Jan Ciechanowski, *The Formation of the Polish Community in Great Britain, 1939–1950* (London: School of Slavonic and East European Studies, University of London, 1989); Jerzy Zubrzycki, *Polish Immigrants in Britain: A Study of Adjustment* (The Hague: Martinus Nijhoff, 1956); an extensive summary of publications on Poles in Australia in Mirosław Boruta and Jan Lencznarowicz, "Polacy w Australii wczoraj i dziś: Przegląd współczesnej literatury przedmiotu," *Przegląd Polonijny* 15, no. 4 (1989): 113–28; Egon F. Kunz, *Displaced Persons: Calwell's New Australians* (Sydney: Australian National University Press, 1988); Henryk Radecki, with Benedykt Heydenkorn, *A Member of a Distinguished Family: The Polish Group in Canada* (Toronto: McClelland and Stewart in Association with the Multicultural Program, Department of the Secretary of State of Canada and the Publishing Centre, Supply and Services Canada, 1976); Henry Radecki, *Ethnic Organizational Dynamics: The Polish Group in Canada* (Waterloo, Ont.: Wilfrid Laurier University Press, 1979).

13. According to the Department of Justice Immigration and Naturalization Service (INS) statistics, between 1939 and 1945 a total of 25,383 Poles identified by country of birth (both quota and non-quota immigrants) arrived in the United States. See Helena Znaniecki Lopata, "Polish Immigration to the United States of America: Problems of Estimation and Parameters," *Polish Review* 21, no. 4 (1976): table 6, p. 96. Numbers of persons arrived from Poland, provided by the *Historical Statistics of the United States, Colonial Times to 1957* (Washington, D.C., 1961) are significantly lower: the total is 3,072 for 1939; 702 for 1940; 451 for 1941; 343 for 1942; 393 for 1943; 292 for 1944; 195 for 1945; the total is 5,448. See Mirosław Francić, "Emigracja z Polski do Stanów Zjednoczonych Ameryki od r. 1918 do lat siedemdziesiątych XX w.," in *Polonia amerykańska: Przeszłość i współczesność,* ed. Hieronim Kubiak, Eugeniusz Kusielewicz, and Tadeusz Gromada (Wrocław: Zakład Narodowy im. Ossolińskich, 1988), 51.

14. American Relief for Poland, manuscript collection in the Polish Museum of America, Chicago, folders: "Polish War Refugees, N.Y. Area, vol. 1–3," and "Polish War Refugees, Chicago Area."

15. Wacław Jędrzejewicz, *Polonia amerykańska w polityce polskiej: Historia Komitetu Narodowego Amerykanów Polskiego Pochodzenia* (New York: National Committee of Americans of Polish Descent, 1954), 15–41.

16. National Committee of Americans of Polish Descent, *Od apelu do Kongresu: Zbiór dokumentów Komitetu Narodowego Amerykanów Polskiego Pochodzenia, 12 maja 1942–28 maja 1944* (New York: Józef Piłsudski Institute of America for Research in the Modern History of Poland, 1944); Richard C. Lukas, *The Strange Allies: The United States and Poland, 1941–1945* (Knoxville: University of Tennessee Press, 1978), 107–16; Peter H. Irons, " 'The Test Is Poland': Polish Americans and the Origins of

the Cold War," *PAS* 30, no. 2 (Autumn 1973): 5–63; Bukowczyk, *And My Children Did Not Know Me,* 92–93; Blejwas, "Old and New Polonias," 62–70.

17. John Bukowczyk, " 'Harness for Posterity the Values of a Nation'—Fifty Years of the Polish American Historical Association and *Polish American Studies,*" *PAS* 50, no. 2 (1993): 5–100; Bukowczyk, "The Polish American Historical Association," in *The Polish Diaspora,* ed. James S. Pula and M. B. Biskupski (Washington, D.C.: Columbia University Press, 1993), vol. 2, *Selected Essays from the Fiftieth Anniversary International Congress of the Polish Institute of Arts and Sciences of America,* 99–102.

18. Michael Budny, "Józef Piłsudski Institute of America for Research in the Modern History of Poland," in Mocha, *Poles in America,* 687–708.

19. Frank Mocha, "The Polish Institute of Arts and Sciences in America, Its Contributions to the Study of Polonia: The Origins of the Polish Historical Association (PAHA)," in Mocha, *Poles in America,* 709–24.

20. *Tygodnik Polski* (since January 1943) superseded *Tygodniowy Przegląd Literacki Koła Pisarzy z Polski,* published in 1941–1942. For Wittlin's views on a writer's life in exile, see Joseph Wittlin, "Sorrow and Grandeur of Exile," *Polish Review* 2, nos. 2–3 (1957): 99–111. See also Czesław Miłosz, *The History of Polish Literature* (Berkeley and Los Angeles: University of California Press, 1983), 387–89, 395–96, 397–98, 423–24, 521–32; Jerzy J. Maciuszko, "Polish Letters in America," in Mocha, *Poles in America,* 531–64.

21. Emil Orzechowski, *Teatr Polonijny w Stanach Zjednoczonych* (Wrocław: Zakład Narodowy im. Ossolińskich, 1989), 226–33.

22. Burstin, *After the Holocaust,* 67–68. See also Loescher and Scanlan, *Calculated Kindness,* 5–6; Dinnerstein, *America and the Survivors,* 163–64. The INS statistics show the total number of Poles entering the United States to be 4,807 in 1946 (quota and non-quota immigrants); 8,156 in 1947 (including 6,494 quota and 1,662 non-quota immigrants); and 8,020 in all of 1948 (including 6,143 quota and 1,877 non-quota immigrants, with 12,117 DPs, and 669 non-immigrants). See Znaniecki Lopata, "Polish Immigration," table 7, p. 97.

23. Proudfoot, *European Refugees,* 189–228, 275–92, 415–18; Stoessinger, *The Refugee,* 51–55.

24. Stoessinger, *The Refugee,* 55–58; Proudfoot, *European Refugees,* 292–98. See also Frank Auerbach, *Admission and Resettlement of the Displaced Persons in the United States: A Handbook of Legal and Technical Information for the Use of Local Social and Civic Agencies* (New York: Common Council for American Unity Incorporated, 1949), 8.

25. George Woodbridge, *UNRRA: The History of the United Nations Relief and Rehabilitation Administration,* vol. 3 (New York: Columbia University Press, 1950), 423; Louis W. Holborn, *The International Refugee Organization, a Specialized Agency of the United Nations: Its History and Work, 1946–1952* (London: Oxford University Press, 1956), 157. John George Stoessinger, *The Refugee Community* (Minneapolis: The University of Minnesota Press, 1956), 55–58. Other large ethnic groups represented among the DPs were Jews, Lithuanians, Latvians, Estonians, Yugoslavs, and Ukrainians. See also Proudfoot, *European Refugees,* 281–85, 291; René Ristelhueber, "The International Refugee Organization," *International Conciliation,* no. 470 (April

1951), 186–87; F. Auerbach, *Admission,* 8. There are some problems with interpretation of the UNRRA's and IRO's statistics, since the division into ethnic groups and corresponding numbers were usually based on the criterion of the country of birth, with less consideration given to the ethnic self-identification of refugees or their religious affiliation. See, for example, Holborn, *The International Refugee Organization,* annex 41, 437–40. In the opinion of Polish DP organizations, the IRO statistics demonstrated numbers below the actual size of the Polish refugee population. The IRO statistics excluded all refugees who after repatriation returned from Poland, those who escaped from Poland, and any others without a legitimate refugee status. For example, the comparison of totals for November 1948 in the American zone indicated 46,987 Polish DPs according to IRO estimates, and 71,000 according to Polish sources. "Główny Referat Osiedleńczy Zjednoczenia polskiego ameriykańskiej okupacji Niemiec," a report, (1948), 4–6, collection "Wysiedleńcy Polscy po 1945 roku w Niemczech," F.# 162, Józef Piłsudski Institute of America, New York.

26. Holborn, *The International Refugee Organization,* 438.

27. *Memo to America, the DP Story: The Final Report of the United States Displaced Persons Commission* (Washington, D.C.: U.S. Government Printing Office, 1952), 9–41; Dinnerstein, *America and the Survivors,* 137–82; Loescher and Scanlon, *Calculated Kindness,* 1–24.

28. Although the precise number is hard to establish, statistics of the Displaced Persons Commission demonstrate that, as of May 31, 1952, 34 percent of immigrants admitted under the DP act indicated Poland as their country of birth, which sets the total at a little below 134 thousand. *Memo to America,* tables 2 and 3, p. 366. DP Commission statistics give 154,556 as a total number of visas issued to DPs from Poland by December 31, 1951. The same number for Polish ex-veterans is 10,472. Ibid., 376. According to IRO statistics, 110,566 DPs from Poland were resettled in the United States between July 1, 1947, and December 31, 1951. Holborn, *The International Refugee Organization,* 438. See also Anna D. Jaroszyńska-Kirchmann, "Communications," *PAS* 46, no. 2 (Autumn 1989): 90; Burstin, *After the Holocaust,* 115–16. Burstin accepts 120,000 as the number of Polish Christians admitted to the United States under the DP act. According to the INS, the following numbers of DPs entered the United States: 17,794 in 1949; 47,871 in 1950; 33,757 in 1951; 25,444 in 1952. The total number of DPs for the years 1947–1952 was 143,504. See Znaniecki Lopata, "Polish Immigration," table 7, p. 97.

29. Dinnerstein, *America and the Survivors,* 183; *Memo to America,* 48–55, 267–70.

30. For PIC, see Thaddeus Theodore Krysiewicz, *The Polish Immigration Committee in the United States: A Historical Survey of the American Committee for Relief of Polish Immigrants, 1947–1952* (New York: The Roman Catholic Church of St. Stanislaus B. M., 1952); Burstin, *After the Holocaust,* 78–82.

For American Relief for Poland, see Franciszek X. Świetlik, *Sprawozdanie z działalności Rady Polonii Amerykańskiej od października 1939 do października 1948, na zjazd Rady Polonii Amerykańskiej odbyty dnia 4go i 5go grudnia, 1948 r. w hotelu Buffalo, w Buffalo, N.Y.* (Chicago: Rada Polonii Amerykańskiej, 1948), 20–28, 30–35, 40–63; Burstin, *After the Holocaust,* 82; Donald E. Pienkos, *For Your Freedom Through Ours: Polish American Efforts on Poland's Behalf, 1863–1991* (New York: Columbia University Press, 1991), 89–98.

For ACRPDP, see Anna D. Jaroszyńska, "The American Committee for the Resettlement of Polish Displaced Persons (1948–1968) in the Manuscript Collection of
the Immigration History Research Center," *PAS* 44 (1987): 63–73; Donald E. Pienkos, "Communications," *PAS* 45 (1988): 98–100; Jaroszyńska-Kirchmann, "Communications," 87–93; Donald A. Pienkos, *For Your Freedom*, 122–30; Anna D. Jaroszyńska-Kirchmann, " 'Nowa Emigracja' and 'Stara Polonia': Transformations of Social
Relations and the DP Resettlement Program in the United States," in *The Polish
Diaspora*, 69–84.

31. Danuta Mostwin, "The Profile of a Transplanted Family," *Polish Review* 19
(1974): 77–89, and "Post World War II Polish Immigrants in the United States," *PAS*
26 (Autumn 1979): 5–14. Some of the social characteristics of the Polish DPs were
examined in unpublished dissertations, such as Rev. Stanislaus T. Sypek, "The Displaced Person in the Greater Boston Community" (Ph.D. diss., Fordham University,
1955); Maria Barbara Korewa, "Casework Treatment of Refugees: A Survey of Selected Professional Periodicals for the Period from January 1, 1939, to January 1, 1956"
(master's thesis, Wayne State University, 1957); Alicja Iwanska, "Values in Crisis Situation" (Ph.D. diss., Columbia University, 1957); Danuta Mostwin, "The Transplanted Family: A Study of Social Adjustment of the Polish Immigrant Family to the
United States After the Second World War" (Ph.D. diss., Ann Arbor, Mich.: University Microfilms, 1971); Sarah Van Atken-Rutkowski, "Integration and Acculturation
of the Polish Veteran of World War II to Canadian Society" (master's thesis, University of Windsor, 1982).

32. Tadeusz Paleczny, *Ewolucja ideologii i przemiany tożsamości narodowej Polonii
w Stanach Zjednoczonych w latach 1870–1970* (Warsaw: Państwowe Wydawnictwo
Naukowe, 1989), 233–42; Aleksander Hertz, *Refleksje amerykańskie* (Paris: Instytut
Literacki, 1966), 90–98; Keith Sword, *The Formation*, 85–213.

33. D. Mostwin labels the entire postwar wave as the "soldiers' immigration."
According to Mostwin, it was the military group who gave the DP immigration its
political and ideological character. See D. Mostwin, *Emigranci polscy w USA* (Lublin:
Redakcja Wydawnictw Katolickiego Uniwersytetu Lubelskiego, 1991), 150–54.

34. Blejwas, "Old and New Polonias," 71; Walter Zachariasiewicz, "Organizational Structure of Polonia," in Mocha, *Poles in America*, 654–56. See also an official
organ of the SPK quarterly *Kombatant w Ameryce* (The combatant in America).

35. Zachariasiewicz, "Organizational Structure," 656, and press releases in *Dziennik Związkowy*, June 10, 1950, p. 3; June 19, 1950, p. 2; June 4, 1951, p. 3; August 6,
1952, p. 8.

36. Józef Wyrwa ("Furgalski," "Stary"), *Pamiętniki Partyzanta* (London: Oficyna
Poetów i Malarzy, 1991), 301–551. The book contains rich and detailed documentation
relating to the case and abundant quotations from the Polish-language press in the
United States. I would like to thank Dr. Wyrwa for providing me with the copy of
his father's book and for his friendly correspondence on the subject.

37. *Dziennik Związkowy* ran a regular weekly column, "Kącik Uchodźców" (renamed subsequently "Kącik Nowej Emigracji" and then "Dział Nowej Emigracji"),
which provided all kinds of legal information that was useful to the Chicago-area DP
population, made announcements about activities of different DP circles, and played

a coordinating role for such events as visits of General Bór Komorowski or General Anders. The Mutual Aid Association of the New Polish Immigration (Stowarzyszenie Samopomocy Nowej Emigracji Polskiej) in Chicago, and a similar organization from Milwaukee, Wisconsin, belonged to the most dynamic associations. Other active organizations included Koło Byłych Wychowawców i Wychowanków Polskich Szkół Średnich z Niemiec (Circle of Former Teachers and Students of Polish High Schools in Germany), Stowarzyszenie Nowych Amerykanów (Association of New Americans), Koło "Nowa Polonia" ("New Polonia" Circle), Związek Lekarzy Polskich na Wychodźstwie (Association of Polish Physicians Abroad), and Polskie Towarzystwo Opieki and Książką "Pielgrzym" (Polish Association for the Care of Books "Pilgrim"). On the scouting movement, see Ewa Gierat, *Powojenna historia harcerstwa w Stanach Zjednoczonych, 1949–1989* (Texas: Language Bridges, 1990); W. Zachariasiewicz, "Organizational Structure," 657–58.

38. Hertz, *Refleksje amerykańskie,* 100; Blejwas, "Old and New Polonias," 55–60; Helena Znaniecka Lopata (with a new chapter by Mary Patrice Erdmans), *Polish Americans* (New Brunswick, N.J.: Transaction Publishers, 1994), 99–102.

39. Blejwas, "Old and New Polonias," 76.

40. Bukowczyk, *And My Children Did Not Know Me,* 95.

41. Several authors discuss the tension between both groups in Polonia: for example, Blejwas, "Old and New Polonias," 72–83; Hertz, *Refleksje amerykańskie,* 99–104; Bukowczyk, *And My Children Did Not Know Me,* 93–96; Znaniecki Lopata, *Polish Americans: Status Competition in an Ethnic Community* (Englewood Cliffs, N.J.: Prentice Hall, 1976), 26–27; Paleczny, *Ewolucja ideologii,* 226–42; Burstin, *After the Holocaust,* 126–37; Jaroszyńska-Kirchmann, " 'Nowa Emigracja' and 'Stara Polonia'," 77–82; Znaniecka Lopata, *Polish Americans,* 103–4.

42. Jaroszyńska-Kirchmann, " 'Nowa Emigracja' and 'Stara Polonia'," 77–82.

43. Jaroszyńska-Kirchmann, " 'Nowa Emigracja' and 'Stara Polonia'," 79–80.

44. Papers of Harry N. Rosenfield, Box 18, folder: DPC—Louisiana Resettlement Problem, Harry S. Truman Library, Independence, Missouri.

45. Blejwas, "Old and New Polonias," 75, 79. For the theater, see E. Orzechowski, *Teatr Polonijny,* 234–73. See also Konstantin Symmons-Symonalewicz, "Polish Contributions to American Scholarship: The Fields of Sociology and Cultural Anthropology, 1918–1976," in Mocha, *Poles in America,* 499–508; Leon Thaddeus Blaszczyk, "Polish Contribution to the Musical Life in America," also in Mocha, *Poles in America,* 565–624; and W. S. Kuniczak, *My Name Is Million: An Illustrated History of the Poles in America* (New York: Doubleday, 1978), 164–72.

The various aspects of the DP experience and adjustment to life in America were also described in numerous literary accounts. Some of the best known are Danuta Mostwin, *Ameryko! Ameryko!* (Paris: Instytut Literacki, 1961); Mostwin, *Asteroidy* (London: Polska Fundacja Kulturalna, 1965); Mostwin, *Ja za wodą, ty za wodą* (Paris: Instytut Literacki, 1972); Flannery O'Connor, "The Displaced Person," in *"A Good Man Is Hard to Find" and Other Stories* (New York: Harcourt, Brace, 1955), 197–251; Florence Hayes, *Joe-Pole, New American* (Boston: Riverside Press, 1952). Literary biographies can be represented by Doug Wead, *Tears of Triumph: The Story of Alicia Gilewicz* (Springfield, Mo.: Restoration Fellowship, 1981).

46. Burstin, *After the Holocaust*, 140–80.

47. Maxine Schwartz Seller, *To Seek America: A History of Ethnic Life in the United States* (Englewood Cliffs, N.J.: Jerome S. Ozer Publisher, 1988), 264. See also Michael C. LeMay, *From Open Door to Dutch Door: An Analysis of U.S. Immigration Policy Since 1820* (New York: Praeger, 1987), 103–8.

48. LeMay, *Open Door*, 108–9.

49. M. Stern Seller, *To Seek America*, 264; LeMay, *Open Door*, 108–14.

50. *Dziennik Związkowy*, April–May 1953 (Jarecki's escape); July 1953 (Jaźwiński's escape).

51. Many others are also mentioned in Kuniczak, *My Name Is Million*, 172–76.

52. Znaniecka Lopata, "Polish Immigration," table 7, p. 97, based on Commissioner of the Bureau of Immigration, *Annual Report* (Washington, D.C.: Government Printing Office, 1947–1972).

53. Dariusz Stola, "Forced Migrations in Central European History," *International Migration Review* 26, no. 2 (1992): 337. According to other authors, 30,000 Jews were forced out of Poland at that time. See M. R. Marrus, *The Unwanted*, 362.

54. Norman Davies, *God's Playground: A History of Poland in Two Volumes*, vol. 2, *1795 to the Present* (New York: Columbia University Press, 1982), 593–609.

55. U.S. Bureau of the Census, *Statistical Abstract of the United States, 1991*, 111th ed. (Washington, D.C.: Governmental Printing Office, 1991), table 7, p. 10; table 10, p. 11.

56. Mostwin received 552 responses. Most came from persons who had immigrated to the United States between 1978 and 1984. According to Mostwin, about 46,000 Poles immigrated to America during that time (8,200 in 1978–1979 and 38,000 in 1980–1984). See Mostwin, *Emigranci polscy*, 44, 55–114.

57. Ryszard Kantor, "Kluby parafii Zaborów w Chicago w okresie międzywojennym i w latach II wojny światowej," *Przegląd Polonijny* 15 (1989): 35–60.

58. Ryszard Kantor, "Kluby parafii Zaborów w Chicago: Geneza, dzieje, i stan obecny," in *Studia nad organizacjami polonijnymi w Ameryce Północnej*, ed. Grzegorz Babiński (Wrocław: Zakład Narodowy im. Ossolińskich, 1988), 141–45.

59. Ryszard Kantor, "Miejsce Chicago we współczesnych migracjach zarobkowych ludności parafii Zaborów (woj. Tarnów)," *Przegląd Polonijny* 10, no. 3 (1984): 57–72.

60. Bukowczyk, *And My Children Did Not Know Me*, 105–24. Znaniecka Lopata, *Polish Americans*, 124; Danuta Mostwin, *Trzecia wartość: Formowanie się nowej tożsamości polskiego emigranta w Ameryce* (Lublin: Instytut Badań Nad Polonią i Duszpasterstwem Polonijnym, Katolicki Uniwersytet Lubelski, 1985), 144.

61. Donald Pienkos, "The Polish American Congress: An Appraisal," *PAS* 36, no. 2 (Autumn 1979): 21 (quotation). Mary Patrice Erdmans, "Recent Political Action on Behalf of Poland: The Interrelationships Among Polonia's Cohorts, 1978–1990," in Znaniecka Lopata, *Polish Americans*, 219.

62. M. R. Marrus, *The Unwanted*, 364.

63. Some issues on the perception of emigration in 1980s Poland, both by the political forces there and the society as a whole, are analyzed by Mary Patrice Erdmans, "The Social Construction of Emigration as a Moral Issue," *PAS*, 49, no. 1

(Spring 1992): 7–25. The author also deals with this and similar problems in her doctoral dissertation, "Emigrés and Ethnics: Patterns of Cooperation Between New and Established Residents in Chicago's Polish Community" (Ph.D. diss., Northwestern University, 1992). The approach of the Catholic Church can be studied through the various church publications on this topic, such as, for instance, Piotr Gach, "Refleksja o współczesnej emigracji polskiej," *Biuletyn Ruchu Apostolatu Emigracyjnego,* no. 2 (6), Rok 3 (1989), 25–28, published by the Christ Society for Polonia Abroad (Towarzystwo Chrystusowe dla Polonii Zagranicznej). The concern of the government is noticeable through the countless propaganda shows and publications in the Polish media at that time, as well as sponsorship of the polls, such as conducted by the Centrum Badania Opinii Społecznej (CBOS) in "Opinie społeczne o osobach wyjeżdżających na Zachód" (Warsaw, June 1988).

64. CBOS poll of 1988; data on the basis of the figures from the Polish Ministry of Foreign Affairs.

65. U.S. Bureau of the Census, *Statistical Abstract, 1991,* table 7, p. 10; table 10, p. 11. Numbers for 1989 are accordingly 15,100 and 3,842 immigrants. See also Stanislaus A. Blejwas, "American Polonia: The Next Generation," *PAS* 49, no. 1 (Spring 1992): 81.

66. Blejwas, "American Polonia," 81–86, on the basis of Andrzej Krajewski, *Region USA: Działacze Solidarności o kraju, o emigracji, o sobie* (London: ANEKS, 1989); Bukowczyk, *And My Children Did Not Know Me,* 122–23.

67. Znaniecka Lopata, *Polish Americans,* 188, 189. Znaniecka Lopata considers the oldest economic wave of immigrants the first cohort, the World War II wave the second cohort, and the most recent wave the third cohort of Polish immigrants to the United States. Ibid., 17–51.

68. "Brief Information Concerning the POMOST Socio-political Movement," Immigration History Research Center (IHRC), University of Minnesota, Papers of Aloysius A. Mazewski, IHRC 127. See also M. P. Erdmans, "Recent Political Action," 219–20.

69. Informational material of POMOST, Chicago, March 1982 (my translation), IHRC 127.

70. See, for example, correspondence between A. A. Mazewski and Christopher Rac, the executive committee coordinator for POMOST, and with Joe Losiak; as well as *Dziennik Związkowy* article by Jan Krawiec (January 6, 1984) and response by James Zmuda of POMOST, IHRC 127.

71. M. P. Erdmans, "Recent Political Action," 214–18. According to Erdmans, "quota immigrants" are those that come within numerical limits of American immigration law; "nonimmigrants" refers to Poles who receive temporary visas for the purposes of business, governmental activity, or tourism; and "refugees" are those who were persecuted or feared persecution in Poland. Ibid., 214.

72. Ibid., 218–42.

73. Publications that appeared in the Polish press in 1980–1987 are collected by Wojciech Chojnacki, "Bibliografia publikacji prasowych o najnowszej emigracji z lat 1980–1987," *Przegląd Polonijny* 4 (1989): 129–43. For social work reports, see Richard

P. Baker, "Eastern Refugees: Implications for Social Work," *Journal of Sociology and Social Welfare* 16, no. 3 (1989): 81–94. Baker bases his analysis on the study of both Polish and Czechoslovakian refugees but does not provide adequate distinction between the specific experiences of both groups. See also Severina Zawistowska-Gorzela, "Problems of Recent Polish Immigrants," *PNCC Studies* 4 (1983): 61–66. A good example of oral history is the interview in "Solidarity: Józef and Krystyna Patyna, Refugees from Trzebinia, Poland—Factory Workers, Providence, Rhode Island," in Al Santoli, *New Americans, an Oral History: Immigrants and Refugees in the U.S. Today* (New York: Viking, 1988), 56–84. See also Mostwin, *Emigranci polscy*, 156–58.

74. M. B. Biskupski, "Aut Caesar, Aut Nulles: Departing Reflections of a PAHA President," *PAS* 48, no. 1 (Spring 1991): 5–6.

75. The literary portrait of immigrants-artists was presented by Janusz Głowacki in his acclaimed play, "Hunting Cockroaches," in *Hunting Cockroaches and Other Plays* (Evanston, Ill.: Northwestern University Press, 1990).

76. Jarosław Rokicki, " 'Wakacjusze' na Jackowie i inni: Szkic o sytuacji współczesnych polskich emigrantów zarobkowych w Chicago," *Przegląd Polonijny* 15, no. 3 (1989): 105–18. See also the review by Ryszard Kantor of a popular fiction book on the problems of Chicago *turyści*, Zofia Mierzyńska, *Wakacjuszka* (Chicago: Z and L Song and Publishing Co., 1983), in *Przegląd Polonijny* 13, no. 3 (1987): 119–20, and also by Kantor, "Współczesne migracje zarobkowe mieszkańców Podhala do USA: Raport z badań terenowych w latach 1987–1988," *Przegląd Polonijny* 27, no. 1 (1991): 13–32; Karen J. Aaroian, "Polish Immigrants in the U.S.: Adjusting to Capitalism," *PAS* 47 (1990): 75–86. For the literary representation of "wakacjusze" circles, see Edward Reliński, *Szczuropolacy* (Warsaw: Polska Oficyna Wydawnicza "BGW," 1994), and *Dolorado* (Warsaw: Polska Oficyna Wydawnicza "BGW," 1994).

77. Znaniecka Lopata, *Polish Americans*, 169. As the demand for "cleaning ladies" remains steady, increasing numbers of Polish immigrants find illegal employment in home elder care. Mary Patrice Erdmans, "Poles and the American Black Market in Eldercare," *2B* 2 (1994): 18–21. D. Mostwin stresses profound psychological crises of many illegal and temporary immigrants who have serious problems dealing with their lives in America. See Mostwin, *Emigranci polscy*, 155–56, 160–62.

78. Mary P. Erdmans, "Immigrants and Ethnics: Conflict and Identity in Chicago Polonia," *Sociological Quarterly* 36 (1995): 175–95.

79. See, for instance, Władysław Miodunka, "O potrzebie badań and najnowszą emigracją z Polski," *Przegląd Polonijny* 4 (1989): 125–28. The Polonia Research Committee of the Polish Academy of Sciences, housed at the Jagiellonian University in Cracow, established that the study of "the fate of Polish emigration after World War II, with research oriented toward developing a political history of the post-war emigration" as one of its principal goals. See *PAHA Newsletter* 48, no. 2 (April 1992): 2; Blejwas, "American Polonia," 86; Biskupski, "Aut Caesar," 5–6.

80. These and other questions regarding future study of the DP wave were previously suggested by Jaroszyńska-Kirchmann in " 'Nowa Emigracja' and 'Stara Polonia'," 83.

81. Pienkos, *PNA*, 282–83.

8. Post-World War II Polish Historiography on Emigration

1. Editor's note: Professor Brożek died in January 1994 before final editing of his essay was completed. In copyediting the present version of his manuscript, I have smoothed out the language, clarified a few opaque usages, and broken up several long paragraphs, while attempting to retain the stylistic flavor of the original text.

2. Editor's note: Another distinct series of migrations involved Poland's Jewish population, in particular between 1945 and the 1960s. Professor Brożek has not engaged this critical subject, nor the large literature dealing with it, in the present essay.

3. A. Brożek, "Historiography of Polish Emigration to North America," *Immigration History Newsletter* 18, no. 1 (May 1986): 1–4; Brożek, "Sources and Historiography of Emigration from Poland Before 1939," in *Overseas Migration from East-Central and Southeastern Europe, 1880–1940*, ed. J. Puskás (Budapest: Akadámiai Kiadó, 1990), 130.

4. Marian M. Drozdowski, ed., *Dzieje Polonii w XIX i XX wieku* (History of Polonia in the nineteenth and twentieth centuries) (Toruń: Polskie Towarzystwo Historyczne, 1974; Warsaw: Państwowe Wydawnictwo Naukowe, 1979); C. Bobińska and A. Pilch, ed., *Employment-Seeking Emigrations of the Poles World-Wide, XIX and XXC.* (Cracow: Uniwersytet Jagielloński, 1975).

5. H. Janowska, *Polska emigracja zarobkowa we Francji, 1919–1939* (Polish employment-seeking emigration in France, 1919–1939) (Warsaw: Książka i Wiedza, 1964).

6. R. Dzwonkowski, *Polska opieka religijna we Francji, 1909–1939* (Polish religious care in France, 1909–1939) (Poznań: Pallotinum, 1988); A. Paczkowski, *Prasa i społeczność polska we Francji w latach 1920–1940* (The press and the Polish ethnic group in France in the years 1920–1940) (Wrocław: Ossolineum, 1979); Paczkowski, *Prasa polonijna w latach 1870–1939: Zarys problematyki* (The Polonian press in the years 1870–1939: Outline of problems) (Warsaw: Biblioteka Narodowa, 1977).

7. W. Śladkowski, *Emigracja polska we Francji* (Polish emigration in France) (Lublin: Wydawnictwo Lubelskie, 1980).

8. B. Drewniak, *Robotnicy sezonowi na Pomorzu Zachodnim, 1890–1918* (Seasonal workers in Western Pomerania, 1890–1918) (Poznań: Instytut Zachodni, 1959); *Emigracja z Pomorza Zachodniego, 1816–1911* (Emigration from Western Pomerania, 1816–1911) (Poznań: Wydawnictwo Poznańskie, 1966).

9. K. Wajda, *Migracje ludności wiejskiej Pomorza Wschodniego w latach 1850–1914* (Migrations of the rural population of Eastern Pomerania in the years 1850–1914) (Wrocław: Ossolineum, 1969).

10. A. Brożek, *Robotnicy spoza zaboru pruskiego w przemyśle na Górnym Śląsku, 1870–1914* (Workers from outside the Prussian partition in the industry of Upper Silesia, 1870–1914) (Wrocław: Ossolineum, 1966).

11. Brożek, *Ostflucht na Śląsku* (Flight from the east in Silesia) (Katowice: Śląsk, 1966); Brożek, *Problematyka narodowościowa ostfluchtu na Śląsku* (Ethnic problems of the flight from the east in Silesia) (Wrocław: Państwowe Wydawnictwo Naukowe, 1969).

12. A. Poniatowska, *Polacy w Berlinie, 1918–1945* (Poles in Berlin, 1918–1945) (Poznań: Wydawnictwo Poznańskie, 1986); Poniatowska, *Polskie wychodźstwo sezonowe na*

Pomorzu Zachodnim, 1918–1939 (Polish seasonal emigration in Western Pomerania, 1918–1939) (Szczecin: Instytut Zachodnio-Pomorski, 1971); B. Drewniak and A. Poniatowska, *Polonia szczecińska, 1890–1939* (The Stettin Polonia, 1890–1939) (Poznań: Wydawnictwo Poznańskie 1961).

13. K. Murzynowska, *Polskie wychodźstwo zarobkowe w Zagłębiu Ruhry w latach 1880–1914* (The Polish employment-seeking emigration in the Ruhr Basin, 1880–1914) (Wrocław: Ossolineum, 1972), published in German as *Die polnischen Erwerbsauswanderer im Ruhrgebiet während der Jahre 1880–1914* (Dortmund: Forschungsstelle Ostmitteleuropa, 1979).

14. J. Kozłowski, *Rozwój organizacji społeczno-narodowych wychodźstwa polskiego w Niemczech w latach 1870–1914* (The development of social and national organizations among the Polish immigration in Germany in the years 1870–1914) (Wrocław: Ossolineum, 1987).

15. W. Wrzesiński, *Plebiscyty na Warmii, Mazurach, i Powiślu w 1920 r.* (Plebiscites in Warmia, Mazuria, and the Vistula region in 1920) (Olsztyn: Ośrodek Badań Naukowych im. W. Kętrzyńskiego, 1974); Wrzesiński, *Ruch polski na Warmii Mazurach i Powiślu w latach 1922–1939* (The Polish movement in Warmia, Mazuria, and the Vistula region, 1922–1939) (Poznań: Instytut Zachodni, 1963); Wrzesiński, *Polski ruch narodowy w Niemczech, 1922–1939)* (The Polish national movement in Germany, 1922–1939) (Poznań: Wydawnicwto Poznańskie, 1970, 1973).

16. H. Chałupczak, *II Rzeczpospolita a mniejszość polska w Niemczech* (The second Polish republic and the Polish minority in Germany) (Poznań: Instytut Zachodni, 1992).

17. A. Nadolny, *Opieka duszpasterska nad dziećmi i młodzieżą polską na terenie Niemiec Zachodnich w latach 1945–1965* (Pastoral care over Polish children and youth in Western Germany, 1945–1965) (Lublin: Katolicki Uniwersytet Lubelski, 1980).

18. U. Kaczmarek, *Aktywność kulturalno-oświatowa Polonii w Bułgarii, Czechosłowacji, Niemieckiej Republice Demokratycznej, Rumunii i na Węgrzech w latach 1945–1989* (Cultural and educational activities of the Polish groups in Bulgaria, Czechoslovakia, German Democratic Republic, Roumania, and Hungary in the years 1945–1989) (Poznań: Uniwersytet Adama Mickiewicza, 1991).

19. A. Poniatowska, S. Liman, and I. Krężałek, *Związek Polaków w Niemczech w latach 1922–1982* (The union of Poles in Germany in the years 1922–1982), ed. Jerzy Marczewski (Warsaw: Wydawnicwto Polonia, 1987).

20. S. Kościelecka, *Dzieje Polaków w Danii w latach 1892–1940* (The history of the Poles in Denmark, 1892–1940) (Szczecin: Wyższa Szkoła Pedagogiczna, 1983); A. Pilch, ed., *Polacy w Austrii: Materiały międzynarodowego sympozjum naukowego, które odbyło się w Uniwersytecie Jagiellońskim w dniach, 20–22 maja 1975* (Poles in Austria: Proceedings of a symposium at the Jagiellonian University, May 20–22, 1975) (Cracow: Uniwersytet Jagielloński, 1976).

21. H. Florkowska-Francić, *Emigracyjna działalność Agatona Gillera po powstaniu styczniowym* (Agaton Giller's emigration activity following the January insurrection) (Wrocław: Ossolineum, 1985); T. Panecki, *Polonia zachodnioeuropejska w planach rządu RP na emigracji, 1940–1944: Akcja Kontynentalna* (Polish communities in Western Europe in the plans of the Polish government in exile, 1940–1944: The continental action) (Warsaw: Państwowe Wydawnictwo Naukowe, 1986).

22. T. Radzik, *Szkolnictwo polskie w Wielkiej Brytanii w latach II wojny światowej* (Polish education in Great Britain during World War II) (Lublin: Polonia, 1986).

23. B. Szydłowska-Ceglowa, ed., *Polonia w Europie* (Polonia in Europe) (Poznań: Zakład Badań Narodowościowych PAN, 1992).

24. Z. Łukawski, *Ludność polska w Rosji, 1863–1914* (Polish population in Russia, 1863–1914) (Wrocław: Ossolineum, 1978).

25. E. Trela, *Edukacja dzieci polskich w Związku Radzieckim w latach 1941–1946* (Education of Polish children in the Soviet Union in the years 1941–1946) (Warsaw: Państwowe Wydawnictwo Naukowe, 1983).

26. *Tygodnik Powszechny*, no. 37 (September 9, 1984): 8; *Vacat*, no. 22 (November 1984): 14–18.

27. M. Iwanow, *Pierwszy naród ukarany: Polacy w Związku Radzieckim 1921–1930* (The First Nation punished: Poles in the Soviet Union, 1921–1939) (Warsaw: Państwowe Wydawnictwo Naukowe, 1991); Iwanow, *Pierwszy naród ukarany: Stalinizm wobec polskiej ludności kresowej* (The First Nation punished: Stalinism versus the Polish frontier population) (Warsaw: Omnipress, 1991); Iwanow, *Polacy w Związku Radzieckim, 1921–1939* (Poles in the Soviet Union, 1921–1939) (Wrocław: Uniwersytet Wrocławski, 1990). I think that M. Iwanow and I could write a unique story about the difficulties in the 1980s of publishing in *Przegląd Polonijny* even a single contribution on Polish communities in the former communist countries.

28. P. Żaroń, *Ludność polska w Związku Radzieckim w czasie II wojny światowej* (Polish people in the Soviet Union during World War II) (Warsaw: Państwowe Wydawnictwo Naukowe, 1990).

29. Editor's note: Professor Brożek might refer here to Hieronim Kubiak.

30. H. Kubiak et al., ed., *Mniejszości polskie i Polonia w ZSRR* (Polish minorities and Polonia in the USSR) (Wrocław: Ossolineum, 1992).

31. H. Kubiak, *Polski Narodowy Kościół Katolicki w Stanach Zjednoczonych Ameryki w latach 1897–1965: Jego społeczne uwarunkowania i społeczne funkcje* (Wrocław: Ossolineum, 1970), published in English as *The Polish National Catholic Church in the United States of America from 1897 to 1980: Its Social Conditioning and Social Functions* (Cracow: Uniwersytet Jagielloński, 1982).

32. J. Miąso, *Dzieje oświaty polonijnej w Stanach Zjednoczonych* (Warsaw: Państwowe Wydawnictwo Naukowe, 1970), published in English as *The History of Education of Polish Immigrants in the United States* (New York and Warsaw: Kosciuszko Foundation and Państwowe Wydawnictwo Naukowe, 1977). Cf. my criticism and polemics in *Kwartalnik Historyczny* (Warsaw), no. 4 (1971): 962–65; no. 3 (1972): 796–98; no. 2 (1973): 527.

Editor's note: Brożek's meaning of "primitive" here is unclear. He appears to have meant "unprofessional," but perhaps also "ideologically rigid."

33. A. Brożek, *Ślązacy w Teksasie: Relacje o najstarszych osadach polskich w Ameryce* (Silesians in Texas: Accounts of the oldest Polish settlements in the United States) (Warsaw: Państwowe Wydawnictwo Naukowe, 1972); F. Stasik, *Polska emigracja polityczna w Stanach Zjednoczonych Ameryki, 1831–1864* (Polish political emigration in the United States, 1831–1864) (Warsaw: Państwowe Wydawnictwo Naukowe, 1973); B. Grzeloński and I. Rusinowa, *Polacy w wojnach amerykańskich, 1775–1783, 1861–1865*

(Poles in American wars, 1775–1783, 1861–1865) (Warsaw: Wydawnictwo Ministerstwa Obrony Narodowej 1973); Grzeloński, *Polacy w Stanach Zjednoczonych Ameryki, 1776–1865* (Warsaw: Interpress, 1976), published in English as *Poles in the United States of America, 1776–1865* (Warsaw: Interpress, 1976).

34. A. Walaszek, *Polscy robotnicy, praca i związki zawodowe w Stanach Zjednoczonych Ameryki, 1880–1922* (Polish workers, labor, and trade unions in the United States, 1880–1922) (Wrocław: Ossolineum, 1988); D. Piątkowska-Koźlik, *Związek Socjalistów Polskich w Ameryce, 1900–1914* (The Polish socialist alliance in America, 1900–1914) (Opole: Wyższa Szkoła Pedagogiczna, 1992); E. Orzechowski, *Teatr polonijny w Stanach Zjednoczonych* (The Polish ethnic theater in the United States) (Wrocław: Ossolineum, 1989); A. Kłossowski, *Na obczyźnie: Ludzie polskiej książki* (Abroad: People of the Polish book) (Wrocław: Ossolineum, 1984).

35. A. Kapiszewski, comp., *Hugh Gibson and Controversy over Polish-Jewish Relations After World War I* (Cracow: Uniwersytet Jagielloński, 1991); Kapiszewski, *Stosunki polsko-żydowskie w Stanach Zjednoczonych* (Polish-Jewish relations in the United States) (Cracow: Uniwersytet Jagielloński, 1978); T. Radzik, *Stosunki polsko-żydowskie w Stanach Zjednoczonych Ameryki w latach 1918–1921* (Polish-Jewish relations in the United States of America in the years 1918–1921) (Lublin: Uniwersytet Marii Curie-Skłodowskiej, 1988).

36. H. Florkowska-Francić, M. Francić, and H. Kubiak, ed., *Polonia wobec niepodległości polski w czasie I wojny światowej* (The Polish ethnic group and Poland's independence during World War I) (Wrocław: Ossolineum, 1979).

37. M. Francić, *Komitet Obrony Narodowej w Ameryce, 1912–1918* (The Committee of National Defense in America, 1912–1918) (Wrocław: Ossolineum, 1983).

38. A. Walaszek, *Reemigracja ze Stanów Zjednoczonych do Polski po I wojnie światowej, 1919–1924* (Re-emigration from the United States to Poland, 1919–1924) (Cracow: Uniwersytet Jagielloński, 1983); T. Radzik, *Społeczno-ekonomiczne aspekty stosunku Polonii amerykańskiej do Polski po I wojnie światowej* (Social and economic aspects of the attitude of the Polish ethnic group in America toward Poland after World War I) (Wrocław: Ossolineum, 1989); T. Radzik, *Polonia amerykańska wobec Polski, 1918–1939* (The American Polonia and Poland, 1918–1939) (Lublin: Uniwersytet Marii Curie-Skłodowskiej, 1986; Lublin: Polonia 1990).

39. W. Wnuk, *Związek Klubów Małopolskich w Ameryce* (The alliance of Little Poland clubs in America) (Warsaw: Pax, 1974).

Editor's note: Małopolska, or Little Poland, is a regional designation referring to the area now roughly coterminous with the southern third of present-day Poland.

40. G. Babiński, ed., *Studia nad organizacjami polonijnymi w Ameryce północnej* (Studies on Polish ethnic organizations in North America) (Wrocław: Ossolineum, 1988).

41. A. Ławrowski, *Reprezentacja polskiej grupy etnicznej w życiu politycznym Stanów Zjednoczonych* (The representation of the Polish ethnic group in the political life of the United States) (Warsaw: Państwowe Wydawnictwo Naukowe, 1979).

42. W. Kula, N. Assorodobraj-Kula, and M. Kula, ed., *Listy emigrantów z Brazylii i Stanów Zjednoczonych, 1890–1981* (Warsaw: Ludowa Spółdzielnia Wydawnicza, 1973), published in English as *Writing Home: Immigrants in Brazil and the United*

States, 1890–1981, trans. J. Wtulich (Boulder, Colo., and New York: East European Monographs, Columbia University Press, 1986). Cf. my critical review in *Acta Poloniae Historica* (Warsaw) 65 (1992): 257–61.

43. *Pamiętniki emigrantów: Stany Zjednoczone* (Memoirs of emigrants: The United States), vols. 1–2 (Warsaw: Instytut Gospodarstwa Społecznego, 1979). Cf. my critical review in *Kwartalnik Historyczny* (Warsaw) no. 1 (1979): 219–25; *Pamiętniki emigrantów, 1878–1958* (Memoirs of emigrants, 1878–1958) (Warsaw: Czytelnik, 1960).

44. B. Grzeloński, ed., *Ameryka w pamiętnikach polaków: Antologia* (America in Polish memoirs: An anthology) (Warsaw: Interpress, 1975); *Burzliwe lata Polonii amerykańskiej: Wspomnienia i listy misjonarzy jezuickich, 1864–1913* (Stormy years of the Poles in America: Recollections and letters of Jesuit missionaries, 1864–1913) (Cracow: Apostolstwo Modlitwy, 1983); D. Piątkowska, ed., *Korespondencja z Ameryki w prasie polskiej na Śląsku* (Reports from America in the Polish press in Silesia) (Wrocław: Ossolineum, 1980); M. M. Drozdowski and E. Kusielewicz, ed., *Polonia Stanów Zjednoczonych Ameryki, 1910–1918: Wybór dokumentów* (Polonia in the United States of America, 1910–1918: Selected documents) (Warsaw: Ludowa Spółdzielnia Wydawnicza, 1989).

45. H. Janowska, T. Jędruszczak, C. Madajczyk, and W. Stankiewicz, ed., *Archiwum polityczne Ignacego Paderewskiego* (Political archives of Ignacy Paderewski), 4 vols. (Wrocław: Ossolineum, 1973).

46. A. Reczyńska, *Emigracja z Polski do Kanady w okresie międzywojennym* (Emigration from Poland to Canada in the interwar period) (Wrocław: Ossolineum, 1986); I. Jost, *Osadnictwo kaszubskie w Ontario* (Kashubian settlement in Ontario) (Lublin: Katolicki Uniwersytet Lubelski, 1983); *Pamiętniki emigrantów: Kanada* (Memoirs of emigrants: Canada) (Warsaw: Instytut Gospodarstwa Społecznego, 1971); J. Samulski, *Pamiętnik emigranta polskiego w Kanadzie* (Memoirs of a Polish emigrant in Canada), ed. B. Szydłowska-Ceglowa, 2 vols. (Wrocław: Ossolineum, 1978, 1982).

47. *Emigracja polska w Brazylii, 100 lat osadnictwa* (Polish emigration in Brazil, a hundred years of settlement) (Warsaw: Ludowa Spółdzielnia Wydawnicza, 1971); K. Groniowski, *Polska emigracja zarobkowa w Brazylii, 1871–1914* (Polish employment-seeking emigration in Brazil, 1871–1914) (Wrocław: Ossolineum, 1972); I. Klarner, *Emigracja z Królestwa Polskiego do Brazylii w latach 1890–1914* (Emigration from the Kingdom of Poland to Brazil in the years 1890–1914) (Warsaw: Książka i Wiedza, 1975); M. Kula, *Polonia brazylijska* (The Polish ethnic group in Brazil) (Warsaw: Ludowa Spółdzielnia Wydawnicza, 1981).

48. Z. Dobosiewicz, ed., *Polonia w Ameryce Łacińskiej* (The Polish ethnic group in Latin America) (Lublin: Wydawnictwo Lubelskie 1977); M. Kula, ed., *Dzieje Polonii w Ameryce Łacińskiej: Zbiór studiów pod redakcją Marcina Kuli* (The history of Polonia in Latin America: Essays edited by Marcin Kula) (Wrocław: Ossolineum, 1983); M. Paradowska, *Polacy w Ameryce Południowej* (Poles in South America) (Wrocław: Ossolineum, 1977); Paradowska, *Polacy w Meksyku i Ameryce Środkowej* (Poles in Mexico and Central America) (Wrocław: Ossolineum, 1985); T. Dworecki, *Zmagania polonijne w Brazylii* (The Polish struggle in Brazil), 4 vols. (Warsaw: Akademia Teologii Katolickiej, 1980–1987).

49. I. Paczyńska and A. Pilch, ed., *Materiały do bibliografii dziejów emigracji oraz*

skupisk polonijnych w Ameryce Północnej i Południowej (Materials concerning bibliography of history of emigration and Polish settlements in North and South America in the nineteenth and twentieth centuries) (Cracow: Uniwersytet Jagielloński, 1979). Reference also might be made to a book on the history of Poles in a rather unfamiliar environment; this is a study by Kazimierz Dopierała on Polish emigration in Turkey. See K. Dopierała, *Emigracja polska w Turcji w XIX i XX wieku* (Polish emigration in Turkey in the nineteenth and twentieth centuries) (Lublin: Polonia, 1988).

50. *Polonia zagraniczna: Bibliografia publikacji* (Foreign Polonia: Bibliography of [Polish] publications [in Poland], comp. Wojciech Chojnacki; Władysław Chojnacki and Wojciech Chojnacki, *Bibliografia kalendarzy polonijnych, 1838–1982* (Bibliography of Polish almanacs abroad, 1838–1982) (Wrocław: Ossolineum, 1984); W. Chojnacki and W. Chojnacki, *Bibliografia kalendarzy wydanych w języku polskim poza granicami polski od roku 1716: Mazury, Śląsk Górny i Dolny oraz Cieszyński* (Bibliography of almanacs published in Polish outside Poland since 1716: Masuria, Upper and Lower Silesia, and Teschen Silesia) (Wrocław: Ossolineum, 1986).

51. J. Kowalik, *Bibliografia czasopism polskich wydanych poza granicami kraju od września 1939 roku* (World index of Polish periodicals published outside Poland since September 1939), 5 vols. (Lublin: Katolicki Uniwersytet Lubelski, 1978–1988); K. Tatarowicz, *Katalog poloników periodycznych wydanych zagranicą do roku 1939: Zbiory Biblioteki Jagiellońskiej* (Catalogue of periodical Polonica published abroad till 1939: Collections of the Jagiellonian Library) (Cracow: Uniwersytet Jagielloński, 1961); A. Kłossowski, comp., *Zbiory i prace polonijne Biblioteki Narodowej: Informator* (Polonia collections and works at the National Library: Directory) (Warsaw: Biblioteka Narodowa, 1982); H. Natuniewicz, *Zbiory i prace polonijne Muzeum Literatury im. Adama Mickiewicza w Warszawie: Informator* (Polonia collections and works at the Adam Mickiewicz Museum of Literature, Warsaw: Directory) (Warsaw: Biblioteka Narodowa, Muzeum Literatury im. A. Mickiewicza, 1984).

52. E. Kołodziej, comp., *Emigracja z ziem polskich i Polonia, 1865–1939: Informator o źródłach przechowywanych w centralnych archiwach państwowych w Polsce* (Emigration from Polish territories and Polonia, 1865–1939: Directory on sources collected in central Polish state archives) (Cracow: Uniwersytet Jagielloński, 1988); E. Kołodziej, comp., *Inwentarz akt Ambasady Polskiej w Berlinie z lat (1919) 1920–1939 (do 1939 roku Poselstwa)* (Catalogue of files of the Polish Embassy in Berlin [1919] 1920–1939 [till 1934 Legation]) (Warsaw: Państwowe Wydawnictwo Naukowe, 1990); E. Kołodziej, comp., *Inwentarze akt konsulatów polskich w Niemczech, 1918–1939* (Catalogs of files of Polish consulates in Germany, 1918–1939) (Opole: Instytut Śląski, 1983); E. Kołodziej, comp., *Polonia zagraniczna: Informator o materiałach źródłowych do 1939 roku przechowywanych w Archiwum Akt Nowych* (Polonia abroad: Directory on source material for the period before 1939, located in the Archives of Recent Documents) (Warsaw: Archiwum Akt Nowych, Biblioteka Narodowa, 1981).

53. M. A. Krąpiec, P. Taras, and J. Turowski, ed., *Wkład polaków do kultury świata* (The contribution of Poles to the culture of the world) (Lublin: Katolicki Uniwersytet Lubelski, 1976); A. Brożek, *Polonia amerykańska, 1854–1939* (Warsaw: Interpress, 1977), published in English as *Polish Americans, 1854–1939* (Warsaw: Interpress, 1985); H. Janowska, *Emigracja zarobkowa z Polski, 1918–1939* (Employment-seeking emigra-

tion from Poland, 1918–1939) (Warsaw: Państwowe Wydawnictwo Naukowe, 1981); E. Kołodziej, *Wychodźstwo zarobkowe z Polski, 1918–1939: Studia nad polityką emigracyjną II Rzeczypospolitej* (Employment-seeking emigration from Poland, 1918–1939: Studies on Polish emigration policy in the Second Republic) (Warsaw: Książka i Wiedza, 1982); W. Wrzesiński, ed., *Liczba i rozmieszczenie Polaków na świecie* (Number and settlement of Poles worldwide) (Wrocław: Uniwersytet Wrocławski, 1981–1985), 1–2.

54. G. Babiński and M. Francić, ed., *Poles in the History and Culture of the United States of America* (Wrocław: Ossolineum, 1979); *Kultura skupisk polonijnych* (The culture of Polonian communities) (Warsaw: Biblioteka Narodowa, 1981, 1987, 1993).

55. A. Pilch, ed., *Emigracja z ziem polskich w czasach nowożytnych i najnowszych, XVIII–XX w.* (Emigration from Polish lands in modern and recent times, from the eighteenth to the twentieth centuries) (Warsaw: Państwowe Wydawnictwo Naukowe, 1984).

56. H. Kubiak, E. Kusielewicz, and T. Gromada, ed., *Polonia amerykańska: Przeszłość i współczesność* (American Polonia: Past and present) (Wrocław: Ossolineum, 1988). The Uppsala project is described in H. Runblom and H. Norman, ed., *From Sweden to America: A History of the Migration* (Minneapolis: University of Minnesota Press; and Uppsala: Acta Universitatis Upsalensis, 1976).

57. W. Miodunka, ed., *Język polski w świecie* (Polish language in the world) (Warsaw, Państwowe Wydawnictwo Naukowe, 1990); E. Kołodziej, *Dzieje Polonii w zarysie, 1918–1939* (History of Polonia, 1918–1939, an outline) (Warsaw: Książka i Wiedza, 1991); *Polacy w historii i kulturze krajów Europy Zachodniej: Słownik biograficzny* (Poles in the history and culture of western European countries: Biographical dictionary) (Poznań: Instytut Zachodni, 1981); B. Grzeloński, *Do New Yorku, Chicago, i San Francisco: Szkice do biografii polsko-amerykańskich* (Warsaw: Interpress, 1983), published in English as *To New York, Chicago, and San Francisco: Polish-American Biographies* (Warsaw: Interpress, 1986).

58. Editor's note: In contrast to recent American and British social history, Polish historical scholarship during the period was not influenced by the so-called cultural Marxism and radical history, viz., E. P. Thompson, Herbert Gutman. Under Polish political circumstances, this is perhaps understandable.

59. Relations of the Polish ethnic group to other groups—for example, Polish-Ukrainian relations in Canada and the United States—are now analyzed in the valuable doctoral thesis by Andrzej Zięba (Jagiellonian University, 1992). A doctoral thesis on the Polish group in Australia by Jan Lencznarowicz is now well advanced at the Jagiellonian University.

Contributors

STANISLAUS A. BLEJWAS is University Professor and Professor of History at Central Connecticut State University. He works in both Polish and Polish-American history. His publications include *Realism in Polish Politics: Warsaw Positivism and National Survival in Nineteenth Century Poland* and *St. Stanislaus B. & M. Parish, Meriden, Connecticut: A Century of Connecticut Polonia, 1891–1991.* He also is the co-editor of *Pastor of the Poles: Polish American Essays* and recipient of the Mieczysław Haiman Medal from the Polish American Historical Association.

ANDRZEJ BROŻEK (1933–1994), Ph.D., graduated from the University of Warsaw and was serving as professor of social and economic history at the Jagiellonian University in Cracow at the time of his death. His main publications include *Wysiedlenia polaków z Górnego Śląska przez Bismarcka* (The expulsion of Poles from Upper Silesia by Bismarck, 1963); *Robotnicy spoza zaboru pruskiego w przemyśle na Górnym Śląsku* (Workers from outside the Prussian Partition in Upper Silesian industry, 1966); *Ostflucht na Śląsku* (Flight from the east in Silesia, 1966); *Problematyka narodowościowa ostfluchtu na Śląsku* (Ethnic problems of the flight from the east in Silesia, 1972); *Ślązacy w Teksasie* (Silesians in Texas, 1972); *Polish Americans: 1854–1939,* 1985; and *Niemcy zagraniczni w polityce kolonizacji pruskich prowincji wschodnich* (Germans from abroad in the policy of colonization of Prussian Eastern Provinces, 1989).

JOHN J. BUKOWCZYK, professor of history at Wayne State University in Detroit, is co-editor of *Detroit Images: Photographs of the Renaissance City* and author of *And My Children Did Not Know Me: A History of the Polish-Americans.* Co-winner of the 1987 Oskar Halecki Award of the Polish American Historical Association (PAHA), and past president of PAHA (1990–1992), Bukowczyk has published articles on Polish immigration and ethnic history in *Labor History, International Labor and Working-Class History,* and *Polish American Studies* and is the 1994 recipient of PAHA's

Haiman Award for sustained scholarly contribution to the Polish-American history field.

WILLIAM FALKOWSKI is coordinator of grants at Erie Community College in western New York. A co-founder of the *Polish-American VOICE* (now merged with and known as the *Polish-American Journal*), he completed his doctoral dissertation, "Accommodation and Conflict: Patterns of Polish Immigrant Adaptation to Industrial Capitalism and American Political Pluralism in Buffalo, New York, 1873–1901," at the State University of New York at Buffalo in 1990. His essay on Leon Czolgosz appears in the *Encyclopedia of the American Left* (1990), and his article "Polka History 101" was included in *History for the Public.*

WILLIAM GALUSH is professor of history at Loyola University of Chicago and editor of *Mid-America.* A contributor to *Immigrants and Religion in Urban America,* edited by R. Miller and T. Marzik, in 1991 Galush won PAHA's Rev. Joseph Swastek Award for his article "Purity and Power: Chicago Polonian Feminists, 1880–1914," which appeared in *Polish American Studies.*

ANNA D. JAROSZYŃSKA-KIRCHMANN received her master's in history and archival administration from Maria Curie-Skłodowska University in Lublin, Poland. While completing her doctoral studies at the University of Minnesota, she worked at the immigration History Research Center as a research assistant for Polish Collections. Her publications relate to the social history of postwar Polish immigration to the United States, as well as to the archival sources on Polonia's history.

THADDEUS C. RADZILOWSKI, professor of history, is president of St. Mary's College in Orchard Lake, Michigan. He took his Ph.D. at the University of Michigan and writes on modern Russian and East Central European history, the social and cultural history of Polish immigration, and historical problems of class, race, and ethnicity.

DANIEL STONE is professor of history at the University of Winnipeg in Canada. He has published extensively on various aspects of eighteenth- and twentieth-century Polish history including the history of Polish Jews.

Index

Abbott, Grace, 69
Adam Mickiewicz Chair of Polish Culture, 23, 24
Addams, Jane, 64, 87
Algren, Nelson, 63
Archacki, Henry, 30
Aronowitz, Stanley, 40–41
Asch, Sholem, 93, 94, 95
Assorodobraj-Kula, Nina, 188

Balch, Emily Greene, 4
Barrett, James R., 45
Barton, Josef, 84
Barzyński, Rev. Vincent, 81, 83, 124
Biskupski, Mieczysław B., 30, 128, 172
Blejwas, Stanislaus A., x, 23, 26, 30, 90, 170
Bodnar, John, 41–41, 60
Bójnowski, Rev. Lucyan, 81
Bolek, Rev. Francis, 14, 18–19, 20
Borowiec, Walter, 137
Brożek, Andrzej, xi, 81, 183–84, 186, 264n1–2
Brzezinski, Zbigniew, 140
Buczek, Daniel, 30, 33, 81, 89–90
Bujak, Franciszek, 3
Bukowczyk, John J., x, 42–43, 81, 87, 88, 89, 138, 164
Burstein, Barbara Stern, 155, 159, 164

Caro, Leopold, 3
Chałupczak, Henryk, 184
Chojnacki, Władysław, 190
Chojnacki, Wojciech, 189–90, 191
Chrobot, Rev. Leonard, 28–29, 35, 90, 205n79
Cieplinski, Mitchell, 140

Class consciousness. *See* Polish Americans, class consciousness of
Cohen, Lizbeth, 52–53
Coleman, Arthur, 22–23
Congregation of the Resurrection. *See* Polish Americans, religious orders of
Cygan, Mary E., 48–50, 66, 67, 206n83
Czolgosz, Leon, 43, 56

Dąbrowski, Rev. Józef, 7, 88
Derwinski, Edwin, 140
Detroit School. *See* Polish-American history
Dingell, John, 139
Dinnerstein, Leonard 154–55
Displaced Persons (DPs), 158–65, 175–76, 257n25, 258n28
Długoszewski, Bolesław Wieniawa, 156
Dmowski, Roman, 3, 49, 115
Dobosiewicz, Zbigniew, 189
Dolan, Jay P., 80, 84, 228n1
Drewniak, Bogusław, 183, 184
Drozdowski, Marian Marek, 188
Dudzik, Sr. Josephine, 87
Dunikowski, Emil, 127
Dworecki, Tadeusz, 189
Dziedzic, Eugene, 46–47
Dziennik Ludowy (people's daily), 48
Dziennik Polski (Polish daily), 16
Dzierozyński, Rev. Francis, 82
Dzwonkowski, Rev. Roman, 183

Echo z Polski, 2, 97
Ehrenkreutz, Andrew, 147
Eisenhower, Dwight D., 140

Erdmans, Mary Patrice, 168, 171–72, 174

Faires, Nora, 54
Falkowski, William G., x, 43–44
Families. *See* Polish American history, and families
Felician Sisters. *See* Polish Americans, religious orders of
Figas, Rev. Justyn, 90
Fink, Leon, 44
Florkowska-Francić, Halina, 185
Fox, Paul, 86
Francic, Miroslaw, 187
Fraser, Steven, 51–52
Fredo, Aleksander, 2
Fudzinski, Rev. Ignatius, 87

Gabbacia, Donna, 71
Galush, William, x, 87
Garrett, Stephen A., 146, 147
German-Jewish Americans, 96, 97
Gieryk, Rev. Theodore, 83
Giller, Agaton, 124–25, 185
Gladsky, Thomas S., xi, 37, 38
Glemp, Józef Cardinal, 149
Głos Robotniczy (the workers' voice), 50
Golab, Caroline, 60, 220*n11*
Goldberg, David J., 47
Góral, Rev. Bolesław, 10
Greene, Victor R., 26, 31, 40, 81, 83, 150
Groniowski, Krzysztof, 189
Gronouski, John, 140
Grzeloński, Bogdan, 187, 191

Haiman, Mieczysław, xiii, 14–15, 17–18, 22, 125, 153, 203*n65*
Halecki, Oskar, 16–17, 22, 25, 157
Haller, Józef, 128, 129
Hapak, Joseph, 88
Haremski, Roman L., 26
Hareven, Tamara, 221–22*n19*
Hodur, Bishop Francis, 84–85, 232*n23*

Immigration, 3–5
Immigration History Research Center (University of Minnesota), 29–30

Iwanow, Mikołaj, 186, 266*n27*
Iwicki, Rev. John, 82, 87

Janowska, Halina, 183
Januszewski, Frank, 156–57
Jaruzelski, Wojciech, 149
Jędrzejewicz, Wacałw, 156–57
Jelavich, Charles, 23
Jews, in Poland, 94–95, 108–12, 166–67. *See also* German-Jewish Americans; Polish-Jewish Americans
John Paul II, 145, 147
Jost, Izabella, 189

Kaczmarek, Urszula, 184
Kadyszewski, Sr. Mary Jane, 86
Kajencki, Francis C., 30
Kalloway, Lois, 58
Kantor, Ryszard, 167–68
Kantowicz, Edward R., 86, 122, 133, 136
Kapiszewski, Andrzej, 187
Karski, Jan, 111
Kikulski, Jan, 46, 50
Kiołbassa, Piotr, 121, 123, 135
Kirchmann, Anna D. Jaroszyńska, x–xi
Klarner, Izabella, 189
Kleczka, John C., 135, 139
Kłobukowski, Stanisław, 3
Klossowski, Andrzej, 187, 190
Knawa, Sr. Anne Marie, 86–87
Kogut, Peter, 133
Kolm, Richard, 26, 31
Kościelecka, Irena, 184
Kosciuszko Foundation, 13, 16, 22, 26, 30, 198*n34–35*
Kosinski, Jerzy, 166
Kostecki, Louis, 136
Kowalik, Jan, 190
Kozłowski, Jerzy, 184
Koźniewski, Kazimierz, 188
Krężałek, Iwona, 184
Krol, John Cardinal, 91
Krupsak, Mary Ann, 136
Kruszka, Michael, 135

Kruszka, Rev. Wacław, 2, 6–7, 81, 83, 85, 122, 125, 130, 138
Krzycki, Leo, 50
Kubiak, Hieronim, 85, 186, 288*n29*
Kucharzewski, Jan, 16
Kula, Marcin, 188, 189
Kula, Witold, 188
Kultura (Paris), 183
Kunz, Stanley, 135
Kusielewicz, Eugene, 188
Kuzniewski, Rev. Anthony, 81, 85–86

Lechon, Jan, 157
Lednicki, Wacław, 23, 24, 31, 157
Lerski, Jerzy, 26
Liman, Stefan, 184
Łukawski, Zygmunt, 185
Łukomirski, Kazimierz, 147, 168

Madaj, Rev. Miecislaus, 34
Malinowski, Bronislaw, 157
Marchlewski, Mieczyslaw, 116
Marrus, M. R., 169
Marshall, Louis, 115
Marzynski, Marian, 37
Matuszewski, Ignacy, 156–57
Maynard, Fredelle Braser, 105–06
Mazewski, Aloysius, 145–47, 149
Mazowiecki, Tadeusz, 149
McCreedy, William, 64
McDowell, Mary, 76
Miąso, Józef, 186, 192
Mierzyńska, Zofia, 173
Mikulski, Barbara, 133, 135–36
Milewski, Jerzy, 148
Miłosz, Czesław, 166
Mink, Gwendolyn, 44–45
Misner, Barbara, 86
Mitana, Thaddeus, 12, 197*n31*
Mizwa, Stephen P., 13, 16
Mocha, Frank, 17, 19
Moczygemba, Rev. Leopold, 81, 87
Morawska, Ewa, 41–42, 60, 75–76
Moskal, Edward, 148–49
Mostwin, Danuta, 26, 161, 164–65, 167

Mrożek, Sławomir, 167
Murkowski, Frank, 135–36
Murzynowska, Krystyna, 184
Muskie, Edward, 135–36, 138

Napierkowski, Thomas, 30
"New Ethnicity," 26–34
Nixon, Richard M., 138
Novak, Michael, 28
Nowak, Jan Jezoranski, 147
Nowak, Margaret Collingwood. *See* Nowak, Stanley
Nowak, Stanley, 50–52
Nuns. *See* Polish Americans, religious orders of
Nyden, Paul John, 53–54
Nyden, Philip W., 54

Oestriecher, Richard Jules, 44
Okołowicz, Józef, 3
Orchard Lake Schools, 7, 8, 16–17, 19, 27, 33, 88, 90
Orton, Lawrence, 30
Orzechowski, Emil, 158
Osada, Stanisław, 7

Pacyga, Dominic A., 45–46
Paczkowski, Andrzej, 183
Paczyńska, Irena, 189
Paderewski, Ignacy Jan, 115, 128–29, 188
Paradowska, Maria, 189
Park, Robert E., 4
Parot, Joseph, 64, 81, 82, 83
Paryski, Anton, 88
Pawlowski, Harriet, 26, 30–31
Philips, Kevin, 138
Piątkowska-Koźlik, Danuta, 187
Pienkos, Angela T., 136, 137
Pienkos, Donald, 168
Pilch, Andrzej, 189, 190–91
Piłsudski, Józef, 49, 116, 128, 156
Pinkowski, Edward, 30
Poles: attitudes of toward history, 1–2; in Australia, 270*n59;* in Austria, 184; in Canada, 188–89, 270*n59;* in Denmark, 184; families

of, 66–68; in France, 183; in Germany, 183–84; in Great Britain, 185; in Latin America, 189; in Russia and the former USSR, 185–86; in the United States. *See also* Polish Americans; Polish-American history

Polish American Congress (PAC), 17, 50, 142–49, 156–57, 160, 168, 171, 172

Polish American Historical Association (PAHA), ix–x, xiii, 175; clergy in, 19, 20–21; membership of, 19, 20–22, 27, 34–35; origins of, 16–22, 157; secularization of 33–34; women in, 21–22, 27, 34

Polish-American history: and assimilation, 10–11; and the Detroit School, 31–32, 35, 208–09*n91;* in Europe, 33, 40, 180–92; and families, 58–79; and filiopietism, 20, 203*n65;* on film, 35–38, 54–57; and marginalized groups, 8; and the "New Ethnicity," 26–34; origins of, 3–5, 6–7; and Poland's millenium, 27; and politics, 121–51; politics of, 35–38, 54–57; and post–World War II immigrants, 172, 174–79; and radicalism, 54–57, 187; and religion, 80–92; source documents for, 188; uses of, 2, 36–38; and women, 58–79, 86–87, 227*n65*

Polish Americans: arrivals since World War II, 152–79; in American politics, 121, 128–41; and assimilation, 9–10, 38; in Catholic-American historiography, 21, 87–88, 231*n20;* Catholicism of, 42, 56, 76, 80–92; class consciousness of, 40–43, 44–46; clergy of, 80–82, 87–88, 89–90, 123, 178; cultural studies of, xi–xii; and history, 2, 5–6, 8–9, 13–14; intermarriage of, 221*n15;* language of, 10–11; literature of, xi; messianism of, 9; and nationalism, 46, 48, 122–30; occupations of, 99; and Poland, 9, 15–16, 22–24, 26, 38, 49, 50, 128–30, 141–51, 153, 156; and Polish culture, 12–13; political divisions among, 7, 121–30, 162–64, 173–74, 243*n9;* politics of 121–51, 156–57, 161–62; poverty among, 65–66, 223*n29;* and Protestantism, 85; publishing activities of, 7; re-emigration of, 129; rela-

tions of with Catholic Church, 6, 76, 84–85, 126; relations of with Jewish Americans, 48, 112–19, 145, 165, 187; religious orders of, 72–74, 82, 86–87, 89; self-definitions of, 9, 152–53, 174–75; social problems of, 59, 63–65, 70, 222*n22–23;* and socialism, 47–51; theater among, 157–58; and unions, 41–42, 43–48, 50–54, 78–79; as workers, 39–57, 74–76; and World War I, 128–30

Polish American Studies, 17–22, 34, 81, 132

Polish Falcons, 54, 125–26, 127, 128

Polish Institute of Arts and Sciences in America (PIASA), ix, 16–17, 19, 25, 30, 157, 158, 175

Polish-Jewish Americans: in business, 104–05; definitions of, 95–96; early history of, 96–97; history of, 93–120; immigration of 95–106, 165, 166–67; literature and theater of, 102; occupations of, 98–99, 100; organizations of, 106–12, 116–17, 118; and Poland, 106–12; poverty among, 99, 118; relations of with Polish Americans, 112–19, 145, 165, 187; religion among, 101; settlement patterns of, 99, 103, 105–106; social problems of, 99, 103; and unions, 101, 103, 117; women's roles among, 104

Polish Microfilm Project, 29–30

Polish Museum of America, 15, 17, 33

Polish National Alliance (PNA), 4, 8, 49, 83, 112, 124–26, 127, 128, 142, 243*n9*

Polish National Catholic Church (PNCC): clergy of, 81; history of, 28, 84–85, 90, 91, 232*n23;* and nationalism, 126

Polish Peasant in Europe and America, 4, 59, 62–65, 66, 70, 113, 126, 128, 188, 218–19*n1,* 222*n20*

Polish Roman Catholic Union (PRCU), 15, 17, 83, 112, 124, 125–26, 128

Polish studies. *See* Slavic studies

Polish Union of America, 125

Polish Women's Alliance. *See* Związek Polek w Ameryce (ZPA)

POMOST, 148, 171, 172

Poniatowska, Anna, 184

Posern-Zielinski, Aleksander, 89
Problemy Polonii Zagranicznej (Problems of Poles abroad), 182
Przegląd Katolicki (Catholic review), 90
Przegląd Polonijny (Polonia review), 182, 185–86, 266*n27*
Przegląd Zachodni (Western review), 182
Pucinski, Roman, 29
Pula, James S., 46–47

Radzik, Tadeusz, 185, 187–88
Radzilowski, Thaddeus C., x, 30, 31–32, 37, 51, 172; surname of, 208–09*n91*
Rajchman, Henryk Florian, 156–57
Reczyńska, Anna, 189
Religious orders. *See* Polish Americans, religious orders of
Renkiewicz, Frank, 34, 40, 77, 90
Resurrectionist Fathers. *See* Polish Americans, religious orders of
Rhode, Bishop Paul, 86, 90–91, 126
Roberts, Peter, 4
Rocznik Polonijny, 182
Rokicki, Jaroslaw, 173
Roosevelt, Franklin D., 111, 117, 119, 134–35, 142–43
Ross, Gaylen, 37, 172
Rostenkowsi, Daniel, 139
Rowny, Edwin, 140
Rozmarek, Charles, 140, 142, 145, 146, 160
Rusinowa, Izabella, 187

Sadlowski, Ed, 53–54
SS. Cyril and Methodius Seminary. *See* Orchard Lake Schools
Salomon, Hyam, 96
Samulski, Józef, 189
Schatz, Ronald, 53
Septek, "Big Mary," 76–77
Shalikashvili, John, 140
Shaw, Clifford, 63
Siekaniec, Rev. Ladislaus J., 20, 21
Siemiradzki, Tomasz, 128
Sienkiewicz, Henryk, 7, 9–10, 12, 123, 130
Skrowaczewski, StanisLaw, 166

Śladkowski, Wieslaw
Slavic studies, 11–12, 15–16, 22–26, 157, 202*nn62–63*
Slayton, Robert A., 45, 46, 47
Sluszka, Sigmund, 24
Smith, Al, 117, 133
Smith, Timothy L., 80, 84, 228*n1*
Smulski, Jan, 135
Stasik, Florian, 186–87
Steerage conditions, 68–69
Stone, Daniel, x
Studia Polonijne (Polonia studies), 182
Swastek, Rev. Joseph, 17, 21, 81, 83
Świetlik, Francis X., 18–19, 153, 159
Świetosławski, Wojciech, 157
Symmons, Konstanty. *See* Symonolewicz, Konstanty
Symmons-Symonolewicz, Konstanty. *See* Symonolewicz, Konstanty
Symonolewicz, Konstanty, 17, 30, 132
Syski, Rev. Alexander, 81
Szalewski, Mieczyslaw, 135
Szymczak, Mieczyslaw, 135, 139

Tatarowicz, Kazimierza, 190
Taubeschlag, Rafał, 157
Thomas, John L., 64–65
Thomas, William I. *See Polish Peasant in Europe and America*
Thompson, Margaret, 86
Thrasher, Frederick, 64
Torosiewicz, M., 81
Trela, Elżbieta, 185
Tuwin, Julian, 157
Tygiel, Zelig, 116
Tygodnik Polski (Polish weekly), 157

Wachtl, Karol, 19
Walaszek, Adam, xii, 187
Waldo, Arthur L., 19
Wałęsa, Lech, 149
Wandycz, Piotr S., 146–47
Węgrzynek, Maksymilian F., 156–57
Wereszycki, Henryk, 127
Wieczerzak, Joseph A., 26, 33

Wierzynski, Kazimierz, 157–58
Wilson, Woodrow, 5, 14, 128
Winter, Benjamin, 116
Wise, Rabbi Stephen, 111
Wittlin, Józef, 157–58
Włoszczewski, Stefan, 17–18, 31, 200
Wolanin, Alphonse S., 19, 201*n53*
Wong, Celia, 30
Wrobel, Paul, 31–32
Wrzesiński, Wojciech, 184
Wrzezokowska, Dr. Anna, 64
Wyman, Mark, 154
Wyrwa, Józef, 162–63
Wyrwa, Tadeusz, 162–63
Wytrwal, Joseph A., 26, 30

Yablonski, Jock, 53–54
Yiddish, 95. *See also* Polish-Jewish Americans

Zablocki, Clement, 139
Zahariasiewicz, Walter, 140
Zand, Helen Stankiewicz, 26, 30–31, 61, 62,
    89
Żaron, Piotr, 186
Zięba, Andrzej, 270*n59*
Znaniecka-Lopata, Helena, 26, 168, 170–71,
    173–74
Znaniecki, Florian, 88. *See also Polish Peasant
    in Europe and America*
Zuk, Mary, 77–78
Związek Polek w Ameryce (ZPA), 17, 54, 71–
    72, 86, 125, 225*n52*, 225*n54*. *See also* Polish
    American history, and women